CliffsNotes®

ACT®

CRAM PLAN™

3rd Edition

William Ma, Jane R. Burstein, and Nichole Vivion

Houghton Mifflin Harcourt
Boston • New York

About the Authors

William Ma was chairman of the Math Department at the Herricks School District on Long Island for many years before retiring. He also taught as an adjunct math instructor at Baruch College, Columbia University, and Fordham University. He is the author of several other review books for subjects including AP Calculus, SAT, and GMAT. He is currently a math consultant.

Jane Burstein taught English at Herricks High School in New Hyde Park, New York, for 36 years. She has been an ACT and SAT tutor for 30 years, an instructor at Hofstra University, and a reader for AP exams. She is the author of several other review books including those for the SAT, GMAT, GRE, and ASVAB.

Nichole Vivion is the author of several biology and test-prep publications including *CliffsNotes AP Biology Flashcards,* and is a contributor to *CliffsNotes Test Success for AP Biology*. She currently teaches upper school science courses in biology, biotechnology, environmental science, and public health at The Nightingale-Bamford School in New York City, where she also acts as chair of the science department.

Acknowledgments

My wife, Mary, and my daughters, Janet and Karen, who gave me much help in putting the book together. Copy editor Lynn Northrup, tech editors Mary Jane Sterling and Tom Page, and especially Christina Stambaugh, the development editor, for their patience and assistance.
—William Ma

I would like to thank my husband, David, and children, Jessica, Jonathan, Beth, and Seth, for their encouragement and helpful suggestions.
—Jane Burstein

Thanks to my husband Aleks for his ongoing support and humor throughout the writing process, and to my incredible colleagues for their constant inspiration and boundless knowledge.
—Nichole Vivion

Editorial

Executive Editor: Greg Tubach
Senior Editor: Christina Stambaugh
Production Editor: Erika West
Copy Editor: Lynn Northrup
Technical Editors: Barbara Swovelin and Mary Jane Sterling
Proofreader: Susan Moritz

CliffsNotes® ACT® Cram Plan™, 3rd Edition

Library of Congress Control Number: 2016962013
ISBN: 978-0-544-83660-0 (pbk)

Printed in the United States of America
DOC 10 9 8 7 6 5 4 3 2   4500697671

For information about permission to reproduce selections from this book, write to trade.permissions@hmhco.com or to Permissions, Houghton Mifflin Harcourt Publishing Company, 3 Park Avenue, 19th Floor, New York, New York 10016.

www.hmhco.com

Table of Contents

Introduction

Many juniors and seniors take the ACT as part of the college admissions process. By taking this test, students give the admissions officers an objective standard that can be used to compare one student to other students. Colleges use these scores, along with the high school transcripts, résumés of extracurricular activities, letters of recommendation, and application essays as a guide to predict how well each individual will do in college-level courses.

Now that you have decided to take this exam, you are ready to begin the preparation process. All you need for success is some time and determination. Whether you have two months, one month, or one week, you can achieve your goals if you are organized, hard-working, and willing to stick to the plan.

This guide introduces you to different sections of the test, provides you with three sample schedules to help you plan your preparation, and presents guided practice to help improve your English, mathematics, reading, and science skills. For those students who are taking the optional Writing Test, Chapter XVI reviews writing strategies.

An Overview of the Cram Plan for the ACT

The ACT is not an intelligence test; it is an achievement test. This means that it tests your ability in four content areas: English, mathematics, reading, and science (and writing if you opt for the Writing Test). The best way to get ready for this test is to first determine exactly how much time you have to prepare and then follow the appropriate plan: the two-month plan, the one-month plan, or the one-week plan.

Each plan has a schedule for you to follow along with the approximate time you will need to allot to each task. In addition, subject review chapters give you strategies for that part of the test. Included in each subject-review chapter are practice exercises to assist you in the areas in which you are weakest and to help you continue to maximize your strengths.

Once you determine which cram plan to follow, the next step is to take the Diagnostic Test. The Diagnostic Test will help you diagnose your areas of weakness: those parts of the test on which you will need to focus your attention. The answer explanations will guide you to the specific chapters that cover the topics in which you need the most help. After the Diagnostic Test, you will find a scoring guide that will give you an indication of your baseline score on each section of the ACT. Then you can begin to focus on the subject review chapters. After you have completed the review, you can take the Practice Test, a full-length simulated ACT.

General Test-Taking Strategies

- Become familiar with the format of the test. If you know what to expect, you will be less nervous and more confident on the day of the test.
- Use this book to familiarize yourself with the directions to each section of the test. Knowing the directions to each section ahead of time will save you precious minutes on the day of the test.

- Work at a steady pace. You do not have the time to get bogged down on any one question. If you are having difficulty with a question, take your best educated guess and move on. The Diagnostic Test and the Practice Test will help you learn to pace yourself properly.

- Read each question very carefully, and be sure you know exactly what it asks. Many questions require you to note very specific details. Watch for **signal words** like *most, seldom, highest,* and *lowest.*

- Always read all the answer choices carefully, and use **POE** (Process of Elimination) to narrow down the choices.

- Use the answer choices to help you when you are unsure. On any multiple-choice test, the answer is always right in front of you.

- If you take the Writing Test, read the prompt and the three perspectives carefully, and be sure to address the issue as it is presented.

- Make sure you completely fill in the corresponding circle on your answer sheet. Check yourself every five questions.

- There is no guessing penalty on the ACT. Answer **EVERY** question. Confirm that you have filled in only one circle for each question. Carefully erase any changed answers.

- Bring everything you will need with you on the day of the test: sharpened no. 2 pencils with good erasers, calculator, and tissues. It is a good idea to bring your own watch; you cannot be sure you will have a visible clock in the testing room, and cell phones are prohibited. Don't forget to have your admission ticket and photo ID with you.

Using a Graphing Calculator

All questions in the math portion of the ACT can be solved without a calculator; however, using a calculator, particularly a graphing calculator, can help you solve a problem faster and avoid making careless errors. In this book, every question that can be solved with the help of a graphing calculator is indicated by a calculator icon. However, this icon does not appear on the actual ACT exam. A special section on how to use a graphing calculator to solve some of the ACT math questions is included in Appendix A.

Please note that some calculators are NOT permitted on the ACT Mathematics Test, for example: Texas Instruments' TI-89, TI-92, and TI-Nspire CAS; Hewlett-Packard's HP 48GII; and Casio's Algebra fx 2.0, ClassPad 300, and ClassPad 330. To see the most up-to-date list of calculators permitted on the ACT Mathematics Test, visit http://www.act.org/content/act/en/products-and-services/the-act/help.html or call 319-337-1270 for a recorded message.

Note: Use of a calculator is not permitted on the ACT Science Test.

Format of the ACT

The ACT is a multiple-choice test comprised of four sections and one optional Writing Test (the essay). Section 1, the English Test, contains questions on grammar, usage, and rhetoric. Section 2, the Mathematics Test, is comprised of questions on pre-algebra, elementary algebra, intermediate algebra, coordinate geometry, plane geometry, trigonometry, and probability and statistics. Section 3, the Reading Test, is comprised of four passages taken from different content areas including fiction, the social sciences, the humanities, and the natural sciences. Section 4, the Science Test, covers the application of science reasoning in biology, chemistry, earth/space sciences, and physics. The optional Writing Test, a persuasive essay in response to a specific prompt with three given perspectives, is offered after the first four sections. The multiple-choice test alone takes 2 hours and 55 minutes; the essay takes an additional 40 minutes.

Test	# of Questions	# of Minutes
English	75	45
Mathematics	60	60
Reading	40	35
Science	40	35
Optional Writing Test	1	40

Security

To ensure that all students have equal opportunity to demonstrate their abilities, the ACT administrators have instituted updated security procedures. When registering for the test, test-takers must electronically submit a current photo (head and shoulders only). This photo will be printed on the roster so proctors will be able to match the test-taker's photo ID to the photo on the roster. The photo will also be printed on the score report.

I. Two-Month Cram Plan for the ACT

	English	Mathematics	Reading	Science
8 weeks before the test	**Study Time:** 3 hours ❑ Take **Diagnostic Test** and review answer explanations. ❑ Based on the questions you missed, identify difficult topics and their corresponding topics. These topics are your targeted chapters. ❑ Compare your Writing Test (essay) to the rubric on pages 70–72 and the samples and target areas to improve.			
7 weeks before the test	**Study Time:** 1½ hours ❑ **English Test:** Chapter V 　❑ Read Sections A–B. 　❑ Read Sections C.1–C.3 and do half the practice questions at the end of each section. For targeted topics, do all practice questions.	**Study Time:** 3 hours ❑ **Using a Graphing Calculator:** Appendix A 　❑ Do all problems. ❑ **Applying Pre-Algebra Skills:** Chapter VIII 　❑ Do all practice problems. ❑ **Strategies for Solving ACT Math Problems:** Chapter VII 　❑ Study.	**Study Time:** 30 minutes ❑ **Reading Test:** Chapter VI 　❑ Read Sections A–B. 　❑ Read Sections C.1–C.4. 　❑ Do Practices 1 and 2.	**Study Time:** 1 hour ❑ **Science Test:** Chapter XV 　❑ Read Sections A–C. 　❑ Practice reading charts and graphs.
6 weeks before the test	**Study Time:** 1½ hours ❑ **English Test:** Chapter V 　❑ Read Sections C.4–C.7 and do half the practice questions at the end of each section. For targeted topics, do all practice questions.	**Study Time:** 2 hours ❑ **Common Math Formulas and Theorems for the ACT:** Appendix B 　❑ Read and review. ❑ **Solving Elementary Algebra Problems:** Chapter IX 　❑ Do all practice problems.	**Study Time:** 30 minutes ❑ **Reading Test:** Chapter VI 　❑ Read Section C.5.a–b. 　❑ Do Practice 3.	**Study Time:** 30 minutes ❑ **Science Test:** Chapter XV 　❑ Read the introduction to Section D. 　❑ Read Passage I and answer questions 1–5. Review answers.

continued

	English	Mathematics	Reading	Science

5 weeks before the test	**Study Time:** 1½ hours
	❏ **English Test:** Chapter V
	   ❏ Read Sections D.1–D.5 and do half the practice questions at the end of each section. For targeted topics, do all practice questions.
		Study Time: 3 hours
		❏ Review targeted areas.
		❏ **Studying Intermediate Algebra:** Chapter X
		   ❏ Do all practice problems.
		❏ **Answering Coordinate Geometry Questions:** Chapter XI
		   ❏ Do all practice problems.
			Study Time: 30 minutes
			❏ **Reading Test:** Chapter VI
			   ❏ Read Sections C.6.a–c. and C.7.
			   ❏ Do Practice 4.
				Study Time: 30 minutes
				❏ **Science Test:** Chapter XV
				   ❏ Read Passages II–III in Section D and answer questions 6–15. Review answers.

4 weeks before the test	**Study Time:** 1½ hours
	❏ **English Test:** Chapter V
	   ❏ Read Sections D.6–D.11 and do half the practice questions at the end of each section. For targeted topics, do all practice questions.
		Study Time: 3 hours
		❏ Review targeted areas.
		❏ **Working with Plane Geometry:** Chapter XII
		   ❏ Do all practice problems.
		❏ **Tackling Trigonometry:** Chapter XIII
		   ❏ Do all practice problems.
			Study Time: 30 minutes
			❏ **Reading Test:** Chapter VI
			   ❏ Read Sections C.8–C.9.
			   ❏ Do Practice 5.
				Study Time: 45 minutes
				❏ **Science Test:** Chapter XV
				   ❏ Review major concepts from past science courses by explaining diagrams, charts, and graphs, and by adding a narrative to images.

Writing Test (Optional essay)
Study Time: 1 hour
❏ If you plan to do the Writing Test, read Chapter XVI. Write Sample Essay A and compare to the rubric on pages 70–72.

	English	Mathematics	Reading	Science

3 weeks before the test	**Study Time:** 1½ hours
	❏ **English Test:** Chapter V
	   ❏ Read Sections E.1–E.3 and do half the practice questions at the end of each section. For targeted topics, do all practice questions.
		Study Time: 2 hours
		❏ Review targeted areas.
		❏ **Understanding Probability and Statistics:** Chapter XIV
		❏ Do all practice problems.
			Study Time: 30 minutes
			❏ **Reading Test:** Chapter VI
			   ❏ Read Section C.10.
			   ❏ Do Practice 6.
				Study Time: 45 minutes
				❏ **Science Test:** Chapter XV
				   ❏ Continue to review major concepts as described at 4 weeks mark.

2 weeks before the test

Writing Test (Optional essay)
Study Time: 1 hour
❏ Review Chapter XVI. Write Sample Essay B and compare to the rubric on pages 70–72.

Practice Test
Study Time: 4 hours
❏ Take the entire **Practice Test** (2 hours, 55 minutes) and review your answers. Note those topics that you still need to work on. These are your targeted topics.

	English	Mathematics	Reading	Science
7 days before the test	**Study Time:** 30 minutes ❑ **English Test:** Chapter V 　❑ Review targeted topics in Sections C.1–C.3. 　❑ For targeted topics, review all practice questions. Do any questions you have not already done.	**Study Time:** 1½ hours ❑ **Using a Graphing Calculator:** Appendix A 　❑ Review. ❑ **Applying Pre-Algebra Skills:** Chapter VIII 　❑ Review. ❑ **Strategies for Solving ACT Math Problems:** Chapter VII 　❑ Study.	**Study Time:** 30 minutes ❑ **Reading Test:** Chapter VI 　❑ Review targeted topics. Look over practice exercises.	**Study Time:** 20 minutes ❑ **Science Test:** Chapter XV 　❑ Review targeted topics.
6 days before the test	**Study Time:** 30 minutes ❑ **English Test:** Chapter V 　❑ Review targeted topics in Sections C.4–C.7. 　❑ For targeted topics, review all practice questions. Do any questions you have not already done.	**Study Time:** 1 hour ❑ **Common Math Formulas and Theorems for the ACT:** Appendix B 　❑ Review. ❑ **Solving Elementary Algebra Problems:** Chapter IX 　❑ Review.	**Study Time:** 30 minutes ❑ **Reading Test:** Chapter VI 　❑ Continue review of targeted topics. Do practice questions 1–3 in Section D.	**Study Time:** 20 minutes ❑ **Science Test:** Chapter XV 　❑ Continue review of targeted topics.
5 days before the test	**Study Time:** 30 minutes ❑ **English Test:** Chapter V 　❑ Review targeted topics in Sections D.1–D.5. 　❑ For targeted topics, review all practice questions. Do any questions you have not already done.	**Study Time:** 1½ hours ❑ **Studying Intermediate Algebra:** Chapter X 　❑ Review.	**Study Time:** 30 minutes ❑ **Reading Test:** Chapter VI 　❑ Continue review of targeted topics. Do practice questions 4–5 in Section D.	**Study Time:** 15 minutes ❑ **Science Test:** Chapter XV 　❑ Practice reading charts and graphs.
4 days before the test	**Study Time:** 30 minutes ❑ **English Test:** Chapter V 　❑ Review targeted topics in Sections D.6–D.11. 　❑ For targeted topics, review all practice questions. Do any questions you have not already done.	**Study Time:** 1½ hours ❑ **Answering Coordinate Geometry Questions:** Chapter XI 　❑ Review.	**Study Time:** 30 minutes ❑ **Reading Test:** Chapter VI 　❑ Continue review of targeted topics. Do practice questions 6–8 in Section D.	**Study Time:** 15 minutes ❑ **Science Test:** Chapter XV 　❑ Practice reading charts and graphs.

continued

	English	Mathematics	Reading	Science

3 days before the test	**Study Time:** 30 minutes
	❑ **English Test:** Chapter V
	  ❑ Review targeted topics in Section E.
	  ❑ For targeted topics, review all practice questions. Do any questions you have not already done.
		Study Time: 1½ hours
		❑ **Working with Plane Geometry:** Chapter XII
		  ❑ Review.
		❑ **Tackling Trigonometry:** Chapter XIII
		  ❑ Review.
			Study Time: 30 minutes
			❑ **Reading Test:** Chapter VI
			  ❑ Continue review of targeted topics. Do practice questions 9–10 in Section D.
				Study Time: 20 minutes
				❑ **Science Test:** Chapter XV
				  ❑ Reread Sections A–B.

2 days before the test	**Study Time:** 15 minutes
	❑ **English Test:** Chapter V
	  ❑ Reread Sections A–B.
		Study Time: 1 hour
		❑ **Understanding Probability and Statistics:** Chapter XIV
		  ❑ Review.
			Study Time: 15 minutes
			❑ **Reading Test:** Chapter VI
			  ❑ Reread Sections A–B.
				Study Time: 15 minutes
				❑ **Science Test:** Chapter XV
				  ❑ Reread Section C.

Night before the test	❑ Relax! You are well prepared for the test. Be confident in your ability to do well. ❑ Exercise. It helps to relieve stress, improve sleep quality, and boost brain performance. ❑ Get a good night's sleep. Try to unplug from electronic devices at least 30 minutes before bedtime and remove any distractions that might wake you during the night.			

Morning of the test	**Reminders:**
	❑ Eat a well-balanced, nutritious breakfast.
	❑ Take the following items with you to the test:
	  ❑ Your admission ticket and photo ID
	  ❑ Several no. 2 pencils and erasers
	  ❑ A calculator with fresh batteries
	  ❑ A watch
	❑ Try to go outside for a few minutes and walk around before the test to relieve stress.
	❑ **Most important:** Stay calm and confident during the test. Take deep, slow breaths and think positive thoughts if you feel nervous. You can do it!			

II. One-Month Cram Plan for the ACT

	English	Mathematics	Reading	Science
4 weeks before the test	**Study Time:** 3 hours ❏ Take **Diagnostic Test** and review answer explanations. ❏ Based on the questions you missed, identify difficult topics and their corresponding topics. These topics are your targeted chapters. ❏ Compare your Writing Test (essay) to the rubric on pages 70–72 and the samples and target areas to improve.			
	Study Time: 3 hours ❏ **English Test:** Chapter V ❏ Read Sections A–B. ❏ Read Sections C.1–C.7 and do half the practice questions at the end of each section. For targeted topics, do all practice questions.	**Study Time:** 5 hours ❏ **Using a Graphing Calculator:** Appendix A ❏ Do all practice problems. ❏ **Common Math Formulas and Theorems for the ACT:** Appendix B ❏ Read and review. ❏ **Applying Pre-Algebra Skills:** Chapter VIII ❏ Do all practice problems. ❏ **Solving Elementary Algebra Problems:** Chapter IX ❏ Do all practice problems. ❏ **Strategies for Solving ACT Math Problems:** Chapter VII ❏ Study. ❏ **Studying Intermediate Algebra:** Chapter X ❏ Do all practice problems.	**Study Time:** 1 hour ❏ **Reading Test:** Chapter VI ❏ Read Sections A–C.7. ❏ Do Practices 1–4.	**Study Time:** 1 hour ❏ **Science Test:** Chapter XV ❏ Read Sections A–C. ❏ Review major concepts from past courses by explaining diagrams, charts, and graphs, and by adding a narrative to images.
3 weeks before the test	**Study Time:** 4½ hours ❏ **English Test:** Chapter V ❏ Read Sections D.1–D.11 and E.1–E.3. ❏ Do half the practice questions at the end of each section. For targeted topics, do all practice questions.	**Study Time:** 6 hours ❏ **Answering Coordinate Geometry Questions:** Chapter XI ❏ Do all practice problems. ❏ **Working with Plane Geometry:** Chapter XII ❏ Do all practice problems. ❏ **Tackling Trigonometry:** Chapter XIII ❏ Do all practice problems. ❏ **Understanding Probability and Statistics:** Chapter XIV ❏ Do all practice problems.	**Study Time:** 1 hour ❏ **Reading Test:** Chapter VI ❏ Read Sections C.8–C.10. ❏ Do Practices 5–6.	**Study Time:** 1 hour ❏ **Science Test:** Chapter XV ❏ Read Section D. ❏ Answer questions 1–15 and review answers.

continued

	English	Mathematics	Reading	Science
2 weeks before the test	**Writing Test (Optional essay)** **Study Time:** 1 hour ❑ If you plan to do the Writing Test (essay), read Chapter XVI. Write Sample Essay A and compare to the rubric on pages 70–72. **Practice Test** **Study Time:** 4 hours ❑ Take the entire **Practice Test** (2 hours, 55 minutes), and review your answers. Note those topics that you still need to work on. These are your targeted topics.			

7 days before the test	**Study Time:**
	30 minutes
	❑ **English Test:**
	Chapter V
	  ❑ Review targeted topics in Sections C.1–C.3.
	  ❑ For targeted topics, review all practice questions. Do any questions you have not already done.
		Study Time: 1½ hours
		❑ **Using a Graphing Calculator:** Appendix A
		  ❑ Review.
		❑ **Applying Pre-Algebra Skills:** Chapter VIII
		  ❑ Read and review.
		❑ **Strategies for Solving ACT Math Problems:** Chapter VII
		  ❑ Study.
			Study Time:
			30 minutes
			❑ **Reading Test:**
			Chapter VI
			  ❑ Review targeted topics. Look over practice exercises.
				Study Time:
				20 minutes
				❑ **Science Test:**
				Chapter XV
				  ❑ Review targeted topics.

6 days before the test	**Study Time:**
	30 minutes
	❑ **English Test:**
	Chapter V
	  ❑ Review targeted topics in Sections C.4–C.7.
	  ❑ For targeted topics, review all practice questions. Do any questions you have not already done.
		Study Time: 1 hour
		❑ **Common Math Formulas and Theorems for the ACT:** Appendix B
		  ❑ Review.
		❑ **Solving Elementary Algebra Problems:** Chapter IX
		  ❑ Review.
			Study Time:
			30 minutes
			❑ **Reading Test:**
			Chapter VI
			  ❑ Continue review of targeted topics. Do practice questions 1–3 in Section D.
				Study Time:
				20 minutes
				❑ **Science Test:**
				Chapter XV
				  ❑ Continue review of targeted topics.

	Essay **Study Time:** 1 hour ❑ If you plan to do the Writing Test (essay), review Chapter XVI. Write Sample Essay B and compare to the rubric on pages 70–72.			

	English	Mathematics	Reading	Science

5 days before the test	**Study Time:** 30 minutes
	❏ **English Test:** Chapter V
	  ❏ Review targeted topics in Sections D.1–D.5.
	  ❏ For targeted topics, review all practice questions. Do any questions you have not already done.
		Study Time: 1½ hours
		❏ **Studying Intermediate Algebra:** Chapter X
		  ❏ Review.
			Study Time: 30 minutes
			❏ **Reading Test:** Chapter VI
			  ❏ Continue review of targeted topics. Do practice questions 4–5 in Section D.
				Study Time: 30 minutes
				❏ **Science Test:** Chapter XV
				  ❏ Continue review of targeted topics.
				  ❏ Practice reading charts and graphs.

4 days before the test	**Study Time:** 30 minutes
	❏ **English Test:** Chapter V
	  ❏ Review targeted topics in Sections D.6–D.11.
	  ❏ For targeted topics, review all practice questions. Do any questions you have not already done.
		Study Time: 1½ hours
		❏ **Answering Coordinate Geometry Questions:** Chapter XI
		  ❏ Review.
			Study Time: 30 minutes
			❏ **Reading Test:** Chapter VI
			  ❏ Continue review of targeted topics. Do practice questions 6–8 in Section D.
				Study Time: 30 minutes
				❏ **Science Test:** Chapter XV
				  ❏ Continue to review major concepts as described at 4 weeks mark.

3 days before the test	**Study Time:** 30 minutes
	❏ **English Test:** Chapter V
	  ❏ Review targeted topics in Section E.
	  ❏ For targeted topics, review all practice questions. Do any questions you have not already done.
		Study Time: 1½ hours
		❏ **Working with Plane Geometry:** Chapter XII
		  ❏ Review.
		❏ **Tackling Trigonometry:** Chapter XIII
		  ❏ Review.
			Study Time: 30 minutes
			❏ **Reading Test:** Chapter VI
			  ❏ Continue review of targeted topics. Do practice questions 9–10 in Section D.
				Study Time: 30 minutes
				❏ **Science Test:** Chapter XV
				  ❏ Reread Sections A–B.
				  ❏ Practice reading charts and graphs.

continued

	English	Mathematics	Reading	Science

2 days before the test	**Study Time:** 15 minutes
	❏ **English Test:** Chapter V
	   ❏ Reread Sections A–B.
		Study Time: 1 hour
		❏ **Understanding Probability and Statistics:** Chapter XIV
		   ❏ Review.
			Study Time: 15 minutes
			❏ **Reading Test:** Chapter VI
			   ❏ Reread Sections A–B.
				Study Time: 15 minutes
				❏ **Science Test:** Chapter XV
				   ❏ Reread Section C.

Night before the test	❏ Relax! You are well prepared for the test. Be confident in your ability to do well. ❏ Exercise. It helps to relieve stress, improve sleep quality, and boost brain performance. ❏ Get a good night's sleep. Try to unplug from electronic devices at least 30 minutes before bedtime and remove any distractions that might wake you during the night.			

Morning of the test	**Reminders:**
	❏ Eat a well-balanced, nutritious breakfast.
	❏ Take the following items with you to the test:
	   ❏ Your admission ticket and photo ID
	   ❏ Several no. 2 pencils and erasers
	   ❏ A calculator with fresh batteries
	   ❏ A watch
	❏ Try to go outside for a few minutes and walk around before the test to relieve stress.
	❏ **Most important:** Stay calm and confident during the test. Take deep, slow breaths and think positive thoughts if you feel nervous. You can do it!			

III. One-Week Cram Plan for the ACT

	English	Mathematics	Reading	Science
7 days before the test	**Study Time:** 3 hours ❏ Take **Diagnostic Test** and review answer explanations. ❏ Based on the questions you missed, identify difficult topics and their corresponding topics. These topics are your targeted chapters. ❏ Compare your Writing Test (essay) to the rubric on pages 70–72 and the samples and target areas to improve.			

	Study Time: 15 minutes
	❏ **English Test:** Chapter V
	  ❏ Read Sections A–B.
		Study Time: 1½ hours
		❏ **Using a Graphing Calculator:** Appendix A
		  ❏ Do all problems.
		❏ **Common Math Formulas and Theorems for the ACT:** Appendix B
		  ❏ Read and review.
		❏ **Strategies for Solving ACT Math Problems:** Chapter VII
		  ❏ Study.
			Study Time: 1 hour
			❏ **Reading Test:** Chapter VI
			  ❏ Read Sections A–C.7.
			  ❏ Do Practices 1–4.
				Study Time: 1 hour
				❏ **Science Test:** Chapter XV
				  ❏ Read Sections A–B.
				  ❏ Review major concepts from past science courses by explaining diagrams, charts, and graphs and by adding a narrative to images.

6 days before the test	**Study Time:** 2 hours
	❏ **English Test:** Chapter V
	  ❏ Read Sections C.1–C.7.
	  ❏ Do a few practice questions at the end of each section.
	  ❏ For targeted topics, do half the practice questions.
		Study Time: 2½ hours
		❏ **Applying Pre-Algebra Skills:** Chapter VIII
		  ❏ Do all practice problems.
		❏ **Solving Elementary Algebra Problems:** Chapter IX
		  ❏ Do all practice problems.
		❏ **Studying Intermediate Algebra:** Chapter X
		  ❏ Do all practice problems.
			Study Time: 30 minutes
			❏ **Reading Test:** Chapter VI
			  ❏ Read Sections C.8–C.9.
			  ❏ Do Practice 5.
				Study Time: 45 minutes
				❏ **Science Test:** Chapter XV
				  ❏ Read Section C.
				  ❏ Continue to review major science concepts as described at 7 days mark.

5 days before the test	**Study Time:** 2 hours
	❏ **English Test:** Chapter V
	  ❏ Read Sections D.1–D.5.
	  ❏ Do a few practice questions at the end of each section.
	  ❏ For targeted topics, do half the practice questions.
		Study Time: 2½ hours
		❏ **Answering Coordinate Geometry Questions:** Chapter XI
		  ❏ Do all practice problems.
		❏ **Working with Plane Geometry:** Chapter XII
		  ❏ Do all practice problems.
			Study Time: 30 minutes
			❏ **Reading Test:** Chapter VI
			  ❏ Read Section C.10.
			  ❏ Do Practice 6.
				Study Time: 30 minutes
				❏ **Science Test:** Chapter XV
				  ❏ Read the introduction to Section D.
				  ❏ Read Passage I and answer questions 1–5. Review answers.

continued

	English	Mathematics	Reading	Science
Writing Test (Optional essay) **Study Time:** 1 hour ❑ If you plan to do the Writing Test (essay), read Chapter XVI. Write Sample Essay A and compare to the rubric on pages 70–72.				

4 days before the test	**Study Time:** 2 hours
	 ❑ **English Test:** Chapter V
	    ❑ Read Sections D.6–D.11 and do a few practice questions at the end of each section.
	    ❑ For targeted topics, do half the practice questions.
	    ❑ Read Sections E.1–E.3 and do practice questions in each section.
		Study Time: 2½ hours
		 ❑ **Tackling Trigonometry:** Chapter XIII
		    ❑ Do all practice problems.
		 ❑ **Understanding Probability and Statistics:** Chapter XIV
		    ❑ Do all practice problems.
			Study Time: 45 minutes
			 ❑ **Reading Test:** Chapter VI
			    ❑ Do additional practice (Section D) at the end of the chapter.
				Study Time: 30 minutes
				 ❑ **Science Test:** Chapter XV
				    ❑ Read Passages II–III in Section D and answer questions 6–15. Review answers.

3 days before the test	**Writing Test (Optional essay)** **Study Time:** 1 hour ❑ If you plan to do the Writing Test (essay), review Chapter XVI. Write Sample Essay B and compare to the rubric on pages 70–72. **Practice Test** **Study Time:** 4 hours ❑ Take the entire **Practice Test** (2 hours, 55 minutes), and review your answers. Note those topics that you still need to work on. These are your targeted topics.			

2 days before the test	**Study Time:** 1 hour
	 ❑ **English Test:** Chapter V
	    ❑ Review the targeted areas. Do a few more practice questions in each section.
		Study Time: 1 hour
		    ❑ Review the targeted areas.
		 ❑ **Common Math Formulas and Theorems for the ACT:** Appendix B
		    ❑ Reread and review.
			Study Time: 1 hour
			 ❑ **Reading Test:** Chapter VI
			    ❑ Reread and review targeted topics.
			    ❑ Look over practice exercises.
				Study Time: 45 minutes
				 ❑ **Science Test:** Chapter XV
				    ❑ Review the targeted topics.
				    ❑ Practice reading charts and graphs.

Night before the test	❑ Relax! You are well prepared for the test. Be confident in your ability to do well. ❑ Exercise. It helps to relieve stress, improve sleep quality, and boost brain performance. ❑ Get a good night's sleep. Try to unplug from electronic devices at least 30 minutes before bedtime and remove any distractions that might wake you during the night.			

Morning of the test	**Reminders:**
	 ❑ Eat a well-balanced, nutritious breakfast.
	 ❑ Take the following items with you to the test:
	    ❑ Your admission ticket and photo ID
	    ❑ Several no. 2 pencils and erasers
	    ❑ A calculator with fresh batteries
	    ❑ A watch
	 ❑ Try to go outside for a few minutes and walk around before the test to relieve stress.
	 ❑ **Most important:** Stay calm and confident during the test. Take deep, slow breaths and think positive thoughts if you feel nervous. You can do it!			

IV. Diagnostic Test

This Diagnostic Test (excluding the essay) is half the length of the actual ACT. You will have a full 40 minutes for the essay.

The Diagnostic Test covers four content areas: English, Mathematics, Reading, and Science. The tests are designed to measure your ability in these four areas and to predict your success in college. Each question on the test is numbered. Choose the best answer for each question and fill in the corresponding circle on the answer sheet provided.

For each question, be sure to fill in only one circle on your answer sheet. If you erase, do so completely as the scoring device will pick up any stray marks. (Although this Diagnostic Test is just for practice and is not being mechanically scored, you should practice the way you would like to perform on the actual test.)

Your score will be based on the number of questions you have answered correctly during the time allowed for each section, so answer **all** questions, even if you are unsure and have to guess. Since no points will be deducted for incorrect answers, it is to your advantage to answer every question on the test.

If you finish a section before the allotted time runs out, you may not work on any other section. You may not go back to a previous section or move ahead to work on the next section.

You may use any open spaces on your test booklet for scrap.

The Diagnostic Test also includes the optional Writing Test. The Writing Test is an essay in which you demonstrate your writing and thinking skills. It is administered after the four sections of the ACT are completed. For more on the Writing Test, see Chapter XVI.

Timing: You will need 2 hours and 9 minutes to complete the Diagnostic Test.

Test	# of Questions	# of Minutes
English	38	23
Mathematics	30	30
Reading	20	18
Science	20	18
Writing	1	40

After you complete the test, use the Answer Key and the Scoring Worksheets to obtain your scaled scores.

To score the Writing Test (Essay), refer to the rubric on pages 70–72 and to the sample essays and their evaluations starting on page 66.

Answer Sheet

Section 1: English Test

1 Ⓐ Ⓑ Ⓒ Ⓓ	26 Ⓕ Ⓖ Ⓗ Ⓙ
2 Ⓕ Ⓖ Ⓗ Ⓙ	27 Ⓐ Ⓑ Ⓒ Ⓓ
3 Ⓐ Ⓑ Ⓒ Ⓓ	28 Ⓕ Ⓖ Ⓗ Ⓙ
4 Ⓕ Ⓖ Ⓗ Ⓙ	29 Ⓐ Ⓑ Ⓒ Ⓓ
5 Ⓐ Ⓑ Ⓒ Ⓓ	30 Ⓕ Ⓖ Ⓗ Ⓙ
6 Ⓕ Ⓖ Ⓗ Ⓙ	31 Ⓐ Ⓑ Ⓒ Ⓓ
7 Ⓐ Ⓑ Ⓒ Ⓓ	32 Ⓕ Ⓖ Ⓗ Ⓙ
8 Ⓕ Ⓖ Ⓗ Ⓙ	33 Ⓐ Ⓑ Ⓒ Ⓓ
9 Ⓐ Ⓑ Ⓒ Ⓓ	34 Ⓕ Ⓖ Ⓗ Ⓙ
10 Ⓕ Ⓖ Ⓗ Ⓙ	35 Ⓐ Ⓑ Ⓒ Ⓓ
11 Ⓐ Ⓑ Ⓒ Ⓓ	36 Ⓕ Ⓖ Ⓗ Ⓙ
12 Ⓕ Ⓖ Ⓗ Ⓙ	37 Ⓐ Ⓑ Ⓒ Ⓓ
13 Ⓐ Ⓑ Ⓒ Ⓓ	38 Ⓕ Ⓖ Ⓗ Ⓙ
14 Ⓕ Ⓖ Ⓗ Ⓙ	
15 Ⓐ Ⓑ Ⓒ Ⓓ	
16 Ⓕ Ⓖ Ⓗ Ⓙ	
17 Ⓐ Ⓑ Ⓒ Ⓓ	
18 Ⓕ Ⓖ Ⓗ Ⓙ	
19 Ⓐ Ⓑ Ⓒ Ⓓ	
20 Ⓕ Ⓖ Ⓗ Ⓙ	
21 Ⓐ Ⓑ Ⓒ Ⓓ	
22 Ⓕ Ⓖ Ⓗ Ⓙ	
23 Ⓐ Ⓑ Ⓒ Ⓓ	
24 Ⓕ Ⓖ Ⓗ Ⓙ	
25 Ⓐ Ⓑ Ⓒ Ⓓ	

Section 2: Mathematics Test

1 Ⓐ Ⓑ Ⓒ Ⓓ Ⓔ	26 Ⓕ Ⓖ Ⓗ Ⓙ Ⓚ
2 Ⓕ Ⓖ Ⓗ Ⓙ Ⓚ	27 Ⓐ Ⓑ Ⓒ Ⓓ Ⓔ
3 Ⓐ Ⓑ Ⓒ Ⓓ Ⓔ	28 Ⓕ Ⓖ Ⓗ Ⓙ Ⓚ
4 Ⓕ Ⓖ Ⓗ Ⓙ Ⓚ	29 Ⓐ Ⓑ Ⓒ Ⓓ Ⓔ
5 Ⓐ Ⓑ Ⓒ Ⓓ Ⓔ	30 Ⓕ Ⓖ Ⓗ Ⓙ Ⓚ
6 Ⓕ Ⓖ Ⓗ Ⓙ Ⓚ	
7 Ⓐ Ⓑ Ⓒ Ⓓ Ⓔ	
8 Ⓕ Ⓖ Ⓗ Ⓙ Ⓚ	
9 Ⓐ Ⓑ Ⓒ Ⓓ Ⓔ	
10 Ⓕ Ⓖ Ⓗ Ⓙ Ⓚ	
11 Ⓐ Ⓑ Ⓒ Ⓓ Ⓔ	
12 Ⓕ Ⓖ Ⓗ Ⓙ Ⓚ	
13 Ⓐ Ⓑ Ⓒ Ⓓ Ⓔ	
14 Ⓕ Ⓖ Ⓗ Ⓙ Ⓚ	
15 Ⓐ Ⓑ Ⓒ Ⓓ Ⓔ	
16 Ⓕ Ⓖ Ⓗ Ⓙ Ⓚ	
17 Ⓐ Ⓑ Ⓒ Ⓓ Ⓔ	
18 Ⓕ Ⓖ Ⓗ Ⓙ Ⓚ	
19 Ⓐ Ⓑ Ⓒ Ⓓ Ⓔ	
20 Ⓕ Ⓖ Ⓗ Ⓙ Ⓚ	
21 Ⓐ Ⓑ Ⓒ Ⓓ Ⓔ	
22 Ⓕ Ⓖ Ⓗ Ⓙ Ⓚ	
23 Ⓐ Ⓑ Ⓒ Ⓓ Ⓔ	
24 Ⓕ Ⓖ Ⓗ Ⓙ Ⓚ	
25 Ⓐ Ⓑ Ⓒ Ⓓ Ⓔ	

Section 3: Reading Test

1 Ⓐ Ⓑ Ⓒ Ⓓ
2 Ⓕ Ⓖ Ⓗ Ⓙ
3 Ⓐ Ⓑ Ⓒ Ⓓ
4 Ⓕ Ⓖ Ⓗ Ⓙ
5 Ⓐ Ⓑ Ⓒ Ⓓ
6 Ⓕ Ⓖ Ⓗ Ⓙ
7 Ⓐ Ⓑ Ⓒ Ⓓ
8 Ⓕ Ⓖ Ⓗ Ⓙ
9 Ⓐ Ⓑ Ⓒ Ⓓ
10 Ⓕ Ⓖ Ⓗ Ⓙ
11 Ⓐ Ⓑ Ⓒ Ⓓ
12 Ⓕ Ⓖ Ⓗ Ⓙ
13 Ⓐ Ⓑ Ⓒ Ⓓ
14 Ⓕ Ⓖ Ⓗ Ⓙ
15 Ⓐ Ⓑ Ⓒ Ⓓ
16 Ⓕ Ⓖ Ⓗ Ⓙ
17 Ⓐ Ⓑ Ⓒ Ⓓ
18 Ⓕ Ⓖ Ⓗ Ⓙ
19 Ⓐ Ⓑ Ⓒ Ⓓ
20 Ⓕ Ⓖ Ⓗ Ⓙ

Section 4: Science Test

1 Ⓐ Ⓑ Ⓒ Ⓓ
2 Ⓕ Ⓖ Ⓗ Ⓙ
3 Ⓐ Ⓑ Ⓒ Ⓓ
4 Ⓕ Ⓖ Ⓗ Ⓙ
5 Ⓐ Ⓑ Ⓒ Ⓓ
6 Ⓕ Ⓖ Ⓗ Ⓙ
7 Ⓐ Ⓑ Ⓒ Ⓓ
8 Ⓕ Ⓖ Ⓗ Ⓙ
9 Ⓐ Ⓑ Ⓒ Ⓓ
10 Ⓕ Ⓖ Ⓗ Ⓙ
11 Ⓐ Ⓑ Ⓒ Ⓓ
12 Ⓕ Ⓖ Ⓗ Ⓙ
13 Ⓐ Ⓑ Ⓒ Ⓓ
14 Ⓕ Ⓖ Ⓗ Ⓙ
15 Ⓐ Ⓑ Ⓒ Ⓓ
16 Ⓕ Ⓖ Ⓗ Ⓙ
17 Ⓐ Ⓑ Ⓒ Ⓓ
18 Ⓕ Ⓖ Ⓗ Ⓙ
19 Ⓐ Ⓑ Ⓒ Ⓓ
20 Ⓕ Ⓖ Ⓗ Ⓙ

CUT HERE

Section 5: Writing Test

CUT HERE

Section 1: English Test

23 Minutes—38 Questions

Directions: The English Test consists of three passages. In each passage, words and phrases are underlined and numbered. Following each passage are corresponding questions (on the actual exam, passages appear in the left-hand column, with corresponding questions in the right-hand column). Each question offers four alternatives for the underlined part. Consider the choices and then select the one that best fits the requirements of standard written English. Be sure to take into account the style and tone of the whole passage. If you think the word or phrase is correct as written, choose "NO CHANGE." For some of the questions, you will see a number in a box, which corresponds to a similar number within the passage. These questions ask about a section of the passage or about the passage as a whole. It is a good idea to read through the entire passage before you begin to answer the questions.

Passage I

The Tale of the Tail

[1]

Famous the world over, the cats of the Isle of Man <u>are famous</u> for the distinct absence of an
[1]
attribute—their tails. These Manx, as the breed is <u>known are solid, stocky cats</u>, with dense coats and a
[2]
distinctive round shape. Sometimes referred to as "rumpies," these cats <u>are either completely tailless or</u>
[3]
<u>have</u> small stumps in place of the long, graceful tails
[3]
of other breeds.

1.
   A. NO CHANGE
   B. is notable
   C. was known
   D. are known

2.
   F. NO CHANGE
   G. known, are solid stocky cats
   H. known, are solid, stocky cats
   J. known are solid stocky cats

3.
   A. NO CHANGE
   B. either are completely tailless or have
   C. are, either completely tailless, or they have
   D. either are completely tailless or having

[2]

Many theories <u>have arose</u> about the origin of the
                    4
Manx. There is a rather humorous story that
explains the cat's tailless state. According to this
tale, Noah <u>was about to closing</u> the door to the ark
                        5
when he realized a cat was missing. This particular
<u>cat; an excellent mouser, was stalking its prey</u> when
                            6
the rains began to fall. <u>Persistently unwilling to</u> give
                                    7
up the chase, the cat continued its hunt as the water
began to rise. Noah, anxious to seal the ark, began
to close the great doors. Suddenly, the door closed,
accidentally severing the cat's tail. ☐8 Thus, the
breed was born.

4.
F. NO CHANGE
G. have arisen
H. arised
J. had arose

5.
A. NO CHANGE
B. has been closing
C. was about to close
D. closed

6.
F. NO CHANGE
G. cat, an excellent mouser, was stalking
their prey
H. cat, an excellent mouser, was stalking its
prey
J. cat, an excellent mouser was stalking its
prey

7. Three of the choices indicate that the cat was
intent on accomplishing its goal. Which
choice does NOT do so?

A. NO CHANGE
B. Loath to
C. Reluctant to
D. Resigned to

8. The writer is considering adding the following
sentence at this point in the paragraph:

> Consequently, that is the story of Noah
> and the cat.

Would this addition be appropriate here?

F. Yes, because it is an appropriate
transitional sentence.
G. Yes, because it effectively concludes the
story.
H. No, because it fails to include any
relevant information.
J. No, because the following sentence
provides a more appropriate conclusion
to the paragraph.

[3]

Another myth about the Manx attributes its tailless state to the proclivity of ancient warriors to decorate <u>the proclivity of ancient warriors to decorate</u>
₉
their helmets with furry tails. Aware that their offspring would face imprisonment and possible death at the hands of the soldiers, mother cats bit off <u>it's kittens' tails</u> so the kittens would not be taken
₁₀
captive.

[4]

<u>Still another</u> conjecture involves the so-called
₁₁
"cabbit." In this legend, long ago on the Isle of Man, a cat and a rabbit mated, producing a round, tailless offspring that combined their physical traits.

9. Which of the following would NOT be an appropriate replacement for the underlined part?

   A. the habit of ancient warriors of decorating

   B. the fact that there was a tendency of ancient warriors who wanted to decorate

   C. the inclination of ancient warriors to decorate

   D. the tendency of ancient warriors to decorate

10.
   F. NO CHANGE

   G. its kitten's tail

   H. their kittens tail

   J. their kittens' tails

11. For the sake of logic and coherence, which would be the best transitional phrase to use?

    A. NO CHANGE

    B. Nevertheless,

    C. In contrast,

    D. Moreover,

[5]

Today, animal biologists consider the Manx to be a genetic mutation <u>at this time</u>. Since the Isle of
12

Man is a rather geographically isolated location, once the dominant mutant tailless gene appeared in the animal population, <u>it became</u> concentrated in
13

the gene pool. Thus, the "typical" cat on the island became the tailless variety. [14] [15]

12.
   F. NO CHANGE
   G. presently
   H. currently
   J. Omit the underlined portion.

13.
   A. NO CHANGE
   B. they became
   C. it has become
   D. it was becoming

14. Suppose after rereading this essay the writer wants to add the following detail:

> The long hind legs of the Manx and its peculiar hopping gait reinforce this speculation.

The most logical and effective place would be after the last sentence in which paragraph?

   F. 2
   G. 3
   H. 4
   J. 5

15. Suppose the writer had intended to write a scholarly essay disproving current theories about the influx of cats in Europe. Would this essay successfully fulfill that goal?

   A. Yes, because the essay is formal in tone and covers the topic thoroughly.
   B. Yes, because the essay cites relevant historical and statistical evidence to disprove the theories.
   C. No, because the essay is not scholarly in tone and does not disprove any theories.
   D. No, because the essay conclusively proves a theory.

Passage II

The Great Wall

[1]

The Great Wall of China is one of the Seven Wonders of the World. Built over 2,000 years ago by Emperor Qin Shi Huang of China during the Qin Dynasty, they wind up and down for 4,000 miles over mountains and plateaus. It is the longest man-made structure in the world.

[2]

The wall was conceived as a defensive fortification to protect the ones inside against marauders coming from outside. Each of the geographical regions along the route was charged with constructing a segment. Thousands of soldiers, prisoners, and local townspeople hauled and packed thousands of tons of stones and earth, some sections are up to

16.
  F. NO CHANGE
  G. Having been built
  H. It was built
  J. It had been built

17.
  A. NO CHANGE
  B. it winds
  C. it is winding
  D. which winds

18.
  F. NO CHANGE
  G. defensive fortification
  H. defensive fortification to protect and defend
  J. way to be a defensive fortification to protect and defend

19.
  A. NO CHANGE
  B. were
  C. were being
  D. was being

20.
  F. NO CHANGE
  G. hauled, and packed thousands of tons of stones
  H. hauled, and packed, thousands of tons of stones
  J. hauled and packed; thousands of tons of stones

21.
  A. NO CHANGE
  B. earth, in some sections
  C. earth. Some sections
  D. earth; with some sections

twenty-five feet high. The wall <u>not only was wide</u>
²²
<u>enough for troops but</u> also for horse-pulled wagons
²²
to travel across. Set at regular intervals along the
wall, watch towers and guard stations provided
lookouts and living quarters for soldiers. ☐23

[3]

The Emperor <u>envisioned the wall as protecting</u>
²⁴
the Chinese Empire from invading armies.
<u>In addition</u>, many segments of the wall were never
²⁵
<u>connected together with each other</u>. Since the
²⁶

22.
   F.   NO CHANGE
   G.   not was wide enough for only troops and
   H.   was wide enough for not only troops as well as
   J.   was wide enough not only for troops but

23. The writer is considering adding the following information to the end of the preceding sentence.

> , who were often on duty for months at a time

If the writer made this addition, the sentence would:

   A.   gain an interesting detail.
   B.   gain a transition.
   C.   become anecdotal.
   D.   contrast with the preceding one.

24. Which of the following choices would be acceptable to replace the underlined words?

   F.   imagined the wall would be to protect
   G.   envisioned the wall to be protection of
   H.   imagined the wall for protecting
   J.   imagined the wall would protect

25.
   A.   NO CHANGE
   B.   For example
   C.   However
   D.   On the other hand

26.
   F.   NO CHANGE
   G.   connected
   H.   able to have a connection with each other
   J.   linked as a connection

sections of the wall <u>is not contiguous</u>, it never
27
achieved its original purpose. It is, however, one of
the most visited tourist sites in the world. <u>People</u>
28
<u>with a camera</u> come from all over the world to pho-
28
tograph this amazing sight. 29

27.
    A. NO CHANGE
    B. is not linked
    C. are not contiguous
    D. has not been connected

28.
    F. NO CHANGE
    G. People who have a camera
    H. People with cameras
    J. People who bring a camera

29. Which of the following sentences, if included here, would best conclude the essay?

    A. I was there last year, and it was a thrill to walk on the wall.
    B. If you go to China, don't miss the wall!
    C. A visit to the wall is a reminder of the great perseverance and determination of the Chinese people.
    D. In China there are also many other great places to visit.

Passage III

Those Popular Penguins

[1]

These tuxedo-clad flightless birds, always fascinating to human beings, have become pop culture icons. No <u>lesser</u> than five films in the past five years
₃₀
have featured the birds. It is not hard to understand the popularity of <u>penguins: They</u> are "well-dressed,"
₃₁
playful, and <u>they are</u> unafraid of people. <u>Indeed,</u>
₃₂ ₃₃
these striking <u>bird's with their</u> distinct waddle <u>have</u>
₃₄ ₃₅
<u>become</u> synonymous with winter fun. Clumsy on
₃₅

30.
- **F.** NO CHANGE
- **G.** less
- **H.** lower
- **J.** fewer

31.
- **A.** NO CHANGE
- **B.** penguins, they
- **C.** penguins being
- **D.** penguins; who

32.
- **F.** NO CHANGE
- **G.** Omit the underlined portion.
- **H.** they have been
- **J.** being

33. The writer would like to use a transitional word for emphasis here. What would best accomplish this?
- **A.** NO CHANGE
- **B.** For instance
- **C.** Nevertheless
- **D.** Similarly

34.
- **F.** NO CHANGE
- **G.** birds with its
- **H.** birds' with their
- **J.** birds with their

35.
- **A.** NO CHANGE
- **B.** has become
- **C.** has became
- **D.** have became

land, yet graceful in the water, <u>scientists have found</u>
₃₆

penguins <u>are superbly adapted to</u> life in the arctic.
₃₇

They have no land predators and need only to be

protected <u>away from</u> eager tourists.
₃₈

36.
    F. NO CHANGE
    G. Omit the underlined portion.
    H. scientists are finding
    J. as found by scientists,

37. Which of the following would NOT be an acceptable replacement for the underlined part?

    A. are well equipped for
    B. are perfectly suited to
    C. are able to be adapted to
    D. are well suited to

38.
    F. NO CHANGE
    G. by
    H. from
    J. with

IF YOU FINISH BEFORE TIME IS CALLED, CHECK YOUR WORK ON THIS SECTION ONLY. DO NOT WORK ON ANY OTHER SECTION IN THE TEST.

Section 2: Mathematics Test

30 Minutes—30 Questions

Directions: Solve each problem and fill in the corresponding circle on the answer sheet. Figures are not necessarily drawn to scale. You may use a permitted graphing calculator.

1. If m and n are integers, which of the following must be an even integer?

   A. $m + n$
   B. $2m + 3n$
   C. $3m + 2n$
   D. $2(m + n)$
   E. $3(m + n)$

2. There are 10 members on the Washington Middle School basketball team. The scatterplot in the accompanying figure shows the length of each player's right foot and the height of the player. The line of best fit is also shown. For the player whose right foot measures 11 inches, his actual height is how many inches greater than the height predicted by the line of best fit?

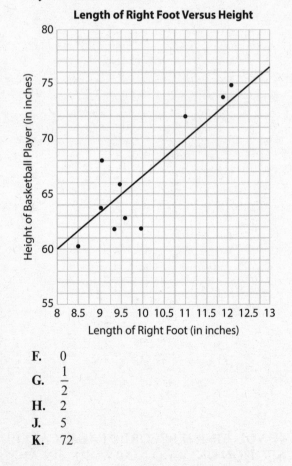

Length of Right Foot Versus Height

   F. 0
   G. $\dfrac{1}{2}$
   H. 2
   J. 5
   K. 72

3. Six years ago, Mary was x years old and Bill was exactly twice as old as Mary. Which of the following represents the sum of their current ages?

   A. $3x - 12$
   B. $3x - 6$
   C. $3x$
   D. $3x + 6$
   E. $3x + 12$

4. If $\overline{DE} \parallel \overline{BC}$, $DE = 3$, $AD = x$, and $DB = 2x$, what is the length of $\overline{BC}$?

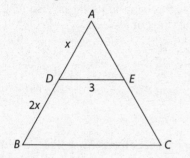

   F.   3
   G.   6
   H.   9
   J.   12
   K.   15

5. A furniture store carries dining room sets consisting of tables and chairs as described here:

Tables	Chairs
Teak	with arms
Walnut	without arms
Oak	

How many different dining room sets, consisting of 1 type of table and 1 type of chair, does the store offer?

   A.   2
   B.   3
   C.   5
   D.   6
   E.   8

6. If x is a negative integer, and $xy = -2$ and $y + x = 1$, what is the value of x?

   F. -2
   G. -1
   H.   0
   J.   1
   K.   2

7. Points B, C, and D lie on a straight line, and $\triangle ABC$ is isosceles. The measure of vertex $\angle A$ is $2x$. If $m\angle ACD = 140$, what is the value of x?

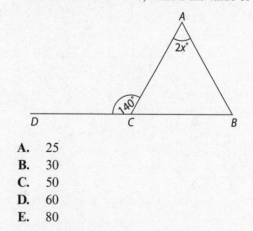

   A.   25
   B.   30
   C.   50
   D.   60
   E.   80

8. In the accompanying diagram, two lines intersect. Which of the following must be true?

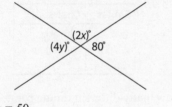

    I. $x = 50$
   II. $y = 40$
  III. $x + y = 90$

   F.   I only
   G.   II only
   H.   I and II only
   J.   II and III only
   K.   I, II, and III

9. If a function f is defined as $f(x) = x^2 + 4$, what is the value of $3f(1) + 2$?

   A.   15
   B.   17
   C.   21
   D.   39
   E.   85

10. Which of the following could be an equation of the accompanying figure?

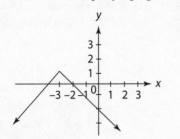

   F. $y = -(x - 3)^2$
   G. $y = -x^2 + 3$
   H. $y = -|x| - 3$
   J. $y = -|x + 3| + 1$
   K. $y = -|x - 3| - 1$

11. What is the slope of the line passing through the points $A(-2,4)$ and $B(-6,-8)$?

   A. -3
   B. $-\dfrac{1}{3}$
   C. $\dfrac{1}{2}$
   D. $\dfrac{1}{3}$
   E.   3

12. Given that k is an integer and if k is decreased by 25 percent of itself, the result is 24, what is the value of k?

   F.   18
   G.   28
   H.   32
   J.   36
   K.   40

13. In the accompanying semicircle with center O, $\overline{AC}$ is a diameter, $AC = 8\sqrt{2}$, and $AB = BC$. What is the sum of the areas of the two shaded regions?

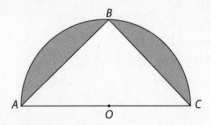

   A. $16\pi + 16\pi$
   B. $16\pi - 32$
   C. $32 + 16\pi$
   D. $16\pi + 32$
   E. $32 + 32$

14. An equation of a circle is given as $x^2 + (y - 3)^2 = 1$. What is the area of this circle?

   F. π
   G. 2π
   H. 3π
   J. 9π
   K. 10π

15. If n is a positive integer, and twice the square of n is the same as four times n, what is the value of n?

    A. −4
    B. −2
    C. 0
    D. 2
    E. 4

16. If the midpoint of $A(2,4)$ and $B(h,k)$ is $(4,2)$, what is the value of k?

    F. −2
    G. 0
    H. 2
    J. 4
    K. 6

17. At a bakery, the price of a doughnut is $0.80. After the first doughnut, each additional doughnut is $0.40. If Mary paid $4.00 for doughnuts, how many doughnuts did Mary buy?

    A. 5
    B. 6
    C. 8
    D. 9
    E. 10

18. In the accompanying diagram, $CB = 12$, $AB = 13$, and $m\angle C = 90$. What is the value of $\cos A$?

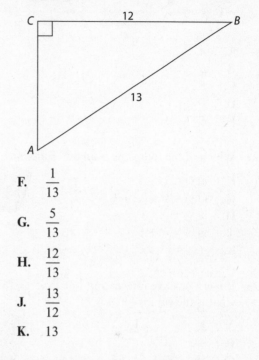

    F. $\dfrac{1}{13}$
    G. $\dfrac{5}{13}$
    H. $\dfrac{12}{13}$
    J. $\dfrac{13}{12}$
    K. 13

19. A square is inscribed in a circle with a radius of 10. What is the area of the square?

    A. 100
    B. $100\sqrt{2}$
    C. 200
    D. $200\sqrt{2}$
    E. 400

20. What is the sum of the 5th and the 15th terms of the sequence 0, 5, 10, 15, . . . ?

    F. 20
    G. 30
    H. 50
    J. 90
    K. 100

21. Which of the following points could represent the coordinate of $B + 2C$?

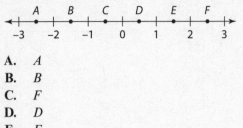

A. A

B. B

C. F

D. D

E. E

22. Which of the following is an odd function?

F. $h(x) = 3x - 5$

G. $k(x) = x^2 - 7x + 9$

H. $p(x) = x^3 - 3$

J. $q(x) = x^3 + 1$

K. $f(x) = x^5 - 2x^3$

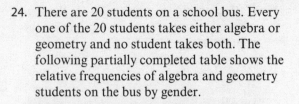

23. If n is a positive integer and $\left(8^{\frac{2}{3}}\right)\left(n^{\frac{1}{4}}\right) = 16$, what is the value of n?

A. 2

B. 8

C. 16

D. 64

E. 256

24. There are 20 students on a school bus. Every one of the 20 students takes either algebra or geometry and no student takes both. The following partially completed table shows the relative frequencies of algebra and geometry students on the bus by gender.

Relative Frequency Table			
	Algebra	Geometry	Total
Male	0.4		0.6
Female		0.15	
Total			1

If a student is picked at random from the school bus, what is the probability that the student is a male and taking geometry?

F. 0.2

G. 0.4

H. 0.6

J. 0.75

K. 0.85

25. If 2 coins are tossed, what is the probability that you will have at least one head?

A. $\dfrac{1}{8}$

B. $\dfrac{1}{4}$

C. $\dfrac{1}{3}$

D. $\dfrac{1}{2}$

E. $\dfrac{3}{4}$

26. Set $A = \{-2, -1, 0, 2, 3, 4\}$. If set B contains only members obtained by multiplying each member of set A by -1, what is the median of set B?

    F. -2
    G. -1
    H. 0
    J. 1
    K. 2

27. In the accompanying diagram, the figure is a rectangular solid. Line segment $\overline{AG}$ is not shown. If $HG = 6$, $GF = 4$, and $CG = 2$, what is the length of $\overline{AG}$?

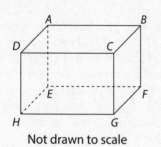

Not drawn to scale

    A. $\sqrt{40}$
    B. $\sqrt{54}$
    C. $\sqrt{56}$
    D. 8
    E. 12

28. If $\log_2 8 + \log_5 25 = \log_3 x$, what is the value of x?

    F. 15
    G. 34
    H. 81
    J. 125
    K. 243

29. If $0 < \theta < \dfrac{\pi}{2}$, which of the following is equivalent to $\dfrac{\cos\theta}{\sqrt{1 - \sin^2\theta}}$?

    A. -1
    B. $-2 - \cos 2\theta$
    C. $2 - \sin\theta$
    D. $1 + \cos\theta$
    E. 1

30. Given $i = \sqrt{-1}$, which of the following is equivalent to $2i(i^3 - 4i)$?

    F. -6
    G. $-6i^2$
    H. 6
    J. 7
    K. 10

IF YOU FINISH BEFORE TIME IS CALLED, CHECK YOUR WORK ON THIS SECTION ONLY. DO NOT WORK ON ANY OTHER SECTION IN THE TEST.

STOP

Section 3: Reading Test

18 Minutes—20 Questions

Directions: The Reading Test consists of four different content area reading passages, each followed by five questions. One content area has a paired reading passage. After reading a passage, select the best answer and fill in the corresponding circle on the answer sheet. You may look back in the passages as you answer the questions.

Passage I

PROSE FICTION: The following is an excerpt from *Anne of Green Gables,* a novel written in 1908 by Lucy Maud Montgomery. The story is set in Green Gables, a farm on Prince Edward Island in Canada owned by siblings Matthew and Marilla Cuthbert. Mrs. Rachel, a neighbor of the Cuthberts, is a well-known gossip.

Mrs. Rachel, before she had fairly closed the door, had taken a mental note of everything that was on that table. There were three plates laid, so that Marilla must be expecting (5) some one home with Matthew to tea; but the dishes were everyday dishes and there was only crab-apple preserves and one kind of cake, so that the expected company could not be any particular company. Yet what of (10) Matthew's white collar and the sorrel mare? Mrs. Rachel was getting fairly dizzy with this unusual mystery about quiet, unmysterious Green Gables.

"Good evening, Rachel," Marilla said (15) briskly. "This is a real fine evening, isn't it? Won't you sit down? How are all your folks?"

Something that for lack of any other name might be called friendship existed and always had existed between Marilla Cuthbert and (20) Mrs. Rachel, in spite of—or perhaps because of—their dissimilarity.

Marilla was a tall, thin woman, with angles and without curves; her dark hair showed some gray streaks and was always twisted up in a (25) hard little knot behind with two wire hairpins stuck aggressively through it. She looked like a woman of narrow experience and rigid conscience, which she was; but there was a saving something about her mouth which, if it had (30) been ever so slightly developed, might have been considered indicative of a sense of humor.

"We're all pretty well," said Mrs. Rachel. "I was kind of afraid YOU weren't, though, when I saw Matthew starting off today. (35) I thought maybe he was going to the doctor's."

Marilla's lips twitched understandingly. She had expected Mrs. Rachel up; she had known that the sight of Matthew jaunting off so unaccountably would be too much for her (40) neighbor's curiosity.

"Oh, no, I'm quite well although I had a bad headache yesterday," she said. "Matthew went to Bright River. We're getting a little boy from an orphan asylum in Nova Scotia and (45) he's coming on the train tonight."

If Marilla had said that Matthew had gone to Bright River to meet a kangaroo from Australia Mrs. Rachel could not have been more astonished. She was actually stricken (50) dumb for five seconds. It was unsupposable that Marilla was making fun of her, but Mrs. Rachel was almost forced to suppose it.

"Are you in earnest, Marilla?" she demanded when voice returned to her. (55)

"Yes, of course," said Marilla, as if getting boys from orphan asylums in Nova Scotia were part of the usual spring work on any well-regulated Avonlea farm instead of being an unheard of innovation. (60)

Mrs. Rachel felt that she had received a severe mental jolt. She thought in exclamation points. A boy! Marilla and Matthew Cuthbert of all people adopting a boy! From an orphan asylum! Well, the world was certainly turning (65) upside down! She would be surprised at nothing after this! Nothing!

"What on earth put such a notion into your head?" she demanded disapprovingly. This had been done without her advice being asked, (70) and must perforce be disapproved.

1. It can be inferred that Mrs. Rachel's dizziness is due to:

   A. the speed with which she hurried to the Cuthbert's farm.

   B. the inexplicable series of events leading up to this conversation.

   C. her fear that Marilla and Matthew were about to embark on a dangerous undertaking.

   D. her concern about Matthew's illness.

2. The physical description of Marilla suggests which of the following?

   F. Despite her circumscribed life, she is capable of seeing humor in life's situations.

   G. She is a warm, motherly woman with a soft, endearing manner.

   H. With very little persuasion, she would be willing to bend her moral code.

   J. Although she lives on a farm, she is sophisticated and urbane.

3. The reference to the kangaroo (line 47) suggests all of the following EXCEPT:

   A. the preposterous nature of the idea that Marilla and Matthew would adopt a child.

   B. Mrs. Rachel's astonishment that this turn of events could have transpired without her awareness.

   C. Avonlea farm is located in the Australian outback.

   D. taking in a child from an orphan asylum is not an everyday occurrence.

4. It can be reasonably inferred from the passage that:

   F. the close relationship between Mrs. Rachel and Marilla is based on the similarity of their lives and circumstances.

   G. Mrs. Rachel's surprise is a direct reflection of her inattention to detail and lack of perceptiveness.

   H. Mrs. Rachel prides herself on her ability to be well informed about events in her neighborhood.

   J. many farmers had previously adopted young orphans to help with the work on the farm.

5. The narrator's tone in the last sentence of the passage (lines 68–70) is:

   A. humorously ironic.

   B. contemptuously hostile.

   C. intensely disapproving.

   D. unabashedly sentimental.

Passage II

SOCIAL SCIENCE: The following passage is adapted from *The Life of Abraham Lincoln* written by Henry Ketcham in 1901. In this excerpt, the author describes the events leading up to Lincoln's taking office.

South Carolina was the first state to secede, and since Fort Sumter commanded Charleston Harbor, it instantly became the focus of national interest. The Secretary of War, Floyd,
(5) had so dispersed the little army of the United States that it was impossible to command the few hundred men necessary adequately to garrison the United States forts. As matters in and about Charleston grew threatening, Major
(10) Anderson, who was in command of the twin forts, Moultrie and Sumter, decided to abandon the former and do his utmost to defend the latter. The removal was successfully accomplished in the night, and when the fact was dis-
(15) covered it was greeted by the South Carolinians with a howl of baffled wrath. Buchanan had endeavored to send provisions. The steamer, *Star of the West,* had gone there for that purpose, but had been fired on by the South
(20) Carolinians and forced to abandon the attempt.

When Lincoln took the government at Washington, it may well be believed that he found matters in a condition decidedly chaotic. His task was many sided, a greater task than
(25) that of Washington as he had justly said. First, of the fifteen slave states seven had seceded. It was his purpose to hold the remaining eight, or as many of them as possible. Of this number, Delaware and Maryland could have been held
(30) by force. Kentucky and Missouri, though slave states, remained in the Union. The Union party in Tennessee, under the lead of Andrew Johnson, made a strong fight against secession, but failed to prevent the ordinance.
(35) The next task of Lincoln was to unite the North as far as possible. The difficulty of doing this has already been set forth. On the other hand there was in the North a sentiment that had been overlooked. It was devotion to
(40) the flag. Benjamin F. Butler, though an ardent democrat, had cautioned his southern brethren that while they might count on a large pro-slavery vote in the North, war was a different matter. The moment you fire on the flag, he
(45) said, you unite the North; and if war comes, slavery goes.

Not the least task of the President was in dealing with foreign nations. The sympathies of these, especially England and France, were
(50) ardently with the South. They would eagerly grasp at the slightest excuse for acknowledging the Southern Confederacy as an independent nation. It was a delicate and difficult matter so to guide affairs that the desired
(55) excuse for this could not be found.

The tactics of the southerners were exceedingly exasperating. They kept "envoys" in Washington to deal with the government. Of course these were not officially received.
(60) Lincoln sent them a copy of his inaugural address as containing a sufficient answer to their questions. But they stayed on, trying to spy out the secrets of the government, trying to get some sort of a pledge of conciliation
(65) from the administration, or, what would equally serve the purpose, to exasperate the administration into some unguarded word or act. Their attempts were a flat failure.

6. It can be reasonably inferred from the passage that the author believes that Lincoln was:

F. overwhelmed by the formidable task he faced in Washington.

G. able to handle the day-to-day practicalities, but unable to deal competently with the larger issues.

H. a shrewd politician who manipulated his enemies into failure.

J. a pragmatic leader who was an accomplished multitasker.

7. All of the following contributed to the "howl of baffled wrath" (line 16) EXCEPT:

   A. the tactics of Secretary of War Floyd regarding the positioning of troops.
   B. Major Anderson's decision to concentrate his forces at Fort Sumter.
   C. the secession of South Carolina.
   D. the attempted landing of the *Star of the West*.

8. It can be inferred from the passage that:

   F. although many in the North were sympathetic to the slaveholders, patriotism and belief in the Union were strong enough to unite the region.
   G. the Northern manufacturers depended on slave labor for raw materials and would not support the Union against the Confederacy.
   H. President Lincoln was so embroiled in domestic issues, international affairs were of little concern.
   J. had President Lincoln agreed to answer questions from leaders of the Confederacy, he could have averted the Civil War.

9. According to the passage, Lincoln faced all of the following difficulties EXCEPT:

   A. the presence of Southern spies in Washington.
   B. keeping Kentucky and Missouri in the Union.
   C. maintaining the support of European nations.
   D. holding on to the support of the pro-slave faction in the North.

10. The word "delicate" in line 53 suggests:

    F. the debated issues concerned matters that could easily erupt in scandal.
    G. without tactful diplomacy by Lincoln, European nations would side with the South.
    H. the relationship between England and France was fragile.
    J. escalating tensions between the North and the South had resulted in an uneasy truce.

Passage III

HUMANITIES: Passage A is adapted from the *Memoir of Jane Austen* written by Austen's nephew, James Edward Austen-Leigh, in 1871. Passage B is adapted from Goldwin Smith. Austen, Jane. *Pride and Prejudice.* Vol. III, Part 2. Harvard Classics Shelf of Fiction. New York: P.F. Collier & Son, 1917; Bartleby.com, 2000. www.bartleby. com/303/2/. [8/15/2016].

Passage A

Jane Austen lived in entire seclusion from the literary world: neither by correspondence, nor by personal intercourse was she known to any contemporary authors. It is probable that
(5) she never was in company with any person whose talents or whose celebrity equaled her own; so that her powers never could have been sharpened by collision with superior intellects, nor her imagination aided by their casual sug-
(10) gestions. Whatever she produced was a genuine home-made article. Even during the last two or three years of her life, when her works were rising in the estimation of the public, they did not enlarge the circle of her acquain-
(15) tance. Few of her readers knew even her name, and none knew more of her than her name. I doubt whether it would be possible to mention any other author of note, whose personal obscurity was so complete. Even those great
(20) writers who hid themselves amongst lakes and

mountains associated with each other; and though little seen by the world were so much in its thoughts that a new term, 'Lakers,' was coined to designate them. A few years ago, a
(25) gentleman visiting Winchester Cathedral desired to be shown Miss Austen's grave. The verger, as he pointed it out, asked, "Pray, sir, can you tell me whether there was anything particular about that lady; so many people
(30) want to know where she was buried?" During her life the ignorance of the verger was shared by most people; few knew that "there was anything particular about that lady."

It was not till towards the close of her life,
(35) when the last of the works that she saw published was in the press, that she received the only mark of distinction ever bestowed upon her; and that was remarkable for the high quarter whence it emanated rather than for
(40) any actual increase of fame that it conferred. It happened thus. In the autumn of 1815 she nursed her brother Henry through a dangerous fever and slow convalescence at his house in Hans Place. He was attended by one of the
(45) Prince Regent's physicians. All attempts to keep her name secret had at this time ceased, and though it had never appeared on a title-page, all who cared to know might easily learn it: and the friendly physician was aware
(50) that his patient's nurse was the author of "Pride and Prejudice." Accordingly he informed her one day that the Prince was a great admirer of her novels; that he read them often, and kept a set in every one of his
(55) residences; that he himself therefore had thought it right to inform his Royal Highness that Miss Austen was staying in London, and that the Prince had desired Mr. Clarke, the librarian of Carlton House, to wait upon her.
(60) The next day Mr. Clarke made his appearance, and invited her to Carlton House, saying that he had the Prince's instructions to show her the library and other apartments, and to pay her every possible attention. The
(65) invitation was of course accepted, and during the visit to Carlton House Mr. Clarke declared himself commissioned to say that if

Miss Austen had any other novel forthcoming she was at liberty to dedicate it to the
(70) Prince. Accordingly such a dedication was immediately prefixed to "Emma," which was at that time in the press.

Passage B

As we should expect from such a circumscribed life, Jane Austen's view of the world is
(75) genial, kindly, and, we repeat, free from anything like cynicism. It is that of a clear-sighted and somewhat satirical onlooker, loving what deserves love, and amusing herself with the foibles, the self-deceptions, the affectation of
(80) humanity. Refined almost to fastidiousness, she is hard upon vulgarity; not, however, on good-natured vulgarity, such as that of Mrs. Jennings in "Sense and Sensibility," but on vulgarity like that of Miss Steele, in the same
(85) novel, combined at once with effrontery and with meanness of soul....

To sentimentality Jane Austen was a foe. Antipathy to it runs through her works. She had encountered it in the romances of the day,
(90) such as the works of Mrs. Radcliffe and in the people who had fed on them. What she would have said if she encountered it in the form of Rousseauism we can only guess. The solid foundation of her own character was good
(95) sense, and her type of excellence as displayed in her heroines is a woman full of feeling, but with her feelings thoroughly under control. Genuine sensibility, however, even when too little under control, she can regard as loveable.
(100) Jane Austen had, as she was sure to have, a feeling for the beauties of nature. She paints in flowing language the scenery of Lyme. She speaks almost with rapture of a view which she calls thoroughly English, though never
(105) having been out of England she could hardly judge of its scenery by contrast.

Questions 11 and 12 ask about Passage A.

11. Which of the following best expresses the main idea of the second paragraph of Passage A?

    A. As Jane Austen interacted more with literary figures of her day, she increased the circle of her acquaintances to include the Prince Regent.

    B. Through an accidental connection occasioned by the illness of her brother, Jane Austen learned of the Prince Regent's affection for her novels.

    C. Jane Austen dedicated her novel *Emma* to the Prince Regent because he was instrumental in saving the life of her brother Henry.

    D. Few people, other than the Prince Regent, knew where Jane Austen was buried.

12. The word "collision" in Passage A line 8 most nearly means:

    F. smash.
    G. explosion.
    H. accident.
    J. interaction.

Questions 13 and 14 ask about Passage B.

13. According to the author, which of the following choices best characterizes Jane Austen's attitude toward vulgarity?

    A. Jane Austen despised vulgarity in any form and wouldn't tolerate it in her characters.

    B. Jane Austen was generally critical of vulgarity but accepted it when it was not mean-spirited.

    C. Jane Austen was too fastidious to encounter vulgarity and never referred to it in her novels.

    D. Jane Austen understood that lower-class characters engaged in vulgarity, so she incorporated it into all her novels.

14. It can be inferred that Jane Austen feels an antipathy to sentimentality because:

    F. she herself was a rather cold woman who preferred her characters to disdain emotional demonstrations.

    G. she agreed with Mrs. Radcliffe that explicit feelings are essential for romance.

    H. she believed a character with good sense would keep her feelings restrained.

    J. she felt sympathy for affected women who display insincere emotions.

Question 15 asks about both Passage A and Passage B.

15. The author of Passage A and the author of Passage B would most likely agree that:

    A. the cynicism that characterizes many of Jane Austen's novels was engendered by her personal exposure to callous aristocrats.

    B. Jane Austen's family belittled her literary attempts and limited her contact with the outside world.

    C. Jane Austen's renown in her lifetime led to many instances of recognition for her superior intellect.

    D. Jane Austen relied on her imagination rather than her extensive experience with the outside world to create her literary works.

Passage IV

NATURAL SCIENCE: The following passage is an excerpt from A History of Science, Volume 2 written by Henry Smith William in 1904. The author discusses experiments by the noted American statesman, author, and scientist Benjamin Franklin (1706–1790) as Franklin investigates the nature of electricity.

According to Franklin's theory, electricity exists in all bodies as a "common stock," and tends to seek and remain in a state of equilibrium, just as fluids naturally tend to seek a

(5) level. But it may, nevertheless, be raised or lowered, and this equilibrium be thus disturbed. If a body has more electricity than its normal amount it is said to be POSITIVELY electrified; but if it has less, it is NEGATIVELY

(10) electrified. An over-electrified or "plus" body tends to give its surplus stock to a body containing the normal amount; while the "minus" or under-electrified body will draw electricity from one containing the normal amount.

(15) Working along lines suggested by this theory, Franklin attempted to show that electricity is not created by friction, but simply collected from its diversified state, the rubbed glass globe attracting a certain quantity of

(20) "electrical fire," but ever ready to give it up to any body that has less. He explained the charged Leyden jar by showing that the inner coating of tin-foil received more than the ordinary quantity of electricity, and in conse-

(25) quence is POSITIVELY electrified, while the outer coating, having the ordinary quantity of electricity diminished, is electrified NEGATIVELY.

These studies of the Leyden jar, and the

(30) studies of pieces of glass coated with sheet metal, led Franklin to invent his battery, constructed of eleven large glass plates coated with sheets of lead. With this machine, after overcoming some defects, he was able to pro-

(35) duce electrical manifestations of great force—a force that "knew no bounds," as he declared ("except in the matter of expense and of labor"), and which could be made to exceed "the greatest know[n] effects of com-

(40) mon lightning."

This reference to lightning would seem to show Franklin's belief, even at that time, that lightning is electricity. Many eminent observers, such as Hauksbee, Wall, Gray, and Nollet,

(45) had noticed the resemblance between electric sparks and lightning, but none of these had more than surmised that the two might be identical. In 1746, the surgeon, John Freke, also asserted his belief in this identity. Winkler,

(50) shortly after this time, expressed the same belief, and, assuming that they were the same, declared that "there is no proof that they are of different natures"; and still he did not prove that they were the same nature.

16. The primary purpose of this passage is to:

F. prove that Benjamin Franklin was the forerunner of modern physicists.

G. argue that much of what scientists now know about electricity is derived from Benjamin Franklin's experiments.

H. explain Benjamin Franklin's theory of electricity and his subsequent experiments to prove it.

J. hypothesize that Benjamin Franklin was not an original thinker but one who copied the efforts of other scientists.

17. Franklin used the Leyden jar to:

    A. show how the inner coating is negatively charged and will thus attract electricity from the positively charged outer coating.

    B. prove conclusively that friction creates electricity.

    C. substantiate his theory that electricity seeks to remain in a state of balance.

    D. re-create conditions under which he could harness electricity to a light bulb.

18. The experiments with the Leyden jar led Franklin to:

    F. reject his theory in favor of that of John Freke.

    G. construct a device with which he could produce forceful electrical manifestations.

    H. theorize that electricity from lightning is of a different nature than that produced by a battery.

    J. overcome the skepticism of those who doubted his findings.

19. The author mentions Hauksbee, Wall, Gray, and Nollet as examples of men who:

    A. published findings similar to Franklin's but received no public credit.

    B. noted many of the same observations as Franklin but failed to make key connections.

    C. decried the experiments of men like Franklin as outlandish and absurd.

    D. jealously guarded their own experiments and prevented Franklin from building on their findings.

20. The purpose of rubbing a glass globe (lines 18–19) is to:

    F. make it clean enough to see the sparks within it.

    G. modify the electrical equilibrium of the glass.

    H. prepare it to receive liquid that will allow the electrical current to pass through.

    J. ground it so that any shock will pass through the jar into the cloth.

IF YOU FINISH BEFORE TIME IS CALLED, CHECK YOUR WORK ON THIS SECTION ONLY. DO NOT WORK ON ANY OTHER SECTION IN THE TEST.

Section 4: Science Test

18 Minutes—20 Questions

Directions: The Science Test consists of five passages; each passage is followed by several questions. After reading each passage, select the best answer to each question and fill in the corresponding circle on the answer sheet. Refer to the information in the passages as often as necessary to respond to the questions. Use of a calculator is NOT permitted on this test.

Passage I

Newton's Law of Cooling states that the rate of loss of heat from a body is proportional to the difference between the temperature of the body and the temperature of the surroundings. This law applies only to small ranges in temperature as are typical in the natural world.

Students were asked to experimentally verify Newton's Law of Cooling by analyzing the cooling of water over time. First, a sample of water was heated to just over 50°C. Then the beaker was transferred to an insulated surface on the lab bench and the initial temperature was immediately recorded at 50°C. As the water in the beaker was allowed to cool, the temperature to 0.1°C was recorded at 2-minute intervals and the change in water temperature (ΔT) over that interval was determined. Later, the average temperature of the water (T_W) over each interval was calculated, as was D_T, the difference between T_W and the temperature of the room (T_R). Finally, the ratio between ΔT and D_T was computed. The collective data were recorded in Table 1. (**Note:** Although the temperature is used here instead of the actual heat of the water sample, the constant mass present in the sample allows the use of temperature as an approximation for heat; $T_R = 20°C$.)

					Table 1
Time (min)	Temperature (°C)	ΔT (°C)	T_W (°C)	$D_T = T_W - T_R$ (°C)	$\dfrac{\Delta T}{D_T}$
0	50.0				
2	46.4	3.6	48.2	28.2	0.128
4	43.2	3.2	44.8	24.8	0.129
6	40.4	2.8	41.8	21.8	0.128
8	37.9	2.5	39.2	19.2	0.130
10	35.7	2.2	36.8	16.8	0.131

1. According to the data in Table 1, the largest change in temperature in any interval was observed after which minute?

    A. 2
    B. 4
    C. 6
    D. 8

2. As the water cools:

    F.   the temperature of the water decreases at a constant rate over the entire 10-minute period.

    G.   the change in the temperature of the water is inversely proportional to the difference between the temperature of the water and the temperature of the room.

    H.   the temperature of the water decreases, reaches room temperature, and then increases slightly.

    J.   the change in the temperature of the water is directly proportional to the difference between the temperature of the water and the temperature of its surroundings.

3. Students generated the following graph of D_T versus ΔT:

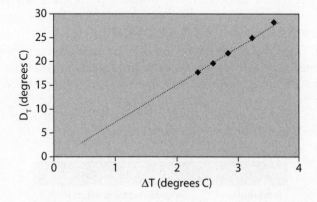

Which of the following statements is supported from the graph and the data in Table 1?

    A.   The increasing slope in the graph is evidence against Newton's Law of Cooling.

    B.   Any slight variation in the data from the slope of 0.13 is evidence against Newton's Law of Cooling.

    C.   The relatively constant slope in the graph supports Newton's Law of Cooling.

    D.   Although a constant rate of cooling is demonstrated by the graph, further calculations need to be made to verify Newton's Law of Cooling.

4. The experiment was continued for several minutes past the 10-minute interval and then stopped. The difference between the temperature of the water and the temperature of the room was calculated to be 10°C at this stopping point. What was the approximate ΔT recorded for the water sample?

    F.   13.0°C

    G.   7.5°C

    H.   1.3°C

    J.   10.3°C

Passage II

The enzyme lactase catalyzes the breakdown of the disaccharide lactose, a sugar common in milk and other dairy foods, into the monosaccharides glucose and galactose according to the following reaction:

$$\text{Lactose + water} \xrightarrow{\text{Lactase}} \text{glucose + galactose}$$

A research group is performing quality-control experiments on commercially available lactase supplements that are designed to combat lactose-intolerance when taken prior to the consumption of lactose-rich foods. The condition of lactose-intolerance can cause painful gastrointestinal symptoms in affected individuals and is often associated with avoidance of the consumption of dairy products.

Experiment 1

Researchers test the effects of temperature on lactase activity when pH remains constant. Samples of lactase are either heated or cooled to various temperatures and then added to the same volume of lactose solution and allowed to react for 60 seconds. The reaction is then stopped by adding a concentrated salt solution. The rate of glucose formation in micromoles (μmol) per milliliter (mL) of solution is then measured and used to assess the reaction rate, and thus the effectiveness of the lactase supplement in digesting lactose. The data collected are shown in Table 1.

Table 1	
Temperature (°C)	Glucose formation (μmol/mL)
10	0.4
25	8.2
40	15.1
55	0.6
70	0.1

Experiment 2

Researchers test the effects of pH on lactase activity when temperature remains constant at 22°C (room temperature). The same general procedure is followed except that the pH of the lactose solution is altered just before the lactase enzyme is added. This is achieved by adding a relative amount of acid or base. The data collected are shown in Table 2.

Table 2	
pH	Glucose formation (μmol/mL)
1.5	0.7
4.0	1.3
6.5	18.8
8.0	10.6
10.5	0.2

The lactase supplement is designed to be swallowed by a lactose-intolerant individual before the consumption of dairy products. The average pH values of some segments of the human digestive tract (at normal body temperature) are presented in Table 3.

Table 3	
Digestive tract structure	Average pH
Mouth	7.0
Upper stomach	5.0
Lower stomach	2.0
Small intestine (upper)	7.5
Large intestine	6.0

Note: Structures are listed in the order in which food flows through the tract.

5. Normal human body temperature is around 37°C. According to the data in Table 1, the product tested:

   A. is likely to be effective at body temperature.

   B. is not likely to be effective at body temperature.

   C. is likely to work at normal body temperatures but not just above or below body temperature.

   D. may or may not be effective at body temperature; it is impossible to tell with the information provided.

6. Which of the following graphs accurately depicts the relationship between pH and the rate of glucose formation presented in Table 2?

F.

G.

H.

J.

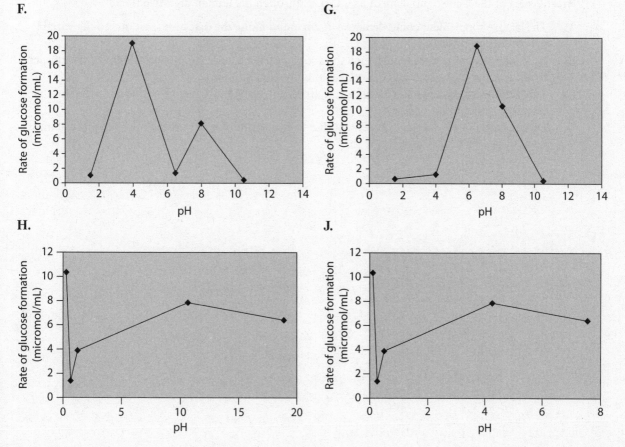

7. Which of the following statements is consistent with the data presented in Tables 1 and 2?

    A. As the temperature or the pH increases, the rate of glucose formation steadily increases.

    B. As the temperature or the pH increases, the rate of glucose formation steadily decreases.

    C. An increase in temperature causes an increase in pH, which in turn causes an increase in glucose formation.

    D. The highest rates of reaction are at a pH of 6.5 and a temperature of 40°C.

8. If a separate trial were run repeating Experiment 2 and the rate of glucose formation was measured at 15.9 μmol/mL, the associated pH is likely to be:

    F. 12

    G. 3

    H. 9

    J. 7

9. The lactase enzyme is a protein, and proteins are known to denature (structurally break down and lose function) at relatively extreme temperatures and pH conditions. Lactase naturally works in the cells lining the small intestine to allow for digestion just before absorption. Given the information presented in Table 3, which of the following statements presents a potential problem with the effectiveness of the lactase supplement as it travels through the human digestive tract?

    A. The lactase supplement could denature at any point along the digestive tract due to the variable pH conditions present.

    B. If denaturation is not reversible, then the activity of the lactase supplement might be diminished by the low pH in the stomach before reaching the small intestine.

    C. The lactase supplement could denature at any point along the digestive tract due to the variable temperature conditions present.

    D. Denaturation of the lactase supplement due to temperature or pH should not take place at any point along the digestive tract.

Passage III

In light of current concerns over global climate change and the perception of an increase in the number and severity of annual hurricanes worldwide, many researchers have further investigated variables that affect hurricane intensity and frequency. A recent study examined the relationship between sea surface temperature (SST) and seasonal hurricane activity in a local region. It was commonly understood by scientists before the study that the SST positively affects the number of hurricanes observed, but debate remained regarding the way in which the SST is measured. Some argued that the only significant variable was the local SST, while others argued that a more accurate measure was the local SST relative to the tropical SST.

Hypothesis 1

The local SST in the region in isolation is responsible for affecting variations in local hurricane activity.

Hypothesis 2

The SST in the region relative to the SST in the tropics affects variations in local hurricane activity.

The actual number of hurricanes was recorded in a local region over a 10-year period and compared to the predications made by Hypotheses 1 and 2. The data are presented in Table 1. The correlation of each set of predictions to the observed values over the 10-year period is also shown; the closer the calculated correlation is to 1, the more reliable the prediction made by that hypothesis. (**Note:** Percent error is a measure of the closeness of the prediction to the observed value: A negative percent error indicates that the prediction was lower than the actual value, and a positive percent error indicates that the prediction was higher than the actual value. Percent errors of ±5 percent are considered reliable.)

Table 1					
Year	Number of Hurricanes Recorded	Hypothesis 1		Hypothesis 2	
		Prediction	% Error	Prediction	% Error
1	79	76	−3.80	82	3.80
2	92	92	0.00	91	−1.09
3	89	80	−10.10	88	−1.12
4	86	90	4.65	93	8.14
5	103	96	−6.80	102	−0.97
6	115	100	−13.00	116	0.87
7	121	117	−3.31	122	0.82
8	109	105	−3.67	113	3.67
9	99	94	−5.05	100	1.01
10	111	103	−7.21	110	−0.90
Total	1004	953	−5.08	1019	1.49
Correlation	(1)	0.93		0.98	

10. According to the information presented in the passage:

    F. the scientific community is debating the cause of the SST change.
    G. the hypotheses are in agreement about the way in which the SST is measured in order to assess its effects on annual hurricane frequency.
    H. global warming is causing an increase in hurricane frequency.
    J. the scientific community was in agreement before the study that the local SST was related to the frequency of hurricanes in a year.

11. In year two of the study:

    A. Hypothesis 2 was a better predictor of hurricane number than Hypothesis 1.
    B. more hurricanes were recorded than in any other year of the study.
    C. both Hypotheses 1 and 2 were good predictors of hurricane number, but Hypothesis 1 was better.
    D. neither hypothesis proved to be a good model for hurricane prediction.

12. According to the data presented in Table 1:

    F. Hypothesis 1 is more strongly supported than Hypothesis 2.
    G. Hypothesis 2 is more strongly supported than Hypothesis 1.
    H. Hypotheses 1 and 2 are supported with equal strength statistically.
    J. Hypothesis 1 is supported more strongly in the second half of the study than Hypothesis 2.

Passage IV

Solubility describes the ability for one substance (the solute) to dissolve in another substance (the solvent) and is affected by temperature, pressure, and other factors. Solubility curves are often generated to easily predict the solubility of a given substance under a certain set of conditions. Above any line, the solution is called supersaturated and some of the solute will not completely dissolve at those same conditions. Below any line, the solution is instead unsaturated, meaning that the solvent could dissolve more solute if added. On the line, the solution is exactly saturated.

Experiment 1

Industrial chemists were interested in the relationship between the temperature of a substance and its solubility. They tested a variety of substances for their solubility in 100 grams (g) of water at varying temperatures and constant pressure. The data are displayed in Figure 1.

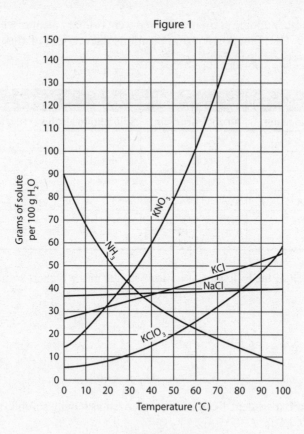

Figure 1

Experiment 2

Of interest also to the chemists was the relationship between the number of carbon atoms present in a substance and the solubility of that substance in water. The solubility of various carbon-containing substances was tested in 110 g of water at room temperature (20°C) and constant pressure. The solubilities of all substances tested that contained the same number of carbon atoms (but possessed different functional groups) were averaged. The data are shown in Figure 2.

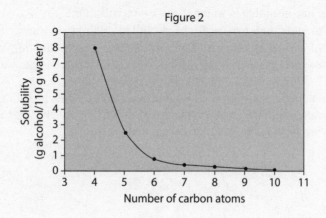

Figure 2

Some of the carbon-containing substances tested were primary alcohols, hydrocarbon molecules that contain the hydroxyl (–OH) functional group positioned at one end of the molecule. The solubility of each alcohol is listed separately in Table 1.

Table 1		
Alcohol name	**Alcohol structure**	**Solubility(g alcohol/110 g H_2O)**
Methanol	CH_3OH	Unlimited
Ethanol	CH_3CH_2OH	Unlimited
Propanol	$CH_3(CH_2)_2OH$	Unlimited
Butanol	$CH_3(CH_2)_3OH$	8.954
Pentanol	$CH_3(CH_2)_4OH$	2.904
Hexanol	$CH_3(CH_2)_5OH$	0.673

13. In Experiment 1, which of the following situations results in the highest solubility in 100 g of water?

   A. NaCl at 90°C
   B. KNO_3 at 45°C
   C. NH_3 at 15°C
   D. $KClO_3$ at 80°C

14. All of the following in Experiment 1 can be characterized as having solubilities in water that increase with temperature EXCEPT:

   F. NaCl
   G. NH_3
   H. KCl
   J. KNO_3

15. According to the information presented in Figure 2 and Table 1:

   A. all alcohols become insoluble in water at some concentration.
   B. any alcohol with more than two carbons has limited solubility in water.
   C. as the number of carbon atoms in an alcohol increases, its solubility in water increases.
   D. as the number of carbon atoms in an alcohol increases, its solubility in water decreases.

16. A chemist desires an aqueous solution of any substance that can keep its solubility fairly constant over a wide temperature range and has a minimum saturation of 20 g of solute per 100 g of water at 0°C. Which of the following substances would be best suited for this purpose?

   F. Hexanol
   G. NaCl
   H. KNO_3
   J. NH_3

Passage V

The life span of a cell from the time it is produced from its parent cell to the point that it completes a division is called the cell cycle. The cell cycle has two main phases: interphase and mitosis. During interphase, the cell metabolizes, grows, regulates its internal environment, and carries out most normal life processes. When a cell is triggered to divide, the mitosis phase begins. Mitosis is technically the division of the cell's nucleus, which may or may not be followed by cytokinesis, the division of the rest of the cell. Mitosis is broken down into four main phases (sequentially: prophase, metaphase, anaphase, and telophase) based upon the coordinated movement of the cell's chromosomes.

Students in a biology class were asked to use a compound light microscope to analyze the length of time needed to complete each phase of mitosis in onion root tip cells, which require 720 minutes to complete the entire cell cycle. They first counted the number of cells observed in each phase (interphase and the phases of mitosis) and calculated the relative percent of cells in each phase; they then used this information to determine the time required to complete each phase according to the following equation:

$$\text{Time for phase X (min)} = \frac{\text{\# of cells in phase X}}{\text{total \# of cells observed}} \times 720 \text{ min}$$

The percent of onion root tip cells observed in each phase and the calculated time needed to complete each phase are presented in Table 1.

Table 1		
Phase	% of cells in phase	Time required to complete phase (min)
Interphase	57	410.4
Prophase	27	194.4
Metaphase	8	57.6
Anaphase	5	36.0
Telophase	3	21.6

The students were then asked to compare this data with results from a research study concerning the cell cycle in normal and cancerous cells. The time needed by normal human skin cells and cancerous human skin cells to complete each phase is listed in Table 2.

Table 2		
Phase	Time required to complete phase (min)	
	Normal human skin cell	Cancerous human skin cell
Interphase	1380	1050
Prophase	41	33
Metaphase	8	8
Anaphase	3	3
Telophase	8	6

17. According to the passage and the data in Table 1, which phase of mitosis requires the longest amount of time to complete?

    A. Interphase
    B. Telophase
    C. Anaphase
    D. Prophase

18. Which of the following graphs correctly represents the data presented in Table 1?

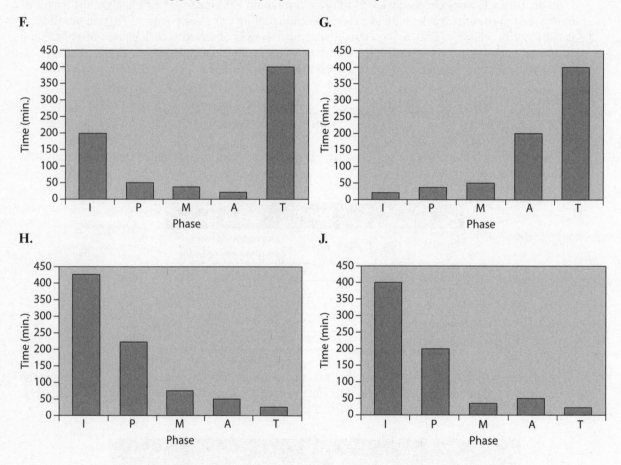

F.

G.

H.

J.

19. Which of the following statements is consistent with the data presented in Tables 1 and 2?

    A. Regardless of the cell type, one should expect to find the smallest proportion of any sample of cells in metaphase.
    B. Regardless of the cell type, one should expect to find the largest proportion of any sample of cells in interphase.
    C. In onion root cells, most cells tend to be in interphase; in human skin cells, most cells tend to be in prophase.
    D. In human skin cells, most cells tend to be in interphase; in onion root cells, most cells tend to be in prophase.

20. Regarding the data shown in Table 2, cancerous human skin cells are different from normal human skin cells in that cancerous cells require:

    F. less time to complete the cell cycle.
    G. more time to complete the cell cycle.
    H. less time to complete each phase of mitosis.
    J. more time to complete each phase of mitosis.

IF YOU FINISH BEFORE TIME IS CALLED, CHECK YOUR WORK ON THIS SECTION ONLY. DO NOT WORK ON ANY OTHER SECTION IN THE TEST.

Section 5: Writing Test

40 Minutes

Maintaining Wilderness Lands

The designation of a piece of land as "wilderness" can be controversial. The designation generally prohibits commercial activities, motorized access, and human infrastructure from the selected areas. Advocates propose wilderness designations to preserve the generally undeveloped conditions of the areas. Opponents see such designations as preventing certain uses and potential economic development in rural areas where such opportunities are relatively limited.

Read the three perspectives below and consider the conflicting positions on maintaining wilderness lands.

Perspective 1	Perspective 2	Perspective 3
The primary benefit of wilderness designation is to maintain such undeveloped conditions and the values that such conditions generate—clean water, undisturbed wildlife habitats, natural scenic views, opportunities for recreation, and unaltered research baselines. Wilderness is also a challenge to human beings because it is inhospitable, alien, and threatening.	Wilderness designation is a defensive and losing strategy. These lands and resources can provide economic opportunities in extracting and developing the resources. While we can calculate the losses in some areas such as timber harvesting, other losses are unknown. The potential for lucrative mineral development cannot be determined without exploration.	The Wilderness Act of 1964 defines wilderness as "an area where the earth and its community of life are untrammeled by man, where man himself is a visitor, ...without permanent improvements or human habitation, which is protected and managed so as to preserve its natural conditions and which (1) generally appears to have been affected primarily by the forces of nature ...; (2) has outstanding opportunities for solitude ...; (3) has at least five thousand acres of land ...; and (4) may also contain ecological, geological, or other features of scientific, educational, scenic, or historical value."

Essay Task

Your task is to construct a well-written, well-organized essay in which you consider the arguments for and against the establishment of wilderness areas. As you plan and write your essay, be sure to

- consider the effectiveness of the three perspectives given above
- develop your own perspective on the issue
- clarify ways in which your perspective is similar to or different from the three perspectives given above

You may choose to defend, challenge, or qualify any part of the three given perspectives. Whatever your position, be sure to back up your assertions with reason and detailed examples.

Planning Your Essay

The space below is for you to plan your essay. As you plan, think about the following ideas:

Strengths and weaknesses of each of the three given perspectives:

- What aspects do they address and what aspects do they disregard?
- Is the perspective persuasive? Why or why not? To whom might each appeal?

Experience or knowledge that will help you evaluate the issue:

- How strong is your position?
- What evidence (reasons, facts, examples) will you offer to support your position?

IF YOU FINISH BEFORE TIME IS CALLED, CHECK YOUR WORK ON THIS
SECTION ONLY. DO NOT WORK ON ANY OTHER SECTION IN THE TEST.

Scoring the Diagnostic Test

Answer Key

Section 1: English Test

1. D (UM)
2. H (UM)
3. B (UM)
4. G (UM)
5. C (UM)
6. H (UM)
7. D (UM)
8. J (RH)
9. B (RH)
10. J (UM)
11. A (RH)
12. J (RH)
13. A (UM)
14. H (RH)

15. C (RH)
16. F (UM)
17. B (UM)
18. G (RH)
19. A (UM)
20. F (UM)
21. C (UM)
22. J (UM)
23. A (RH)
24. J (UM)
25. C (RH)
26. G (RH)
27. C (UM)
28. H (UM)

29. C (RH)
30. J (RH)
31. A (UM)
32. G (UM)
33. A (RH)
34. J (UM)
35. A (UM)
36. G (UM)
37. C (UM)
38. H (UM)

UM = Usage/Mechanics

RH = Rhetorical Skills

Section 2: Mathematics Test

1. D (EA)
2. H (PS)
3. E (EA)
4. H (GT)
5. D (PS)
6. G (AG)
7. C (GT)
8. F (GT)
9. B (AG)
10. J (GT)
11. E (AG)
12. H (EA)

13. B (GT)
14. F (AG)
15. D (EA)
16. G (AG)
17. D (EA)
18. G (GT)
19. C (GT)
20. J (AG)
21. A (EA)
22. K (AG)
23. E (EA)
24. F (PS)

25. E (PS)
26. G (PS)
27. C (GT)
28. K (AG)
29. E (GT)
30. K (AG)

EA = Pre-Algebra/Elementary Algebra

AG = Intermediate Algebra/ Coordinate Geometry

GT = Plane Geometry/ Trigonometry

PS = Probability/Statistics

Section 3: Reading Test

1. B (AL)
2. F (AL)
3. C (AL)
4. H (AL)
5. A (AL)
6. J (SS)
7. C (SS)
8. F (SS)

9. B (SS)
10. G (SS)
11. B (AL)
12. J (AL)
13. B (AL)
14. H (AL)
15. D (AL)
16. H (SS)

17. C (SS)
18. G (SS)
19. B (SS)
20. G (SS)

AL = Arts/Literature

SS = Social Studies/ Sciences

Section 4: Science Test

1. A (DR)
2. J (DR)
3. C (DR)
4. H (DR)
5. A (RS)
6. G (RS)
7. D (RS)
8. J (RS)
9. B (RS)

10. J (CV)
11. C (CV)
12. G (CV)
13. B (RS)
14. G (RS)
15. D (RS)
16. G (RS)
17. D (DR)
18. H (DR)

19. B (DR)
20. F (DR)

DR = Data Representation

RS = Research Summaries

CV = Conflicting Viewpoints

Answer Explanations

Section 1: English Test

Passage I

1. **D.** The subject of the sentence is **cats,** so the verb must be the plural **are known.** Choice A is redundant because the word **famous** is already in the sentence. Choices B and C are incorrect because both use the singular form of the verb. (*Chapter V: Section D.9.*)

2. **H.** Commas are necessary between the parenthetical phrase **as the breed is known** and the rest of the sentence and between parallel adjectives **solid, stocky.** (*Chapter V: Section C.4.*)

3. **B.** In any sentence, to achieve parallelism with correlative conjunctions (**either…or**) whatever follows the word **either** must be in the same structure as what follows the word **or.** Choices A, C, and D are not parallel. (*Chapter V: Section D.5.*)

4. **G.** The present perfect tense is formed by the present tense of **have** and the past participle of the verb. The past participle of **arise** is **arisen.** Choice H incorrectly uses the simple past tense, and Choices F and J incorrectly use the past tense form of the verb **arose** instead of the past participle **arisen.** (*Chapter V: Section D.10.*)

5. **C.** This question tests your ability to recognize correct verb form in context. The context of the sentence should lead you to the correct form **was about to close.** Be sure to read the whole sentence as you make your choice. Choice A is not idiomatic English; Choice B is the incorrect tense; Choice D gives the wrong meaning to the sentence. (*Chapter V: Section D.10.*)

6. **H.** This punctuation question tests your understanding of the semicolon and the comma. The semicolon is incorrectly used in the passage, so Choice F is incorrect. (*Chapter V: Section C.3.*) Choice G uses the incorrect plural pronoun **their** to refer to the singular antecedent **cat.** (*Chapter V: Section D.1.*) Choice J incorrectly omits the comma after **mouser.** (*Chapter V: Section C.4.*)

7. **D.** This is a rhetoric question designed to test your understanding of writing style. It also tests your knowledge of vocabulary. Choices A, B, and C all indicate the cat's persistence. Choice D, **resigned to,** does not. **Resigned to** in this sentence would mean the cat is sadly accepting defeat. (*Chapter V: Section E.1.*)

8. **J.** Another rhetoric question, this question tests your understanding of organization. If you read the sentence in the passage that would follow the additional sentence in the question, you will see that both sentences say essentially the same thing, and the original sentence is a more fitting conclusion in any case. Therefore, the addition would be unnecessary. (*Chapter V: Section E.3.*)

9. **B.** Rhetoric again. Stylistically, Choice B is very wordy. All of the other choices are appropriate. (*Chapter V: Section D.2.*)

10. **J.** This question involves both pronoun and apostrophe issues. The correct pronoun is **their** because the antecedent is the plural noun **cats.** Thus, Choices F and G are incorrect. (*Chapter V: Section D.1.*) Also, the possessive pronoun **its** never takes an apostrophe (Choice F), and Choice G uses the singular possessive **kitten's** rather than the plural possessive **kittens'.** Choice H correctly uses **their** but omits the necessary apostrophe for **kittens.** (*Chapter V: Section C.1.*)

11. **A.** This rhetoric question tests your understanding of the correct transitional words for this situation. Choices B and C use contrast words; no contrast is indicated in the sentence. Choice D is not appropriate to begin paragraph 4 because it does not logically follow the previous transitional word that begins paragraph 3. (*Chapter V: Section E.3.*)

12. **J.** The sentence begins with the word **Today,** so it would be redundant to use any of the other choices. The underlined portion should be omitted. (*Chapter V: Section D.2.*)

13. **A.** No change is needed because the pronoun **it** refers to the gene and **became** is the proper verb form. (*Chapter V: Sections D.1 and D.10.*)

14. **H.** This is a rhetoric question about organization. The best place to put this sentence would be after the last sentence of paragraph 4 because it logically continues the information about the "cabbit." (*Chapter V: Section E.3.*)

15. **C.** This is not a formal, scholarly essay. It contains no statistical information, and it does not conclusively disprove any theories. (*Chapter V: Section E.*)

Passage II

16. **F.** No change is needed. The past participle **built** is the proper verb form to begin the participial phrase. (*Chapter V: Section D.10.*)

17. **B.** The singular antecedent **wall** takes the singular pronoun **it.** (*Chapter V: Section D.1.*) Logically, the present tense verb **winds** is preferable to the present progressive tense **is winding** in this sentence. (*Chapter V: Section D.10.*)

18. **G.** This is a wordiness error. Choices F, H, and J are all redundant in that they add unneeded words that restate what a defensive fortification is. (*Chapter V: Section D.2.*)

19. **A.** No change is needed. The singular subject **Each** takes the singular form of the verb **was.** (*Chapter V: Section D.1.*)

20. **F.** No change is needed. Choices G and H incorrectly add commas, and Choice J incorrectly uses a semicolon. (*Chapter V: Sections C.3 and C.4.*)

21. **C.** This sentence has a comma splice error. (*Chapter V: Section D.11.*) Choice B also is a comma splice, and Choice D incorrectly uses the semicolon (if **with** were deleted, Choice D would be correct). Choice C correctly divides the sentence into two sentences.

22. **J.** This is a question about parallelism and correlative conjunctions. The conjunctions "not only" and "but also" are correlative conjunctions (conjunctions that occur in pairs). The words or phrases that follow one correlative conjunction must be parallel to those that follow the other conjunction. In this sentence, **not only** is followed by a verb (**was**) while **but also** is followed by an adjective modifying a noun (**horse-pulled wagons**). The correct phrasing would be: "The wall was wide enough not only for troops but also for horse-pulled wagons . . ." The only parallel answer is Choice J. (*Chapter V: Section D.5.*)

23. **A.** The information is an interesting detail about the soldiers. It is not a transition (Choice B), it is not an anecdote (a short, personal story, Choice C), and it does not contrast with the preceding sentence (Choice D). (*Chapter V: Section E.*)

24. **J.** This is an idiom question. Only Choice J is idiomatically correct. (*Chapter V: Section D.3.*)

25. **C.** The correct transitional word to begin this sentence is Choice C, **However.** The information in the sentence contrasts the idea in the preceding sentence, and only Choice C provides the logical transition to a different idea. (*Chapter V: Section E.3.*)

26. **G.** The original phrase **connected together with each other** is redundant, as are Choices H and J. (*Chapter V: Section D.2.*)

27. **C.** The plural subject **sections** needs the plural form of the verb **are.** (*Chapter V: Section D.9.*)

28. **H.** This is a noun agreement problem. The plural noun **people** must match the plural noun **cameras.** (*Chapter V: Section D.9.*)

29. **C.** Choices A and B are irrelevant to the passage and inconsistent with its tone. Choice D is not an effective conclusion. (*Chapter V: Section E.1.*)

Passage III

30. **J.** The correct word is **fewer,** which should be used with the plural phrase "five films." Use **less** or **lesser** for singular or whole quantities. (*Chapter V: Section D.7.*)

31. **A.** No change is needed. This is a correct use of the colon. (*Chapter V: Section C.2.*)

32. **G.** The underlined portion should be omitted to achieve parallelism of items in the series. (*Chapter V: Section D.5.*)

33. **A.** The best transitional word for emphasis is **Indeed.** (*Chapter V: Section E.3.*)

34. **J.** The possessive form **bird's** is incorrect here. Choice G uses the incorrect singular pronoun **its** to refer to the plural antecedent **birds.** Choice J correctly uses the plural (not the possessive) form of **birds** and the correct plural pronoun **their.** (*Chapter V: Section C.1.*)

35. **A.** No change is needed because the plural subject **birds** needs the plural form of the verb **have** and the past participle **become.** (*Chapter V: Sections D.9 and D.10.*)

36. **G.** You must omit the underlined portion because the modifying phrase that begins the sentence (**Clumsy on land, yet graceful in the water**) modifies **penguins,** not **scientists.** (*Chapter V: Section D.4.*)

37. **C.** Choice C is idiomatically incorrect. All the other choices are acceptable. (*Chapter V: Section D.3.*)

38. **H.** The correct idiom is **protected from** not **protected away from.** (*Chapter V: Section D.3.*)

Section 2: Mathematics Test

1. **D.** The sum of m and n could be even or odd. However, 2 times this sum, $2(m + n)$, is always even, thus Choice D is correct. Another way to approach the question is to substitute different integers for m and n and to check each choice. (*Chapter VIII: Section B.*)

2. **H.** Inspecting the scatterplot and the line of best fit, the actual height of the player whose right foot measures 11 inches is 72 inches high, and the predicted height by the line of best fit is 70 inches. Thus, the difference is 2 inches. (*Chapter XIV: Section G.*)

3. **E.** Since Mary was x years old 6 years ago, she is now $(x + 6)$. Bill was $2x$ years old 6 years ago, and thus, he is now $(2x + 6)$. The sum of their current ages is $(x + 6) + (2x + 6)$, which is $(3x + 12)$. (*Chapter IX: Section G.*)

4. **H.** Triangles ADE and ABC are similar. The ratio of AD to AB is $\frac{1}{3}$, and thus, the ratio of DE to BC is $\frac{1}{3}$. Therefore, $\frac{DE}{BC} = \frac{1}{3}$ and $\frac{3}{BC} = \frac{1}{3}$. So, $BC = 9$. *(Chapter XII: Section D.)*

5. **D.** There are 3 types of tables and 2 types of chairs. For each type of table, there are two choices for chairs. Therefore, there are 6 different dining room sets. *(Chapter XIV: Section A.)*

6. **G.** Since $y + x = 1$, you have $y = 1 - x$. Thus, $xy = -2$ becomes $x(1 - x) = -2$ and $x - x^2 = -2$ and $x^2 - x - 2 = 0$. Factor and you have $(x - 2)(x + 1) = 0$ and $x = 2$ or $x = -1$. Since x is negative, $x = -1$ is the only solution. *(Chapter X: Section F.)*

7. **C.** Since the $m\angle ACD = 140$, the $m\angle ACB = 40$. The $m\angle ACB$ and the $m\angle ABC$ are the same because they are base angles of an isosceles triangle. Therefore, $2x + 40 + 40 = 180$ and $x = 50$. *(Chapter XII: Section A.)*

8. **F.** The two intersecting lines create two pairs of vertical angles. Thus, $4y = 80$ and $y = 20$, and $2x = 100$, which leads to $x = 50$. Therefore, only statement I is true. *(Chapter XII: Section A.)*

9. **B.** You have $f(1) = 1^2 + 4 = 5$. Thus, $3f(1) = 15$ and $3f(1) + 2 = 17$. *(Chapter X: Section G.)*

10. **J.** The figure can be obtained by translating the graph of $y = -|x|$ (which is in the shape of an upside-down "v") 3 units to the left and 1 unit up. You could also enter the given equations into your calculator and examine their graphs. *(Chapter XII: Section I.)*

11. **E.** The slope of a line is defined as $m = \frac{y_2 - y_1}{x_2 - x_1}$. Therefore, the slope of the line $\overleftrightarrow{AB}$ is
$$m = \frac{4 - (-8)}{-2 - (-6)} = \frac{4 + 8}{-2 + 6} = \frac{12}{4} = 3.$$ *(Chapter XI: Section E.)*

12. **H.** You have $k - 0.25k = 24$, and, thus, $0.75k = 24$. Dividing both sides by 0.75 gives you $k = 32$. *(Chapter VIII: Section G.)*

13. **B.** Since $\overline{AC}$ is a diameter, angle B is inscribed in a semicircle, and thus, it is a right angle, and $\triangle ABC$ is a right triangle. You are given that $AB = BC$. Using the Pythagorean theorem, you obtain 8 for both AB and BC:

$$x^2 + x^2 = \left(8\sqrt{2}\right)^2$$
$$2x^2 = 128$$
$$x^2 = 64$$
$$x = \pm 8$$

Thus $AB = 8$ and $BC = 8$.

Since the diameter of the circle is $8\sqrt{2}$, the radius of the circle is $4\sqrt{2}$, and thus the area of the semicircle is 16π: $A = \frac{\pi r^2}{2} = \frac{\pi\left(4\sqrt{2}\right)^2}{2} = \frac{\pi(4)(4)(2)}{2} = \frac{32\pi}{2} = 16\pi$.

The area of the triangle is $\left(\frac{1}{2}\right)(8)(8)$, which is 32. The area of the two shaded regions is the difference of the semicircle and the triangle. Thus, the area of the two shaded regions is $16\pi - 32$. (*Chapter XII: Section G.*)

14. **F.** The standard equation of a circle is $(x - h)^2 + (y - k)^2 = r^2$, where (h,k) is the center and r is the radius. In this case, the radius is 1. Thus, the area of the circle is $\pi(1)^2$ or simply π. (*Chapter XI: Section B.*)

15. **D.** Begin with the equation $2n^2 = 4n$ and rewrite it as $2n^2 - 4n = 0$. Factor and obtain $2n(n - 2) = 0$, and thus $n = 0$ or $n = 2$. Since n is positive, n is 2. (*Chapter IX: Section F.*)

16. **G.** The midpoint formula is $\left(\frac{x_1 + x_2}{2}, \frac{y_1 + y_2}{2}\right)$. Therefore, $\frac{(4 + k)}{2} = 2$ or $4 + k = 4$ or $k = 0$. (*Chapter XI: Section G.*)

17. **D.** Mary paid $0.80 for the first doughnut and had $3.20 left. Divide $3.20 by $0.40, and you have 8. Thus, Mary bought a total of 9 doughnuts. (*Chapter IX: Section G.*)

18. **G.** The cosine function is defined as $\frac{\text{adjacent leg}}{\text{hypotenuse}}$. The adjacent leg to $\angle A$ is $\overline{AC}$. Using the Pythagorean theorem, you have $(AC)^2 + 12^2 = 13^2$ or $AC = 5$. Thus, $\cos A = \frac{5}{13}$. (*Chapter XIII: Section A.*)

19. **C.** The diameter of the circle is 20, and the diameter is also a diagonal of the square. The area of a square can be obtained by either $(s)^2$ or $\frac{(d)^2}{2}$, where s is a side and d is a diagonal. Thus, the area of the square is $\frac{(20)^2}{2}$ or 200. You could also have found the side of the square by using the Pythagorean theorem or the special 45°-45° right triangle relationship. (*Chapter XII: Section E.*)

20. **J.** This is an arithmetic sequence. The formula for the nth term of an arithmetic sequence is $a_0 + (n - 1)d$. Thus, the 5th term $= 0 + (5 - 1)(5) = 20$, and the 15th term $= 0 + (15 - 1)(5) = 70$. The sum of the two terms is 90. (*Chapter X: Section K.*)

21. **A.** The coordinate of B is -1.5 and $2C$ is -1. The sum of $B + 2C$ is -2.5. Thus, the point is A. (*Chapter VIII: Section C.*)

22. **K.** If a function f is an odd function, then $f(x) = -f(-x)$. In Choice K, $f(x) = x^5 - 2x^3$ and $-f(-x) = -[(-x)^5 - 2(-x)^3] = -(-x^5 + 2x^3) = x^5 - 2x^3$. Thus, $f(x)$ is an odd function. An alternate solution is to enter the given functions into your calculator and see which graph has point symmetry at the origin. (*Chapter X: Section G.*)

23. **E.** Using your calculator, you have $\left(8^{\frac{2}{3}}\right) = 4$. Then, $4\left(n^{\frac{1}{4}}\right) = 16$ and $\left(n^{\frac{1}{4}}\right) = 4$. Raise both sides of the equation to the 4th power; you have $n = 256$. (*Chapter IX: Section B.*)

24. **F.** Inspecting the table, you note that the relative frequency of male students taking algebra is 0.4, and that the relative frequency of male students taking either algebra or geometry is 0.6. Therefore, the relative frequency of male students taking geometry is $0.6 - 0.4 = 0.2$. Thus, the probability of picking a male student taking geometry is 0.2.

Relative Frequency Table			
	Algebra	Geometry	Total
Male	0.4	0.2	0.6
Female	0.25	0.15	0.4
Total	0.65	0.35	1

Complete the relative frequency table as shown above. (*Chapter XIV: Section C.*)

25. **E.** The probability of "getting at least one head" = 1 – the probability of getting 2 tails. The probability of getting 2 tails is $\left(\frac{1}{2}\right)\left(\frac{1}{2}\right) = \frac{1}{4}$. Thus, the probability of getting at least one head is $\frac{3}{4}$. (*Chapter XIV: Section B.*)

26. **G.** Set B = {2, 1, 0, –2, –3, –4}. The median is the middle number, and in this case, $\frac{(0 + -2)}{2}$ or –1. (*Chapter XIV: Section D.*)

27. **C.** Triangle EHG is a right triangle. Using the Pythagorean theorem, you can find EG. You have $6^2 + 4^2 = EG^2$ or $EG = \sqrt{52}$. Similarly, triangle AEG is a right triangle. Using the Pythagorean theorem again, you have $2^2 + \sqrt{52}^2 = AG^2$ or $AG = \sqrt{56}$. (*Chapter XII: Section F.*)

28. **K.** Since $\log_2 8 = 3$ and $\log_5 25 = 2$, you have $3 + 2 = \log_3 x$, or $5 = \log_3 x$. Thus, $x = 3^5$ or 243. (*Chapter X: Section H.*)

29. **E.** Since $\sin^2 \theta + \cos^2 \theta = 1$, you have $\cos^2 \theta = 1 - \sin^2 \theta$ or $\cos \theta = \pm\sqrt{1 - \sin^2 \theta}$. Since $0 < \theta < \frac{\pi}{2}$, $\cos \theta = \sqrt{1 - \sin^2 \theta}$. Thus, the expression $\frac{\cos \theta}{\sqrt{1 - \sin^2 \theta}}$ is equivalent to $\frac{\cos \theta}{\cos \theta}$ or 1. (*Chapter XIII: Section E.*)

30. **K.** Applying the distributive property, you have $2i(i^3 - 4i) = 2i^4 - 8i^2$. Since $i^4 = 1$ and $i^2 = -1$, the expression $2i^4 - 8i^2$ becomes $2(1) - 8(-1) = 2 + 8$ or 10. (*Chapter X: Section J.*)

Section 3: Reading Test

Passage I

1. **B.** According to the passage, Mrs. Rachel is getting dizzy because of "this unusual mystery about quiet, unmysterious Green Gables." It is clear from the passage that she is a woman who likes to know everything that is going on. The idea that a major event could occur in her neighborhood without her knowledge is extremely disturbing to her. (*Chapter VI: Section C.5.*)

2. **F.** The passage implies that Marilla has led a circumscribed (restricted) life. She is described as a "woman of narrow experience" (line 27). The details about her mouth (lines 28–31) suggest she has a sense of humor. (*Chapter VI: Section C.5.*)

3. **C.** In an EXCEPT question, three of the answers are correct and one is incorrect. Since the information in the introductory notes states that the Green Gables farm is in Canada, Choice C is clearly wrong. (*Chapter VI: Section C.5.*)

4. **H.** This is a generalization question. The whole passage suggests that Mrs. Rachel has a need to be informed on every event that occurs in Avonlea. In fact, she becomes upset at the notion that a major event is taking place without her knowledge. (*Chapter VI: Section C.7.*)

5. **A.** In the last sentence, the narrator sums up Mrs. Rachel's attitude, that anything done without her advice MUST be disapproved of, with an ironic tone. The humor is gentle, but the tone of the entire passage does not indicate any hostility, so Choice B is incorrect. Eliminate Choice C because the narrator does not share Mrs. Rachel's disapproval. The sentence is not sentimental at all, so Choice D is incorrect. (*Chapter VI: Section C.8.*)

Passage II

6. **J.** This question asks you to generalize about Lincoln, to take everything that you learned about him in the passage and boil it down to one statement that summarizes his character. Since the passage makes clear that Lincoln handled the crises well, Choices F and G are incorrect. Since the evidence in the passage suggests that Lincoln was a practical man rather than a manipulator (Choice H) and that he was able to handle multiple problems simultaneously, Choice J is the best answer. (*Chapter VI: Section C.7.*)

7. **C.** The "howl of baffled wrath" was the reaction of the South Carolinians to the news that Fort Moultrie was no longer being defended. This retreat occurred because Floyd did not have enough men (Choice A), so Major Anderson decided to remove his troops from Fort Moultrie and concentrate on defending Fort Sumter (Choice B). The South Carolinians had been expecting provisions from the *Star of the West,* but these could not be unloaded (Choice D). Thus, all of the choices except Choice C contributed to the feelings of anger. (*Chapter VI: Section C.5.*)

8. **F.** The answer to this implied detail question can be inferred from paragraph 3 (lines 35–46). It suggests that while some Northerners were sympathetic to the pro-slave position, the preservation of the Union was their priority. (*Chapter VI: Section C.5.*)

9. **B.** Choices A, C, and D are all mentioned in the passage as difficulties Lincoln faced. Kentucky and Missouri had remained in the Union (lines 30–31). Nowhere in the passage does it state that keeping these states in the union posed a problem for Lincoln. (*Chapter VI: Section C.5.*)

10. **G.** This vocabulary question requires that you consider the context carefully. Any "delicate" political situation will need careful diplomacy. The passage does not indicate that the relationship between England and France was fragile (Choice H) or that a truce was likely (Choice J) or that a scandal might erupt (Choice F). (*Chapter VI: Section C.9.*)

Passage III

11. **B.** All of the choices have some connection to events in the second paragraph, but only Choice B is accurate. Choice A is inaccurate because there is no evidence Jane Austen actually met the Prince Regent. Choice C is inaccurate because there is no evidence that the prince had anything to do with saving Jane Austen's brother. Choice D is off topic. There is no indication the prince knew where Jane Austen was buried. (*Chapter VI: Section C.5.*)

12. **J.** This vocabulary question tests your ability to understand the meaning of a simple word with multiple meanings. In the context of the passage, the word does not indicate any smash, explosion, or accident. It is used to emphasize Jane Austen's isolation in that she had no "interaction" with other intellectuals. (*Chapter VI: Section C.9.*)

13. **B.** The passage indicates that Jane Austen "is hard upon vulgarity," but she accepts "good-natured vulgarity" in some characters. This evidence contradicts choices A and C. No evidence from the passage supports Choice D. (*Chapter VI: Section C.1.*)

14. **H.** The passage states that Jane Austen's "foundation of her own character was good sense, and her type of excellence…is a woman full of feeling, but with her feelings thoroughly under control." From this statement, you can infer that she disliked sentimentality because it suggests unrestrained emotions. No evidence from the passage suggests Austen was a cold woman, so Choice F is incorrect. The passage implies that Austen disliked Mrs. Radcliffe's romances, so Choice G is incorrect. Choice J is contradicted by the evidence that Austen liked "genuine sensibility." (*Chapter VI: Section C.1.*)

15. **D.** This question asks you to find a choice with which both authors would agree. Both passages mention that Jane Austen lived a refined life with little contact with the world outside her town and family. Passage A specifically states that Austen wasn't cynical, so Choice A is incorrect. No evidence from either passage supports Choice B. Choice C is contradicted by the information in Passage A ("Jane Austen lived in entire seclusion from the literary world.") (*Chapter VI: Section C.5.*)

Passage IV

16. **H.** The primary purpose is to explain Franklin's theory. Choices F and G are not supported by textual evidence and Choice J is not accurate according to the passage. (*Chapter VI: Section C.1.*)

17. **C.** According to the passage, Franklin used the Leyden jar to prove that electricity seeks to "remain in a state of equilibrium" (lines 3–4). Franklin disagreed with Choice B. Choice A reverses the charges of the coating on the jar. Choice D is not covered in the passage. (*Chapter VI: Section C.5.*)

18. **G.** This cause and effect and sequence of events question asks you to follow the logic of the passage. Franklin took what he learned from the Leyden jar and applied it to the construction of a battery which, in turn, enabled him to "produce electrical manifestations of great force" (lines 34–36). He did not reject his theory (Choice F) or theorize that electricity is different from lightning (Choice H). There is no evidence in the passage to support his having to overcome skepticism (Choice J). (*Chapter VI: Section C.6.*)

19. **B.** To answer this detail question correctly, you must go back to the text, identify the four men, and note why they are mentioned. The passage indicates they all saw the "resemblance between electric sparks and lightning, but none of these had more than surmised that the two might be identical" (lines 45–48). Thus, they failed to make key connections. (*Chapter VI: Section C.5.*)

20. **G.** You must infer the answer to this detail question from lines 18–21 which state, "the rubbed glass globe attracting a certain quantity of 'electrical fire,' but ever ready to give it up to any body that has less." Choice H is incorrect because no liquid is placed in the jar. There is no indication that the jar will cause a shock (Choice J), and the cleanliness of the jar does not seem to be an issue (Choice F). (*Chapter VI: Section C.5.*)

Section 4: Science Test

Passage I

1. **A.** The largest change in temperature ($\Delta T = 3.6°C$) is observed after the first 2-minute interval. All other observed ΔT values in Table 1 are lower than $3.6°C$.

2. **J.** Although the temperature of the water does decrease, it is not at a constant rate (ΔT changes in each interval). Since $\dfrac{\Delta T}{D_T}$ is approximately equal to 0.13 in each interval, Choice J is strongly supported by the data.

3. **C.** The graph clearly demonstrates a strong correlation between ΔT and D_T such that $\dfrac{\Delta T}{D_T}$ is constant (lies approximately on a straight line). Although there are very slight variations from $\dfrac{\Delta T}{D_T} = 0.13$ in the data, this is insignificant and negligible. This could very easily be attributed to equipment error (low accuracy or poor calibration), human error in taking the measurement, and/or rounding in the calculations.

4. **H.** If $D_T = 10°C$, then $\Delta T = 10°C \times 0.13 = 1.3$. This is true because $\dfrac{\Delta T}{D_T} = 0.13$ (constant).

Passage II

5. **A.** The value lies between 25°C and 40°C, and in that range there is moderate to high glucose production (8.2–15.1 µmol/mL). The enzyme would therefore be effective at that temperature. There is also sufficient evidence to suggest that just above and below normal body temperature (36°–38°C), the enzyme would be either as effective or slightly less effective than at 37°C. It appears to only significantly lose effectiveness at more extreme temperatures.

6. **G.** Table 2 demonstrates that as pH increases, the rate of glucose formation increases, peaks, and then decreases. This graph is consistent with that relationship, for as the curve is read in the direction of increasing x-values, the corresponding y-values first increase, peak (around 19 µmol/mL), and then decrease.

7. **D.** Table 1 indicates that the highest rate of glucose formation observed is 15.1 µmol/mL, which corresponds to 40°C. Table 2 demonstrates that the highest rate of glucose formation is 18.8 µmol/mL, which corresponds to a pH of 6.5. Table 1 indicates that as temperature increases, the rate of glucose formation increases, peaks, and then decreases. A similar pattern is observed in Table 2 for pH.

8. **J.** The new value of 15.9 µmol/mL lies between two possible sets of observed values for glucose formation: 1.3–18.8 or 18.8–10.6 (i.e., just before or after the maximum rate of glucose production). The possible pH value then is somewhere between 4.0 and 8.0, but likely very close to 6.5. The closest answer is 7.

9. **B.** Table 3 indicates that just before the lactase supplement reaches the cells of the small intestine (where it will be working at a pH of 7.5), it passes through the stomach where the pH of 2 is much lower. Using Table 2, it is logical to predict that the lactase supplement would not be very effective in the stomach at that pH, which is consistent with the notion that the supplement would denature at low pH. If the denaturation is not reversible, when the supplement reaches the small intestine, it may no longer function properly.

Passage III

10. **J.** The passage states that even before the study, the scientific community was in agreement about a relationship between SST and hurricane frequency. The debate concerned the way in which the local SST was determined (i.e., whether the local SST should be measured relative to the tropical SST or on its own).

11. **C.** According to Table 1, Hypothesis 1 predicted the exact number of hurricanes observed in that year (0% error). Hypothesis 2 was also very close, but underpredicted the value by 1 (–1.09% error). Therefore, both hypotheses could be considered reliable since they fall within the ±5% range. Regarding hurricane numbers, there were more hurricanes recorded in years 5–10 than in year 2, when they numbered only 92.

12. **G.** According to Table 1, the correlation of Hypothesis 1 is 0.93 and the correlation of Hypothesis 2 is 0.98. Because the closer the correlation value is to 1, the stronger the hypothesis is considered, Hypothesis 2 is more strongly supported by the data overall.

Passage IV

13. **B.** According to Figure 1, the curve with the highest solubility at 45°C is KNO_3. The corresponding y-value on that curve where $x = 45$ is approximately 70 g of KNO_3 per 100 g of water. Each of the other suggested solubilities (40 g for NaCl at 90°C, 60 g for NH_3 at 15°C, and 40 g for $KClO_3$ at 80°C) is below that of KNO_3.

14. **G.** Examining the solubility curve for NH_3, it is obvious that as the temperature increases (moving along the x-axis from left to right), the solubility decreases (values along the y-axis become smaller). Each of the other solubility curves (NaCl, KCl, $KClO_3$, and KNO_3) demonstrates an increase in solubility with an increase in temperature (i.e., the y-values increase as the x-values increase).

15. **D.** According to Figure 2, as the number of carbon atoms present in any carbon-containing molecule increases (i.e., the x-values increase), the solubility of that molecule in 110 g of water decreases (i.e., the y-values decrease). According to Table 1, the solubilities of alcohols with 1–3 carbon atoms are unlimited, but as the number of carbon atoms present in an alcohol increases beyond 4, the solubility decreases sharply.

16. **G.** NaCl has a minimal change in solubility over a wide range of temperatures (e.g., 37 g at 0°C and 40 g at 100°C) and a minimum saturation of 37 g of solute in 100 g of water. It meets both criteria desired by the chemist. Hexanol demonstrates a lower solubility than desired (<1 g/110 g water), while KNO_3 and NH_3 vary widely as temperature increases. The solubility for KNO_3 increases from 12 g at 0°C to 150 g at 77°C, while the solubility for NH_3 decreases from 91 g at 0°C to 7 g at 100°C.

Passage V

17. **D.** According to the passage, mitosis includes prophase, metaphase, anaphase, and telophase (it does not include interphase). Table 1 demonstrates that the longest phase of mitosis then is prophase at 194.4 minutes. Both telophase and anaphase were calculated to require times lower than that of prophase (21.6 minutes and 36.0 minutes, respectively).

18. **H.** Of all the phases studied, interphase was found to be the most commonly observed (57% of all cells examined were in this phase) and thus required the longest time to complete (57% of 720 minutes, or 410.4 minutes). From there, the length of time required to complete the phase decreased for each successive phase as the cell progressed through mitosis.

19. **B.** According to Table 1, most onion root cells examined were in interphase. According to Table 2, interphase took the longest time to complete of any phase for both normal and cancerous human skin cells. It can be deduced then that most of the human skin cells observed under the microscope were in interphase. The smallest percentage of onion root cells observed in any phase was in telophase (see Table 1) and the smallest percentage of human skin cells observed was in anaphase (regardless of whether normal or cancerous, see Table 2).

20. **F.** According to Table 2, cancerous human skin cells require less time than normal human skin cells to complete each phase except metaphase and anaphase. For those two phases, the same amount of time is required for normal and cancerous cells. The entire cell cycle (interphase + mitosis) must then be shorter for cancerous cells (1100 minutes) than for normal cells (1440 minutes).

Section 5: Writing Test

Sample Scored Essay A

By designating a piece of land a "wilderness," we have the opportunity to protect our wonderful environment. Many of us forget that there is only one earth, and that it is therefore our responsibility to protect it for future generations and ourselves. If we do not take these measures, big business will capitalize on this land, using it for commercial activities, and we will lose a very precious resource.

Areas that are designated "wilderness" are heavily protected, which benefits the entire community. As stated in Perspective 1, creating "wilderness" areas allows for conditions that provide undisturbed wildlife habitats, natural scenic views, and opportunities for recreation. We live in a society that is notorious for its hustle and bustle, which results in a plethora of stressed individuals, desperate for some form of relaxation. As a high school student, I can certainly attest to this pressure, which is why preserving untouched areas is so important. Whenever I have had an extremely stressful week at school, my parents take my siblings and I for a hike to a local nature preserve. Walking up the mountain, taking in the view, and listening to the silence allow me to forget all of my problems and just be in the moment. Recognizing the benefits of spending time in unspoiled nature, some colleges and universities have established hiking clubs, specifically designed to help students escape from the pressures of schoolwork.

Moreover, preserving designated "wilderness" areas can have a positive effect on the environment. Setting aside "no build" areas would cut down on air and water pollution, while the converse—building on every square inch of uninhabited land—will have the opposite effect: more air and water pollution. Leaving these lands as pristine as they were before human encroachment will always remind us that the earth is fragile and we have to protect this planet.

It is also imperative to consider all forms of life in wilderness areas. Have scientists identified every living organism? Is it not possible that some unique and previously unidentified flora or fauna will be discovered in the wilderness? As urban sprawl covers the landscape, plants and animals are losing their habitats and disappearing. For all we know, some plant that could have amazing curative properties might disappear from earth to make way for a new strip mall or a housing development. It is these serious considerations that led to The Wilderness Act of 1964. Perspective 3 offers an excerpt from this Act, which emphasizes the relationship between human beings and the wilderness lands. I agree with the premise of this act, that human beings must consider themselves "visitors" rather than owners of nature. The "untrammeled" nature of these designated areas must be protected or there will no longer be any reminders of raw nature.

Some individuals believe it is in the best interest of our society to take advantage of every resource. After all, forests can be cut down to provide wood for needed housing, and hunted animals can provide food for hungry people. Factories that employ thousands can be built on unused land and can produce goods that will bolster the economy. There might even be valuable minerals, as Perspective 2 acknowledges, that can help industry or health care. But, all these resources come at too great a price. Wilderness areas are not "renewable energy." Once developed, they can never be returned to their natural state.

By setting aside land and designating it as untouchable "wilderness," the U.S. is taking a stand on an important ecological issue. By putting the environment before financial gain, it is taking a position that I strongly support. We owe it to our children and future generations to leave evidence that this country was once filled with unspoiled forests and deserts and fields.

Domain Scores

Ideas and Analysis: 6 (× 2 = 12)

The writer presents an effective analysis of the three perspectives, using Perspectives 1 and 3 to support her claims and refuting Perspective 2. The introductory paragraph presents a strong thesis, which is developed in the body paragraphs. The writer shows insight into the context of the issue and recognizes its complexities by giving multiple reasons to support wilderness areas.

Development and Support: 5 (× 2 = 10)

The evidence the writer uses to support her argument is varied and reveals her understanding of the issue. She draws on multiple reasons (relieving stress, protecting the environment, saving flora and fauna).

Organization: 6 (× 2 = 12)

The organizational pattern is skillful and the writer effectively uses transitional words (*Moreover, also*) and phrases to highlight relationships between ideas (*Some individuals believe…, After all…*). The controlling idea (*there is only one earth, and that it is therefore our responsibility to protect it for future generations and ourselves*) unifies the essay.

Language Use: 5 (× 2 = 10)

Language use is competent and appropriate (*Leaving these lands as pristine as they were before human encroachment will always remind us that the earth is fragile and we have to protect this planet*). Word choice demonstrates accuracy (*As urban sprawl covers the landscape, curative properties*) and sentence structure is often varied (*Is it not possible that some unique and previously unidentified flora or fauna will be discovered in the wilderness?*). Errors in grammar are minor (*my parents take my siblings and I for a hike*).

To calculate the Essay Score, add the Domain Scores: 12 + 10 + 12 + 10 = 44.

Using the conversion table on page 371, a Domain Score of **44** equals a scaled score of **34**.

Sample Scored Essay B

When I think about the wilderness I think about the wild west. When I went camping with my family we went to some national parks that have places where you can set up a tent and camp out. We had a great time and we like the scenary which is where we go. I don't think builders should come in and just built where ever they want.

There are three perspectives on the wilderness issue. Perspective number 1 is what I agree with because there should be places where people can go to enjoy the nature. Perspective number 1 says we need clean water and clean air and places where no one lives. it is important to get away from all your troubles and nature is the place to go there.

I agree with perspective number 2 because we need to use our resources and make money from the land. The propspecters went out west and they found gold which made us rich.

I'm not sure about perspective number 3 because it just tell you what the law says. I guess I agree with the law.

In conclusion, it is good to have places to go where there is no traffic and no Big Macs. That is what the wilderness means to me. We need to have laws to save it.

Domain Scores

Ideas and Analysis: 2 (× 2 = 4)

While the writer responds to the perspectives, he agrees with all three, demonstrating his limited understanding of the perspectives. The thesis is imprecise (*I don't think builders should come in and just built where ever they want*). The argument shows some understanding of the context (personal experience with camping in the national parks), but any analysis is vague.

Development and Support: 2 (× 2 = 4)

The evidence the writer uses to support his argument is superficial (*there should be places where people can go to enjoy the nature*) and confused (*I agree with perspective number 2 because we need to use our resources and make money from the land*).

Organization: 2 (× 2 = 4)

Although the writer covers one idea in each paragraph, the organizational pattern is simple and basic. The writer uses no transitions between or within paragraphs.

Language Use: 2 (× 2 = 4)

Language use is unclear and inaccurate (*it is important to get away from all your troubles and nature is the place to go there*). Word choice is basic (*I guess I agree with the law*). Sentence structure is unclear (*We had a great time and we like the scenary which is where we go*). Multiple errors in grammar hinder understanding (*The propspecters went out west and they found gold which made us rich*).

To calculate the Essay Score, add the Domain Scores: 4 + 4 + 4 + 4 = 16.

Using the conversion table on page 371, a Domain Score of **16** equals a scaled score of **12**.

Scoring Worksheets

Sections 1–4

English Test

Number Correct

Usage/Mechanics (UM) Subscore Area   _____ (25)

Rhetorical Skills (RH) Subscore Area   _____ (13)

Total Number Correct for English Test (UM + RH)   _____ (38)

Raw Score (Total Number Correct × 2)   _____

Mathematics Test

Number Correct

Pre-Algebra/Elementary Algebra (EA) Subscore Area   _____ (7)

Intermediate Algebra/Coordinate Geometry (AG) Subscore Area   _____ (9)

Plane Geometry/Trigonometry (GT) Subscore Area   _____ (9)

Probability/Statistics (PS) Subscore Area   _____ (5)

Total Number Correct for Math Test (EA + AG + GT + PS)   _____ (30)

Raw Score (Total Number Correct × 2)   _____

Reading Test

Number Correct

Social Studies/Sciences (SS) Subscore Area   _____ (10)

Arts/Literature (AL) Subscore Area   _____ (10)

Total Number Correct for Reading Test (SS + AL)   _____ (20)

Raw Score (Total Number Correct × 2)   _____

Science Test

Number Correct

Data Representation (DR) Subscore Area   _____ (8)

Research Summaries (RS) Subscore Area   _____ (9)

Conflicting Viewpoints (CV) Subscore Area   _____ (3)

Total Number Correct for Science Test (DR + RS + CV)   _____ (20)

Raw Score (Total Number Correct × 2)   _____

Test	Raw Score	Scale Score
English		
Mathematics		
Reading		
Science		
Sum of Scale Scores (English + Mathematics + Reading + Science)		
Composite Score (sum ÷ 4)		

Note: To obtain your scale score, refer to the conversion table on page 371.

Section 5: Writing Test

To obtain your Writing Test score, refer to the following rubric. Then compare your essay to the scored essays on pages 66–68. It may be helpful to have another person, ideally your English teacher, give feedback on your essay.

The ACT Writing Test Rubric

Score	Ideas and Analysis	Development and Support	Organization	Language Use
6	❑ Essay presents effective analysis of the three given perspectives ❑ Thesis addresses the nuances of the complexity of the issue ❑ Argument shows insightful understanding of the context ❑ Analysis thoroughly addresses implications and validity of claims in given perspectives	❑ Evidence develops insightful understanding of context ❑ Skillful reasoning illustrates the argument ❑ Ideas and analysis are deepened and broadened by understanding of the complexities of the issue	❑ Organizational strategy is skillful and effective ❑ Controlling idea unifies the response and ideas progress logically ❑ Transitions provide strong connections and establish logical relationships among ideas	❑ Skillful language enriches the essay ❑ Word choice demonstrates fluency and accuracy ❑ Sentence structure is varied and effective ❑ Style reflects strong voice and effective use of tone ❑ Errors in grammar are few and/or minor

Score	Ideas and Analysis	Development and Support	Organization	Language Use
5	❑ Essay presents reasonable analysis of the three given perspectives ❑ Thesis precisely addresses the complexity of the issue ❑ Argument shows thoughtful understanding of the context ❑ Analysis addresses implications and validity of claims in given perspectives	❑ Evidence develops clear understanding of context ❑ Well-defined reasoning illustrates the argument ❑ Ideas and analysis demonstrate astute understanding of the complexities of the issue	❑ Organizational strategy is purposeful ❑ Controlling idea mostly unifies the response and ideas progress logically ❑ Transitions provide consistent connections and clarify relationships among ideas	❑ Language use is competent and appropriate ❑ Word choice demonstrates accuracy ❑ Sentence structure is often varied and effective ❑ Style reflects voice and competent use of tone ❑ Errors in grammar are minor
4	❑ Essay presents some reasonable analysis of the three given perspectives ❑ Thesis addresses the complexity of the issue ❑ Argument shows understanding of the context ❑ Analysis recognizes implications and validity of claims in given perspectives	❑ Evidence clarifies understanding of context ❑ Reasoning adequately illustrates the argument ❑ Ideas and analysis demonstrate understanding of the complexities of the issue	❑ Organizational strategy is clear ❑ Ideas progress logically from an implied controlling idea ❑ Transitions provide connections and clarify relationships among ideas	❑ Language use is appropriate ❑ Word choice is adequate and sometimes accurate ❑ Sentence structure is clear and shows some variety ❑ Style choices are appropriate ❑ Some errors in grammar are present, but they rarely hinder understanding
3	❑ Essay responds to the three given perspectives ❑ Thesis addresses some of the complexity of the issue ❑ Argument shows limited understanding of the context ❑ Analysis of given perspectives is simplistic or vague	❑ Evidence of understanding of context is vague or simplistic ❑ Reasoning to illustrate the argument is vague or imprecise ❑ Ideas and analysis demonstrate some understanding of the issue	❑ Organizational strategy is formulaic and/or basic ❑ Most ideas are logically arranged ❑ Transitions to provide connections are uneven	❑ Language use is simplistic and sometimes unclear ❑ Word choice is vague and sometimes inaccurate ❑ Sentence structure is clear but shows little variety ❑ Style choices may occasionally be inappropriate ❑ Errors in grammar are distracting but mostly don't hinder understanding

continued

Score	Ideas and Analysis	Development and Support	Organization	Language Use
2	❏ Essay weakly responds to perspectives ❏ Thesis is imprecise, unclear, or missing ❏ Argument shows little understanding of the context ❏ Analysis of given perspectives is superficial, vague, or merely a summary	❏ Understanding of context is weak, vague, or jumbled ❏ Reasoning is unclear, insufficient, or mistaken ❏ Ideas and analysis are confused or absent	❏ Organizational strategy is very simple and basic ❏ Ideas are disorganized ❏ Transitions fail to provide logical connections	❏ Language use is unclear and inaccurate ❏ Word choice is basic and frequently inaccurate ❏ Sentence structure is sometimes unclear ❏ Style choices may be inappropriate ❏ Errors in grammar are distracting and sometimes hinder understanding
1	❏ Essay fails to present an argument ❏ Thesis is absent or irrelevant to the task ❏ Argument shows no understanding of the context ❏ Analysis is absent or irrelevant	❏ Ideas are unclear, underdeveloped, or absent ❏ Reasoning is unsupported ❏ Analysis is incoherent or absent	❏ Organizational strategy is absent ❏ Ideas show no logical organizational plan ❏ Transitions are absent or illogical	❏ Language use is incompetent ❏ Word choice is inaccurate and may be incomprehensible ❏ Sentence structure is often unclear ❏ Style choices are illogical and/or inappropriate ❏ Errors in grammar are distracting, widespread, and often hinder understanding

Calculating Your Writing Test Score

1. **Using the rubric, find** your four domain scores and enter them below. **Then, multiply each by 2.**

	Score	× 2	= Domain Score
Ideas and Analysis			
Development and Support			
Organization			
Language Use and Conventions			
			Total

2. The total of the Domain Scores after multiplying by 2 =_____.
3. To obtain your scaled score, refer to the conversion table on page 371.

V. English Test

Format

The English Test consists of five passages. There are about 15 questions per passage for a total of 75 questions to be completed in 45 minutes. On the ACT English Test, the passages are on the left side of the page and the questions are on the right side.

Content

The purpose of the ACT English Test is to test your knowledge of standard written English. This is the formal "language" used by educated Americans. For the most part, you do not have to know how to identify nouns, verbs, participles, or gerunds; you just have to know how to use them correctly. Since the ACT English Test is an editing and revising test, you will have to know the grammatical rules only as they apply to the context of the passages.

There are two categories of questions on the English Test:

- 40 **Usage/Mechanics** questions test your knowledge of punctuation, grammar and usage, and sentence structure.
- 35 **Rhetorical Skills** questions test your understanding of the decisions writers make about diction, style, organization, and writing strategy.

Parts of each of the passages are underlined. Some questions ask you to consider the underlined portion and determine whether or not a usage or mechanics error is present. You are offered four answer choices. If you think the underlined part is correct, you may select the NO CHANGE option (if it is offered as a choice). Or, you may consider the other options. Some questions ask you to consider the sentence, paragraph, or passage as a whole.

What is *NOT* on the ACT English Test: You will not be tested on spelling or vocabulary (other than an occasional diction question that asks you to choose the best word for the context). You will not have to identify the parts of speech or the parts of a sentence. No reading comprehension questions are given on the English Test. The reading comprehension questions are found in Section 3 of the ACT (the Reading Test).

A. Usage and Mechanics

The Usage and Mechanics questions will test your ability to recognize and use standard written English. You will be tested on your knowledge of punctuation, such as the proper use of apostrophes, colons, semicolons, commas, question marks, dashes, and exclamation points. In addition, you will be tested on your skills in revising sentence structure and correcting grammatical errors.

- Begin each passage by reading through the entire passage quickly, noting the organization, style, and tone.
- Consider the correctness of the underlined portion of the text within the context of the sentence and the whole essay.

- Note the differences among the answer choices. Be aware that some choices will correct the original error but create a new error.
- After you select an answer, reread the entire sentence to make sure it makes sense within the original context.
- Watch out for redundancies. Examine the phrasing **before or after** the underlined part for words or phrases that make the answer you have chosen redundant.
- Be careful about two-part questions and interrelated questions. In some cases, your answer to one question will impact your answer to the next question.
- Watch out for questions that ask you which answer would **NOT** be correct in the context of the passage. Some questions will state, "All of the following are acceptable EXCEPT …" In these questions, three of the choices are **correct;** your task is to find the one that is **incorrect.**

B. Important Terms to Know

- A **clause** is group of words that contains a subject and a verb.
- A **main clause** or **independent clause** is a clause that expresses a complete thought.
  Example: The music on my iPhone is a mixture of rock and country songs.
- A **subordinate clause** or **dependent clause** does not express a complete thought.
  Example: Since the music on my iPhone is a mixture of rock and country songs
- A **sentence** contains a subject and a verb and expresses a complete thought.
  Example: Max is so excited about his new computer.
- A **sentence fragment** is missing one of the elements of a complete sentence.
  Example: Max being excited about his new computer (no verb)
  Example: Being excited about his new computer (no subject, no verb)
  Example: Since Max is excited about his new computer (incomplete thought)
- A **run-on sentence** combines two or more sentences with incorrect punctuation.
  Example: Max is excited about his new computer he just got it last night.

C. Understanding Mechanics

Mechanics refers to the little details of standard written English. On the ACT, mechanics questions test your knowledge of the rules of punctuation.

1. The Apostrophe

The apostrophe is used to indicate possession in nouns and to indicate missing letters in contractions.

a. To Indicate Possession

Singular nouns: The possessive form of singular nouns is made by adding **'s** to the word.

Example: cat + 's = cat's
The **cat's** bowl is filled with milk.

Example: Noah + 's = Noah's

The blanket is tucked into **Noah's** crib.

Singular nouns that end in s: In most cases, singular nouns that end in **s** follow the same rule. However, in some cases, it becomes difficult to pronounce the word in its possessive form. In these cases, just the apostrophe alone may be added after the last **s** in the word.

Example: Lois + **'s** = Lois's

Lois's car is parked behind the school.

Exception: The possessive form of **witness** is **witness' (or witness's)**

The witness' (or witness's) testimony was the deciding factor in the case.

Plural nouns: If the plural form of the noun does not end in **s,** form the plural by adding **'s.**

Example: children + **'s** = children's

The children's murals decorated the auditorium.

Plural nouns that end in s: If the plural form of the noun ends in **s,** add only the apostrophe to make it possessive.

Example: teachers + **'** = teachers'

The teachers' cafeteria is located in the rear of the building.

Joint ownership: When two people own something together, the apostrophe is used only with the name of the last person mentioned.

Example: Jane and David's house

Indefinite pronouns: The possessive form of indefinite pronouns is formed by adding **'s.**

Example: one + **'s** = one's

It is important to protect one's identity from theft.

> **IMPORTANT: The possessive forms of personal pronouns never require an apostrophe.**
>
> **Never use the apostrophe with these pronouns: my, his, hers, its, ours, yours, theirs, who.**
>
> **These apostrophe errors will appear frequently on the test, and you can quickly eliminate choices that contain** *its', yours', theirs', ours', hers',* **or** *his'.*
>
> **Note:** *Who's* **is the contraction of** *who is;* **the possessive form of** *who* **is** *whose.*
>
> **Example: We should determine who's going on the field trip so we know whose car to take.**

b. In Contractions

The apostrophe indicates that one or more letters have been omitted in a contraction.

Example: it is = it's (**Note:** This is not the possessive form of **its,** which has no apostrophe.)

Example: who is = who's (**Note:** This is not the possessive of **who,** which is **whose.**)

Example: would have = would've (**Note:** It is never correct to write **would of, could of,** or **should of.**)

Examples

For the following sentences, choose the correct word:

> 1. The (rivers, rivers', river's) current was so strong we hardly had to paddle the canoe.

river's. The possessive of a singular noun is formed by adding **'s.**

> 2. I have found (its, it's) not hard to understand the lyrics to the song.

it's. The contraction of *it is* is **it's.**

> 3. The four (reader's, readers, readers') responses were recorded in their logs.

readers'. The possessive of a plural noun is formed by adding the apostrophe after the **s.**

> 4. After the summer, the song lost (its, it's, its') meaning to me.

its. The possessive pronoun *its* is already in the possessive form. It does not take an apostrophe.

> 5. The juniors wished that (their's, theirs', theirs) had been the winning float.

theirs. The possessive pronoun *theirs* is already in the possessive form. It does not take an apostrophe.

> 6. I would (of, have) left earlier if I had known it was going to snow.

have. *Would of* is never correct.

2. Colons

The colon indicates a pause in the sentence. It is used before a list; before a long, formal statement; and before an explanatory statement.

a. Before a List

Use a colon before a list of items, including a list that is introduced by the words *the following* or *as follows*.

> Example: Our tour included all of the following cities: London, Paris, Rome, and Florence.

Note: Do not use a colon right after a verb or a preposition.

Example: The distinguishing characteristics of collies <u>are</u> long pointy snouts, distinctive color coats, bushy tails, and affectionate dispositions. (no colon after a verb)

Example: You can learn about cities in France <u>by</u> looking in an encyclopedia, reading a book about Europe, or looking on the Internet. (no colon after a preposition)

b. Before a Long, Formal Statement

Use a colon to introduce a formal quotation. In this case, begin the quotation with a capital letter.

> Example: President Lincoln began the Gettysburg Address with these words: "Four score and seven years ago our fathers brought forth on this continent, a new nation, conceived in Liberty, and dedicated to the proposition that all men are created equal."

c. Before an Explanatory Statement

Use a colon after a main clause when it is followed by a second clause or phrase that offers an explanation or a restatement of the first clause. In this case, if the statement after the colon is a complete clause and is important, you may begin it with a capital letter. (This is not a hard-and-fast rule. You will see it both ways: both with and without the capital letter.)

> Example: Our all-day fishing expedition did not live up to our expectations: The weather was nasty and the fish did not bite. (complete clause after the colon)

> Example: Iago was driven by one deep desire: to destroy Othello. (phrase after the colon)

Examples

Rewrite the following sentences, correcting the punctuation:

> 1. I love the words of Queen Elizabeth's speech to her troops "Let tyrants fear, I have always so behaved myself that, under God, I have placed my chiefest strength and safeguard in the loyal hearts and good-will of my subjects."

I love the words of Queen Elizabeth's speech to her troops: "Let tyrants fear, I have always so behaved myself that, under God, I have placed my chiefest strength and safeguard in the loyal hearts and good-will of my subjects."

> 2. My chemistry teacher covered all of the following topics atomic structure, thermodynamics, and bonding.

My chemistry teacher covered all of the following topics: atomic structure, thermodynamics, and bonding.

> 3. Only four students were chosen to go to the finals Ellen, Stan, Charlie, and Devika.

Only four students were chosen to go to the finals: Ellen, Stan, Charlie, and Devika.

> 4. My favorite writers are Dostoyevsky, Fitzgerald, Faulkner, and Wharton.

My favorite writers are Dostoyevsky, Fitzgerald, Faulkner, and Wharton. (no colon needed after a verb)

> 5. My grandfather had one ambition in life to live to be one hundred years old.

My grandfather had one ambition in life: to live to be one hundred years old.

> 6. Galileo spent the last years of his life under house arrest he was condemned by the church for his heliocentric views.

Galileo spent the last years of his life under house arrest: He was condemned by the church for his heliocentric views.

3. Semicolons

The semicolon is used to join main clauses, between main clauses connected by a conjunctive adverb or a connecting phrase, between main clauses if there is a comma within one or both clauses, and between items in a series if there are commas within the series.

a. Join Main Clauses

Use the semicolon between closely related main clauses in a compound sentence when the main clauses are not connected by a conjunction.

> Example: You may find the movie appropriate for young children; Sydney does not.

b. Connection between Main Clauses

The semicolon is used between main clauses connected by a conjunctive adverb or a connecting phrase.

> Example: We enjoyed watching *Iron Man 2;* however, we thought the special effects were better in the first movie. (**Note:** Use a semicolon before the conjunctive adverb and a comma after it.)

> Example: My computer has been causing many problems; in fact, it totally crashed last week. (**Note:** Use a semicolon before the connecting phrase and a comma after it.)

Common conjunctive adverbs: indeed, furthermore, however, moreover, besides, consequently, nevertheless, therefore, yet, instead

Common connecting phrases: in fact, for example, for instance, that is, at the same time, on the other hand (**Note:** Use the semicolon only when these phrases connect two **main** clauses.)

c. Separate Main Clauses

The semicolon is used between main clauses if there is a comma within one or both clauses, or between items in a series if there are commas within the series.

Use the semicolon for clarity between clauses when there are commas within a clause.

> Example: If you leave early, we will not finish the project; but if you stay, we will complete the assignment.

Use the semicolon for clarity between items in a series that contains a comma.

Example: On our cruise, we stopped at Miami, Florida; San Juan, Puerto Rico; and Nassau, Bahamas.

Examples

Punctuate the following sentences correctly:

> 1. I enjoyed seeing Madonna perform live my mother did not.

I enjoyed seeing Madonna perform live; my mother did not.

> 2. My social studies teacher, a graduate of UCLA, is an expert on the history of California in fact, he is writing his thesis on the Gold Rush.

My social studies teacher, a graduate of UCLA, is an expert on the history of California; in fact, he is writing his thesis on the Gold Rush.

> 3. I thought I could handle two AP courses at the same time however, I find I am too stressed to do well in either class.

I thought I could handle two AP courses at the same time; however, I find I am too stressed to do well in either class.

> 4. Justin Timberlake's North American tour includes stops in Memphis, Tennessee Atlanta, Georgia Boston, Massachusetts and Toronto, Canada.

Justin Timberlake's North American tour includes stops in Memphis, Tennessee; Atlanta, Georgia; Boston, Massachusetts; and Toronto, Canada.

> 5. When I finish the report, I will be glad to help you together we will complete the diagrams.

When I finish the report, I will be glad to help you; together we will complete the diagrams.

Or: When I finish the report, I will be glad to help you, and together we will complete the diagrams.

4. Commas

Commas are used for many purposes:

- To separate items in a series
- Before a conjunction that joins main clauses
- To set off any expressions that interrupt the sentence
- With a direct quotation
- To set off an appositive

- With a non-restrictive clause or phrase
- To set off geographical names, addresses, and dates
- To separate two adjectives when the word **and** can be inserted between them
- To separate contrasting parts of a sentence
- After an introductory phrase or clause

a. Separate Items in a Series

Commas are used to separate items in a series.

> Example: Michael likes to listen to Ne-Yo, John Legend, and Coldplay. (words in a series)
>
> Example: We put up new wallpaper in our bedroom, in the dining room, and in the kitchen. (phrases in a series)
>
> Example: I told you that the taxi arrived late, that the concert was disappointing, and that the entire evening was a disaster. (clauses in a series)

b. Join Main Clauses

Use a comma before a coordinating conjunction that joins main clauses. FANBOYS is an acronym that will help you remember the coordinating conjunctions: For, And, Nor, But, Or, Yet, So.

> Example: *C.S.I.* is my favorite TV program, but my friend finds it too gory to watch.

c. Set Off Expressions

Commas are used to set off expressions that interrupt the sentence. Parenthetical expressions are set off with commas.

> Example: The winner of *American Idol,* I am sure, will have a great-selling album.
>
> Example: Phillip Phillips, for example, was number 1 on the charts.

Words used in direct address are set off with commas.

> Example: Sunil, your brother is looking for you.

Introductory words are set off with commas.

> Example: Well, there certainly are a lot of comma rules.

d. Direct Quotation

Commas are used with a direct quotation.

> Example: My English teacher announced, "All students should be reading for thirty minutes every night."
>
> Example: "Run four laps," the coach yelled, "and then meet me on the field."

e. Set Off an Appositive

Commas are used to set off an appositive. An **appositive** is a word or phrase that follows a noun or pronoun to explain or identify it.

> Example: The movie, a horror film starring Courteney Cox, grossed 120 million dollars. (*a horror film starring Courteney Cox* is the appositive phrase.)

Note: You do not have to use commas with a one-word appositive that is closely related to the word it modifies.

Example: My aunt Judy wears the most glamorous outfits.

Example: My friend Myrna is a fabulous tennis player.

f. Nonrestrictive Clause or Phrase

Commas are used with nonrestrictive clauses or phrases. A nonrestrictive clause or phrase is not essential to the meaning of the sentence.

> Example: My cousin, the one who lives in Chicago, worked for Habitat for Humanity last summer. (*the one who lives in Chicago* is the nonrestrictive clause: it is not essential to the meaning of the sentence.)

> Example: The book that is on reserve is the one I need for my research. (*that is on reserve* is a restrictive clause: it is essential to the meaning of the sentence.)

> Example: The book, which I got as a gift last year, has been very valuable for my research. (*which I got as a gift last year* is a nonrestrictive clause: it is not essential to the meaning of the sentence.)

If you are not sure if the clause or phrase is essential or nonessential, here are some clues to help you:

> Try leaving out the clause or phrase. Does the sentence still make sense?

> Try moving the clause or phrase to a different position in the sentence. Does the sentence still make sense?

If your answer is *yes* to one or both of these questions, then the clause or phrase is nonrestrictive (not essential to the sentence) and should be set off with commas.

g. Geographical Names, Addresses, and Dates

Use commas to set off geographical names, addresses, and dates.

> Example: We visited the pumpkin farm in Weston, Connecticut, last week.

> Example: The presidential election will determine who lives at 1600 Pennsylvania Avenue, Washington, D.C.

> Example: Rona met her husband on August 6, 1999, in Omaha, Nebraska.

h. Separate Two Adjectives

Use a comma to separate two adjectives when the word *and* can be inserted between them.

Example: The basketball coach wants to recruit Josh for the team because of his tall, muscular physique.

> Note: Do not use a comma if you would not use the word *and* between the adjectives.
>
> Example: Sun Valley is an expensive winter resort. (You would not say "expensive and winter resort.")

i. Separate Contrasting Parts of a Sentence

Use a comma to separate contrasting parts of a sentence.

Example: The red car parked in my space is Jan's, not Jeff's.

j. Introductory Phrase or Clause

Use a comma after an **introductory adverb clause** that begins with a subordinating conjunction such as after, although, as, because, before, if, since, though, until, unless, when, whenever, where, while.

Example: Until I save all the work I have done, do not turn off the computer.

Use a comma after a **participial phrase** (a participle is a form of a verb that functions like an adjective to modify a noun or pronoun).

Example: Stamping her foot angrily, Ella refused to leave the toy store. (The phrase *Stamping her foot angrily* is a participial phrase modifying Ella.)

Use a comma after an **infinitive phrase** (to + verb).

Example: To make a call on the iPhone, simply say the name of the person to whom you wish to speak.

Use a comma after a long prepositional phrase or a series of prepositional phrases.

Example: In the middle of a long conversation, my cell phone battery died.

k. Avoid the Comma Splice Error

A frequent error on the ACT is the **comma splice error:** two main clauses joined by a comma. Do not use a comma to join two main clauses *unless* they are very brief.

Acceptable: I came, I saw, I conquered.

Not acceptable: I entered the classroom quietly, all the students were silently reading their response journals.

Correct a comma splice by using a semicolon, adding a conjunction, or making one of the main clauses into a subordinate clause.

Examples

Punctuate the following sentences correctly:

> 1. The European Conference on Artificial Intelligence will be held in Lisbon Portugal on April 10 2014.

The European Conference on Artificial Intelligence will be held in Lisbon, Portugal, on April 10, 2014.

> 2. Well I thought the class trip to Mount Rushmore National Memorial Keystone South Dakota would be fabulous but the reality surpassed my expectations.

Well, I thought the class trip to Mount Rushmore National Memorial, Keystone, South Dakota, would be fabulous, but the reality surpassed my expectations.

> 3. My uncle a math teacher in Memphis went to China on a teacher exchange.

My uncle, a math teacher in Memphis, went to China on a teacher exchange.

> 4. I have always found that my best subject is science not math.

I have always found that my best subject is science, not math.

> 5. The new science lab was amazing and we couldn't wait to try the new microscopes.

The new science lab was amazing, and we couldn't wait to try the new microscopes.

> 6. Although I am a good golfer I am unable to defeat my younger brother at Wii golf.

Although I am a good golfer, I am unable to defeat my younger brother at Wii golf.

> 7. "The winner of the debate contest" the principal announced "will go on to compete in the state finals."

"The winner of the debate contest," the principal announced, "will go on to compete in the state finals."

> 8. On the day of the ACT Test be sure to bring no. 2 pencils an eraser your ID and your admission ticket.

On the day of the ACT Test, be sure to bring no. 2 pencils, an eraser, your ID, and your admission ticket.

> 9. My old class picture which was packed in a carton in the garage clearly shows the braces I wore on my teeth for two years.

My old class picture, which was packed in a carton in the garage, clearly shows the braces I wore on my teeth for two years.

10. Barking loudly enough to wake the neighbors my new dog was a noisy unhappy pet.

Barking loudly enough to wake the neighbors, my new dog was a noisy, unhappy pet.

5. The Dash

Use the dash to indicate an important or abrupt break in thought or before a summary.

a. Abrupt Break in Thought

The dash gives the information that is set off special emphasis or indicates a sudden change in thought.

> Example: When I left my laptop on the plane, it was lost—or so I thought until the flight attendant came running after me.

> Example: Those rights that Americans hold dear—life, liberty, the pursuit of happiness—are not universally respected.

Note: When the dash sets off a part of the sentence, unless the sentence ends with that part, be sure to use a second dash (not a comma as you'll see in some incorrect answer choices).

Not acceptable: Four of the horses entering the starting gate—Afleet Alex, Trampoline, Winner Takes All, and Fascinating Filly, struggled impatiently against the handlers trying to calm them.

Acceptable: Four of the horses entering the starting gate—Afleet Alex, Trampoline, Winner Takes All, and Fascinating Filly—struggled impatiently against the handlers trying to calm them.

b. Before a Summary

Use the dash before a summary. In these cases, the dash and the colon are interchangeable. The dash is used after items in a series to indicate a summarizing statement.

> Example: Cupcakes, ice cream, cookies—the dessert buffet was filled with all my favorite confections.

6. The Parentheses

Use the parentheses to enclose additional material or explanatory information that might be interesting to know but is not of major importance to the text. Information that is enclosed in parentheses can usually be removed from the text without changing the meaning or losing any essential information.

> Example: When she moved to Indiana, Ms. North had to go through the complete process (certification, competency tests, interviews) to get her teaching license.

You could use a colon here for more emphasis since it is a list, or use a dash for strong emphasis. In this sentence, the material is rather unimportant to the main meaning of the sentence, so the parentheses are the proper punctuation.

Punctuation of parentheses can be tricky. Periods and other end punctuation are placed outside the close of a parenthesis. No punctuation mark may be placed before a parenthesis, but a comma can follow one. When the information enclosed in the parentheses is a complete sentence, treat it as such: Start with a capital letter and end with a period. A question mark or exclamation point, if it is part of the parenthetical material, can go inside a parenthesis, but another punctuation mark is needed to close the sentence:

> Example: I brought a ghoulish selection of costumes to the Halloween party (skeletons, goblins, and zombies!).

> Example: The Stone family has built a new home overlooking the river. (Their apartment in the city was too small.)

Examples

Punctuate the following sentences correctly:

---

1. Cilantro, chipotle, wasabi these spices have become popular with adventurous cooks.

Cilantro, chipotle, wasabi—these spices have become popular with adventurous cooks.

---

2. Florence called Firenze in Italy is a small city of breathtaking beauty.

Florence (called Firenze in Italy) is a small city of breathtaking beauty.

---

3. My sister Ann can you believe it got the lead role in the school play.

My sister Ann—can you believe it—got the lead role in the school play.

---

4. Most of the boys on the basketball team in fact all but two made all-state.

Most of the boys on the basketball team—in fact, all but two—made all-state.

---

5. It is a tradition in my family that holidays even Thanksgiving are potluck.

It is a tradition in my family that holidays (even Thanksgiving) are potluck.

7. Question Marks and Exclamation Points

Question marks and exclamation points are end marks that indicate the writer's intention: to ask a question or to make a strong or startling statement.

a. Question Marks

Use a question mark at the end of an interrogative sentence. An interrogative sentence is one that asks a question.

> Example: Do you have plans for vacation?

Do not use a question mark with an indirect question.

Example: Mr. Ramirez wants to know who won the game.

b. Exclamation Points

Use an exclamation point after a startling statement or at the end of an exclamatory sentence.

Example: Wow! I passed my road test!

Examples

Punctuate the following sentences:

> 1. Did you see that funny pets video on *YouTube*

Did you see that funny pets video on *YouTube*?

> 2. It was great

It was great!

> 3. I wonder if Louis saw the game last week

I wonder if Louis saw the game last week. (indirect question)

> 4. We won Can you believe it

We won! Can you believe it?

> 5. Have we changed quarterbacks

Have we changed quarterbacks?

D. Grammar and Usage

"PRIMPED CATS" is a mnemonic (a formula used to improve the memory). Each letter stands for a grammatical error you will encounter on the ACT English Test. Remember this mnemonic, and you are well on your way to ACT English success.

P—Pronoun errors   **C**—Comparisons
R—Redundancy   **A**—Agreement
I—Idioms   **T**—Tense
M—Modification   **S**—Sentence structure
P—Parallelism
E—Errors with adjectives/adverbs
D—Diction

1. Pronoun Errors

Pronouns are words that are used to replace nouns. The noun that the pronoun replaces is called the **antecedent.** Usually, but not always, the antecedent comes before the pronoun.

a. Pronoun Antecedent Agreement Errors

A pronoun must agree with its antecedent in gender and number. On the ACT English Test, always go back and reread the entire sentence to find the antecedent for the pronoun.

If the antecedent of a pronoun is singular, the pronoun must be singular. If the antecedent is plural, the pronoun must be plural.

If the antecedent is feminine, the pronoun must be feminine. If the antecedent is masculine, the pronoun must be masculine.

> Example: Debbie brought her laptop to the Math Challenge. (**Debbie** is the feminine singular antecedent for the feminine singular pronoun **her.**)

> Example: The **students** brought **their** laptops to the Math Challenge. (**Students** is the plural antecedent for the plural pronoun **their.**)

If the antecedent refers to both genders, the phrase "his or her" is acceptable to avoid sexist language. When this phrasing is repeated several times in a sentence or paragraph, it may become awkward; avoid the problem by using the plural form.

> Awkward: Every one of the students put his or her laptop on his or her desk.

> Better: The students put their laptops on their desks.

b. Indefinite Pronouns

When indefinite pronouns are antecedents, determine whether they are singular or plural.

Singular indefinite pronouns:

anybody	everybody	nobody
anyone	everyone	one
each	neither	somebody
either	no one	someone

Example: **Each** of the boys on the team took **his** trophy home.

Example: **Everyone** chose **his or her** favorite novel.

Exceptions: Sometimes, with **everyone** and **everybody,** the sense of the sentence is compromised when the singular pronoun is used. In these cases, the plural form is acceptable.

Awkward: **Everyone** in the crowd stood and applauded when **he or she** saw the float.

Better: **Everyone** in the crowd stood and applauded when **they** saw the float.

Plural Indefinite Pronouns:

both	many
few	several

Singular or Plural Indefinite Pronouns (depending on how they are used):

all	most	some
any	none	

Example: Some of the play has lost **its** meaning. (singular in meaning)

Example: Some of the houses have lost **their** roofs. (plural in meaning)

c. Singular Antecedents and Singular Pronouns

Two or more singular antecedents joined by *or* or *nor* take the singular pronoun.

Example: Either Marlee or Olivia will bring **her** car to the football game.

Example: Neither Eli nor Jaxon has taken **his** road test.

d. Clear Antecedents

To avoid vague pronoun references on the ACT English Test, be sure you can pinpoint the antecedent of the pronoun. Every pronoun must clearly refer to a specific antecedent.

Vague: In the newspaper **it** says that more young people voted this year than last year. (The pronoun **it** has no antecedent.)

Better: The article in the *Tribune* states that more young people voted this year than last year.

Vague: Jessica wants to be a doctor because **it** is so rewarding. (The pronoun **it** has no antecedent.)

Better: Jessica wants to be a doctor because the work is so rewarding.

Vague: Barbara came late to every meeting, **which** annoyed her supervisor. (**Which** is a vague pronoun because it has no antecedent.)

Better: Barbara came late to every meeting, a habit that annoyed her supervisor.

Or even better: Barbara's chronic lateness annoyed her supervisor.

Vague: Students are coming to school on time, bringing their books to class, and taking notes regularly. **This** helps the school receive federal funds. (**This** is a vague pronoun because it has no antecedent.)

Better: Students are coming to school on time, bringing their books to class, and taking notes regularly. The improved attendance helps the school receive federal funds.

e. Pronoun Case Errors

If you have ever wondered whether to write *I* or *me*, you have encountered a **pronoun case** problem. Pronouns change their form depending on how they are used. The different forms of the pronouns are called **cases**. Pronouns have three cases: **nominative, objective,** and **possessive.**

Nominative	Objective	Possessive
I	me	my, mine
we	us	our, ours
you	you	your, yours
he	him	his
she	her	her, hers
it	it	its
they	them	their, theirs
who	whom	whose

The **nominative case** of pronouns is used when the pronoun is the subject or the predicate nominative.

The **objective case** is used when the pronoun is the object of a verb or the object of a preposition.

The **possessive case** is used to indicate possession.

On the ACT English Test, you will have to decide which form of the pronoun to select. First, look at the whole sentence and determine what role the pronoun plays in the sentence. Is it the subject or the predicate nominative? Then use the nominative case. Is it the object of a verb or the object of a preposition? Then choose the objective case. Is the pronoun showing ownership? Then use the possessive case.

Nominative case: The pronoun is the subject.

> Example: **He** and **I** want to be lab partners in chemistry.
> Example: Judy and **she** went shopping for decorations for the prom.
> Example: **Who** is going to be class president next year?

The pronoun is the **predicate nominative** (word in the predicate part of the sentence that is linked to the subject).

> Example: The winners must have been **they.**
> Example: The team captains are Sophie and **she.**

Objective case: The pronoun is the **object of a verb** (direct object or indirect object).

> Example: Alexis gave **her** the gift. (**Her** is the indirect object of the verb **gave.**)

> Example: Hayley invited Juan and **him** to the dance. (**Juan** and **him** are the direct objects of the verb **invited.**)

The pronoun is the **object of a preposition.**

> Example: The head of the committee wanted to share the responsibility with **them.** (**Them** is the object of the preposition **with.**)

> Example: To **whom** should I address the letter of recommendation? (**Whom** is the object of the preposition **to.**)

Possessive case: Use the possessive case to show ownership and before a gerund (-ing form of a verb used as a noun).

> Example: The director appreciates **your** being prompt for all rehearsals. (**Your** is the possessive pronoun used before the gerund **being.**)

> Example: **His** quick thinking saved the day. (**His** is the possessive pronoun used before the gerund **thinking.**)

Examples

Select the correct pronoun:

> 1. This birthday present is from Julia and (I, me).

This birthday present is from Julia and **me.**

> 2. The Intel Corporation awarded Ronni and (she, her) the prize.

The Intel Corporation awarded Ronni and **her** the prize.

> 3. No one objected to (he, him, his) bringing a date to the prom.

No one objected to **his** bringing a date to the prom.

> 4. Neither the seniors nor (us, we) have won the play contest.

Neither the seniors nor **we** have won the play contest.

> 5. Neither of these journals has all (its, their) entries.

Neither of these journals has all **its** entries.

6. Each of the participants presented (his or her, their) experiment(s) to the panel.

Each of the participants presented **his or her** experiment to the panel.

7. Russ and Jenn brought (his, their) calculators to the exam.

Russ and Jenn brought **their** calculators to the exam.

8. It is silly to let this disagreement come between you and (she, her).

It is silly to let this disagreement come between you and **her.**

9. I can't wait to find out if the champion is (her, she).

I can't wait to find out if the champion is **she.**

10. (Who, Whom) do you think should lead the group?

Who do you think should lead the group?

2. Redundancy

In standard written English, conciseness is a goal. It is best to express your ideas in as few well-chosen words as possible. On the ACT English Test, always be alert for such repetitive and wordy expressions as:

true fact	round in shape
important essentials	close proximity
two equal halves	new innovations
consensus of opinion	the future to come
unexpected surprise	due to the fact that
various different	ten years in age
extreme in degree	problem that needs a solution
large in size	

On the English Test, you will often have to go back to the beginning of a sentence (before the underlined part) and read all the way to the end of the sentence (past the underlined part) to check for redundancies.

Example. At the present time, the problem the community is currently facing must be addressed.

At first reading, you may think the underlined part of the sentence is grammatically correct. You'd be right. *However,* if you reread the sentence from the beginning, you will see the phrase *At the present time.* This phrase makes the word *currently* redundant. You will have to find a choice that eliminates this redundancy. You will also be expected to recognize words whose meanings are so similar that to use both words is redundant.

Example: In the **predictable** and **foreseeable** future new sources of energy will be necessary for survival.

The use of both **predictable** and **foreseeable** is redundant; you would choose an answer that eliminates one of these words.

Examples

Rewrite the following sentences to avoid redundancies and wordiness. Your answers might be slightly different. Do not worry if this is the case; your goal is to eliminate the redundant expressions.

> 1. By associating and connecting together, the two teams were able to come up with a new innovation.

By connecting, the two teams were able to come up with an innovation.

> 2. We chose a sign that was large in size due to the fact that we hoped every person and all people would be able to see it.

We chose a large sign so everyone could see it.

> 3. Every year the teachers do an annual review of their classroom supplies.

The teachers do an annual review of their classroom supplies.

> 4. I told you the reason why you should take the ACT is because it is a good test.

I told you to take the ACT because it is a good test.

> 5. Larry will tell you the honest truth about his past experience.

Larry will tell you the truth about his experience.

> 6. It is the consensus of opinion that we should advance forward and join together to solve the problems that need solutions.

The consensus is that together we can advance and solve the problems.

> 7. The population of cougars began to decline and wane following the influx of humans into the area.

The population of cougars began to decline following the influx of humans into the area.

3. Idioms

Idioms are expressions or verb phrases that are used in English. The problem on the ACT English Test arises when a cliché appears (avoid them) or when the incorrect preposition is used with a verb. Unfortunately, there are no rules ... you just need to know what is accepted as correct. Usually, you can trust your "ears"—go with what sounds right.

Some common idioms are as follows:

abide by	conform to	opinion of
agree to (something)	consists of	participate in
agree with (someone)	depend on	prefer to
apply for	differ from	preoccupied with
approve of	discriminate against	prohibited from
argue about (something)	escape from	protect from
argue with (someone)	in contrast to	relevant to
arrived at	insensitive to	subscribe to
believe in	insight into	succeeded in
capable of	insist upon	tendency to
comment on	method of	
complain about	object to	

Some common clichés to avoid are as follows:

the whole nine yards	selling like hotcakes
white (pale) as a ghost (sheet)	as easy as stealing candy from a baby
faster than the speed of light	quiet as a mouse
as light as a feather	slow as a turtle
fought an uphill battle	slept like a baby
sadder but wiser	free as a bird
blind as a bat	hit the nail on the head
since the dawn of time	bite the bullet

Examples

Correct the idiom errors in the following sentences:

> 1. Ignacio proved that he was capable to rebuild the engine on the '62 Chevy.

Ignacio proved that he was **capable of rebuilding** the engine on the '62 Chevy.

> 2. While I was reading *Macbeth,* I was amazed that Shakespeare had such insight on ambitious leaders who ruthlessly seize power.

While I was reading *Macbeth,* I was amazed that Shakespeare had such **insight into** ambitious leaders who ruthlessly seize power.

3. Alex tried to get his mother's attention, but she was preoccupied on the complicated recipe she was preparing.

Alex tried to get his mother's attention, but she was **preoccupied with** the complicated recipe she was preparing.

4. Contrasting with the ornate style of Gothic architecture, modern geometric buildings have clean lines and sharp edges.

In contrast to ornate Gothic architecture, modern geometric buildings have clean lines and sharp edges.

5. Because my dad is such a great cook, my family prefers eating at home rather than eating in restaurants.

Because my dad is such a great cook, my family prefers eating at home **to** eating in restaurants.

6. Arthur went into the new sales program as blind as a bat, but faster than the speed of light his product was selling like hotcakes.

Arthur was inexperienced at selling but quickly became successful. (eliminate all clichés)

4. Modification

On the ACT English Test, always go back and reread the entire sentence to check for proper modification. Modifiers are words, phrases, or clauses that describe, change, or specify other parts of a sentence.

a. Misplaced Modifiers

Modifiers are often participial phrases:

> Example: **Riding on the bus,** we read the article in the paper. (**Riding on the bus** describes **we.**)
>
> Example: As I turned the corner, I heard my dog **barking loudly. (Barking loudly** describes the **dog.**)

Sometimes modifiers are infinitive phrases:

> Example: **To understand English grammar,** students must practice writing and speaking correctly. (**To understand English grammar** modifies **students.**)

In English, changes in word order (syntax) lead to changes in meaning. A modifier that is misplaced can cause confusion.

> Examples:
>
> Maria spotted an orange cat sitting on a bench eating a sandwich. (The cat is sitting and eating.)
>
> Sitting on a bench eating a sandwich, Maria spotted an orange cat. (Maria is sitting and eating.)
>
> Sitting on a bench, Maria spotted an orange cat eating a sandwich. (Maria is sitting and the cat is eating.)

To avoid confusion, always place modifying phrases and clauses as close as possible to the words they modify.

b. Dangling Modifiers

Dangling modifiers have no word or phrase to modify.

> Confusing: Standing on the bridge overlooking the city, the buildings look like children's toys. (Who is standing? Certainly not the buildings.)

To correct dangling modifiers, add the missing words or revise the sentence.

> Revised: Standing on the bridge overlooking the city, George thought the buildings looked like children's toys.
>
> Or: As George stood on the bridge overlooking the city, the buildings looked like children's toys.

Examples

Revise the following sentences to correct the modification errors. Your answers may vary, but be sure to eliminate all modification confusion.

---

1. Athena found her cell phone walking home from practice.

Walking home from practice, Athena found her cell phone.

---

2. To order safely from the Internet, your credit card should be protected.

To order safely from the Internet, you should be sure your credit card is protected.

---

3. Looking up at the sky, the eclipse was both magnificent and frightening.

Looking up at the sky, we discovered the eclipse was both magnificent and frightening.

---

4. While working out in the gym, my leg muscle cramped.

While I was working out in the gym, my leg muscle cramped.

---

5. Ashley wore her new bag over her shoulder which she had just purchased at the mall.

Ashley wore her new bag, which she had just purchased at the mall, over her shoulder.

---

6. Perhaps best known for convincing her husband to murder the king, Lady Macbeth's rampant ambition became uncontrollable.

Perhaps best known for convincing her husband to murder the king, Lady Macbeth allowed her rampant ambition to become uncontrollable.

5. Parallelism

Parallel ideas should be in the same grammatical form. On the ACT English Test, always go back and reread the entire sentence to check the parallelism.

When you join ideas using conjunctions, they should be in the same form. Nouns should be joined with nouns, prepositional phrases joined with prepositional phrases, and clauses joined with clauses.

Unparallel nouns: Martin Luther King, Jr., was honored for his courage, faith, and he was willing to stick to his beliefs.

Parallel nouns: Martin Luther King, Jr., was honored for his courage, faith, and perseverance.

Unparallel verb phrases: I like to ski, to hike, and swimming.

Parallel verb phrases: I like to ski, to hike, and to swim. (Also: I like to ski, hike, and swim.)

Unparallel prepositional phrases: We left the party early because of the inclement weather, and it was late.

Parallel prepositional phrases: We left the party early because of the inclement weather and because of the lateness of the hour.

Unparallel clauses: Hamlet found it difficult to believe that his father had died of natural causes and in the innocence of his uncle.

Parallel clauses: Hamlet found it difficult to believe that his father had died of natural causes and that his uncle was innocent.

Correlative conjunctions, which always occur in pairs, can be tricky; be sure what comes after the first conjunction is parallel to what comes after the second conjunction.

Correlatives are as follows: both … and, either … or, neither … nor, not only … but also.

Unparallel: The car wash **not only** did a great job on my car, **but also** on my brother's.

Parallel: The car wash did a great job **not only** on my car, **but also** on my brother's.

Unparallel: The general had **neither** the support of his troops **nor** did he have the loyalty of his officers.

Parallel: The general had **neither** the support of his troops **nor** the loyalty of his officers.

Examples

Revise the following sentences to correct the errors in parallelism. Your answers may vary slightly.

1. Julius Caesar could not be sure that he had the support of the common people or if the other senators would stand by him.

Julius Caesar could not be sure that he had the support of the common people or the other senators.

> 2. Brutus was ambitious, gullible, and he thought a lot about his own motives.

Brutus was ambitious, gullible, and introspective.

> 3. I either want to do my English research paper on Ernest Hemingway or F. Scott Fitzgerald.

I want to do my English research paper on either Ernest Hemingway or F. Scott Fitzgerald.

> 4. Galileo not only believed that the earth was round but also that it rotated around the sun.

Galileo believed not only that the earth was round but also that it rotated around the sun.

> 5. Those who try sky diving both know the thrill of freefall and the excitement of flying.

Those who try sky diving know both the thrill of freefall and the excitement of flying.

6. Errors with Adjectives/Adverbs

To answer these questions on the ACT English Test, you will need to know the difference between adjectives and adverbs. Adjectives are used to modify nouns. They usually answer such questions as "Which?" "What kind?" and "How many?" Adverbs are used to modify verbs, adjectives, or other adverbs. They usually answer such questions as "How?" "When?" and "To what extent?"

a. Comparisons

Use the **comparative** form of the adjective to compare *two* nouns or pronouns. The comparative is formed in two ways. For one-syllable adjectives, add *–er* (also used for some two-syllable adjectives).

> Example: Of the two boys, Troy is the younger.
> Example: Samantha is the funnier of the two sisters.

For most two-syllable-or-more adjectives, put "more" in front of the word.

> Example: Sydney's flowers are more fragrant than mine.
> Example: My computer is more efficient than Herb's.

Use the **superlative** form of the adjective to compare *three or more* nouns or pronouns. The superlative form is formed in two ways: For one-syllable adjectives, add *–est* (also used for some two-syllable adjectives).

> Example: Amy is the youngest girl in the class.
> Example: The happiest (or most happy) teacher in the district is Sarah.

For most two-syllable adjectives, put "most" in front of the word.

> Example: Jana won the award for the most cautious driver.

Some irregular comparison forms are as follows:

	Comparative	Superlative
good	better	best
bad	worse	worst
little	less or lesser	least
much	more	most
far	farther or further	farthest or furthest

Some adjectives are absolute values and cannot be intensified with **more** or **most:**

complete	round	totally
correct	square	unique
perfect	superior	
preferable	supreme	

b. Adjective/Adverb Confusion

Use an adjective to modify a noun or a pronoun and use an adverb to modify a verb, an adjective, or another adverb.

Incorrect: The children's choir sang so beautiful that the audience was moved to tears. (incorrectly uses the adjective **beautiful** instead of the adverb **beautifully** to modify the verb "sang")

Correct: The children's choir sang so beautifully that the audience was moved to tears. (correctly uses the adverb **beautifully** to modify the verb "sang")

Examples

Correct the errors in the following sentences:

> 1. Of the jaguar and the hyena, the jaguar is the fastest.

Of the jaguar and the hyena, the jaguar is the **faster.**

> 2. When she won the lottery, my neighbor was the most happiest woman in town.

When she won the lottery, my neighbor was the **happiest** (or **most happy**) woman in town.

> 3. The fire chief was impressed by how speedy we all exited the building during the fire drill.

The fire chief was impressed by how **speedily** we all exited the building during the fire drill.

4. I thought the stuffed animal I bought for my little sister was more cuter than the one she has on her bed.

I thought the stuffed animal I bought for my little sister was **cuter** than the one she has on her bed.

5. When we measured all ten basketball players, Jamal was the taller.

When we measured all ten basketball players, Jamal was the **tallest.**

6. Among all the pottery on display, Russell's was the most unique.

Among all the pottery on display, Russell's was **unique.**

7. Diction

Diction means word choice. A diction error occurs when a word is used incorrectly or inappropriately.

Commonly misused words:

among/between:	use **between** for two people or things (between my brother and me)
	use **among** for three or more (among all my friends)
fewer/less:	use **fewer** for anything you can count (fewer times at bat)
	use **less** for whole quantities (less pain)
their/there/they're:	use **their** for the plural possessive pronoun (their notebooks)
	use **there** for place (I put it there)
	use **they're** as a contraction of *they are* (they're coming home)
amount/number:	use **amount** for whole quantities (amount of homework)
	use **number** for things you can count (number of math problems)
who's/whose:	use **who's** as a contraction of *who is* (who's your buddy)
	use **whose** for possessive form of who (whose book is that)
bad/badly:	use **bad** (adjective) after a linking verb (Sue feels bad)
	use **badly** (adverb) to describe how something is being done (he sings badly)

Examples

Correct the diction errors in the following sentences:

1. The chemistry teacher divided the unknowns between the four groups.

The chemistry teacher divided the unknowns **among** the four groups.

2. I hope I have less pages to read than you do.

I hope I have **fewer** pages to read than you do.

3. The coach took a survey to see whose going to the clinic on Saturday.

The coach took a survey to see **who's** going to the clinic on Saturday.

4. Tracy and Lauren left there books outside, and their going to be so sorry when they're is a thunderstorm.

Tracy and Lauren left **their** books outside, and **they're** going to be so sorry when **there** is a thunderstorm.

5. The amount of physics problems we have to do is not terrible, especially if we divide them among the two of us.

The **number** of physics problems we have to do is not terrible, especially if we divide them **between** the two of us.

6. I tried to find Linda so I could apologize because I felt so badly about the argument.

I tried to find Linda so I could apologize because I felt so **bad** about the argument.

8. Comparisons

To check comparisons on the ACT English Test, always go back and reread the entire sentence.

a. Illogical Comparisons

Use the word *other* or the word *else* to compare one thing or person to the rest of the group.

> Illogical comparison: Our debate team won more prizes than any team. (illogical because your team is one of the competing teams)
>
> Logical comparison: Our debate team won more prizes than any **other** team.

b. Unbalanced Comparisons

Comparisons must be balanced and parallel. Use the word *than* or *as* to balance the sentence.

> Unbalanced: The mathletes won as many points, if not more than, their opponents.
>
> Balanced: The mathletes won **as** many points **as,** if not more **than,** their opponents.

c. Faulty Comparisons

You must compare like things … apples to apples, not apples to oranges.

> Faulty: After tasting all the exotic dishes at the ethnic food fair, I found I like the foods from India better than China. (comparing **foods** to **China**)

> Correct: After tasting all the exotic dishes at the ethnic food fair, I found I like the foods from India better than the foods (or those) from China. (comparing foods to foods)

> Faulty: Our track star was more dominant than the previous years. (comparing the track star to years)

> Correct: Our track star was more dominant than those in previous years. (comparing **star** to **those** or **track stars**)

Examples

Correct the comparison errors in the following sentences:

> 1. The music of Rascal Flatts is as good as Sugarland.

The music of Rascal Flatts is as good as **that of** Sugarland.

> 2. Rachel felt her poetry was better than any other student in the writing class.

Rachel felt her poetry was better than **that of** any other student in the writing class.

> 3. My car is cleaner than any car in the parking lot.

My car is cleaner than any **other** car in the parking lot.

> 4. It was clear that the flowers from the local garden shop were fresher than the florist.

It was clear that the flowers from the local garden shop were fresher than **those from** the florist.

> 5. The movie *Diehard 3* was as suspenseful, if not more suspenseful than, the prequel.

The movie *Diehard 3* was as suspenseful **as,** if not more suspenseful than, the prequel.

> 6. The Spanish restaurant on South Street is better than any restaurant in town.

The Spanish restaurant on South Street is better than any **other** restaurant in town.

9. Agreement

Agreement questions usually refer to errors in subject-verb agreement or noun agreement. Your task will be to make sure all verbs agree with their subjects in gender and number and all noun references agree in number.

a. Agreement of Subject and Verb

A verb must agree with its subject in number. A singular subject takes the singular form of a verb; a plural subject takes the plural form of the verb.

> Singular: My **answer agrees** with yours. (one answer)
>
> Plural: My **answers agree** with yours. (more than one answer)

Note: While most nouns form the plural by adding the letter *s*, most verbs in their plural form do not end in the letter *s*.

Phrases may intervene between the subject and the verb. In most cases, to ensure agreement, ignore the intervening phrase.

> Example: My answers **on the test** agree with yours. (**on the test** is a prepositional phrase)

Intervening **prepositional phrases** do not affect agreement of subject and verb, so the best approach is to cross out or bracket intervening phrases. This will avoid confusion.

Note: The subject of a sentence is *NEVER* part of a prepositional phrase.

> Example: The sleeping **cabin** with a bathroom and two beds **is** available.

To check agreement on the ACT, go back and reread the entire sentence. Bracket the intervening phrase:

> The sleeping **cabin** [with a bathroom and two beds] **is** available.

Be sure to find the subject and match it with the verb.

> Example: Studying for final exams helps me do well on the test.

Bracket the intervening phrases:

> **Studying** [for final exams] **helps** me do well on the test.
>
> **Studying** is the singular subject; **helps** is the singular form of the verb.

Sometimes on the ACT English Test passages, multiple phrases intervene.

> Example: The photographs of the family taken in the field beyond the house show a group of smiling people of all ages.

Follow the same procedure and reread the entire sentence bracketing the phrases.

> The **photographs** [of the family taken in the field beyond the house] **show** a group of smiling people of all ages.

Photographs is the plural subject; **show** is the plural form of the verb.

Intervening **parenthetical or explanatory phrases** also do not affect agreement of subject and verb, so the best approach is to cross out or bracket intervening phrases. This will avoid confusion.

> Example: My cousin, along with ten of her closest friends, volunteers in a hospital.

Bracket the intervening phrase or phrases and match the subject with the verb:

> My **cousin,** [along with ten of her closest friends,] **volunteers** in a hospital.

> Example: Our chapter of DECA, like all the other chapters in the surrounding districts, attends the state competition.

> Our **chapter** [of DECA,] [like all the other chapters in the surrounding districts,] **attends** the state competition.

> Example: Julius Caesar, accompanied by many of the deceitful senators, was approached by a soothsayer who warned him of danger.

> **Julius Caesar,** [accompanied by many of the deceitful senators,] **was** approached by a soothsayer who warned him of danger.

Singular **indefinite pronouns** take the singular form of the verb; plural indefinite pronouns take the plural form of the verb.

> Example: **Each** of the games on the computer **requires** skillful manipulation. (singular)

> Example: **Both** of the games on the computer **require** skillful manipulation. (plural)

Agreement problems also occur with *either ... or* and *neither ... nor*. Singular subjects joined by these correlative conjunctions are singular.

> Example: Either the **novel** or the **play is** acceptable.

Plural subjects joined by these correlative conjunctions are plural.

> Example: Neither the **trees** nor the **bushes were** damaged by the fire.

When one subject is singular and one subject is plural, the verb agrees with the closer subject.

> Example: Neither the **parents** nor the little **girl is** afraid of spiders.

> Example: Either the **coach** or my **parents are driving** to the game.

Inverted sentences will be tricky on the ACT because you will encounter the verb before the subject. Again, the key to success is to find the subject, wherever it is in the sentence.

> Note: The words *here* and *there* are never subjects.

> Example: Two months before the hurricane there **were** warning **signs.** (Plural subject **signs** agrees with the plural form of the verb **were.**)

> Example: There **are** many **problems** with the economy today. (Plural subject **problems** agrees with the plural form of the verb **are.**)

Be sure to read the whole sentence through to find the subject.

> Example: Onto the field **march** the **band** and **the color guard.** (Plural subjects **band** and **color guard** agree with the plural form of the verb **march.**)

> Example: Over the trees **flies** a small **bird.** (Singular subject **bird** agrees with singular form of the verb **flies.**)

b. Noun Agreement

Use a singular noun to refer to a singular noun and a plural noun to refer to a plural noun … sounds logical, right? Yet, problems do arise.

> Example: People who wish to be a teacher should apply here.

This sentence is incorrect because the plural noun **people** requires the plural noun **teachers** to be logical.

> Correct: **People** who wish to be **teachers** should apply here.
> Incorrect: Tourists with a visa must sign in at Passport Control.
> Correct: **Tourists** with **visas** must sign in at Passport Control.

Examples

Select the best word in the following sentences:

1. Into every life (come, comes) some issues that perplex us.

Into every life **come** some issues that perplex us.

2. A carton of books (is, are) ready to be opened and stacked on the shelves.

A carton of books **is** ready to be opened and stacked on the shelves.

3. Neither the cats nor the dog (is, are) in the house.

Neither the cats nor the dog **is** in the house.

4. Each of the sentences on the bulletin boards (was, were) written by a student.

Each of the sentences on the bulletin boards **was** written by a student.

5. (Does, Do) either of the maps show the Himalayan Mountains?

Does either of the maps show the Himalayan Mountains?

6. One of the puzzling aspects of the physics equations (is, are) the vector analysis.

One of the puzzling aspects of the physics equations **is** the vector analysis.

10. Tense

Verbs tell the action or state of being in a sentence. They are also the **time** words, the principal indicators of **tense.** Tense errors come up fairly frequently on the ACT. As you read, be aware of the tense of the passage and note any inconsistencies.

The six tenses in English are as follows:

Present	Past	Future
(action taking place in the present)	(action that has already taken place in the past)	(action that will take place in the future)
I walk	I walked	I will walk
He, she, it walks	He, she, it walked	He, she, it will walk
They walk	They walked	They will walk

Present Perfect	Past Perfect	Future Perfect
(action that began in the past and continues into the present)	(action that began in the past and was completed before some other action)	(action completed in the future before some other action in the future)
I have walked	I had walked	I will have walked
He, she, it has walked	He, she, it had walked	He, she, it will have walked
They have walked	They had walked	They will have walked

Perfect tenses are always formed by using **have, has,** or **had** + the **past participle** form of the verb.

You also have the option of using the **progressive** form (-ing) in each tense to show ongoing action:

Present Progressive: I am walking	*Present Perfect Progressive:* I have been walking
Past Progressive: I was walking	*Past Perfect Progressive:* I had been walking
Future Progressive: I will be walking	*Future Perfect Progressive:* I will have been walking

The **present participle** is the –ing form of the verb: walking. (These –ing forms cannot be verbs alone; they need a helping verb.)

The **past participle** is the –ed, –d, –t, –en, –n form of the verb: walked. Many verbs have irregular forms:

Present	Past	Past Participle
arise	arose	(have) arisen
become	became	(have) become
bring	brought	(have) brought
catch	caught	(have) caught
do	did	(have) done
drink	drank	(have) drunk
drive	drove	(have) driven
eat	ate	(have) eaten
fall	fell	(have) fallen
fly	flew	(have) flown
lend	lent	(have) lent
ring	rang	(have) rung
sing	sang	(have) sung
swim	swam	(have) swum
write	wrote	(have) written

Often verbs occur in verb phrases with a helping verb and a main verb. Some verbs like **do, have,** and **be** can be either main verbs or helping verbs.

> Example: Roberto will **do** his homework. (main verb)

> Example: Roberto and Anna **do need** to practice their duet. (helping verb)

As you read the passages on the ACT English Test, watch for sentences that have illogical shifts in tense or that use incorrect verb forms.

> Illogical shift: He **searched** for signs of deer when he **notices** the tracks.

> Correct: He **is searching** for signs of deer when he **notices** the tracks. (present)

> Or: He **was searching** for signs of deer when he **noticed** the tracks. (past)

Check the tense of the passage to determine whether the sentence should be in the present or past.

> Incorrect verb form: We were shocked that he **had drank** all the water in the canteen.

> Correct: We were shocked that he **had drunk** all the water in the canteen.

Examples

Write the correct form of the italicized verb in the blank:

1. I was pleased to discover that I had _____ a mile. *swim*

swum

2. By the next meet, I will have _____ my own record. *beat*

beaten

3. When I woke up, I found that two inches of snow had _____. *fall*

fallen

4. At last week's meeting, I _____ a presentation. *give*

gave

5. Joan _____ her dog to school yesterday. *bring*

brought

6. Once the bell has _____, we can leave for the beach. *ring*

rung

11. Sentence Structure

Questions on sentence structure test your ability to recognize run-on sentences, sentence fragments, and complete sentences. They also test your ability to recognize the relationship between main clauses and subordinate clauses.

a. Run-On Sentences

Two or more complete thoughts joined in one sentence without proper punctuation constitute a run-on sentence.

> Example: The lecture was on the life cycle of the frog it seemed to go on for hours.

The run-on can be corrected in several ways:

1. Break the sentence up into separate sentences.
   The lecture was on the life cycle of the frog. It seemed to go on for hours.
2. Join the main clauses with a semicolon.
   The lecture was on the life cycle of the frog; it seemed to go on for hours.
3. Change one or more of the main clauses to a subordinate clause.
   Because the lecture was on the life cycle of the frog, it seemed to go on for hours.
4. Use a comma and a conjunction.
   The lecture was on the life cycle of the frog, and it seemed to go on for hours.
5. Use the semicolon and a conjunctive adverb.
   The lecture was on the life cycle of the frog; consequently, it seemed to go on for hours.

The comma splice: The most common run-on occurs when a comma joins two sentences.

> Example: Serena really likes Aaron, she thinks he can help her achieve her goals.

Correct the comma splice by any one of the run-on correction methods.

> Example: Serena really likes Aaron; she thinks he can help her achieve her goals.

b. Sentence Fragments

Most sentence fragments are phrases or subordinate clauses. Very often on the ACT English Test a participial phrase or an infinitive phrase will be a choice, but a complete sentence is needed.

> Example: Being interested in setting up a charity auction. (participial phrase)
> Example: To be interested in setting up a charity auction. (infinitive phrase)
> Example: Since we are all interested in setting up a charity auction. (subordinate clause)

To avoid fragments, remember:

- A sentence must have a subject and a verb and express a complete thought.
- No word ending in –ing can stand alone as a verb without a helping verb (except one-syllable verbs like sing and ring).

Examples

Correct the following sentences. Answers may vary.

> 1. Raghav being the highest scoring quarterback on the football team.

Raghav has been the highest scoring quarterback on the football team.

> 2. Many people think dogs make the best pets, cats are affectionate, too.

Many people think dogs make the best pets, but cats are affectionate, too.

> 3. Hoping to fill all the seats in the auditorium for the school musical.

We are hoping to fill all the seats in the auditorium for the school musical.

> 4. Pearl loves to go to Florida, she has so many friends and relatives to visit there.

Pearl loves to go to Florida because she has so many friends and relatives to visit there.

> 5. Not only did the class picnic get rained out on Saturday, but cancelled forever.

Not only did the class picnic get rained out on Saturday, but it was also cancelled forever.

> 6. The TV show *Lost* was filmed in Hawaii, the lucky cast got to live there.

The TV show *Lost* was filmed in Hawaii; the lucky cast got to live there.

E. Rhetoric

Rhetoric questions focus on style, writing strategy, and organization. You are asked to make decisions similar to those that writers make when they revise their work.

1. Style

The five passages on the ACT English Test will vary in style. You are expected to note the style (sometimes referred to as the writer's voice) and take it into consideration as you answer questions about the writers' decisions. Some passages, especially those written in first person (I) by a teenager, will have an informal, even breezy, style, but rarely will slang expressions be correct. Many passages are objective and informational; these will have a straightforward and unemotional style. Most questions will involve choices in diction and wordiness.

---

1. My cousin Larry is one of the funniest people I know. I see him every day because we attend the same school. He is very clever and never fails to make me laugh with his <u>nutty, crazy stuff that makes me giggle</u>.

   A. NO CHANGE
   B. idiosyncratic and comedic jocularity.
   C. quirky humor and silly jokes.
   D. perspicacious awareness of absurdity.

In this question, you should note that the excerpt is written in an informal style. Therefore, Choice B and Choice D are far too formal for this passage. Choice A, although informal, borders on slang and is wordy and imprecise. Choice C is the best phrasing for the underlined words.

---

2. The Board of Education has issued a statement regarding the dress code for high schools in the district. The code includes a definition of what constitutes "proper attire." The reason for the new code is <u>because some kids come to school dressed to the nines.</u>

   F. NO CHANGE
   G. that some students have been dressing too formally.
   H. because of kids' wearing formal clothes.
   J. because of kids who wear formal attire.

This excerpt is written in a more formal style than the previous example. The underlined portion is not acceptable; it contains a usage error and a cliché. *The reason … is because* is not standard English. It should be rewritten as *The reason … is that.* In addition, *dressed to the nines* is a cliché and should be changed to more original phrasing. Choice H repeats the usage error. Choice J also has the usage error. Choice G is correct.

In answering style questions, keep in mind that active verbs are preferable to passive ones.

Example: **He designed the posters.** (active verb) is preferable to **The posters were designed by him.** (passive).

2. Writing Strategy

These questions ask you to consider the appropriateness of the writer's strategy in either a portion of the passage or the entire passage. As you read, consider the following questions: Which is the best choice for the writer to accomplish his or her purpose? Which choice shows his or her awareness of the audience? Which choice is more effectively written? Is every piece of information relevant to the focus of the passage?

(The following is an adaptation of an essay written in 1921 by T. S. Eliot)

The modern dramatist, and probably the modern audience, is terrified of the myth. The myth is imagination and it is also criticism, <u>and the two are one.</u> The Seventeenth Century had its own machinery of virtues

1
and vices, as we have, but its drama is a <u>criticism about humanity</u> far more serious than its conscious moral

2
judgments. "Volpone" does <u>not merely show</u> that wickedness is punished; it criticises humanity by intensifying

3
wickedness. <u>When I read "Volpone," I found it difficult to follow the stage directions.</u>

4

---

1. If the writer were to delete the underlined portion, the paragraph would primarily lose

    A. a contrast to the idea that preceded it.
    B. an emphatic assertion.
    C. a detail that adds specificity to the sentence.
    D. a foreshadowing of the conclusion.

B. If the writer deletes the underlined portion, he will lose an emphatic assertion (Choice B). An emphatic assertion is a strong statement. The writer has stated that myth is both imagination and criticism. Now he reiterates the point with emphasis. The statement is not a contrast (Choice A) or a detail (Choice C). In no way does it foreshadow a conclusion (Choice D).

---

2. Which of the following is the best alternative to the underlined part?

    F. criticism towards humanity
    G. criticism toward humanity
    H. criticism referring to humanity
    J. criticism of humanity

J. This is an idiom question. The correct preposition to use with **criticism** is **of** (Choice J).

---

3. Which of the following alternatives to the underlined part would NOT be acceptable?

    A. not only show
    B. not show
    C. not merely illustrate
    D. not only demonstrate

B. In this sentence, **merely** and **only** can be used interchangeably before the verb. The verbs **show, demonstrate,** and **illustrate** are equally appropriate in this sentence. Choice B, which omits the word **merely,** changes the meaning of the sentence and is not acceptable.

4. The writer is considering leaving out this sentence. Should he delete it?

    F.   No, because his opinion adds liveliness to the essay.

    G.   No, because the reader always wants to know what the writer is thinking.

    H.   Yes, because it is irrelevant to the focus of the essay.

    J.   Yes, because it is a detail that might enhance the reader's understanding of the paragraph.

H. The writer should delete the sentence (Choice H) because it is irrelevant to the paragraph. The writer never mentioned stage directions, and his opinion, at this point in the paragraph, is not relevant.

3. Organization

Questions on organization deal with the order and coherence of ideas in the passages. One of the keys to achieving coherence is the effective use of transitional words and phrases.

a. Order and Coherence

You will notice as you read the ACT English Test passages that sometimes the sentences in the passage are numbered, and sometimes the paragraphs are numbered. This numbering tells you that you will encounter questions about order. Use the context clues to help you determine the best order. For example, if a person or place is mentioned by name, ask yourself, "Has this name been introduced or identified?" If the introduction comes later in the passage, then you know you must logically rearrange the order of the sentences. The same holds true for paragraph order. Use logic and look for clues to what happens next within the passage.

    (1) Last summer I went on vacation with my family to England. (2) Since we had landed in London, we had to rent a car to drive to their house. (3) Several times we got lost and had to ask for directions. (4) While we were there, we decided to visit some cousins who live in Ludlow, a small city near the border of Wales. (5) To our embarrassment and to the amusement of those we stopped, we frequently mispronounced the names of the towns along the way. (6) The drive itself was an adventure. (7) How could we know the British often drop syllables from names?

1. The passage is best organized in which order?

    A.   1, 4, 2, 3, 5, 6, 7

    B.   2, 1, 6, 5, 4, 7, 3

    C.   2, 6, 1, 3, 7, 4, 5

    D.   1, 4, 2, 6, 3, 5, 7

D. The logical order is Choice D:

    (1) Last summer I went on vacation with my family to England. (4) While we were there, we decided to visit some cousins who live in Ludlow, a small city near the border of Wales. (2) Since we had landed in London, we had to rent a car to drive to their house. (6) The drive itself was an adventure. (3) Several times we got lost and had to ask for directions. (5) To our embarrassment and to the amusement of those we stopped, we frequently mispronounced the names of the towns along the way. (7) How could we know the British often drop syllables from names?

b. Transitional Words and Phrases

Transitional words and phrases link ideas and indicate the relationship of ideas within a sentence, a paragraph, or a passage. They are essential tools for a writer who wants to achieve a clear and logical flow of ideas.

Important Transitional Words and Phrases			
Words used to indicate an example		**Words used to show a result**	
for example for instance specifically		consequently hence accordingly therefore	
Words used to indicate a reason		**Words used to indicate more information**	
as because since due to		besides in addition moreover furthermore	
Words used to contrast		**Words used to show similarity**	
although but however in contrast nevertheless whereas while yet on the other hand still despite		another similarly likewise also again in the same way too equally	
Words used to establish time relationships		**Words used for emphasis**	
before during after at last at this point	later soon next until recently	then then again once at the same time assuredly	indeed clearly to be sure without doubt

Examples

Select the best transitional word or phrase to fit in the sentences:

---

1. Our lacrosse team has lost every game so far; _____, they are expected to win today.

   A. similarly
   B. nevertheless
   C. in addition
   D. recently

B. nevertheless (contrast)

---

2. I heard it is raining heavily in Denver, _____ it is sunny in Topeka.

   F. then
   G. but
   H. likewise
   J. consequently

G. but (contrast)

---

3. The report on upgrading the reading program showed serious weaknesses in some programs; _____, it recommended several steps to redress the problems.

   A. although
   B. furthermore
   C. likewise
   D. whereas

B. furthermore (more information)

---

4. I have traveled to many states; _____, I have been to New York, California, Florida, and Nevada.

   F. in addition
   G. however
   H. therefore
   J. for example

J. for example (an example)

VI. Reading Test

A. Overview of the ACT Reading Test

The Reading Test consists of four passages: Prose Fiction, Humanities, Social Science, and Natural Science. After each section, there are 10 questions based on the information stated or implied in the passage. One of the four passages will include a paired reading: two short passages (about one-half the length of a regular passage) on related topics. You have 35 minutes to read all the passages and answer the 40 questions.

Prose Fiction: This passage is usually an excerpt from a short story or a novel. You are reading to understand the mood of the selection, the narration of events (plot), and the characters as they are revealed by their words, their actions, and the responses of the other characters to them.

Humanities: This passage describes or analyzes works of art, presents information about an artist, or is a memoir. The Humanities passage tests your ability to comprehend, analyze, and ascertain point of view.

Social Science: This passage is an informative presentation of material that has been gathered by research. It is similar to a chapter in your social studies textbook. To answer the questions, you will often have to follow the chronology of the events in the passage, understand the ramifications of political actions, or make conclusions about psychological experiments.

Natural Science: This passage tests your ability to read about science-related topics. The questions require you to understand the sequence of events, recall facts, and draw conclusions.

B. General Strategies for the Reading Test

- Read the passage actively. Think about what you are reading as you read.
- Answer all questions based on information directly stated in the passage or implied by the passage. Do not rely on your own knowledge of the topic.
- Take note of names, dates, places, and events that may show up in the questions. Circle or underline them as you read.
- As you read, think about the main idea of the passage and the author's purpose in writing it.
- Don't get bogged down with a difficult sentence or two. Keep reading; the point may become clear as you go on.
- Read the questions carefully; be sure you know exactly what you are being asked.
- The questions do not go in the order of the passage. The first question, for example, may deal with information in the last paragraph of the passage.
- Some questions are EXCEPT or NOT questions. In these cases, you are looking for the answer choice that is NOT true.
- Do not feel you must rely on your memory; go back and refer to the text as often as necessary.
- For detail questions, go back and skim until you find the reference. Some of the questions will ask you to recall very specific information.

- For the paired reading passages, answer the questions on each passage first; then answer the questions that ask you about both passages.

- If you are unsure of an answer, make your best guess and move on. Remember, there is no guessing penalty on the ACT, so do not leave any answers blank.

- Be aware of time; you can't leisurely read the passages. You have about 8½ minutes to read and answer the 10 questions on each passage.

C. Types of Reading Questions

The reading questions will test your ability to read and comprehend passages similar to those you will encounter in college. To answer the questions, you will need to understand both what is directly stated in the passage and what is implied by the author. You don't need any previous knowledge of the topics; all the information you need to answer the questions is contained in the passages, so don't hesitate to look back as you answer.

1. Main Idea

Main idea questions test your ability to figure out the author's primary point in writing the passage. Often, rereading the first two sentences in each paragraph will help you. Most authors refer to their main idea in the topic sentence(s) of each paragraph. Look for the common thread, the idea that each paragraph supports.

2. Main Conflict Questions

Main conflict questions refer to the opposing sides in the primary struggle within the prose fiction passage. The struggle may be between two characters, between a character and a facet of nature, or between two facets of nature.

3. Passage-as-a-Whole Questions

Questions about the passage as a whole refer to the main point of the entire passage, not just a portion.

4. Main Point of a Paragraph

These questions ask you to identify the main point of one particular paragraph. First, be sure you are looking at the correct paragraph; perhaps mark in brackets as a reminder. Check the line numbers in the questions carefully. Then identify the topic sentence of the paragraph (usually, but not always, the first sentence). Follow the author's logic in the paragraph. Ask yourself, "What point is he/she trying to prove?" The answer to this question should correspond to one of the answer choices.

Practice 1: Main Conflict Question

The following excerpt is from *The Autobiography of Benjamin Franklin* written in 1771.

> It was about this time I conceiv'd the bold and arduous project of arriving at moral perfection. I wish'd to live without committing any fault at any time; I would conquer all that either natural

inclination, custom, or company might lead me into. As I knew, or thought I knew, what was right and wrong, I did not see why I might not always do the one and avoid the other. But I soon found I had
(5) undertaken a task of more difficulty than I had imagined. While my care was employ'd in guarding against one fault, I was often surprised by another; habit took the advantage of inattention; inclination was sometimes too strong for reason. I concluded, at length, that the mere speculative conviction that it was our interest to be completely virtuous was not sufficient to prevent our slipping; and that the contrary habits must be broken, and good ones acquired and established, before we can have any depen-
(10) dence on a steady, uniform rectitude of conduct.

---

1. The main conflict in this passage is between:

   A. Franklin's need for independence and his employer's need for assistance.
   B. Franklin's desire to be virtuous and his tendency toward wrongdoing.
   C. Franklin's belief in good habits and his code of conduct.
   D. Franklin's inclination to be alone and his natural need for company.

B is correct. Franklin states he conceived the idea of living a life of "moral perfection." Then he writes, "But I soon found I had undertaken a task of more difficulty than I had imagined." It was more difficult because he found his desire to be good "was not sufficient to prevent our slipping." So, even though he wanted to be good, he could not help slipping back into bad habits. All the wrong answer choices (Choices A, C, and D) count on your reading quickly and pouncing on words in the choices that look familiar because they are also in the passage.

Practice 2: Main Idea Question

The following excerpt is from *Democracy in America* written by Alexis de Tocqueville in 1840.

In the United States the majority undertakes to supply a multitude of ready-made opinions for the use of individuals, who are thus relieved from the necessity of forming opinions of their own. Everybody there adopts great numbers of theories, on philosophy, morals, and politics, without inquiry, upon public trust; and if we look to it very narrowly, it will be perceived that religion herself holds her sway there, much less
(5) as a doctrine of revelation than as a commonly received opinion. The fact that the political laws of the Americans are such that the majority rules the community with sovereign sway, materially increases the power which that majority naturally exercises over the mind. For nothing is more customary in man than to recognize superior wisdom in the person of his oppressor. This political omnipotence of the majority in the United States doubtless augments the influence which public opinion would obtain without it over the
(10) mind of each member of the community; but the foundations of that influence do not rest upon it.

---

2. Which of the following best states the main idea of this paragraph?

   F. America is a nation founded on the premise that the convictions of the individual are more powerful than the will of the majority.
   G. The foundation of political power in this country rests in the hands of those with superior wisdom.
   H. The beliefs of the majority in America are sovereign and inform the opinions of the individual.
   J. Because it is a country ruled by the majority, the United States is politically omnipotent.

H is correct. The main idea is stated in the first sentence of the passage. Choice F is the opposite of his thesis, Choice G is a misreading of his point that the individual believes the majority has superior wisdom, and Choice J is unsupported by any evidence in the passage.

5. Detail Questions

Questions about details in a passage will ask you to identify and analyze details that the author uses to support his or her thesis. Details will usually be in the form of facts, names, examples, illustrations, places, or evidence from research.

a. Directly Stated Details

Directly stated details should be locatable within the passage. Identify the paragraph that most likely contains the information; then skim until you find the specific piece of information you need.

b. Implied Details

Some details are implied by the information in the text. In these cases, you must "read between the lines" to find the implied detail.

Practice 3: Detail Questions

This passage is an excerpt from *The Birds of America* written by John James Audubon in 1839.

Previous to my visit to the Florida Keys, I had seen but few Frigate-birds, and those only at some distance, while I was on the Gulf of Mexico, so that I could merely recognize them by their mode of flight. On approaching Indian Key, however, I observed several of them, and as I proceeded farther south, their numbers rapidly increased; but on the Tortugas very few were observed. This bird rarely
(5) travels farther eastward than the Bay of Charleston in South Carolina, although it is abundant in all seasons from Cape Florida to Cape Sable, the two extremes of the peninsula. How far south it may be found I cannot tell.

3. Before the author traveled to the Florida Keys, he had:
    A. widely studied the Frigate-birds in their natural habitat.
    B. been part of a scientific expedition that had explored all of the Florida peninsula to find the rare Frigate-bird.
    C. doubted the existence of the nearly extinct bird.
    D. not seen Frigate-birds close up, but had observed them in flight.

D is correct. The author directly states: "Previous to my visit to the Florida Keys, I had seen but few Frigate-birds, and those only at some distance." None of the other choices are supported by the text.

4. Where would one be most likely to see a flock of Frigate-birds?
    F. On the islands in the Bay of Charleston off the east coast of South Carolina
    G. Off the coast of Miami Beach
    H. On Cape Sable Island in Canada
    J. On an American Indian reservation in Arizona

G is correct. The author states the Frigate-bird "is abundant in all seasons from Cape Florida to Cape Sable, the two extremes of the peninsula." From this statement, you may infer that the birds are abundant anywhere along the coast of Florida. Choice F is incorrect because the author states, "This bird rarely travels farther eastward than the Bay of Charleston in South Carolina." Choice H is meant to distract you with an island that has the same name as Cape Sable in Florida; however, this passage solely concerns Florida. Choice J is obviously wrong; however, it is a distracter because Indian Key was mentioned in the passage.

6. Relationships

Some questions will test your ability to note relationships among ideas, facts, examples, or illustrations.

a. Comparison/Contrast

Comparison/contrast questions test your ability to note similarities and differences between the elements in a passage. For these questions, you must make connections between ideas, engage in critical thinking, and reflect on similarities and differences. Look for words like **compare, contrast, similarities,** and **differences** to help you locate the answer in the text.

b. Cause and Effect

Cause and effect questions test your ability to see how one event or situation is responsible for another. The cause is what made something happen; the effect is the result of the cause.

c. Sequence of Events

Sequence of events questions test your ability to follow a series of events in the order in which they occurred. Some order may be chronological (time) or spatial (large to small, east to west, top to bottom) or specific to general (or general to specific).

7. Generalizations

A **generalization** question asks you to consider the information in the passage and reduce it to a single statement. You may have to characterize a person about whom you have been reading, condense a process, or draw a conclusion about a subject.

Practice 4: Relationship and Generalization Questions

The following is adapted from "The Custom-House," the introductory chapter of *The Scarlet Letter,* written by Nathaniel Hawthorne in 1850.

But, one idle and rainy day, it was my fortune to make a discovery of some little interest. Poking and burrowing into the heaped-up rubbish in the corner, unfolding one and another document, and reading the names of vessels that had long ago foundered at sea or rotted at the wharves . . . I chanced to lay my hand on a small package, carefully done up in a piece of ancient yellow parchment. This envelope had
(5)   the air of an official record . . . There was something about it that quickened an instinctive curiosity, and made me undo the faded red tape that tied up the package, with the sense that a treasure would here be brought to light. Unbending the rigid folds of the parchment cover, I found it to be a commission . . . in favour of one Jonathan Pue, as Surveyor of His Majesty's Customs for the Port of Salem . . . Nothing, if I rightly call to mind, was left of my respected predecessor, save an imperfect skeleton, and some frag-
(10)   ments of apparel, and a wig of majestic frizzle, which, unlike the head that it once adorned, was in very

satisfactory preservation. But, on examining the papers which the parchment commission served to envelop, I found more traces of Mr. Pue's mental part, and the internal operations of his head . . .

They were documents, in short, not official, but of a private nature, or, at least, written in his private capacity, and apparently with his own hand. I could account for their being included in the heap of
(15) Custom-House lumber only by the fact that Mr. Pue's death had happened suddenly, and that these papers, which he probably kept in his official desk, had never come to the knowledge of his heirs, or were supposed to relate to the business of the revenue. On the transfer of the archives to Halifax, this package, proving to be of no public concern, was left behind, and had remained ever since unopened.

The ancient Surveyor—being little molested, I suppose, at that early day with business pertaining to his
(20) office—seems to have devoted some of his many leisure hours to researches as a local antiquarian . . .

But the object that most drew my attention to the mysterious package was a certain affair of fine red cloth, much worn and faded. There were traces about it of gold embroidery, which, however, was greatly frayed and defaced, so that none, or very little, of the glitter was left. It had been wrought, as was easy to perceive, with wonderful skill of needlework; and the stitch (as I am assured by ladies conversant with such
(25) mysteries) gives evidence of a now forgotten art, not to be discovered even by the process of picking out the threads. This rag of scarlet cloth—for time, and wear, and a sacrilegious moth had reduced it to little other than a rag—on careful examination, assumed the shape of a letter. It was the capital letter A. . . .

---

5. What is the correct sequence of events?

   A. The narrator found the cloth, discovered the commission of Mr. Pue, and poked around the accumulated garbage in the corner of the room.

   B. The narrator opened the parchment package, did research, and found the scarlet cloth before Mr. Pue died.

   C. The narrator poked around the rubbish, found and opened the parchment package, discovered Mr. Pue's documents, and found the scarlet cloth.

   D. After Mr. Pue died, the narrator found the scarlet cloth, undid the faded red tape, and read the documents.

C is correct. Refer to the passage and locate each event. Choice A is incorrect because the narrator found the package when he poked around the rubbish. In Choice B, Mr. Pue dies last; since he left the package when he died, the order is incorrect. Choice D reverses the order: The cloth is in the package tied with the red tape.

---

6. The author is intrigued by the scarlet cloth for all of the following reasons EXCEPT:

   F. It is evidence of the forgotten art of needlework.

   G. It is a curious find among the papers of a surveyor.

   H. Although it is quite old, it has been mysteriously preserved in good condition.

   J. He is an instinctively curious man.

H is correct. The narrator states the cloth has been reduced to little more than a rag by time and wear and moths.

---

7. In the passage, the author creates a contrast between:

   A. idle curiosity and fascinating discovery.

   B. sensationalistic expectation and official bookkeeping.

   C. eager anticipation and disappointing reality.

   D. youthful enthusiasm and mature practicality.

A is correct. The narrator is just passing time on an idle, rainy day when he unexpectedly discovers the mysterious embroidered cloth. He appears fascinated by his discovery, not disappointed (Choice C) or practical (Choice D). He certainly had no sensationalistic expectation, and bookkeeping does not figure into his reaction (Choice B).

---

8. Based on the evidence in the passage, the narrator is best described as:

   F. a humorless and pompous bureaucrat.
   G. an unromantic and meticulous organizer.
   H. an imaginative and somewhat ironic observer.
   J. a piously devoted antiquarian.

H is correct. The narrator's imagination is captured by the scrap of scarlet cloth; his irony is apparent in his comments about his deceased predecessor, Mr. Pue: "a wig of majestic frizzle, which, unlike the head that it once adorned, was in very satisfactory preservation" (lines 10–11). There is no evidence of pomposity, and he does display ironic humor, so Choice F is incorrect. Choice G does not consider his imagination (unromantic), and he is just poking around rubbish, not organizing it. The narrator refers to Mr. Pue, not himself, as an antiquarian (Choice J).

8. Author's Voice and Method

These questions refer to the author's tone and attitude toward his or her subject and the way in which he or she presents ideas. Questions may be about the author's craft as well as his or her point of view. Look for clues in the diction (word choice) in the passage. Is it positive and generally a tribute to the person or event? Does it point out the weaknesses or failures of a plan or a design? Also, if a question asks you to consider the purpose of a paragraph, think about what that paragraph contributes to the passage as a whole. Ask yourself what the passage would lose if that paragraph were to be omitted.

9. Vocabulary in Context

Vocabulary-in-context questions ask about the meaning of a word or a short phrase as it is used in the passage. Often words that have multiple meanings are selected. You must find the appropriate choice for the context. The best technique is to go back to the text, circle the word or phrase, and reread the whole sentence. Then replace the circled word or phrase with the words in the answer choices. Select the answer choice that is consistent with the original meaning of the sentence.

Practice 5: Author's Voice and Method and Vocabulary Questions

The following passage is an excerpt from *The Age of Innocence* written by Edith Wharton in 1920. Newland Archer, a wealthy young gentleman, is at the opera observing an innocent young woman whom he plans to marry.

He did not in the least wish the future Mrs. Newland Archer to be a simpleton. He meant her (thanks to his enlightening companionship) to develop a social tact and readiness of wit enabling her to hold her own with the most popular married women of the "younger set," in which it was the recognised custom to attract masculine homage while playfully discouraging it. If he had probed to the bottom of his vanity (as
(5)   he sometimes nearly did) he would have found there the wish that his wife should be as worldly-wise and

as eager to please as the married lady whose charms had held his fancy through two mildly agitated years; without, of course, any hint of the frailty which had so nearly marred that unhappy being's life, and had disarranged his own plans for a whole winter.

(10) How this miracle of fire and ice was to be created, and to sustain itself in a harsh world, he had never taken the time to think out; but he was content to hold his view without analyzing it, since he knew it was that of all the carefully-brushed, white-waistcoated, button-hole-flowered gentlemen who succeeded each other in the club box, exchanged friendly greetings with him, and turned their opera-glasses critically on the circle of ladies who were the product of the system. In matters intellectual and artistic Newland Archer felt himself distinctly the superior of these chosen specimens of old New York gentility;

(15) he had probably read more, thought more, and even seen a good deal more of the world, than any other man of the number. Singly they betrayed their inferiority; but grouped together they represented "New York," and the habit of masculine solidarity made him accept their doctrine on all the issues called moral. He instinctively felt that in this respect it would be troublesome—and also rather bad form—to strike out for himself.

---

9. It can be inferred from the passage that the author views Newland Archer as:

   A. a confident man who does not rely on the judgments of others to give him authority.
   B. a rather egotistical gentleman with pretensions to superiority.
   C. a naïve fellow who lacks the sophistication of "New York gentility."
   D. a newcomer to society who believes he must conform to the standards of those who set the rules.

B is correct. Archer is presented as a man with an inflated sense of his own self-worth. He believes he is "superior" to the other men. Choice A is incorrect: Although Archer is confident, he does rely on the judgments of others. Choice C is incorrect because Archer is quite sophisticated. Choice D is also incorrect; nothing in the passage indicates that Archer is a newcomer to society.

---

10. Which of the following best describes the function of the author's parenthetical comments in lines 1–2 and lines 4–5?

    F. They underscore her faith in Archer's good judgment.
    G. They ironically comment on Archer's egotism.
    H. They present the first indication that the author is hostile to Archer.
    J. They present a contrast between the public Archer and the private Archer.

G is correct. The author's parenthetical comments are ironic and reveal her acknowledgment of Archer's vanity. Choice F is incorrect because the comments don't emphasize Archer's good judgment. Choice H is incorrect because the author isn't hostile to Archer. Choice J is incorrect because no contrast is evident in the passage.

---

11. The reference to "this miracle of fire and ice" (line 9) indicates that the narrator believes:

    A. Archer has set unreasonable standards for his future wife.
    B. Archer's future will be juxtaposed between the joy of passion and the bleakness of despair.
    C. the harshness of the world will intrude on Archer's neat plan for marriage to his intended bride.
    D. the tragedy of the opera will be a direct contrast to the happiness of Archer's marriage.

A is correct. By using the term "miracle," the author implies Archer has set unreasonable standards for his wife. Choices B, C, and D are incorrect because the phrase refers only to Archer's future wife, not to his future, the world, or the opera.

---

12. The word "fancy" in line 6 most nearly means:

    F. embellishment.
    G. interest.
    H. daydream.
    J. enthusiasm.

G is correct. A "lady whose charms had held his fancy" held his *interest.* None of the other choices fit the context.

---

13. The sentence "Singly they betrayed their inferiority; but grouped together they represented 'New York,' and the habit of masculine solidarity made him accept their doctrine on all the issues called moral" (lines 16–18) functions in the passage to present the narrator's view that:

    A. Archer's arrogance does not extend to challenging the collective values of his clique in society.
    B. because Archer believes himself a cut above the other men, he is unwilling to conform to their collective values.
    C. Archer feels betrayed by the members of society who disapprove of his choice of his future bride.
    D. because of the superiority of his education and the breadth of his reading, Archer believes he should be the moral compass of his social set.

A is correct. The fact that Archer would "accept their doctrine on all the issues called moral" suggests that he didn't challenge the moral values of the group, an implication that makes Choice B incorrect. There is no indication that Archer feels betrayed, so Choice C is incorrect. Archer doesn't believe he should be the moral compass (Choice D) because he isn't a leader; he's a follower of the values of the group.

---

14. The description of the men as "carefully-brushed, white-waistcoated, button-hole-flowered gentlemen" (line 11) reveals all of the following EXCEPT:

    F. the importance of conformity in appearance.
    G. the habit of masculine solidarity.
    H. the emphasis on individualism and assertiveness.
    J. the superficiality of a society that values conventionality.

H is correct. The lines indicate that the men are concerned about their appearance (Choice F), believe in masculine superiority (Choice G), and accept the importance of conventionality (Choice J).

10. Paired Readings

The paired reading passages test your ability to integrate knowledge and ideas from two texts. This section consists of two topically related short passages, each about one-half the length of a regular passage. You will get 2 to 4 questions on each individual passage and 2 to 4 questions that ask you to synthesize (combine or integrate) information from both passages. The paired reading may occur in any one of the four content areas on the Reading Test.

The best strategy for the paired reading passages is to answer the questions on each passage first so that you have a clear understanding of each author's main points, purpose, and point of view. Then, tackle the synthesis questions, keeping in mind your understanding of each short passage.

Practice 6: Paired Reading Questions

HUMANITIES: Passage A is an excerpt adapted from *A Wheel within a Wheel,* a memoir by Frances E. Willard (1895). Passage B is an excerpt from the essay "Taming the Bicycle" by Mark Twain (1884).

Passage A

Living in the country, far from the artificial restraints and conventions by which most girls are hedged from the activities that would develop a good physique, and endowed with the companionship of a mother who let me have my own sweet will, I "ran wild" until my sixteenth birthday, when the hampering long skirts were brought, with their accompanying corset and high heels; my hair was clubbed up
(5)   with pins, and I remember writing in my journal, in the first heartbreak of a young human colt taken from its pleasant pasture, "Altogether, I recognize that my occupation is gone." From that time on I always realized and was obedient to the limitations thus imposed, though in my heart of hearts I felt their unwisdom even more than their injustice.

My work then changed from my beloved and breezy outdoor world to the indoor realm of study,
(10)   teaching, writing, speaking, and went on almost without a break or pain until my fifty-third year, when the loss of my mother accentuated the strain of this long period in which mental and physical life were out of balance.... Thus ruthlessly thrown out of the usual lines of reaction on my environment, and sighing for new worlds to conquer, I determined that I would learn the bicycle. Already I knew well enough that tens of thousands who could never afford to own, feed, and stable a horse, had by this
(15)   bright invention enjoyed the swiftness of motion which is perhaps the most fascinating feature of material life, the charm of a wide outlook upon the natural world, and that sense of mastery which is probably the greatest attraction in horseback-riding. But the steed that never tires, and is "mettlesome" in the fullest sense of the word, is full of tricks and capers, and to hold his head steady and make him prance to suit you is no small accomplishment.

(20)   I always felt a strong attraction toward the bicycle, because it is the vehicle of so much harmless pleasure, and because the skill required in handling it obliges those who mount to keep clear heads and steady hands. Nor could I see a reason in the world why a woman should not ride the silent steed so swift and blithesome. I knew perfectly well that when, some ten or fifteen years ago, Miss Bertha von Hillern, a young German artist in America, took it into her head to give exhibitions of her skill in riding the
(25)   bicycle she was thought by some to be a sort of semi-monster; and liberal as our people are in their views of what a woman may undertake, I should certainly have felt compromised, at that remote and benighted period, by going to see her ride, not because there was any harm in it, but solely because of what we call in homely phrase "the speech of people." But behold! it was long ago conceded that women might ride the tricycle indeed, one had been presented to me by my friend Colonel Pope, of Boston, a
(30)   famous manufacturer of these swift roadsters, as far back as 1886; and I had swung around the garden-paths upon its saddle a few minutes every evening when work was over at my Rest Cottage home. I had even hoped to give an impetus among conservative women to this new line of physical development and outdoor happiness; but that is quite another story and will come in later. Suffice it for the present that it did me good, as it doth the upright in heart, to notice recently that the Princesses Louise and Beatrice
(35)   both ride the tricycle at Balmoral; for I know that with the great mass of feminine humanity this precedent will have exceeding weight and where the tricycle prophesies the bicycle shall ere long preach the gospel of outdoors.

Passage B

I thought the matter over, and concluded I could do it. So I went down and bought a barrel of Pond's Extract and a bicycle. The Expert came home with me to instruct me. We chose the back yard, for the
(40) sake of privacy, and went to work.

Mine was not a full-grown bicycle, but only a colt—a fifty-inch, with the pedals shortened up to forty-eight— and skittish, like any other colt. The Expert explained the thing's points briefly, then he got on its back and rode around a little, to show me how easy it was to do. He said that the dismounting was perhaps the hardest thing to learn, and so we would leave that to the last. But he was in error there. He found, to his surprise and joy, that all
(45) that he needed to do was to get me on to the machine and stand out of the way; I could get off, myself. Although I was wholly inexperienced, I dismounted in the best time on record. He was on that side, shoving up the machine; we all came down with a crash, he at the bottom, I next, and the machine on top.

We examined the machine, but it was not in the least injured. This was hardly believable. Yet the Expert assured me that it was true; in fact, the examination proved it. I was partly to realize, then, how
(50) admirably these things are constructed. We applied some Pond's Extract, and resumed. The Expert got on the OTHER side to shove up this time, but I dismounted on that side; so the result was as before.

The machine was not hurt. We oiled ourselves again, and resumed. This time the Expert took up a sheltered position behind, but somehow or other we landed on him again. He was full of admiration; said it was abnormal. She was all right, not a scratch on her, not a timber started anywhere. I said it was
(55) wonderful, while we were greasing up, but he said that when I came to know these steel spider-webs I would realize that nothing but dynamite could cripple them. Then he limped out to position, and we resumed once more. This time the Expert took up the position of short-stop, and got a man to shove up behind. We got up a handsome speed, and presently traversed a brick, and I went out over the top of the tiller and landed, head down, on the instructor's back, and saw the machine fluttering in the air between
(60) me and the sun. It was well it came down on us, for that broke the fall, and it was not injured.

Five days later I got out and was carried down to the hospital, and found the Expert doing pretty fairly. In a few more days I was quite sound. I attribute this to my prudence in always dismounting on something soft. Some recommend a feather bed, but I think an Expert is better.

Questions 15–18 ask about Passage A.

---

15. The author presents Miss Bertha von Hillern as an example of:

   A. an artist who has chosen to exhibit her paintings despite widespread criticism.
   B. a woman generally considered a semi-monster for her radical political views.
   C. an early bicyclist who publically displayed her riding skills.
   D. a follower of Princesses Louise and Beatrice who believed women should flaunt their physical attributes.

C is correct. According to the passage, Miss Bertha von Hillern "took it into her head to give exhibitions of her skill in riding the bicycle." She was an artist, but there is no evidence that she exhibited her paintings or that they received criticism, so Choice A is incorrect. Her political views are never stated or implied, so Choice B is incorrect. There is no evidence in the passage that she was "a follower of Princesses Louise and Beatrice who believed women should flaunt their physical attributes," so Choice D is incorrect.

---

16. In paragraph 3 the author indicates that she would feel "compromised" by her:

   F. concerns about being the subject of gossip.
   G. need to keep peace in her family.
   H. fear that she would be unable to ride skillfully.
   J. desire to mediate between conservatives and liberals.

125

F is correct. In the context of the passage, "compromised" means put in jeopardy. The author feels she would have been compromised by "the speech of the people," the gossip that she would have caused by going to see Miss von Hillern ride. There is no evidence in the passage that the author needs to keep peace in her family (Choice G) or has to mediate between conservatives and liberals (Choice J). She never expresses fear that she would be unable to ride skillfully (Choice H).

---

17. It can be inferred that to the author, the "corset" and "long skirts" are symbols of:

    A. the required dress code for cyclists.

    B. the inevitable end of the freedom of youth.

    C. the escape from childhood restrictions.

    D. her connection to her beloved mother.

B is correct. In the first paragraph, the author refers to the "corset" and "long skirts" as symbols of the end of her "wild" days and the beginning of the limitations of being a nineteenth-century woman. They are not the dress code for cyclists (Choice A). She describes this change in dress as both restrictive and inevitable, the opposite of an escape from childhood restrictions, so Choice C is incorrect. Nowhere in the passage does she connect this change of dress to her mother (Choice D).

---

18. In line 32 the word "impetus" most nearly means:

    F. an encouragement.

    G. a force.

    H. a compulsion.

    J. a concession.

F is correct. As it is used in the context of the passage, "impetus" most nearly means an encouragement. Choices G (a force) and H (a compulsion) are too strong for this context, and Choice J (a concession) is illogical.

Questions 19–21 ask about Passage B.

---

19. The author's attitude toward learning to ride a bicycle is best described as:

    A. serious.

    B. satirical.

    C. technical.

    D. gloomy.

B is correct. The author is satirizing both his partner, "the Expert," who professes to know what he is doing, and himself in the process of learning how to ride. The passage amusingly mocks both their efforts. He is not serious (Choice A) or technical (Choice C) or gloomy (Choice D).

---

20. According to the Expert, the most difficult part of learning to ride a bicycle is:

    F. getting the bicycle started.

    G. balancing on the sidewalks.

    H. learning to dismount.

    J. steering around obstacles.

H is correct. The Expert believes that "the dismounting was perhaps the hardest thing to learn." The other choices are incorrect because the Expert either doesn't refer to them or doesn't refer to them as difficult.

21. It can be inferred that during the author's process of learning to ride, all of the following occurred EXCEPT:

    A. The bicycle is damaged by crashing down on the ground.
    B. The Expert is hurt enough to be hospitalized.
    C. The author suffers injuries from falling off the bicycle.
    D. The bicycle crashes down on top of the author.

A is correct. The author describes the bicycle crashing down on him as he falls on top of the Expert so you can eliminate Choice D, but he maintains that throughout the process, the bicycle remains unhurt (Choice A). He has to be carried to visit the Expert in the hospital, so choices B and C are incorrect.

Questions 22–24 ask about both passages.

22. The authors of both passages draw a parallel between the bicycle and a:

    F. boat.
    G. monster.
    H. myth.
    J. horse.

J is correct. The author of Passage A compares the bicycle to "the steed that never tires" and the author of Passage B describes his bicycle as "only a colt." Neither of the passages compares the bicycle to a boat (Choice F), a monster (Choice G), or a myth (Choice H).

23. Which of the following best describes the relationship between the two passages?

    A. Passage A sees the symbolic freedom implied by cycling, while Passage B finds cycling to be daunting and discouraging.
    B. Passage A acknowledges the recklessness cycling entails, while Passage B sees only the joy in cycling.
    C. Passage A describes the bicycle as a tool of empowerment, while Passage B views it as a source of humor.
    D. Passage A is reluctant to embrace the fascination of cycling, while Passage B fully accepts the lure of the open road.

C is correct. The author of Passage A sees the bicycle as liberating her from the limitations her world imposes on women. The author of Passage B humorously describes the process of learning to ride a bicycle and pokes fun at both himself and the so-called Expert who is teaching him. Choice A is incorrect because the author of Passage B doesn't become discouraged. Choice B is incorrect because the author of Passage A doesn't acknowledge the recklessness cycling entails. Choice D is incorrect because the author of Passage A isn't reluctant to embrace cycling.

24. Compared to the narrator of Passage B, the narrator of Passage A provides more information about the:

    F.   process of mounting and dismounting a bicycle.

    G.   mechanics of the invention of the bicycle.

    H.   care and maintenance of a bicycle.

    J.   advantages of riding a bicycle.

J is correct. The author of Passage A explains that bicycle riding has afforded her "the swiftness of motion which is perhaps the most fascinating feature of material life, the charm of a wide outlook upon the natural world, and that sense of mastery which is probably the greatest attraction in horseback-riding." Choice F is incorrect because Passage B provides more information about mounting and dismounting a bicycle. Choices G and H are incorrect because neither passage explains the mechanics of the invention of the bicycle or its care and maintenance.

D. Practice Questions

SOCIAL SCIENCE: The following passage is adapted from *Manners, Customs, and Dress During the Middle Ages and During the Renaissance Period* written by Paul Lacroix circa 1874.

    Charlemagne took as much pains with the administration of his palace as he did with that of his States. For instance, he not only interested himself in his warlike and hunting equipages, but also in his kitchen and pleasure gardens. He insisted upon knowing every year the number of his oxen, horses, and goats; he calculated the produce of the sale of fruits gathered in his orchards, which were not required
(5)   for the use of his house; he had a return of the number of fish caught in his ponds; he pointed out the shrubs best calculated for ornamenting his garden, and the vegetables which were required for his table.

    The Emperor generally assumed the greatest simplicity in his dress. His daily attire consisted of a linen shirt and drawers, and a woolen tunic fastened with a silk belt. Over this tunic he threw a cloak of blue stuff, very long behind and before, but very short on each side, thus giving freedom to his arms to
(10)   use his sword, which he always wore. On his feet he wore bands of stuffs of various colors, crossed over one another, and covering his legs also. In winter, when he traveled or hunted on horseback, he threw over his shoulders a covering of otter or sheepskin.

    He was most simple as regards his food and drink, and made a habit of having pious or historical works read to him during his repasts. He devoted the morning, which with him began in summer at
(15)   sunrise, and in winter earlier, to the political administration of his empire. He dined at twelve with his family; the dukes and chiefs of various nations first waited on him, and then took their places at the table, and were waited on in their turn by the counts, prefects, and superior officers of the court who dined after them. When these had finished the different chiefs of the household sat down, and they were succeeded lastly by servants of the lower order, who often did not dine till midnight, and had to content
(20)   themselves with what was left. When occasion required, however, this powerful Emperor knew how to maintain the pomp and dignity of his station; but as soon as he had done what was necessary, either for some great religious festival or otherwise, he returned, as if by instinct, to his dear and native simplicity.

    It must be understood that the simple tastes of Charlemagne were not always shared by the princes
(25)   and princesses of his family, nor by the magnates of his court. Poets and historians have handed down to us descriptions of hunts, feasts, and ceremonies, at which a truly Asiatic splendor was displayed.

Eginhard, however, assures us that the sons and daughters of the King were brought up under their father's eye in liberal studios; that, to save them from the vice of idleness, Charlemagne required his sons to devote themselves to all bodily exercises, such as horsemanship, handling of arms, etc., and his (30) daughters to do needlework and to spin. From what is recorded, however, of the frivolous habits and irregular morals of these princesses, it is evident that they but imperfectly realized the end of their education.

Science and letters, which for a time were brought into prominence by Charlemagne and also by his son Louis, who was very learned and was considered skilful in translating and expounding Scripture, (35) were, however, after the death of these two kings, for a long time banished to the seclusion of the cloisters, owing to the hostile rivalry of their successors, which favored the attacks of the Norman pirates. All the monuments and relics of the Gallo-Roman civilization, which the great Emperor had collected, disappeared in the civil wars, or were gradually destroyed by the devastations of the northerners.

During the first period of feudalism, that is to say from the middle of the ninth to the middle of the (40) twelfth centuries, the inhabitants of castles had little time to devote to the pleasures of private life. They had not only to be continually under arms for the endless quarrels of the King and the great chiefs; but they had also to oppose the Normans on one side, and the Saracens on the other, who, being masters of the Spanish peninsula, spread like the rising tide. It is true that the Carlovingian warriors obtained a handsome and rich reward for these long and sanguinary efforts, for at last they seized upon the prov- (45) inces and districts which had been originally entrusted to their charge, and the origin of their feudal possession was soon so far forgotten, that their descendants pretended that they held the lands, which they had really usurped regardless of their oath, from heaven and their swords. It is needless to say, that at that time the domestic life in these castles must have been dull and monotonous; although, according to M. Guizot, the loneliness which was the result of this rough and laborious life, became by degrees the (50) pioneer of civilization.

"When the owner of the fief left his castle, his wife remained there, though in a totally different position from that which women generally held. She remained as mistress, representing her husband, and was charged with the defense and honor of the fief. This high and exalted position, in the center of domestic life, often gave to women an opportunity of displaying dignity, courage, virtue, and intelli- (55) gence, which would otherwise have remained hidden, and, no doubt, contributed greatly to their moral development, and to the general improvement of their condition.

"The importance of children, and particularly of the eldest son, was greater in feudal houses than elsewhere. The eldest son of the noble was, in the eyes of his father and of all his followers, a prince and heir-presumptive, and the hope and glory of the dynasty. These feelings, and the domestic pride and (60) affection of the various members one to another, united to give families much energy and power. Add to this the influence of Christian ideas, and it will be understood how this lonely, dull, and hard castle life was, nevertheless, favorable to the development of domestic society, and to that improvement in the condition of women which plays such a great part in the history of our civilization."

Whatever opinion may be formed of chivalry, it is impossible to deny the influence which this institu- (65) tion exercised on private life in the Middle Ages. It considerably modified custom, by bringing the stronger sex to respect and defend the weaker. These warriors, who were both simple and externally rough and coarse, required association with women to soften them. In taking women and helpless widows under their protection, they were necessarily more and more thrown in contact with them. A deep feeling of veneration for woman, inspired by Christianity, and, above all, by the worship of the Virgin (70) Mary, ran throughout the songs of the troubadours, and produced a sort of sentimental reverence for the gentle sex, which culminated in the authority which women had in the courts of love.

1. In this passage, Charlemagne is generally characterized as:

   A. a ruthless dictator driven by ambition.
   B. an elegant courtier with refined manners and rarefied tastes.
   C. an uncouth barbarian who disdained the trappings of civilization.
   D. a strong but unassuming ruler who was involved in all aspects of his domain.

2. The author's purpose in writing this passage is most likely to:

   F. point out the differences between life in France before and after the rule of Charlemagne.
   G. present a portrait of the internal workings of the household of the Emperor.
   H. argue that the Age of Chivalry was actually marred by serious religious conflicts.
   J. hypothesize that Charlemagne was responsible for the improvement in the lives of the peasants.

3. The purpose of the second and third paragraphs (lines 7–23) is to:

   A. show how Charlemagne brought an emphasis on science and learning to the court.
   B. explain why Charlemagne was regarded as the ruler who most democratized the court in the Middle Ages.
   C. argue that Charlemagne was responsible for reorganizing the hierarchy of the social order in Medieval France.
   D. substantiate the assertion that Charlemagne did not leave the administration of his household to others.

4. According to the passage, all of the following were habits of Charlemagne EXCEPT:

   F. He enjoyed listening to religious tracts while he dined.
   G. He usually appeared dressed in simple apparel.
   H. He insisted upon knowing exactly how many goats were born each year.
   J. He rose at sunrise, summer and winter.

5. It can be inferred from the passage that the position of women in the Middle Ages:

   A. changed radically in that they no longer had the right to govern their households.
   B. improved during those periods when their husbands were not in residence.
   C. was unprecedented in that for the first time women were no longer considered property of their husbands.
   D. degenerated as the status of first-born sons was elevated to new heights.

6. According to M. Guizot, the loneliness and monotony of castle life had what effect?

   F. It led warriors to fight among themselves to combat boredom.
   G. Clinical depression reached epidemic proportions.
   H. Lords declared war on neighboring fiefs to gain land and power.
   J. It led to the rise of civilization as it fostered the development of domestic society.

7. According to the passage, both Christianity and chivalry:

   A. engendered feelings of respect and protectiveness in men toward women.
   B. increased the likelihood that the eldest son would become a scholar.
   C. stimulated scientific thought and inspired a renewed interest in the Gallo-Roman relics.
   D. elevated the status of servants in the household of Charlemagne.

8. It can be inferred from the passage that the daughters of Charlemagne:

    F. inspired the troubadours to write love songs dedicated to them.

    G. disappointed their father by their frivolous and immoral behavior.

    H. were highly skilled in martial arts including horsemanship and weaponry.

    J. displayed the dignity, courage, and elegance expected of royal princesses.

9. According to the passage, what was a direct result of the deaths of Charlemagne and his son Louis?

    A. Women achieved prominence in the fields of art and music.

    B. Studies in science and religion were relegated to religious orders.

    C. New rulers arose who restored pomp and dignity to the court.

    D. Feelings of domestic pride diminished, and household rivalries marred family gatherings.

10. The phrase "but imperfectly realized the end of their education" (lines 31–32) suggests:

    F. the princesses did not know when they had completed their education.

    G. Charlemagne thought it unwise to educate the daughters in the royal household.

    H. education was so primitive during the Middle Ages that most knowledge was inaccurate or incomplete.

    J. the outcome of the princesses' education was not what had been intended.

Answer Explanations

1. **D.** Charlemagne is presented as a man of simple dress who involved himself in the internal workings of his empire. The passage doesn't indicate that he is ruthless (Choice A), elegant (Choice B), or uncouth (Choice C).

2. **G.** The focus of the passage is a description of how Charlemagne ran his household. Nothing is mentioned of the differences in life in France before and after his rule, so Choice F is incorrect. The passage doesn't argue or hypothesize, so Choices H and J are incorrect.

3. **D.** The second and third paragraphs continue the description of Charlemagne's involvement in the day-to-day running of his household. A discussion of science and learning doesn't occur until paragraph 5 (Choice A). The passage doesn't indicate that Charlemagne democratized the court (Choice B) or reorganized the hierarchy of the social order (Choice C).

4. **J.** According to lines 14–15 of the passage, Charlemagne rose "in summer at sunrise, and in winter earlier."

5. **B.** See paragraph 7 (lines 51–56). A wife's position was elevated when her husband was away from home, but the passage doesn't state that wives were no longer property of their husbands (Choice C). Their position didn't degenerate (Choice D) or change radically (Choice A).

6. **J.** According to M. Guizot, "this lonely, dull, and hard castle life was, nevertheless, favorable to the development of domestic society" (lines 61–62). This contradicts Choice G. No mention is made in the passage of the boredom causing fights (Choice F) or wars (Choice H).

7. **A.** The last two paragraphs of the passage discuss the effects of chivalry and Christianity, especially their emphasis on the defense of women. Choices B, C, and D are not mentioned in the passage as relevant to the principles of chivalry and Christianity.

8. **G.** The passage makes it clear that Charlemagne wanted his children to occupy themselves with useful skills. The reader can infer that the "frivolous habits and irregular morals" (lines 30–31) of the princesses would have disappointed their pragmatic father. Choice F is not mentioned in the passage with regard to the princesses. Choice H refers to Charlemagne's sons, not his daughters. Choice J is contradicted by the description of the princesses in the passage.

9. **B.** According to the passage, the study of science and letters declined after the deaths of Charlemagne and his son Louis (paragraph 5, lines 33–38). Choices A, C, and D aren't mentioned as results of the deaths of these two men.

10. **J.** The phrase suggests that the princesses' education didn't fulfill Charlemagne's intentions for them. Because they are described as frivolous and immoral, it can be inferred that they lacked maturity and engaged in idle foolishness. The passage indicates that Charlemagne did value education, so Choice G is incorrect. Choice F is a misreading of the phrase, and Choice H is an inaccurate representation of the information in the passage.

VII. Strategies for Solving ACT Math Problems

You have 60 minutes to answer 60 questions in the Math Section. The 60 questions consist of seven major types of problems, as listed below:

- Pre-Algebra
- Elementary Algebra
- Intermediate Algebra
- Coordinate Geometry
- Plane Geometry
- Trigonometry
- Probability and Statistics

Generally, the ACT Mathematics Test has fewer problems on trigonometry than on the other six topics. On the average, you have about 1 minute per question. Do not linger on any question. Move on.

Do the easy questions first. All questions are worth the same amount of credit. There is no partial credit for any of the questions. You do not need to show work for your answers.

There is no penalty for an incorrect answer. For questions that you do not know how to solve, make an educated guess.

Read, Read, Read. Read each question carefully, particularly with a word problem. Know what information is given to you and determine what the question is asking you to find. Be sure to answer the question.

If a problem contains a graph or a chart, read the labeling of the chart and the scale for the axes carefully. For example, one unit on the x-axis may represent 1 hour, but one unit on the y-axis may represent 10 miles.

Be careful if a problem changes its unit of measurement. For example, a problem may state that a train traveled 180 miles in 3 hours and ask you to find the number of minutes the train will take to cover a distance of 20 miles. You will need to convert hours to minutes.

If a problem involves an equation, sometimes the solution to the equation may not be the final answer to the question. Be sure to know what the question is asking you to find and answer the question.

Sometimes it is easier to work backward by trying each of the given choices as the final answer. Often, you will be able to eliminate a couple of the choices immediately.

If you have trouble solving a problem involving a literal equation with several variables, try substituting numbers for some of the variables and then solve. For example, to solve the equation $at + b = c$ for t, you might substitute numbers for a, b, and c, such as 2, 4, and 8, respectively, and obtain $2t + 4 = 8$. Solve $2t + 4 = 8$ and obtain $t = 2$. Check the given choices for t using $a = 2$, $b = 4$, and $c = 8$ and see which choice is equivalent to $t = 2$. It is possible that substituting random numbers may produce a solution that satisfies more than one of the given choices, especially with problems involving inequalities. In that case, try substituting another set of numbers, find a solution, and look among the given choices for the one that satisfies both solutions.

If a problem contains decimal numbers, do not round off these numbers until the final answer. Carry all decimal numbers at least two more decimal places than the question requires for the final answer, and round the final answer at the last step.

 Before the ACT Mathematics Test, clear all entries (for variables) in your graphing calculator by resetting your RAM. For example, you might have stored a numerical value to the variable x; clear all such entries before the test.

Be sure to remember whether your calculator is set to degree mode or radian mode.

Lastly, trust your instincts. Your first approach to solve a problem is usually the correct one.

Good luck! You can do it.

VIII. Applying Pre-Algebra Skills

On the ACT Mathematics Test, you'll be tested on your pre-algebra skills, which include the concepts of real numbers, linear equations, simple probability, data interpretation, and simple statistics. The practice problems in this chapter are designed to help you review many of the pre-algebra skills. Work the problems, and check your answers with the given explanations.

A. Real Numbers

---

1. If $x^2y = 16$ and $xyz = 0$, which of the following must be true?

   A. $x > 0$
   B. $y < 0$
   C. $y = 0$
   D. $z < 0$
   E. $z = 0$

E is correct because $xyz = 0$; at least one of the variables x, y, or z must be 0. If either $x = 0$ or $y = 0$, the product x^2y would have to equal 0. Since $x^2y = 16$, which implies that neither x nor y is 0, the factor that equals zero must be z.

---

2. Which of the following expressions has a negative value if $p < 0$ and $q < 0$?

   F. $2pq$
   G. $-p^2q$
   H. $\dfrac{p}{q}$
   J. $|-p + q|$
   K. $2p + 3q$

K is correct. One approach is to assign numerical values to p and q and substitute them in the algebraic expression of each of the five choices. For example, let $p = -2$ and $q = -3$. Thus, in Choice F, $2pq = 2(-2)$ $(-3) = 12$; in Choice G, $-p^2q = -(-2)^2(-3) = 12$; in Choice H, $\dfrac{p}{q} = \dfrac{-2}{-3} = \dfrac{2}{3}$; in Choice J, $|-p + q| = |-(-2) +$ $(-3)| = 1$; and in Choice K, $2p + 3q = 2(-2) + 3(-3) = -13$, which is a negative value. When evaluating the numerical expressions, you must follow PEMDAS, the order of operations: **P**arentheses, **E**xponents, **M**ultiplication, **D**ivision, **A**ddition, and **S**ubtraction. Multiplication and division are performed from left to right. For example, $40 \div 4 \times 2 = 10 \times 2 = 20$. Addition and subtraction are also performed from left to right. If you are using a calculator, you could just enter the entire numerical expression as shown above. The calculator will follow PEMDAS.

B. Integers

1. Which of the following is NOT a factor of 72?

   A. 8
   B. 16
   C. 24
   D. 36
   E. 72

B is correct. A number is a factor of 72 if the remainder is zero when 72 is divided by the number. If you divide 72 by 8, 24, 36, or 72, the remainder is zero. If you divide 72 by 16, the remainder is 8. Thus, 16 is not a factor of 72. Alternatively, the prime factorization of 72 is (2)(2)(2)(3)(3), and the prime factorization of 16 is (2)(2)(2)(2). Since 16 has four factors of 2 and 72 has only three factors of 2, 16 cannot be a factor of 72.

2. If n is a positive integer, which of the following expressions always represents an odd integer?

   F. $n + 5$
   G. $2n - 4$
   H. $3n + 3$
   J. $6n + 3$
   K. $n^2 + 1$

J is correct. Test each choice by substituting values for n. Because even/odd results are influenced by whether the number substituted is even or odd, you must use an even number and an odd number when you test. When you substitute 4 for n, $n + 5 = 9$, $2n - 4 = 4$, $3n + 3 = 15$, $6n + 3 = 27$, and $n^2 + 1 = 17$. Choice G is eliminated. Then substitute 3 for n in the remaining choices: $n + 5 = 8$, $3n + 3 = 12$, $6n + 3 = 21$, and $n^2 + 1 = 10$. The expression that represents an odd integer is $6n + 3$.

3. If n and k are both prime numbers, which of the following is NOT a possible value of nk?

   A. 10
   B. 13
   C. 33
   D. 35
   E. 49

B is correct. Each choice, except for Choice B, may be expressed as a product of two prime numbers: $10 = (5)(2)$, $33 = (3)(11)$, $35 = (7)(5)$, $49 = (7)(7)$. Choice B, 13, can never be expressed as a product of primes because 13 is a prime number and has only 1 and itself as factors, and 1 is not a prime number.

4. If a positive integer, n, is divisible by 2, 5, and 6, which of the following must also be divisible by 2, 5, and 6?

    F. $n + 10$

    G. $n + 12$

    H. $n + 13$

    J. $n^2 - 13$

    K. $2n + 30$

K is correct. Since n is a positive integer divisible by 2, 5, and 6, a possible value for n is 30. Now substitute 30 for n in the given choices, and you have $n + 10 = 40$, $n + 12 = 42$, $n + 13 = 43$, $n^2 - 13 = 887$, and $2n + 30 = 90$. Only Choice K produces an answer that is divisible by 2, 5, and 6. Thus, $2n + 30$, Choice K, is the correct answer. You could also use a different approach that is based on the fact that if two numbers are divisible by 2, 5, and 6, then their sum, difference, and product are also divisible by 2, 5, and 6. Inspecting the given choices, you have n, n^2, and $2n$ all divisible by 2, 5, and 6. Looking at the constants in the given choices, you have 10, 12, and 13 not divisible by 2, 5, and 6, and thus, Choices F, G, H, and J are eliminated. For Choice K, you know that 30 is divisible by 2, 5, and 6. Therefore, the sum $2n + 30$, Choice K, is divisible by 2, 5, and 6.

C. Fractions and Decimals

1. If $b < -1 < a < 0$, which of the following has the smallest value?

    A. $-b^3$

    B. $-b$

    C. ab

    D. $-a^2$

    E. a^3

D is correct. You can either consider each choice or select values and substitute. If you consider each choice:

- Choice A: Since b is less than -1, b^3 is also less than -1, and $-b^3$ is greater than 1.
- Choice B: Since b is less than -1, $-b$ is more than 1.
- Choice C: Since a and b are both negative, their product is positive, and ab is positive.
- Choice D: Since a^2 is always positive, $-a^2$ is negative.
- Choice E: Since a is negative, a^3 is negative.

Since negative numbers are smaller than positive numbers, Choices A, B, and C are eliminated. For example, a^3 and $-a^2$ are both between -1 and 0; if you let $a = -0.5$, then $a^3 = -0.125$ and $-a^2 = -0.25$. Thus, $-a^2 < a^3$. The smallest value is $-a^2$.

If you substitute values, let $b = -10$ and $a = -0.5$, then $-b^3 = 1000$, $-b = 10$, $ab = 5$, $-a^2 = -0.25$, and $a^3 = -0.125$. The smallest value is -0.25, which is $-a^2$.

---

2. On the number line, a, b, c, d, and e are equally spaced between -2 and 1. Which of the following fractions has the greatest value?

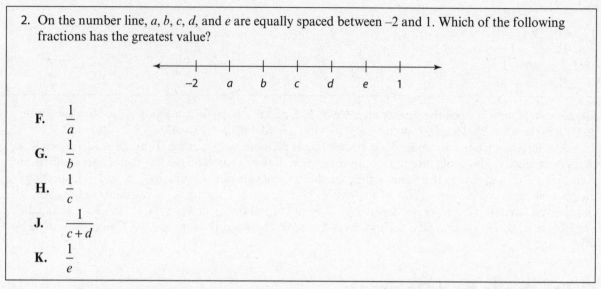

   F. $\dfrac{1}{a}$

   G. $\dfrac{1}{b}$

   H. $\dfrac{1}{c}$

   J. $\dfrac{1}{c+d}$

   K. $\dfrac{1}{e}$

K is correct. The length of the segment from -2 to 1 is 3. Because the interval from -2 to 1 has been divided into 6 equal segments, each segment is 0.5 in length, and $a = -1.5$, $b = -1$, $c = -0.5$, $d = 0$, and $e = 0.5$. Since a, b, and c are negative and $d = 0$, when evaluated, Choices F, G, H, and J will be negative. Since e is positive, only the value of Choice K is positive.

The greatest value must be $\dfrac{1}{e}$.

---

3. As part of the high school physical fitness program, each of the 180 students in a school was required to sign up for exactly one activity: soccer, baseball, table tennis, or volleyball. If $\dfrac{1}{2}$ of the students signed up for soccer, $\dfrac{1}{3}$ signed up for baseball, and of the remaining students, twice as many signed up for volleyball as table tennis, how many students signed up for table tennis?

   A. 5
   B. 10
   C. 15
   D. 20
   E. 30

B is correct. Since $\dfrac{1}{2}$ of the students signed up for soccer, $\dfrac{1}{2}(180)$ or 90 students signed up for soccer. Since $\dfrac{1}{3}$ of the students signed up for baseball, $\dfrac{1}{3}(180)$ or 60 students signed up for baseball. The $180 - (90 + 60)$ or 30 remaining students played table tennis or volleyball, and of these students, twice as many signed up for volleyball than signed up for table tennis. The number of students who signed up for table tennis, x, can be obtained from the equation $2x + x = 30$. Thus $x = 10$.

---

4. What is the least common denominator when adding the fractions $\frac{x}{6}$, $\frac{1}{12}$, and $\frac{y}{18}$?

    F. 6
    G. 18
    H. 36
    J. 216
    K. 1,296

H is correct. One approach to the problem is to test each number in the choices beginning with the smallest. Remember that the least common denominator (LCD) must be divisible by all three denominators: 6, 12, and 18. Thus, 36 is the LCD. Another approach is to express each denominator as a product of its prime factors. Thus, $6 = 2 \times 3$, $12 = 2 \times 2 \times 3$, and $18 = 2 \times 3 \times 3$. The LCD must contain the prime factors of all three denominators. Therefore, the LCD $= 2 \times 2 \times 3 \times 3$ or 36.

D. Absolute Value

---

1. What is the value of $|-6 + 4(-5)|$?

    A. −26
    B. −10
    C. 10
    D. 26
    E. 50

D is correct. Remember the absolute value of a number is always greater than or equal to zero. First, evaluate the expression by following PEMDAS, the order of operations (see page 135). Thus,

$$|-6 + 4(-5)| = |-6 - 20| = |-26| \text{ or } 26$$

---

2. If a and b are nonzero numbers and $|a + b| = |a| + |b|$, then which of the following must be true?

    F. $a = b$
    G. $ab > 0$
    H. $ab < 0$
    J. $a > b$
    K. $b > a$

G is correct. The equation $|a + b| = |a| + |b|$ is true only when both a and b are positive or both are negative. For example, $|3 + 4| = |3| + |4|$ and $|(-3) + (-4)| = |-3| + |-4|$. If a and b have different signs, the equation is false, $|-3 + 4| \neq |-3| + |4|$. Therefore, the choice that must be true is $ab > 0$.

3. In the xy-plane, which of the following points lies on the graph of the equation $-2|x| + y = 2$?

   A. $(-3,8)$
   B. $(-1,0)$
   C. $(0,-2)$
   D. $(4,-1)$
   E. $(6,-2)$

A is correct. If a point lies on the graph of an equation, then the coordinates of the point satisfy the equation. Substitute the coordinates of each point in the five choices into the equation and check. In Choice A, using $x = -3$ and $y = 8$, you have $-2|-3| + 8 = 2$, or $-6 + 8 = 2$, or $2 = 2$. Thus, the coordinates satisfy the equation. The point that is on the graph is $(-3,8)$. Since Choice A worked, there is no need to try the other answer choices.

E. Scientific Notation

1. What is the value of $(3.5 \times 10^8)(4.8 \times 10^{-2})$?

   A. 16.8×10^{-14}
   B. 1.68×10^5
   C. 1.68×10^4
   D. 1.68×10^7
   E. 16.8×10^7

D is correct. Apply the commutative property of multiplication and rewrite $(3.5 \times 10^8)(4.8 \times 10^{-2})$ as $(3.5 \times 4.8) \times (10^8 \times 10^{-2})$, which is equivalent to $16.8 \times 10^{8 + (-2)}$ or 16.8×10^6.

Then express 16.8×10^6 in scientific notation, and you have $1.68 \times 10 \times 10^6$ or 1.68×10^7.

2. What is the value of $\dfrac{2.4 \times 10^{-2}}{6 \times 10^{-6}}$?

   F. 4×10^{-7}
   G. 4×10^{-4}
   H. 4×10^3
   J. 4×10^4
   K. 4×10^7

H is correct. Dividing 2.4 by 6, you have 0.4, and dividing 10^{-2} by 10^{-6}, you have $10^{-2-(-6)}$ or 10^4. Thus, $\dfrac{2.4 \times 10^{-2}}{6 \times 10^{-6}} = 0.4 \times 10^4$, which is equivalent to $(4 \times 10^{-1}) \times 10^4$ or 4×10^3.

F. Exponents and Radicals

---

1. If $5^4(5^a) = 5^{20}$, what is the value of a?

   A. 5
   B. 6
   C. 10
   D. 16
   E. 80

D is correct. Since you are trying to find an exponent, express each side as a power with the same base and set the exponents equal. Since $5^4(5^a) = 5^{(4+a)}$, you can set $5^{(4+a)} = 5^{20}$ and $4 + a = 20$ or $a = 16$.

---

2. If $\sqrt[3]{x} = 2$ and $y^2 = 16$, which of the following could be a value of $x - y$?

   F. −8
   G. −2
   H. 6
   J. 8
   K. 12

K is correct. Since $\sqrt[3]{x} = 2$, raise both sides to the third power, and you have $\left(\sqrt[3]{x}\right)^3 = (2)^3$ or $x = 8$, and since $y^2 = 16$, $y = \pm 4$. Therefore, $x - y$ could be $8 - 4 = 4$ or $8 - (-4) = 12$, which is the only correct answer shown in the choices.

---

3. What is the value of $\sqrt[3]{8} + \left(\dfrac{1}{2}\right)^{-2} - 4^0$?

   A. 0
   B. $\dfrac{5}{4}$
   C. 3
   D. 5
   E. 7

D is correct. Evaluating each term, you have $\sqrt[3]{8} = 2$, $\left(\dfrac{1}{2}\right)^{-2} = \left(\dfrac{2}{1}\right)^2 = 4$, and $-4^0 = -1$. Therefore,

$$\sqrt[3]{8} + \left(\frac{1}{2}\right)^{-2} - 4^0 = 2 + 4 - 1 \text{ or } 5.$$

G. Percents

1. If n is a positive number, which of the following represents $2n$ percent of 150?

   A. $3n$
   B. $30n$
   C. $60n$
   D. $75n$
   E. $300n$

A is correct. Since $2n\%$ is $\dfrac{2n}{100}$, then $2n\%$ of 150 is equivalent to $\dfrac{2n}{100}(150) = 3n$.

2. The accompanying circle graph shows how John's salary in 2013 was determined. If John earned a total of \$18,000 in overtime pay in 2013, how much did he receive as bonuses?

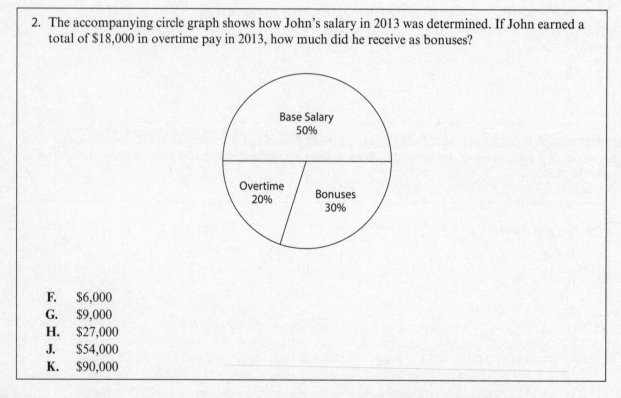

   F. \$6,000
   G. \$9,000
   H. \$27,000
   J. \$54,000
   K. \$90,000

H is correct. Let x be John's annual salary. Since the overtime pay was 20% of John's salary, $0.2x = 18,000$ or $x = 90,000$. Since the bonuses were 30% of John's salary, $0.3x = 0.3(90,000) = 27,000$. Thus, John's bonuses for 2013 were \$27,000. You can also do this problem by setting up a proportion to find the bonuses. Let y be the bonuses. Then $\dfrac{0.2}{18,000} = \dfrac{0.3}{y}$ or $0.2y = (0.3)(18,000)$. Thus, $y = 27,000$.

3. Two rounds of auditions were being held to select 40 students for a new chorus that was being formed. In the first round of auditions, 30 students were selected, 80% of whom were girls. If 25% of the members of the chorus had to be boys, how many boys had to be selected in the second round of auditions?

    A.   4
    B.   6
    C.   8
    D.   10
    E.   12

A is correct. If 25% of the 40 chorus members must be boys, there must be a total of 0.25(40) = 10 boys selected. In the first round, since 80% of the 30 students were girls, 20% of the 30 students were boys and 20% of 30 is 0.20(30) = 6. Since 10 boys are needed and 6 were already selected, in the second round, the number of boys selected must be 10 – 6 or 4.

H. Ratios and Proportions

1. If $\frac{2}{5}$ of a number is 30, what is $\frac{1}{3}$ of the number?

    A.   4
    B.   10
    C.   12
    D.   25
    E.   75

D is correct. Let x be the number. Since $\frac{2}{5}$ of the number is 30, you have $\frac{2}{5}x = 30$ or $x = 75$. Thus, $\frac{1}{3}$ of the number is $\frac{1}{3}(75)$ or 25. You can also do this problem by using a proportion: $\frac{\frac{2}{5}}{30} = \frac{\frac{1}{3}}{x}$. Thus, $\frac{2}{5}x = \frac{1}{3}(30)$, or $x = 25$.

2. On a blueprint for an office building, 6 in represents 45 ft. Using this scale, how many inches on the blueprint represent 30 ft?

    F.   1.5
    G.   2
    H.   2.5
    J.   3
    K.   4

K is correct. To find the number of inches on the blueprint, x, use the proportion $\frac{6}{45} = \frac{x}{30}$.

Thus, $45x = 6(30)$ or $x = 4$. Notice that you do not have to convert inches to feet. When you set up a proportion, corresponding quantities must have the same unit of measurement. In this problem, you are comparing inches on the blueprint to height measured in feet. Both blueprint numbers are in the same units, inches, and both heights are in the same units, feet, and so the proportion may be set up. If the height of one building were given in feet and the height of the other building were given in inches, you would have to convert both to feet or both to inches before the proportion could be set up.

---

3. Erica and Niki were the only candidates running for president of the senior class. When the votes were tallied, the ratio of the number of votes that Erica received to the number of votes that Niki received was 3 to 2. If 60 students voted for Erica, how many students voted in the election?

    A.   20
    B.   40
    C.   60
    D.   80
    E.   100

E is correct. To find the number of votes that Niki received, x, solve the proportion $\dfrac{3}{2} = \dfrac{60}{x}$ or $x = 40$. Since 60 students voted for Erica and 40 voted for Niki, the number of students who voted is $60 + 40$ or 100.

I. Linear Equations

---

1. If $2x + 3y = 10$, what is the value of $4x + 6y$?

    A.   15
    B.   20
    C.   30
    D.   40
    E.   60

B is correct. The question did not ask for the individual values of x and y, but instead the value of $4x + 6y$. Notice that $4x + 6y = 2(2x + 3y)$. Multiply both sides of the equation $2x + 3y = 10$ by 2 and you have $2(2x + 3y) = 20$. Thus, $4x + 6y = 20$.

---

2. If $8 - 2(x + 1) = 4x$, what is the value of x?

    F. -3
    G. -1
    H.   1
    J. $\dfrac{7}{6}$
    K.   3

H is correct. Begin by applying the distributive property, and you have $8 - 2x - 2 = 4x$, which is equivalent to $6 - 2x = 4x$. Adding $2x$ to both sides of the equation, you have $6 = 6x$ or $x = 1$.

---

3. What is the value of n if $\frac{1}{2}n - \frac{1}{3}n = 6$?

   A. -36
   B. -6
   C. 1
   D. 6
   E. 36

E is correct. One approach to the problem is to multiply every term of the equation by 6, the least common denominator (LCD) of 2 and 3: $6\left(\frac{1}{2}n\right) - 6\left(\frac{1}{3}n\right) = 6(6)$, which is equivalent to $3n - 2n = 36$ or $n = 36$.

J. Sets

---

1. If A is the set of positive odd integers less than 24 and B is the set of prime numbers less than 20, how many numbers are common to both sets?

   A. 7
   B. 8
   C. 9
   D. 10
   E. 12

A is correct. Because Set B has fewer elements than Set A, list the elements in Set B and see how many elements in Set B are odd integers. The elements in Set B are {2, 3, 5, 7, 11, 13, 17, 19}. The elements in Set B that are positive odd integers less than 24 are {3, 5, 7, 11, 13, 17, 19}. The number of common elements is 7.

---

2. Each of the 24 students in Mr. Martin's class plays tennis, soccer, or both. If 4 students play both sports and 8 play only tennis, how many students play only soccer?

   F. 12
   G. 14
   H. 16
   J. 18
   K. 20

F is correct.

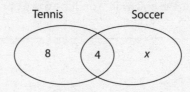

Tennis   Soccer

8   4 x

Set up a Venn diagram with x representing the number of students who only play soccer. Because 4 students play in both sports and 8 students play only tennis, the number of students who only play soccer is $24 - (8 + 4) = 24 - 12 = 12$.

---

3. When x is a member of Set A, the value of $\sqrt{x^2} + x$ is also a member of Set A. Which of the following could be Set A?

   A. $\{-2, 1\}$
   B. $\{-1, 0\}$
   C. $\{-1, 0, 1\}$
   D. $\{0, 1\}$
   E. $\{0, 1, 2\}$

B is correct. Substituting gives the results listed in the following table.

x	-2	-1	0	1	2
$\sqrt{x^2} + x$	0	0	0	2	4

Of the choices, the only set that satisfies the condition is $\{-1, 0\}$.

IX. Solving Elementary Algebra Problems

On the ACT Mathematics Test, you'll be tested on your elementary algebra skills, which include working with algebraic expressions, polynomials, exponents, and quadratic equations. The practice problems in this chapter are designed to help you review many of the elementary algebra skills. Work the problems, and check your answers with the given explanations.

A. Rational Expressions

---

1. For all values of x not equal to 4, which of the following expressions is equivalent to $\dfrac{x^2 - 16}{2x - 8}$?

    A. $\dfrac{x - 4}{2}$

    B. $\dfrac{x}{2} + 4$

    C. $x + 2$

    D. $\dfrac{x + 2}{2}$

    E. $\dfrac{x + 4}{2}$

E is correct. Factoring both the numerator and denominator of $\dfrac{x^2 - 16}{2x - 8}$, you have $\dfrac{(x + 4)(x - 4)}{2(x - 4)}$, which is equivalent to $\dfrac{x + 4}{2}$.

---

2. For all values of x not equal to ± 2, which of the following is equivalent to the sum of $\dfrac{1}{x + 2} + \dfrac{1}{2 - x}$?

    F. $\dfrac{1}{x + 1}$

    G. $\dfrac{2}{x + 2}$

    H. $\dfrac{1}{x^2 - 1}$

    J. $\dfrac{1}{x^2}$

    K. $\dfrac{-4}{x^2 - 4}$

K is correct. Multiply both the numerator and denominator of $\dfrac{1}{2 - x}$ by -1 and you have $\dfrac{-1}{x - 2}$. Now $\dfrac{1}{x + 2} + \dfrac{1}{2 - x}$ becomes $\dfrac{1}{x + 2} - \dfrac{1}{x - 2}$. The least common denominator (LCD) of $(x + 2)$ and $(x - 2)$ is $(x + 2)$ $(x - 2)$. Therefore, $\dfrac{1}{x + 2} - \dfrac{1}{x - 2} = \dfrac{1(x - 2) - 1(x + 2)}{(x + 2)(x - 2)} = \dfrac{x - 2 - x - 2}{(x + 2)(x - 2)}$ or $\dfrac{-4}{x^2 - 4}$.

B. Properties of Exponents

---

1. If $3^n + 3^n + 3^n = 9^6$, what is the value of n?

   A. 2
   B. 3
   C. 4
   D. 11
   E. 12

D is correct. Since you are trying to find an exponent, express each side as a power with the same base and then set the exponents equal.

Since $3^n + 3^n + 3^n = 3(3^n) = (3^1)(3^n) = 3^{n+1}$ and since $9^6 = (3^2)^6 = 3^{12}$, you know that $3^{n+1} = 3^{12}$ and $n + 1 = 12$ or $n = 11$.

---

2. If $(2x^2)^3 = 8x^n$ for all values of x, what is the value of n?

   F. 3
   G. 4
   H. 5
   J. 6
   K. 7

J is correct. Since you are trying to find an exponent, express each side as a power with the same base and set the exponents equal. Since $(2x^2)^3 = 8x^6$ and $(2x^2)^3 = 8x^n$, you know that $8x^6 = 8x^n$ or $n = 6$.

---

3. If $n^a = 5$ and $n^b = 25$, what is the value of n^{2a+b}?

   A. 25
   B. 35
   C. 125
   D. 625
   E. 3,125

D is correct. Since $n^{2a+b} = (n^a)(n^a)(n^b)$ and $n^a = 5$ and $n^b = 25$, you know that $n^{2a+b} = (5)(5)(25)$. The value of n^{2a+b} is 625.

C. Factoring Polynomials

---

1. Which of the following is equivalent to $3x^2 - 11x + 10$ for all values of x?

   A. $(x + 5)(3x + 2)$
   B. $(x - 5)(3x - 2)$
   C. $(x + 2)(3x + 5)$
   D. $(x - 2)(3x + 5)$
   E. $(3x - 5)(x - 2)$

E is correct. One approach to the problem is to multiply the two binomials in each of the five choices and check the results. In Choice E, $(3x - 5)(x - 2) = 3x^2 - 6x - 5x + 10$, which is equivalent to $3x^2 - 11x + 10$, the result that we want. Another approach is to factor the trinomial $3x^2 - 11x + 10$. The possible pairs of factors of $+10$ are $\{1, 10\}$, $\{-1, -10\}$, $\{2, 5\}$, and $\{-2, -5\}$. Since the coefficient of x is -11, only the pairs $\{-1, -10\}$ and $\{-2, -5\}$ are possible. Thus, checking the possible pairs of factors, you have $(3x - 2)(x - 5)$, $(3x - 5)(x - 2)$, $(3x - 1)(x - 10)$, and $(3x - 10)(x - 1)$. Only the product $(3x - 5)(x - 2)$ is $3x^2 - 11x + 10$.

---

2. What is the value of c if $(x - 5)$ is a factor of $3x^2 - 14x + c$ for all values of x?

   F. -15
   G. -5
   H. 5
   J. 6
   K. 15

G is correct. If $(x - 5)$ is a factor of $3x^2 - 14x + c$, then $x = 5$ is a root of the equation $y = 3x^2 - 14x + c$. In other words, if you substitute $x = 5$ in the equation, you'll have $y = 0$. Thus, $3(5)^2 - 14(5) + c = 0$, which is equivalent to $75 - 70 + c = 0$ or $c = -5$.

---

3. For all values of x and y, which of the following is a factor of $x^2 - 4y^2$?

   A. -4
   B. $x - y$
   C. $x + 4y$
   D. $x - 2y$
   E. $2(x + y)$

D is correct. Rewrite $x^2 - 4y^2$ as $(x)^2 - (2y)^2$, which is now expressed as the difference of two squares. Thus, $(x)^2 - (2y)^2 = (x - 2y)(x + 2y)$, with $x - 2y$ as a factor.

4. What is the greatest common factor of $12x^2y$, $15xy^2$, and $18xy$ for all values of x and y?

    F. $2xy$

    G. $3xy$

    H. $3x^2y^2$

    J. $180xy$

    K. $180x^2y^2$

G is correct. Begin with the coefficients 12, 15, and 18. The prime factors are $12 = 2 \times 2 \times 3$, $15 = 3 \times 5$, and $18 = 2 \times 3 \times 3$. Therefore, the greatest common factor (GCF) is 3. The GCF of x^2y, xy^2, and xy is xy. Thus, the GCF of $12x^2y$, $15xy^2$, and $18xy$ is $3xy$.

D. Adding and Subtracting Polynomials

1. What polynomial must be subtracted from $x^2 - 4$ so that the difference is $2x^2 - 3x + 1$?

    A. $-x^2 + 3x - 5$

    B. $x^2 - 3x + 5$

    C. $-x^2 - 3x + 1$

    D. $x^2 + 3x + 5$

    E. $3x^2 - 3x - 3$

A is correct. Subtract each polynomial in the five choices from $x^2 - 4$ and check the result. Begin with Choice A and you have $(x^2 - 4) - (-x^2 + 3x - 5) = x^2 - 4 + x^2 - 3x + 5$ or $2x^2 - 3x + 1$, the desired result. There is no need to check the other answer choices.

2. If the length of a rectangle is represented by $2x$ and the width by $3x + 1$, what is the perimeter of the rectangle in terms of x?

    F. $x + 1$

    G. $5x + 1$

    H. $10x + 2$

    J. $10x + 4$

    K. $6x^2 + 2x$

H is correct. The perimeter of a rectangle equals twice the length plus twice the width. Thus, the perimeter is $2(2x) + 2(3x + 1)$, which is equivalent to $4x + 6x + 2$ or $10x + 2$.

E. Multiplying and Dividing Polynomials

---

1. For all values of x, which of the following is equivalent to $(2x - 1)^2$?

   A. $4x - 2$
   B. $4x^2 + 1$
   C. $4x^2 - 2x + 1$
   D. $4x^2 - 4x + 1$
   E. $4x^2 + 4x + 1$

D is correct. Rewrite $(2x - 1)^2$ as $(2x - 1)(2x - 1)$ and multiply. Thus, $(2x - 1)(2x - 1) = 4x^2 - 2x - 2x + 1$ or $4x^2 - 4x + 1$.

---

2. For all values of $x \neq 0$, which of the following is equivalent to $\dfrac{3x^6 - 2x^4 + x^2}{x^2}$?

   F. $3x^3 - 2x^2 + x$
   G. $3x^3 - 2x^2 + 1$
   H. $3x^4 - 2x^2$
   J. $3x^4 - 2x^2 + 1$
   K. $3x^4 - 2x^4$

J is correct. The expression $\dfrac{3x^6 - 2x^4 + x^2}{x^2}$ is equivalent to dividing each term in the numerator by the denominator x^2. Thus $\dfrac{3x^6}{x^2} - \dfrac{2x^4}{x^2} + \dfrac{x^2}{x^2} = 3x^4 - 2x^2 + 1$. Remember that when you divide monomials with the same base, you subtract exponents.

F. Quadratic Equations

---

1. If x is a real number, how many values of x satisfy the equation $(x + 10)^2 = 25$?

   A.   0
   B.   1
   C.   2
   D.   3
   E.   4

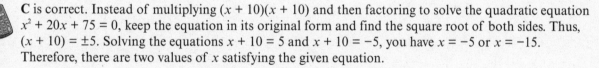

C is correct. Instead of multiplying $(x + 10)(x + 10)$ and then factoring to solve the quadratic equation $x^2 + 20x + 75 = 0$, keep the equation in its original form and find the square root of both sides. Thus, $(x + 10) = \pm 5$. Solving the equations $x + 10 = 5$ and $x + 10 = -5$, you have $x = -5$ or $x = -15$. Therefore, there are two values of x satisfying the given equation.

2. Which of the following is a solution to the equation $y^2 = 4y$?

    F.   −4
    G.   −2
    H.   0
    J.   8
    K.   16

H is correct. Rewrite $y^2 = 4y$ by subtracting $4y$ from both sides of the equation. Thus, you have $y^2 − 4y = 0$. Factor $y^2 − 4y = 0$, and you have $y(y − 4) = 0$. Therefore, either $y = 0$ or $y − 4 = 0$, which is equivalent to $y = 4$. The solutions are 0 and 4, but only 0 is shown among the given choices.

3. Which of the following equations has both $x = h$ and $x = −k$ as roots?

    A. $x^2 + x(h − k) − hk = 0$
    B. $x^2 − x(h − k) + hk = 0$
    C. $x^2 + x(k − h) + hk = 0$
    D. $x^2 + x(h − k) + hk = 0$
    E. $x^2 + x(k − h) − hk = 0$

E is correct. Since the roots of the equation are $x = h$ and $x = −k$, then the equation could be written as $(x − h)(x − (−k)) = 0$, which is equivalent to $(x − h)(x + k) = 0$. Multiplying $(x − h)(x + k)$, you have $x^2 + kx − hx − hk = 0$ or $x^2 + x(k − h) − hk = 0$.

G. Word Problems

1. Three times a number is the same as the number added to 60. What is the number?

    A.   15
    B.   20
    C.   30
    D.   45
    E.   180

C is correct. Let x be the number. Then you have $3x = x + 60$, which is equivalent is to $2x = 60$, or $x = 30$. The number is 30. You could also solve the problem by substituting each answer choice to see which one works.

2. Rebecca has twice as much money as Rachel. If Rebecca gives Rachel $60, then the two of them will have the same amount of money. How much money did Rebecca have originally?

   F. $60
   G. $90
   H. $120
   J. $180
   K. $240

K is correct. Let x be the amount of money that Rachel has. Then $2x$ represents the amount of money that Rebecca has. Since Rebecca gave Rachel $60 and they have the same amount of money, you can write the equation $2x - 60 = x + 60$. Subtracting x from both sides of the equation, you have $x - 60 = 60$ or $x = 120$. Thus, Rachel has $120, and Rebecca has $240. You could also solve this problem by substituting each answer choice to see which one works.

3. There are 200 marbles in a box. All the marbles are either red or blue. If there are 40 more red marbles than blue marbles, how many red marbles are there in the box?

   A. 40
   B. 80
   C. 120
   D. 160
   E. 180

C is correct. Let x be the number of blue marbles and $x + 40$ be the number of red marbles. Since there are 200 marbles in the box, you have $x + x + 40 = 200$, which is equivalent to $2x + 40 = 200$ or $x = 80$. Thus, the number of red marbles is $x + 40$ or 120. You could also solve this problem by substituting each answer choice to see which one works.

4. Erica used a car service that charges $5 per mile plus an initial fee of $20. If the total cost for the car service was $110, what was the distance traveled in miles?

   F. 16
   G. 18
   H. 20
   J. 22
   K. 26

G is correct. Let x be the number of miles of Erica's trip. Then $5x + 20 = 110$, which is equivalent to $5x = 90$ or $x = 18$. Thus, the distance of Erica's trip is 18 miles. You could also solve this problem by substituting each answer choice to see which one works.

X. Studying Intermediate Algebra

On the ACT Mathematics Test, you'll be tested on your intermediate algebra skills, which include working with rational and algebraic expressions, equations and inequalities, logarithmic and exponential functions, complex numbers, sequences, and matrices. The practice problems in this chapter are designed to help you review many of the intermediate algebra skills. Work the problems, and check your answers with the given explanations.

A. Algebraic Expressions

1. If you hire Mary's Car Service to drive you across town, you will be charged $10 plus $2 for each $\frac{1}{4}$ mile. Which of the following represents the total number of dollars that you would be charged if the trip is n miles?

   A. $2n$
   B. $10 + 2n$
   C. $10 + 4n$
   D. $10 + 8n$
   E. $12n$

D is correct. Because you are charged $2 for each $\frac{1}{4}$ mile, the charge for each mile is 4($2) = $8 and the charge for n miles would be $8n$. The total charge, in dollars, is $10 + 8n$.

2. If Janet is n years old, Karen is 2 years younger than Janet, and Mary is 4 years more than twice Janet's age, which of the following represents how many years older Mary is than Karen?

   F. 2
   G. $n - 2$
   H. n
   J. $n + 2$
   K. $n + 6$

K is correct. Because Janet's age is n, Karen's age is $(n - 2)$ and Mary's age is $2n + 4$. Since Mary is older than Karen, the difference in their ages is $(2n + 4) - (n - 2)$, which is equivalent to $2n + 4 - n + 2$ or $n + 6$.

3. Points A, B, C, and D lie on the same line. If B is the midpoint of $\overline{AC}$, C is the midpoint of $\overline{BD}$, and $AD = 12k$, what is the length of $\overline{BD}$ in terms of k?

   A. $2k$
   B. $4k$
   C. $6k$
   D. $8k$
   E. $10k$

D is correct.

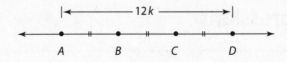

Since B is the midpoint of $\overline{AC}$, $AB = BC$. Since C is the midpoint of $\overline{BD}$, $BC = CD$. Since $AB = BC$ and $BC = CD$, you know that $AB = BC = CD$. Because $AB + BC + CD = AD$ and $AD = 12k$, each segment is $4k$ in length. $BC + CD = 4k + 4k = 8k$ and thus $BD = 8k$.

4. Let n^* be defined as $n^* = n^2 - 3n$ for all integers n. What is the value of n^* if $n = -4$?

   F. -28
   G. -4
   H. 4
   J. 16
   K. 28

K is correct. Substitute -4 for n and do the arithmetic: $(-4)^2 - 3(-4) = 16 + 12$ or 28.

B. Algebraic Expressions Involving Absolute Value

1. $10 - |n + 2| = 4$

   If n is a negative number, what is the value of n?

   A. -2
   B. -6
   C. -8
   D. -10
   E. -16

C is correct. The equation is equivalent to $6 = |n + 2|$. In this form you can see that $n + 2 = 6$ or $n + 2 = -6$, and you have $n = 4$ or $n = -8$. Since n is a negative number, $n = -8$.

2. If x is a negative integer, $\left|\dfrac{x}{2}-1\right|<2$, what is the value of x?

    F. -4

    G. -3

    H. -2

    J. -1

    K. 0

J is correct. The inequality $\left|\dfrac{x}{2}-1\right|<2$ is equivalent to $-2<\left(\dfrac{x}{2}-1\right)<2$. Adding 1 to all three parts, you have $-1<\dfrac{x}{2}<3$. Multiplying by 2, you have $-2<x<6$. Since x is a negative integer, $x=-1$.

3. If $\left|\dfrac{k}{3}-4\right|=\dfrac{k}{3}-4$, what is the smallest possible value for k?

    A. -12

    B. 0

    C. 8

    D. 12

    E. 15

D is correct. The absolute value of a quantity must be greater than or equal to 0. Since $\left|\dfrac{k}{3}-4\right|=\dfrac{k}{3}-4$, you have $\dfrac{k}{3}-4\geq 0$. Solve the inequality, and you have $\dfrac{k}{3}\geq 4$ or $k\geq 12$. Thus, the smallest value for k is 12.

C. Algebraic Expressions Involving Exponents and Radicals

1. If x is a positive integer, $x^a=\dfrac{x^4}{x^b}$, and $x^a=x^2(x^b)$, what is the value of b?

    A. 4

    B. 2

    C. 1

    D. 0

    E. -2

C is correct. Since you are trying to find an exponent, express each side as a power with the same base and set the exponents equal. Since $x^a=\dfrac{x^4}{x^b}$ and $\dfrac{x^4}{x^b}=x^{4-b}$, you know that $x^a=x^{4-b}$ and $a=4-b$. Since $x^a=x^2(x^b)$ and $x^2(x^b)=x^{2+b}$, you know that $x^a=x^{2+b}$ and $a=2+b$. Solving the system $a=4-b$ and $a=2+b$, you have $4-b=2+b$, or $b=1$.

2. What is the value of $x^2 + x^{\frac{1}{4}}$ if $\sqrt{x} = 4$?

   F. 4.5
   G. 5
   H. 20
   J. 254
   K. 258

K is correct. Squaring both sides of the equation $\sqrt{x} = 4$, you have $x = 16$. Therefore, $x^2 + x^{\frac{1}{4}} = (16)^2 + (16)^{\frac{1}{4}} = 256 + 2$ or 258.

3. Which of the following has the greatest value if $0 < x < 1$?

   A. $\sqrt[3]{x}$
   B. $\sqrt{x}$
   C. x
   D. x^2
   E. x^3

A is correct. One approach to the problem is to assign a numerical value to x. For example, let $x = 0.5$, then $\sqrt[3]{x} = \sqrt[3]{0.5} \approx 0.79$, $\sqrt{x} = \sqrt{0.5} \approx 0.71$, $x = 0.5$, $x^2 = (0.5)^2 = 0.25$, and $x^3 = (0.5)^3 = 0.125$. Therefore, $\sqrt[3]{x}$ has the greatest value.

4. If $\sqrt{x+1} - 2 = 7$, what is the value of x?

   F. 24
   G. 26
   H. 80
   J. 81
   K. 82

H is correct. Isolate the radical by adding 2 to both sides of the equation, and you have $\sqrt{x+1} = 9$. Squaring both sides gives you $x + 1 = 81$ or $x = 80$. Checking $x = 80$ with the original equation, you have $\sqrt{80+1} - 2 = 7$ or $7 = 7$.

D. Equations

1. For which positive number is 16 times the cube root of the number the same as the number?

   A. 4
   B. 8
   C. 10
   D. 32
   E. 64

E is correct. If x is the number, then $16\left(\sqrt[3]{x}\right) = x$. Cubing both sides, you have $4{,}096x = x^3$ or $x^3 - 4{,}096x = 0$. Factoring the equation $x^3 - 4{,}096x = 0$, you have $x(x^2 - 4{,}096) = 0$. Thus $x = 0$ or $x = \pm\sqrt{4{,}096} = \pm 64$. Since x is a positive number, $x = 64$.

2. If $a > b$ and $ay - by = 4$, what is the value of y when $(a - b)^2 = 4$?

   F. 0
   G. 1
   H. 2
   J. 4
   K. 8

H is correct. Since $(a - b)^2 = 4$, you know that $(a - b) = \pm 2$. Because $a > b$, you know $a - b > 0$ and $a - b = 2$. To find y when $a - b = 2$, express $ay - by = 4$ in the factored form: $y(a - b) = 4$. Now substitute 2 for $(a - b)$. Then $(y)(2) = 4$ and $y = 2$.

3. If $(a - 1)(b + 2)(c - 3) = 0$, what is the smallest value for $a^2 + b^2 + c^2$?

   A. 0
   B. 1
   C. 4
   D. 9
   E. 14

B is correct. In order for $(a - 1)(b + 2)(c - 3)$ to have a value of zero, only one of the following three conditions must be met: $a = 1$ or $b = -2$ or $c = 3$. If you let $a = 1$ and then choose to let $b = 0$ and $c = 0$, the product of $(a - 1)(b + 2)(c - 3)$ will be zero and the value of $a^2 + b^2 + c^2$ will be the smallest value possible or $(1)^2 + (0)^2 + (0)^2 = 1$.

E. Inequalities

---

1. If $\dfrac{1}{6} < \dfrac{3}{n} < \dfrac{1}{4}$, how many integral values of n are possible?

    A. 1
    B. 3
    C. 5
    D. 6
    E. 7

C is correct. The inequality $\dfrac{1}{6} < \dfrac{3}{n} < \dfrac{1}{4}$ is equivalent to $\dfrac{1}{6} < \dfrac{3}{n}$ and $\dfrac{3}{n} < \dfrac{1}{4}$. Solving $\dfrac{1}{6} < \dfrac{3}{n}$, you have $n < 18$. Similarly, solving $\dfrac{3}{n} < \dfrac{1}{4}$, you have $12 < n$ or $n > 12$. Since $n > 12$ and $n < 18$, n must be 13, 14, 15, 16, or 17. There are 5 integral values for n.

---

2. Five years ago, Mary was at least 3 more than twice Karen's age. If k represents Karen's age now and m represents Mary's age now, which of the following describes the relationship of their ages 5 years ago?

    F. $m > 2k + 3$
    G. $m > 2k - 3$
    H. $m + 5 > 2(k + 5) - 3$
    J. $m - 5 \le 2(k + 5) + 3$
    K. $m - 5 \ge 2(k - 5) + 3$

K is correct.

	Current age	Age 5 years ago
Mary	m	$m - 5$
Karen	k	$k - 5$

Five years ago, Mary's age was $m - 5$ and Karen's age was $k - 5$. If 5 years ago Mary had been 3 years more than twice Karen's age, the relationship of their ages would have been described as $m - 5 = 2(k - 5) + 3$. Since 5 years ago, Mary was *at least* 3 years more than twice Karen's age, the equation becomes an inequality: $m - 5 \ge 2(k - 5) + 3$.

3. If a and b are positive integers and $(a - b)^2 = 36$, which of the following must be true?

   A. $a^2 + b^2 < 36$
   B. $a^2 + b^2 > 36$
   C. $a^2 + b^2 = 36$
   D. $a^2 - b^2 = 36$
   E. $a - b = 6$

B is correct. Since $(a - b)^2 = a^2 - 2ab + b^2$, you know that $a^2 - 2ab + b^2 = 36$ or $a^2 + b^2 = 36 + 2ab$. Because a and b are positive integers, $2ab$ is positive. Thus, $a^2 + b^2 = 36 + 2ab$ is equivalent to $a^2 + b^2 = 36 +$ (a positive number). Therefore, $a^2 + b^2 > 36$.

F. Systems of Equations

1. If $4a - 5b = 20$ and $b = 4$, what is the value of $2b + 5a$?

   A. -42
   B. 0
   C. 8
   D. 30
   E. 58

E is correct. Since $b = 4$ and $4a - 5b = 20$, you know that $4a - 5(4) = 20$ or $4a = 40$ or $a = 10$. Because $a = 10$ and $b = 4$, $2b + 5a = 2(4) + 5(10)$ or 58.

2. If $a > 0$, $c > 0$, $a^2b = 9$, and $bc^2 = 25$, what is the value of abc?

   F. 15
   G. 25
   H. 45
   J. 75
   K. 225

F is correct. When you multiply the equations $a^2b = 9$ and $bc^2 = 25$, you have $(a^2b)(bc^2) = (9)(25)$ or $a^2b^2c^2 = 225$ and $abc = \pm15$. Because $a > 0$ and $c > 0$ and $a^2b = 9 > 0$, you know that $b > 0$. Thus, $abc = 15$.

3. At the beginning of the school year, Caitlin paid $22 for 4 pens and 3 notebooks. Two months later, she decided to buy 6 more of the same pens and 5 more of the same notebooks before the price changed. If she spent $35 on these additional pens and notebooks, what was the cost, in dollars, of 1 notebook?

A. 2

B. $2\dfrac{1}{2}$

C. 4

D. 5

E. 8

C is correct. Let p be the price of a pen and n be the price of a notebook, then $4p + 3n = 22$ and $6p + 5n = 35$. To solve for n, multiply the first equation by -3 and the second by 2 and then add them together:

$$
\begin{aligned}
-12p - 9n &= -66 \\
\underline{12p + 10n} &= \underline{70} \\
n &= 4
\end{aligned}
$$

The number of dollars that 1 notebook cost was 4.

G. Functions

1. If $f(x) = x^2 - 4$ and $g(x) = x + 2$, then what is the value of $f(g(-4))$?

A. −8

B. −4

C. 0

D. 4

E. 8

C is correct. Begin by evaluating $g(-4)$, which is $g(-4) = (-4) + 2$ or -2. Therefore, $f(g(-4)) = f(-2)$, and evaluating $f(-2)$, you have $f(-2) = (-2)^2 - 4 = 4 - 4$ or 0.

2. If the function f is defined by $f(x) = 2x - 6$, which of the following is equivalent to $5f(x) + 10$?

F. $10x - 40$

G. $10x - 20$

H. $10x + 4$

J. $10x + 20$

K. $7x + 4$

G is correct. Since $f(x) = 2x - 6$, you have $5f(x) + 10 = 5(2x - 6) + 10$, which is equivalent to $10x - 20$.

3. The life expectancy of a certain virus is given by the function $L(t) = \dfrac{12t + 36}{t + 1}$, $t \le 120$, where t is the temperature in Celsius of the environment in which the virus is placed, and L is the number of minutes that the virus will survive in that environment. What is the change in life expectancy, in minutes, if the temperature is raised from 7°C to 23°C?

   A.   −16
   B.   −2
   C.   15
   D.   16
   E.   30

B is correct. At 7°C, the life expectancy of the virus is $L(7) = \dfrac{12(7) + 36}{7 + 1} = \dfrac{120}{8} = 15$ minutes, and at 23°C it is $L(23) = \dfrac{12(23) + 36}{23 + 1} = \dfrac{312}{24} = 13$ minutes. Therefore, the change in life expectancy is $13 - 15$ or -2 minutes.

4. Some of the values of the function f are shown in the accompanying table. If a function h is defined by $h(x) = 2f(x - 1)$, what is the value of $h(2)$?

x	f(x)
−3	−1
−2	0
−1	4
0	2
1	−3
2	4
3	5

   F.   −6
   G.   −3
   H.   4
   J.   5
   K.   7

F is correct. Since $h(x) = 2f(x - 1)$, $h(2) = 2f(2 - 1)$ or $h(2) = 2f(1)$. The table shows that $f(1) = -3$. Thus, $2f(1) = 2(-3)$ or -6.

H. Logarithmic and Exponential Functions

1. If $\log_x 16 = 2$, what is the value of x?

   A. -4

   B. $\dfrac{1}{4}$

   C. $\dfrac{1}{2}$

   D. 4

   E. 8

D is correct. One of the properties of a logarithm is that if $a > 0$, $a \neq 1$, and $\log_a b = c$, then $a^c = b$. Since $\log_x 16 = 2$, you have $x^2 = 16$ and $x = \pm 4$. Since $x > 0$, you have $x = 4$.

2. If $3(5^x) = 375$, what is the value of x?

   F. 3

   G. 25

   H. 120

   J. 125

   K. 625

F is correct. Begin by dividing both sides of the equation by 3, and you have $5^x = 125$. Notice that $125 = 5^3$ and rewrite $5^x = 125$ as $5^x = 5^3$. Thus, $x = 3$.

3. If $\log_4 32 + \log_4 2 = \log_2 x$, what is the value of x?

   A. 3

   B. 8

   C. 32

   D. 68

   E. 128

B is correct. One of the properties of a logarithm is that if a, b, and $c > 0$, and $a \neq 1$, then $\log_a(bc) = \log_a b + \log_a c$. Therefore, rewrite $\log_4 32 + \log_4 2$ as $\log_4 (32)(2)$, which is equivalent to $\log_4 (64)$ and $\log_4 (64) = 3$ since $4^3 = 64$. Now that the left side of the equation is 3, you have $3 = \log_2 x$, which is equivalent to $2^3 = x$ or $x = 8$.

I. Modeling

> 1. In a printing company, if one machine can print 600 copies in 12 hours, how many hours would it take to print 1,200 copies with three identical machines working together?
>
>   **A.** 4
>   **B.** 6
>   **C.** 8
>   **D.** 10
>   **E.** 12

C is correct. Since it takes 12 hours for one machine to print 600 copies, it would take 24 hours for one machine to print 1,200 copies. If three machines worked together to print 1,200 copies, it would take $\frac{24}{3}$ or 8 hours. You could also use an inverse proportion. The more machines you use, the less time it would require to print 1,200 copies.

Number of machines	Hours	# of copies
1	24	1,200
3	x	1,200

Since the number of copies is the same, you have $(1)(24) = (3)(x)$ or $x = 8$ hours.

> 2. If Marissa drove for h hours at an average rate of m miles per hour and then she drove for k hours at an average rate of n miles per hour, what is the total distance, in miles, that she drove?
>
>   **F.** $m + n$
>   **G.** $\dfrac{m + n}{h + k}$
>   **H.** $\dfrac{m}{h} + \dfrac{n}{k}$
>   **J.** $(h + k)(m + n)$
>   **K.** $mh + nk$

K is correct. Since Distance = Rate × Time, when Marissa drove for h hours at an average of m miles per hour, the distance was mh miles. Similarly, when she drove for k hours at an average rate of n miles per hour, the distance was nk miles. The total distance, in miles, is $mh + nk$.

3. In a music class with 22 students, each student plays only the violin, plays only the cello, or plays both. If 4 students play both the violin and the cello, and of the remaining students, twice as many play the violin as play the cello, how many students play only the cello?

   A.   4
   B.   6
   C.   8
   D.   10
   E.   12

B is correct.

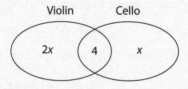

Set up a Venn diagram with x representing the number of students who play only the cello and $2x$ representing the number of students who play only the violin. Since there are 22 students in the class, $2x + x + 4 = 22$. Solve the equation, and you find $x = 6$. The number of students who play only the cello is 6.

4. Mrs. Cohen bought a box of individually wrapped chocolates and decided to give the chocolates to her students. If she gave each student 2 pieces of chocolate, 25 pieces would be left in the box. If she gave each student 3 pieces, 5 pieces would be left in the box. How many students are in her class?

   F.   15
   G.   20
   H.   30
   J.   40
   K.   65

G is correct. If x is the number of students in Mrs. Cohen's class and y is the number of pieces of chocolate in the box, then $2x + 25 = y$ and $3x + 5 = y$ or $2x + 25 = 3x + 5$ and $x = 20$. The number of students in Mrs. Cohen's class is 20.

J. Complex Numbers

1. Given $i^2 = -1$, what is the value of $(3 - i)(3 + i)$?

   A. 5
   B. 8
   C. 10
   D. 12
   E. 13

C is correct. Multiply $(3 - i)$ and $(3 + i)$ by applying the distributive property, and you have $9 + 3i - 3i - i^2$ or $9 - i^2$. Since $i^2 = -1$, $9 - i^2 = 9 - (-1)$ or 10.

2. For $i^2 = -1$, what is the value of $2i^4 + i^3 - 3i^2 + i$?

   F. -1
   G. 1
   H. 5
   J. $-1 + 2i$
   K. $5 + 2i$

H is correct. Since $i^2 = -1$, you have $2i^4 = 2(1)$, $i^3 = -i$, and $-3i^2 = -3(-1) = 3$. Therefore, $2i^4 + i^3 - 3i^2 + i = 2 - i + 3 + i$ or 5.

3. For $i^2 = -1$, which of the following is equivalent to $\dfrac{1}{1+i} + \dfrac{1}{1-i}$?

   A. -2
   B. $-i$
   C. 0
   D. i
   E. 1

E is correct. Express both $\dfrac{1}{1+i}$ and $\dfrac{1}{1-i}$ in $a + bi$ form. Rewrite $\dfrac{1}{1+i}$ as $\dfrac{1}{1+i} \cdot \dfrac{1-i}{1-i} = \dfrac{1-i}{1-i^2} = \dfrac{1-i}{1-(-1)} = \dfrac{1-i}{2}$ or $\dfrac{1}{2} - \dfrac{i}{2}$. Also, rewrite $\dfrac{1}{1-i}$ as $\dfrac{1}{1-i} \cdot \dfrac{1+i}{1+i} = \dfrac{1+i}{1-i^2} = \dfrac{1+i}{1-(-1)} = \dfrac{1+i}{2}$ or $\dfrac{1}{2} + \dfrac{i}{2}$. Therefore, $\dfrac{1}{1+i} + \dfrac{1}{1-i} = \dfrac{1}{2} - \dfrac{i}{2} + \dfrac{1}{2} + \dfrac{i}{2}$ or 1.

An alternate solution is to add the two fractions as follows: $\dfrac{1}{1+i} + \dfrac{1}{1-i} = \dfrac{1-i+1+i}{(1+i)(1-i)} = \dfrac{2}{1-i^2} = \dfrac{2}{2} = 1$.

K. Patterns and Sequences

1. If the kth term of a sequence is defined as $5k - 1$, what is the value of the smallest term greater than 100?

   A. 20
   B. 21
   C. 104
   D. 109
   E. 504

C is correct. Since the value of the kth term is $5k - 1$, solve $5k - 1 > 100$, and you have $5k > 101$ or $k > 20.2$. Since k has to be an integer, and the smallest integer greater than 20.2 is 21, $k = 21$ and $5k - 1 = 104$, which is the smallest term greater than 100. Note that you can eliminate Choices A and B right away since they are both less than 100.

2. If the first term of a sequence is 2 and each successive term is found by multiplying the preceding term by -3, what is the sum of the fourth and fifth terms?

   F. -216
   G. -108
   H. 108
   J. 162
   K. 216

H is correct. Since this is a geometric sequence, using the formula $a_n = a_1(r^{n-1})$, you have the fourth term $a_4 = (2)(-3)^{(4-1)} = 2(-3)^3 = -54$ and the fifth term $a_5 = 2(-3)^{(5-1)} = 162$. The sum of the fourth and fifth terms is $162 + (-54)$ or 108.

3. $1^2, 2^2, 3^2, 4^2, \ldots$

   The first 4 terms of a sequence are shown here. If the sum of the first nth terms is greater than 100, what is the smallest value of n?

   A. 6
   B. 7
   C. 8
   D. 10
   E. 17

B is correct. To find when the sum will be more than 100, start adding the terms: $1^2 + 2^2 = 5$; $1^2 + 2^2 + 3^2 = 14$. When you reach $1^2 + 2^2 + 3^2 + 4^2 + 5^2 + 6^2 = 91$, and $1^2 + 2^2 + 3^2 + 4^2 + 5^2 + 6^2 + 7^2 = 140$, you know that the first time the sum is greater than 100 occurs when $n = 7$. The smallest value of n is 7.

L. Matrices

1. The matrices A and B are given here:

$$A = \begin{bmatrix} -4 & 0 \\ 2 & 1 \end{bmatrix} \text{ and } B = \begin{bmatrix} 3 & 2 \\ -1 & 5 \end{bmatrix}$$

If $X = 3A - 2B$, which of the following is X?

A. $\begin{bmatrix} -4 & 0 \\ 2 & 1 \end{bmatrix}$

B. $\begin{bmatrix} -1 & -2 \\ 3 & -4 \end{bmatrix}$

C. $\begin{bmatrix} -15 & -2 \\ 7 & 2 \end{bmatrix}$

D. $\begin{bmatrix} -6 & 4 \\ 4 & -13 \end{bmatrix}$

E. $\begin{bmatrix} -18 & -4 \\ 8 & -7 \end{bmatrix}$

E is correct. Since $X = 3A - 2B$, you have $X = 3\begin{bmatrix} -4 & 0 \\ 2 & 1 \end{bmatrix} - 2\begin{bmatrix} 3 & 2 \\ -1 & 5 \end{bmatrix} = \begin{bmatrix} -12 & 0 \\ 6 & 3 \end{bmatrix} - \begin{bmatrix} 6 & 4 \\ -2 & 10 \end{bmatrix}$

$$= \begin{bmatrix} -12-6 & 0-4 \\ 6-(-2) & 3-10 \end{bmatrix} = \begin{bmatrix} -18 & -4 \\ 8 & -7 \end{bmatrix}.$$

2. If $\begin{bmatrix} x & -6 \\ 3 & 10 \end{bmatrix} = \begin{bmatrix} 4 & 2y \\ 3 & 10 \end{bmatrix}$, what is the value of $x + y$?

F. -8
G. -4
H. -2
J. 1
K. 2

J is correct. Since the two matrices are equal, you have $x = 4$ and $-6 = 2y$ or $-3 = y$. Therefore, $x + y = 4 + (-3)$ or 1.

3. What is the matrix product of $\begin{bmatrix} 2 & -1 & 0 \end{bmatrix} \begin{bmatrix} 4 \\ 6 \\ -3 \end{bmatrix}$?

  A. $[-48]$
  B. $[-1]$
  C. $[2]$
  D. $\begin{bmatrix} 8 & -6 & 0 \end{bmatrix}$

  E. $\begin{bmatrix} 8 \\ -6 \\ 0 \end{bmatrix}$

C is correct. Since $\begin{bmatrix} 2 & -1 & 0 \end{bmatrix}$ is a 1×3 matrix and $\begin{bmatrix} 4 \\ 6 \\ -3 \end{bmatrix}$ is a 3×1 matrix, their product is a 1×1 matrix.

The product is $[2(4) + (-1)(6) + 0(-3)]$ or $[8 - 6 + 0]$, which is $[2]$.

XI. Answering Coordinate Geometry Questions

On the ACT Mathematics Test, you'll be tested on many concepts of coordinate geometry, including your understanding of graphing points, lines, inequalities, conics, and other curves. You are also expected to know and apply the distance, midpoint, and slope formulas (see below). The practice problems in this chapter are designed to help you review many of the coordinate geometry concepts. Work the problems, and check your answers with the given explanations. Here are the distance, midpoint, and slope formulas for reference:

Given $A(x_1, y_1)$ and $B(x_2, y_2)$:

- The **distance** between A and B (the length of $\overline{AB}$): $d_{\overline{AB}} = \sqrt{(x_2 - x_1)^2 + (y_2 - y_1)^2}$

- The **midpoint** of $\overline{AB}$: $\left(\dfrac{x_1 + x_2}{2}, \dfrac{y_1 + y_2}{2}\right)$. Think of a midpoint as the "average."

- The **slope** of $\overline{AB}$: $m_{\overline{AB}} = \dfrac{y_2 - y_1}{x_2 - x_1}$.

A. Points, Lines, and Planes

1. Which of the following is a relation that contains the three ordered pairs (x, y) listed in the table?

x	0	1	2
y	0	3	8

   A. $y = 3x$
   B. $y = 3x^2$
   C. $y = x^3$
   D. $y = x^2 + 2x$
   E. $y = x^3 + 2x$

D is correct. A relation contains the given ordered pair if substituting the given value of x produces the given value of y. To determine which of the equations contains all three pairs, choose an equation and substitute $x = 0$. If the answer is $y = 0$, test the next value of x by substituting $x = 1$. If that answer is $y = 3$, test the third value of x by substituting $x = 2$. If the answer is $y = 8$, then the relation contains all three ordered pairs. Only $y = x^2 + 2x$ contains all three pairs.

> Note: If you use a graphing calculator, you can solve this problem without substitution. Just use the [$y_=$] function to enter each equation, and check for the three ordered pairs using [Table].

2. Which of the following points on the accompanying graph has coordinates that satisfy the equation $-|x| + y = 2$?

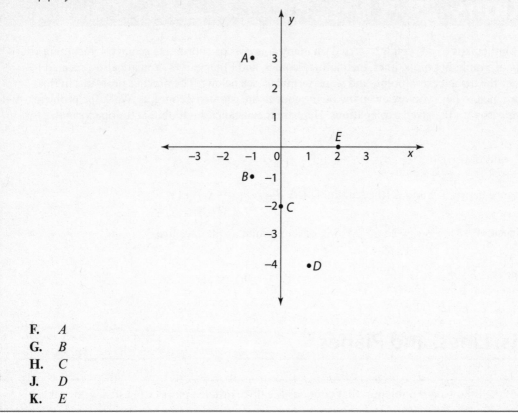

F. A
G. B
H. C
J. D
K. E

F is correct. A point satisfies an equation if substituting produces an equation that is true. Substitute the coordinates of each point into the equation $-|x| + y = 2$. Only when the coordinates of A $(-1,3)$ are substituted is the resulting equation true: $-|-1| + 3 = -1 + 3 = 2$.

3. In the xy-plane, the point $(-4,-2)$ is on the line $-3x + y = k$. What is the value of k?

A. -14
B. -10
C. 10
D. 12
E. 18

C is correct. The coordinates of a point on a line satisfy the equation of the line. Therefore, substitute -4 for x and -2 for y in the equation $-3x + y = k$, and you have $-3(-4) + (-2) = k$ or $k = 10$.

4. In the xy-plane, two lines intersect at point $(1,k)$. If the equations of the two lines are $y = -x$ and $y = 2x + h$, what is the value of h?

   F. -3
   G. -1
   H. 0
   J. 1
   K. 3

F is correct. If two lines intersect, the coordinates of the intersection point satisfy the equations of both lines. Substitute $(1,k)$ into both equations, and you have $k = -1$ and $k = 2(1) + h$. Therefore, $-1 = 2 + h$ or $h = -3$.

B. Conic Sections and Other Curves

1. In an xy-coordinate plane, point C with coordinates $(2,1)$ is the center of a circle and point A with coordinates $(7,1)$ is on the circle. Which of the following could be the coordinates of point B, if B is also a point on the circle?

   A. $(-7,1)$
   B. $(1,7)$
   C. $(4,6)$
   D. $(6,4)$
   E. $(7,6)$

D is correct.

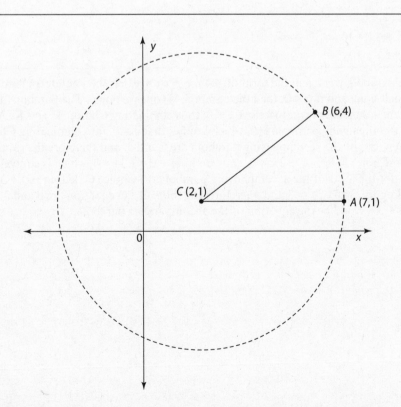

173

Since $\overline{CA}$ is a radius of the circle, the length of the radius of the circle is $\sqrt{(7-2)^2+(1-1)^2}=5$. Because B is a point on the circle, $\overline{CB}$ must also be a radius with length 5. Using the distance formula with each choice, only when the coordinates of B are (6,4) does the length equal 5: $\sqrt{(6-2)^2+(4-1)^2}=5$.

> **Note:** You can save time if you graph the points. Since $\overline{CA}$ is horizontal, you can find the length of the radius using 7 − 2 = 5, and you can see that Choices A, B, and E appear to be too far from C to be on the circle. Now only two points require checking with the distance formula.

---

2. Which of the following could be the equation of the graph in the accompanying figure?

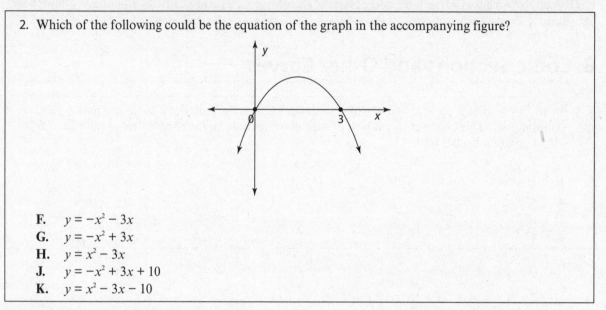

    F. $y = -x^2 - 3x$
    G. $y = -x^2 + 3x$
    H. $y = x^2 - 3x$
    J. $y = -x^2 + 3x + 10$
    K. $y = x^2 - 3x - 10$

G is correct. For a parabola written in the form of $y = ax^2 + bx + c$, c is the y-intercept, and if $a > 0$, then the parabola is concave up, and if $a < 0$, then the parabola is concave down. The parabola in the accompanying figure is concave down; therefore $a < 0$, thus eliminating Choices H and K. Also, the y-intercept in the accompanying parabola is 0, which implies that $c = 0$, thus eliminating Choice J. In addition, the x-intercepts of the accompanying parabola are 0 and 3, and therefore the roots of the equation must be 0 and 3. In Choice F, let $-x^2 - 3x = 0$, and you have $-x(x + 3) = 0$, which is equivalent to $x = 0$ or $x = -3$, which are not the roots of the accompanying parabola. In Choice G, letting $-x^2 + 3x = 0$, you have $x(-x + 3) = 0$ leading to $x = 0$ or $x = 3$ and, therefore, the roots of the equation are 0 and 3, which means Choice G, $y = -x^2 + 3x$, could be the equation of the accompanying parabola.

3. In an xy-coordinate plane, a circle in the second quadrant is tangent to the x-axis, the y-axis, and the line $x = -8$. If point $C(h,k)$ is the center of the circle, what is the value of $h + k$?

   A. -8
   B. -4
   C. 0
   D. 4
   E. 8

C is correct.

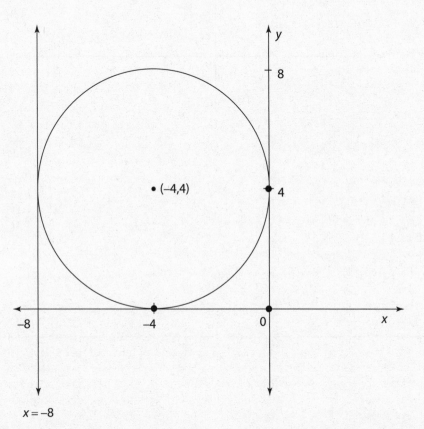

Draw a sketch of the coordinate plane and the line $x = -8$. Since the circle is tangent to both axes and the line $x = -8$, its diameter must be 8, which implies the radius is 4. Therefore, the center must be 4 units from all three lines, making its coordinates $(-4,4)$. Thus, the value of $h + k$ is $(-4) + (4)$ or 0.

4. In the standard (x,y) coordinate plane below, line ℓ is shown in the accompanying diagram. The graph of which of the following equations is the reflection of line ℓ on the y-axis?

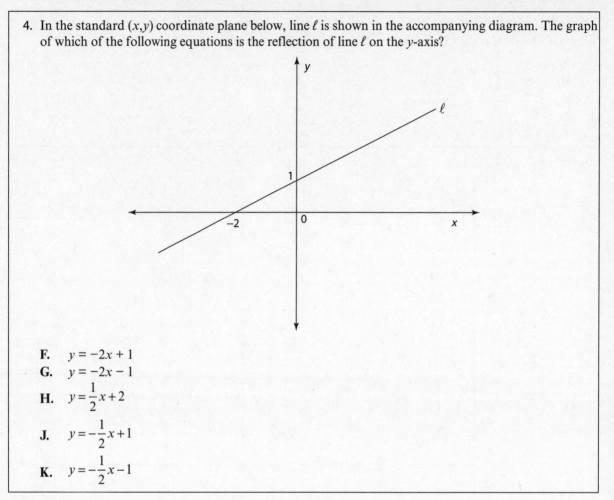

   F. $y = -2x + 1$

   G. $y = -2x - 1$

   H. $y = \dfrac{1}{2}x + 2$

   J. $y = -\dfrac{1}{2}x + 1$

   K. $y = -\dfrac{1}{2}x - 1$

J is correct.

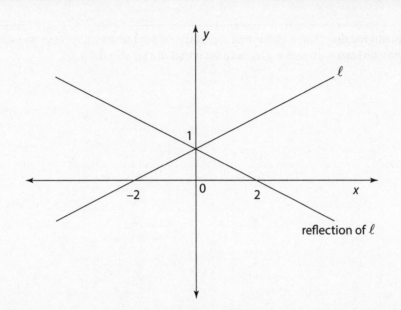

reflection of ℓ

The reflection of line ℓ on the y-axis is the mirror image of line ℓ with the y-axis as the mirror. The mirror image of the point $(-2,0)$ is $(2,0)$. This point $(0,1)$ is on the y-axis, and therefore, the mirror image of $(0,1)$ is itself. Now you have two points on the mirror image of line ℓ: $(2,0)$ and $(0,1)$. The slope of this mirror image is $\dfrac{1-0}{0-2} = -\dfrac{1}{2}$, and the equation is $y - 1 = -\dfrac{1}{2}(x - 0)$ or $y = -\dfrac{1}{2}x + 1$.

Note: You could also enter the equations into your graphing calculator and see which one is the reflection of line ℓ.

5. In the accompanying diagram, a portion of the graph of $h(x)$ is shown. If $h(x) = h(x + 4)$ for all values of x, how many distinct values of x are there such that $h(x) = 0$ and $0 \le x \le 40$?

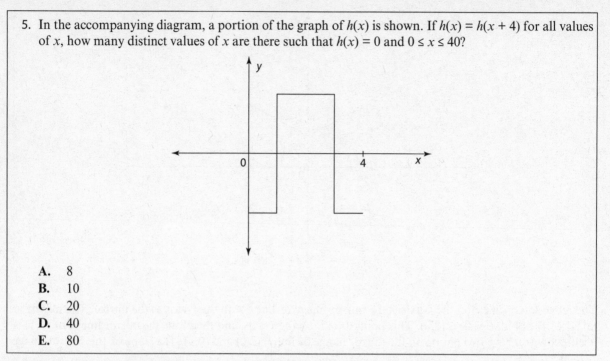

   A. 8
   B. 10
   C. 20
   D. 40
   E. 80

C is correct. The fact that $h(x) = h(x + 4)$ implies that $h(x)$ is periodic. That is to say that the graph repeats itself every 4 units. In this case, the portion of the graph will appear 10 times on the interval [0,40]. Also, the x-values satisfying $h(x) = 0$ are the x-intercepts. Since the graph crosses the x-axis twice for $0 \le x \le 4$, it will cross the x-axis 2(10) or 20 times for $0 \le x \le 40$.

C. Odd and Even Functions

1. A function f is an even function if $f(x) = f(-x)$ for all x in the domain of f. Which of the following is an even function?

   A. $f(x) = 4x$
   B. $f(x) = 2x^2 - 4x$
   C. $f(x) = (x - 2)^2$
   D. $f(x) = x^3 + 2$
   E. $f(x) = x^4 - 3$

E is correct. Apply the property $f(x) = f(-x)$ to the five choices by finding $f(-x)$ and comparing it with $f(x)$: Choice A, $f(-x) = 4(-x) = -4x \ne 4x$; Choice B, $f(-x) = 2(-x)^2 - 4(-x) = 2x^2 + 4x \ne 2x^2 - 4x$; Choice C, $f(-x) = (-x - 2)^2 = (-(x + 2))^2 = (x + 2)^2 \ne (x - 2)^2$; Choice D, $f(-x) = (-x)^3 + 2 = -x^3 + 2 \ne x^3 + 2$; and Choice E, $f(-x) = (-x)^4 - 3 = x^4 - 3$, which is the same as $f(x)$.

2. Which of the following functions is neither an odd function nor an even function?

F.

G.

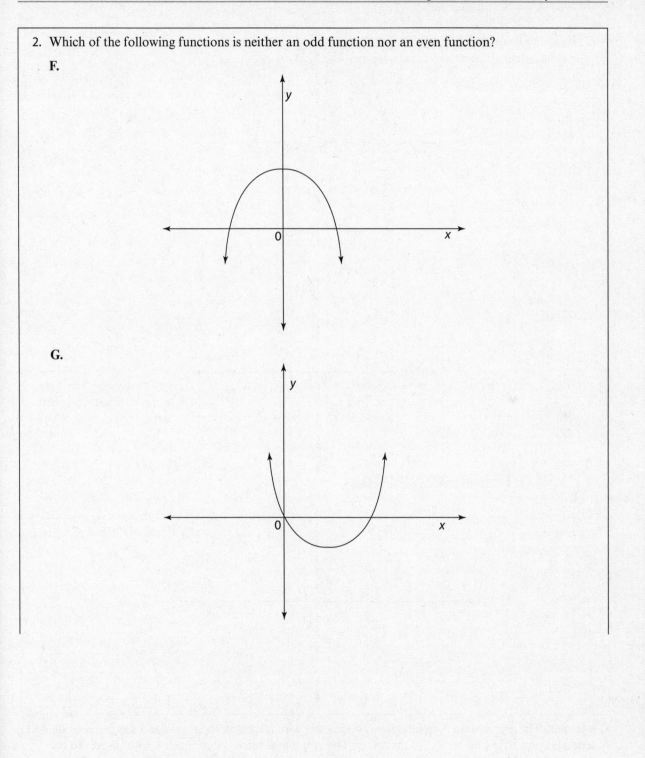

H.

J.

K.

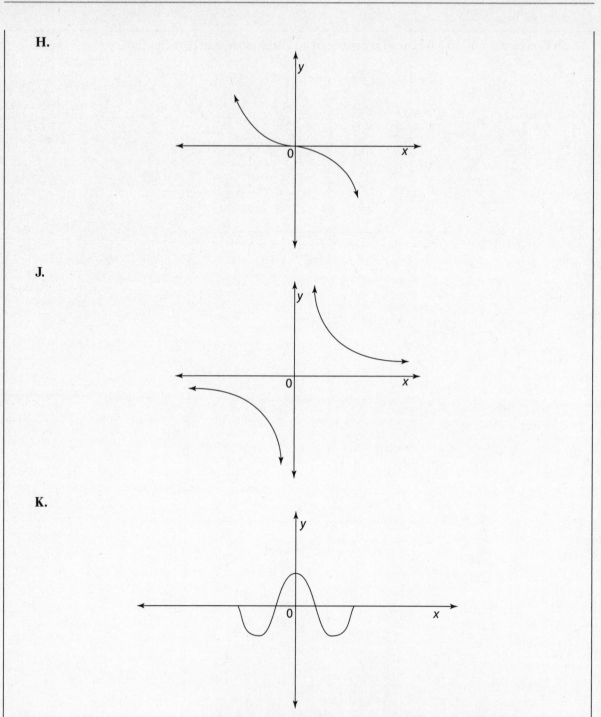

G is correct. The graph of an even function is symmetric with respect to the y-axis, and the graph of an odd function is symmetric with respect to the origin. The graph in Choice F is symmetric with respect to the y-axis; in Choice H, the origin; in Choice J, the origin; and in Choice K, the y-axis. The graph in Choice G is not symmetric with respect to the y-axis or the origin; thus, it is neither an even nor an odd function.

3. A function f is an odd function if $f(x) = -f(-x)$. Which of the following is an odd function?

  A. $f(x) = 3x + 5$
  B. $f(x) = x^2 - 1$
  C. $f(x) = (x + 1)^3$
  D. $f(x) = |x|$
  E. $f(x) = \dfrac{1}{x}$

E is correct. Apply the property $f(x) = -f(-x)$ to the five choices by finding $-f(-x)$ and checking it with $f(x)$. In Choice A, $-f(-x) = -(3(-x) + 5) = -(-3x + 5) = 3x - 5 \ne f(x)$. In Choice B, $-f(-x) = -((-x)^2 - 1) = -(x^2 - 1) = -x^2 + 1 \ne f(x)$. In Choice C, $-f(-x) = -(-x + 1)^3 = -((-(x-1))^3) = -(-(x-1)^3) = (x-1)^3 \ne f(x)$. In Choice D, $-f(-x) = -|-x| = -|x| \ne f(x)$. In Choice E, $-f(-x) = -\dfrac{1}{-x} = \dfrac{1}{x} = f(x)$; therefore, the function in

Choice E is an odd function.

D. Graphing Inequalities

1. Which of the following inequalities has the graph shown in the accompanying figure?

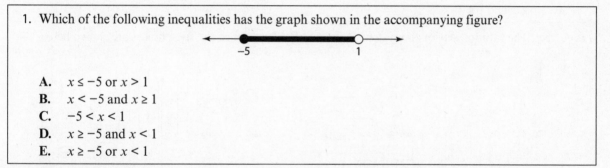

  A. $x \le -5$ or $x > 1$
  B. $x < -5$ and $x \ge 1$
  C. $-5 < x < 1$
  D. $x \ge -5$ and $x < 1$
  E. $x \ge -5$ or $x < 1$

D is correct. The graph in the accompanying figure indicates a set of real numbers between -5 and 1 including -5 but not including 1. Using interval notation, this set is written as $[-5, 1)$. Using set builder notation, this set may be written as either $\{x | -5 \le x < 1\}$ or $\{x | x \ge -5$ and $x < 1\}$. Thus, the inequality in Choice D is the correct choice.

2. Which of the following systems of inequalities is represented by the shaded region in the accompanying figure?

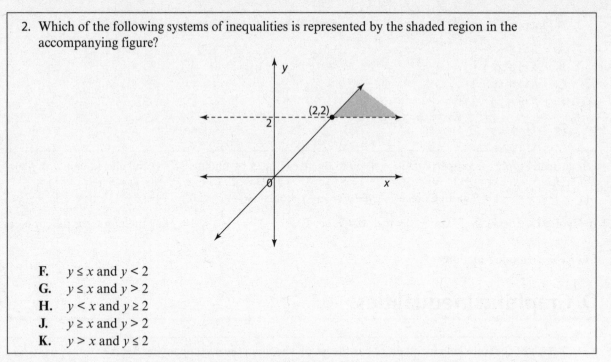

    F. $y \leq x$ and $y < 2$
    G. $y \leq x$ and $y > 2$
    H. $y < x$ and $y \geq 2$
    J. $y \geq x$ and $y > 2$
    K. $y > x$ and $y \leq 2$

G is correct. The solution sets of the system of inequalities for each of the five choices are shown here:

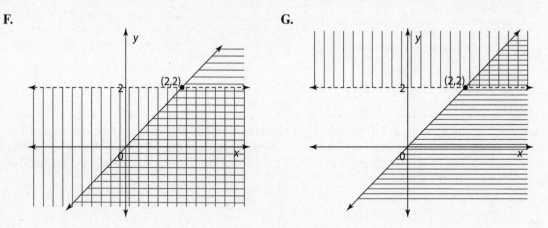

H.

J.

K.

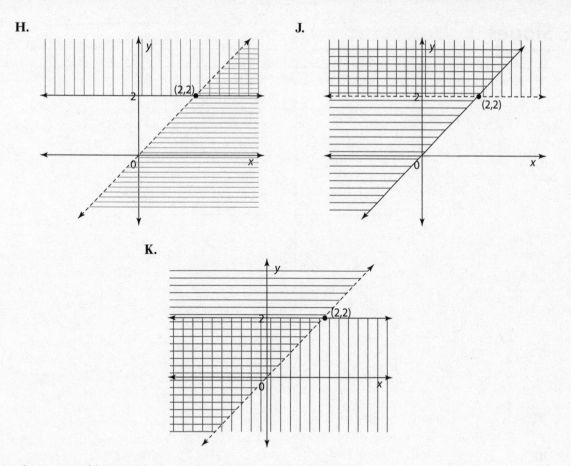

Thus, the system of inequalities in Choice G is the correct choice.

E. Slopes

1. In the accompanying diagram, what is the slope of line ℓ?

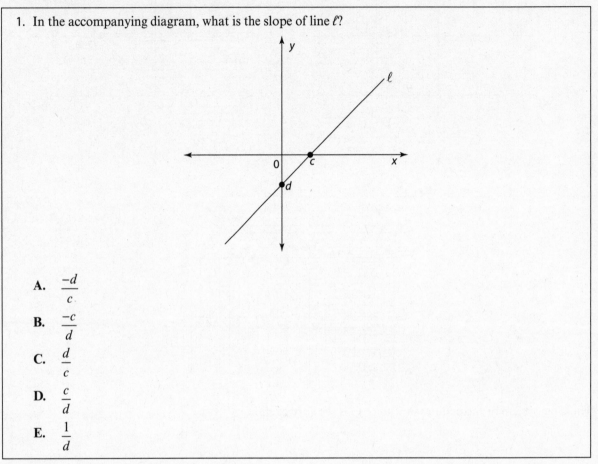

A. $\dfrac{-d}{c}$

B. $\dfrac{-c}{d}$

C. $\dfrac{d}{c}$

D. $\dfrac{c}{d}$

E. $\dfrac{1}{d}$

A is correct. The coordinates of the two points are $(c,0)$ and $(0,d)$. The slope of a line passing through two given points is defined as $m = \dfrac{\Delta y}{\Delta x}$ or $\dfrac{y_2 - y_1}{x_2 - x_1}$. In this case, the slope of line ℓ is $m = \dfrac{0 - d}{c - 0}$ or $\dfrac{-d}{c}$. Remember that you must use the same order when subtracting the x and y coordinates.

2. In the accompanying diagram, if a line is drawn through any two of the given points, which of the following is the smallest possible value for the slope of the line?

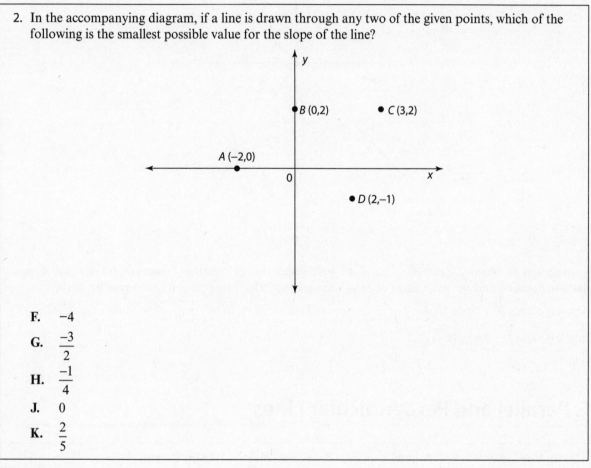

F.   −4

G. $\dfrac{-3}{2}$

H. $\dfrac{-1}{4}$

J.   0

K. $\dfrac{2}{5}$

G is correct.

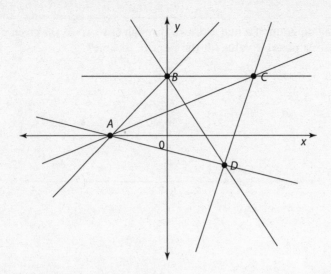

Six lines can be drawn. Lines $\overrightarrow{AB}$, $\overrightarrow{DC}$, and $\overrightarrow{AC}$ have slopes that are positive. Lines $\overrightarrow{AD}$ and $\overrightarrow{BD}$ have slopes that are negative, and $\overrightarrow{BC}$ has a slope of zero. The smallest value for slope will be the smaller of the two negative slopes. The slope of $\overrightarrow{AD} = \dfrac{-1-0}{2-(-2)} = \dfrac{-1}{4}$ and the slope of $\overrightarrow{BD} = \dfrac{-1-2}{2-0} = \dfrac{-3}{2}$. Since $\dfrac{-3}{2} < \dfrac{-1}{4}$, the smallest value for the slope is $\dfrac{-3}{2}$.

F. Parallel and Perpendicular Lines

1. In the xy-plane, $y = 4x + 1$ and $cx + 2y = d$ are parallel lines. What is the value of c?

   A. -8

   B. -4

   C. $-\dfrac{1}{4}$

   D. 4

   E. 8

A is correct. If two lines are parallel, their slopes are equal. The line $y = 4x + 1$ is written in slope-intercept form $y = mx + b$. The slope of this line is $m = 4$. To find the slope of $cx + 2y = d$, rewrite the equation in $y = mx + b$ form. Subtracting cx from both sides of the equation, you have $2y = -cx + d$, and dividing both sides by 2, you have $y = \dfrac{-cx}{2} + \dfrac{d}{2}$. Therefore, the slope of this line is $m = -\dfrac{c}{2}$. Since the two lines are parallel, the slopes are equal. Set $-\dfrac{c}{2} = 4$, and you have $c = -8$.

2. In the xy-plane, the coordinates of three given points are $A(2,4)$, $B(1,1)$, and $C(4,2)$. If line ℓ is drawn passing through point A and perpendicular to $\overrightarrow{BC}$, what is the slope of line ℓ?

    F. -3

    G. -1

    H. $-\dfrac{1}{3}$

    J. $\dfrac{1}{3}$

    K. 1

F is correct. Draw a sketch of the xy-plane including the points A, B, and C.

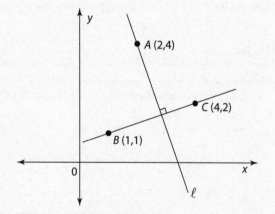

If two lines are perpendicular, their slopes are negative reciprocals. The slope of $\overrightarrow{BC}$ is $m_{\overline{BC}} = \dfrac{2-1}{4-1} = \dfrac{1}{3}$.

Therefore, the slope of a line perpendicular to $\overrightarrow{BC}$ is -3.

> **Note:** The fact that the line passes through point A is not relevant. There are infinitely many lines perpendicular to $\overrightarrow{BC}$, and the slopes of all of these lines are -3.

G. Midpoints

1. On a number line, what is the midpoint of the line segment whose endpoints are -12 and -2?

    A. -14

    B. -7

    C. -5

    D. 5

    E. 7

B is correct. The midpoint of a line segment whose endpoints are two given numbers on a number line is equivalent to the average of the two numbers. In this case, the coordinate of the midpoint of -12 and -2 is $\dfrac{(-12)+(-2)}{2}$ or -7.

2. In the coordinate plane, if $M(2,-1)$ is the midpoint of the line segment joining points $A(4,a)$ and $B(0,b)$, what is the value of $a + b$?

   F. -2
   G. -1
   H.   0
   J.   3
   K.   6

F is correct. Applying the midpoint formula (see page 171), you have the coordinates of M as $\left(\dfrac{4+0}{2}, \dfrac{a+b}{2}\right)$. Since the coordinates of M are given as $(2,-1)$, you have $\dfrac{a+b}{2} = -1$ or $a + b = -2$. Notice that you do not need to find the individual values of a and b. They are not relevant to the question.

H. Distance Formula

1. In the xy-plane, what is the distance between the points $(-10,1)$ and $(2,6)$?

   A.   12
   B.   13
   C.   17
   D. $\sqrt{89}$
   E. $\sqrt{189}$

B is correct. The distance between two points can be found using the distance formula, $d = \sqrt{(x_2 - x_1)^2 + (y_2 - y_1)^2}$. In this case, $d = \sqrt{(2-(-10))^2 + (6-1)^2} = \sqrt{12^2 + 5^2} = \sqrt{144 + 25} = \sqrt{169}$ or 13.

2. In a coordinate plane, the distance between point $A(10,5)$ and point $B(-2,b)$ is 13. If $b > 0$, what is the value of b?

   F. -5
   G.   0
   H.   5
   J.   10
   K.   15

J is correct. Using the distance formula, you have $d_{\overline{AB}} = \sqrt{(10-(-2))^2 + (5-b)^2} = 13$, or $\sqrt{144 + (5-b)^2} = 13$. Square both sides of the equation, and you have $144 + (5 - b)^2 = 169$ or $(5 - b)^2 = 25$. Take the square root of both sides, and you get $5 - b = 5$ or $5 - b = -5$, which implies $b = 0$ or $b = 10$. Since $b > 0$, $b = 10$.

XII. Working with Plane Geometry

On the ACT Mathematics Test, you'll be tested on many concepts of plane geometry, including properties of angles, line segments, triangles, quadrilaterals, polygons, and circles. You are also expected to demonstrate an understanding of transformations, surface areas, volumes, and the techniques of proof. The practice problems in this chapter are designed to help you review many of the plane geometry concepts. Work the problems, and check your answers with the given explanations.

A. Measurement of Angles and Line Segments

1. The measure of the vertex angle of an isosceles triangle is 40 degrees. What is the measure, in degrees, of a base angle of the triangle?

   A. 40
   B. 60
   C. 70
   D. 80
   E. 90

C is correct.

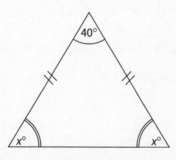

In the accompanying diagram, x represents the degree measure of one of the base angles. Since the given triangle is isosceles, the measures of the base angles are equal. The sum of the measures of a triangle is 180 degrees. Therefore, you have $x + x + 40 = 180$ or $2x = 140$. Thus $x = 70$.

2. Line ℓ intersects $\overline{AB}$ and $\overline{BC}$ at D and E, respectively. What is the value of x?

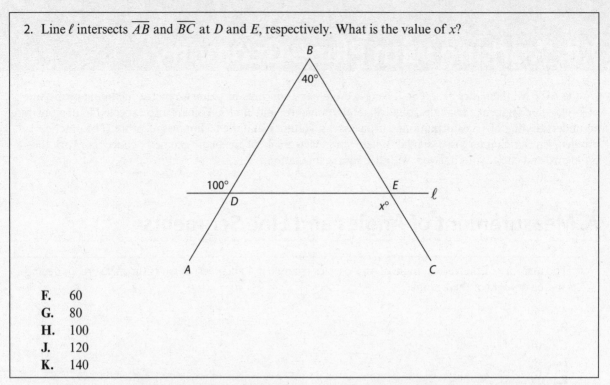

    F.   60
    G.   80
    H.   100
    J.   120
    K.   140

J is correct. Since $m\angle BDE + 100 = 180$, $m\angle BDE = 80$. You know that the sum of the measures of the three angles of a triangle is 180 degrees. Therefore, $80 + 40 + m\angle BED = 180$ or $m\angle BED = 60$. Since $m\angle BED + x = 180$, you have $60 + x = 180$, or $x = 120$.

3. In the accompanying diagram, $ABCD$ is a parallelogram. What is the value of x?

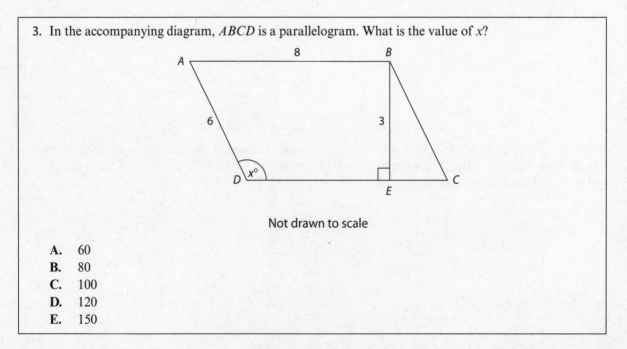

Not drawn to scale

    A.   60
    B.   80
    C.   100
    D.   120
    E.   150

E is correct. Opposite sides of a parallelogram are congruent; therefore, $BC = 6$. In the right triangle $\triangle BEC$, $BE = 3$ and $BC = 6$. Note that $\overline{BC}$ is the hypotenuse and $\overline{BE}$ is a leg. Since the length of the hypotenuse is twice the length of a leg, $\triangle BEC$ is a 30°-60° right triangle. Thus, the $m\angle C = 30$. Also, in parallelogram $ABCD$, $\angle D$ and $\angle C$ are supplementary. Therefore, $m\angle D = 150$.

---

4. Points A, B, C, and D lie on a line in that order. If C is the midpoint of $\overline{BD}$, $CD = 2AB$ and $AD = 60$, what is the length of $\overline{AC}$?

   F. 12
   G. 24
   H. 36
   J. 40
   K. 48

H is correct. Let $AB = x$. Since $CD = 2AB$, you have $CD = 2x$. Also, C is the midpoint of $\overline{BD}$; therefore, $BC = CD = 2x$. Since $AD = 60$, you have $x + 2x + 2x = 60$ or $5x = 60$, which leads to $x = 12$. The length of $\overline{AC}$ is $3x$ or $3(12)$, which is 36.

B. Properties of Triangles

1. Starting from home, Mary drove 5 miles due east to Bill's house. She then drove 6 miles due south to Karen's house. Mary then drove 3 miles due east to Janet's house. What is the distance, in miles, between Mary's house and Janet's house?

   A. 4
   B. 8
   C. 10
   D. 14
   E. 16

C is correct.

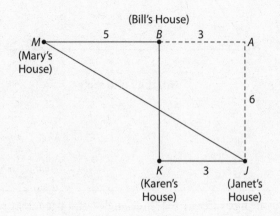

In the accompanying diagram of Mary's trip, if you extend $\overline{MB}$ to A and draw $\overline{AJ}$, ΔMAJ is a right triangle and quadrilateral $BAJK$ is a rectangle with $BA = KJ = 3$ and $BK = AJ = 6$. Since $AM = 8$, $(AM)^2 + (AJ)^2 = (MJ)^2$ or $8^2 + 6^2 = (MJ)^2$ and $MJ = 10$.

---

2. In ΔDEF, $DE = 6$ and $DF = 10$. What is the smallest possible integer length of side $\overline{EF}$?

 F. 4
 G. 5
 H. 6
 J. 15
 K. 16

G is correct.

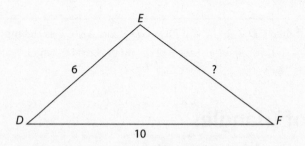

Since you are looking for the smallest possible length of $\overline{EF}$, assume that $\overline{EF}$ is not the longest side of ΔDEF. Applying the triangle inequality, you have $DE + EF > DF$ or $6 + EF > 10$, which is equivalent to $EF > 4$. Since EF is an integer, the smallest possible value for EF is 5.

---

3. In the accompanying diagram, a, b, and c are the lengths of the three sides of the triangle. Which of the following must be true?

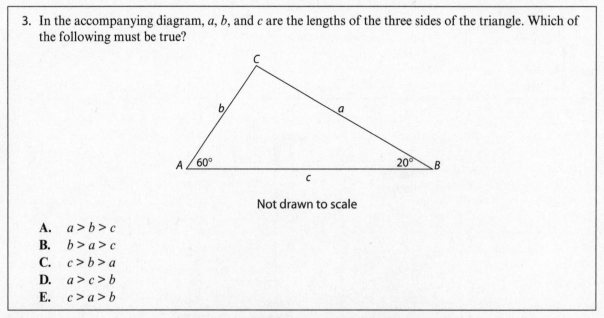

Not drawn to scale

 A. $a > b > c$
 B. $b > a > c$
 C. $c > b > a$
 D. $a > c > b$
 E. $c > a > b$

E is correct. Since the sum of the measures of the three angles of a triangle is 180 degrees, $m\angle C = 180 - 60 - 20 = 100$. In a triangle, the longest side is always opposite the biggest angle. Thus, $c > a > b$.

4. Given three points A, B, and C, if the distance between A and B is 5 and the distance between B and C is 12, what is the shortest possible distance between A and C?

    F.   5

    G.   7

    H.   12

    J.   13

    K.   17

G is correct. Points A, B, and C either form a triangle, or they lie on the same line. If A, B, and C form a triangle, then $7 < AC < 17$ because the sum of the lengths of any two sides of the triangle must be greater than the third. If the points are collinear, then the shortest distance occurs when A is between B and C. Thus, $AC = 12 - 5 = 7$.

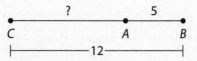

C. Properties of Quadrilaterals

1. In the accompanying diagram, $DEFG$ is a parallelogram. What is the length of $\overline{GH}$?

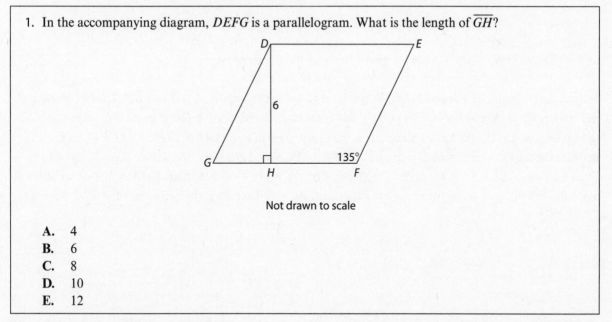

Not drawn to scale

    A.   4

    B.   6

    C.   8

    D.   10

    E.   12

B is correct. Since $DEFG$ is a parallelogram, $m\angle G + m\angle F = 180$ degrees, which means $m\angle G + 135 = 180$ or $m\angle G = 45$. In the right triangle DGH, $m\angle G = 45$ implies that $m\angle GDH$ is also 45, and thus ΔDGH is isosceles. Therefore, $GH = DH$ or $GH = 6$.

2. In the accompanying diagram, *ABCD* is an isosceles trapezoid with $\overline{AB} \parallel \overline{DC}$. If *AB* = 8, *DC* = 16, and the height of the trapezoid is 3, what is the perimeter of trapezoid *ABCD*?

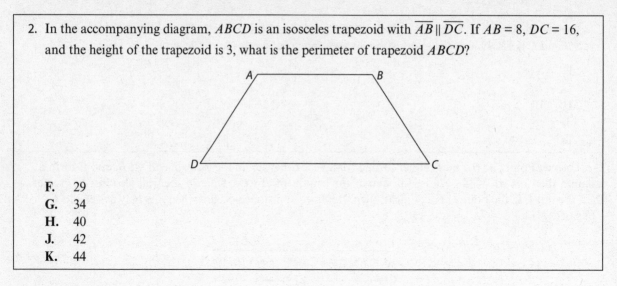

F. 29
G. 34
H. 40
J. 42
K. 44

G is correct.

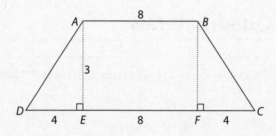

To find the perimeter of trapezoid *ABCD*, you need to know the lengths of $\overline{AD}$ and $\overline{BC}$. To start, draw a line from point *A* intersecting $\overline{DC}$ at point *E* and from point *B* intersecting $\overline{DC}$ at point *F* to form two right triangles: $\triangle ADE$ and $\triangle BCF$. Since $\overline{AD}$ is the hypotenuse in right $\triangle ADE$, $(AD)^2 = (AE)^2 + (DE)^2$. Because the trapezoid is isosceles, $\overline{AD} \cong \overline{BC}$, $\triangle ADE \cong \triangle BCF$, and *DE* = *FC*. And since *AB* = 8, *EF* = 8. Therefore, *DE* + *EF* + *FC* = 16, making the lengths of $\overline{DE}$ and $\overline{FC}$ both 4. Also, $(AD)^2 = 3^2 + 4^2$, so *AD* = 5. Since the legs of an isosceles trapezoid are congruent, *BC* = 5. Therefore, the perimeter of *ABCD* = 5 + 8 + 5 + 16 = 34.

3. In the accompanying diagram, $ABCD$ is a rectangle with side $\overline{AB}$ containing points E and F and $AE = EF = FB$. If the area of $\triangle ADF$ is 12, what is the area of quadrilateral $FBCD$?

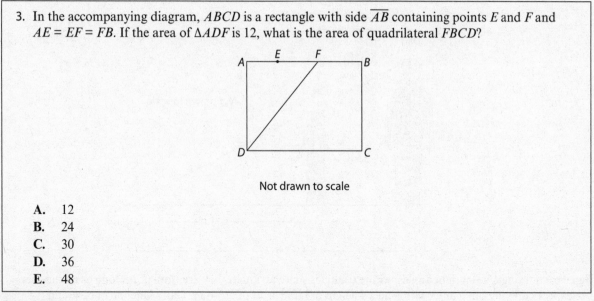

Not drawn to scale

    A.   12
    B.   24
    C.   30
    D.   36
    E.   48

B is correct.

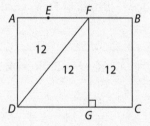

Draw a perpendicular line from F to $\overline{DC}$, meeting $\overline{DC}$ at point G. Note that the area of $\triangle AFD$ equals the area of $\triangle FDG = 12$. Since $AE = EF = FB$, you have $FB = \dfrac{1}{2}AF$. The area of rectangle $FBCG = \dfrac{1}{2}AFGD$. The area of rectangle $AFGD = 24$, making the area of rectangle $FBCG = 12$. Therefore, the area of quadrilateral $FBCD$ is $12 + 12$ or 24.

D. Similarity

1. Kaela is 5 ft 6 in tall and casts a shadow that is 11 ft long. If Dan is standing behind Kaela, and he is 6 ft tall, how long is his shadow?

    A.   10 ft
    B.   11 ft
    C.   11 ft 6 in
    D.   12 ft
    E.   12 ft 6 in

D is correct.

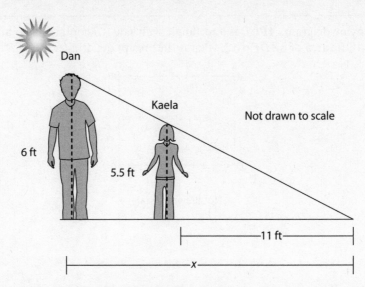

Since each triangle has a right angle and the triangles share an angle, they are similar. As long as all numbers are expressed in the same units with Kaela's height 5.5 ft instead of 5 ft 6 in, Dan's height can be found using the equation $\dfrac{\text{Kaela's height}}{\text{length of Kaela's shadow}} = \dfrac{\text{Dan's height}}{\text{length of Dan's shadow}}$ or $\dfrac{5.5}{11} = \dfrac{6}{x}$ or $5.5x = 66$ or $x = 12$. Dan's shadow is 12 ft long.

---

2. In the accompanying diagram, $\overline{DE} \parallel \overline{BC}$. If $AE = 2$, $EC = 4$, and $BC = 12$, find the length of $\overline{DE}$.

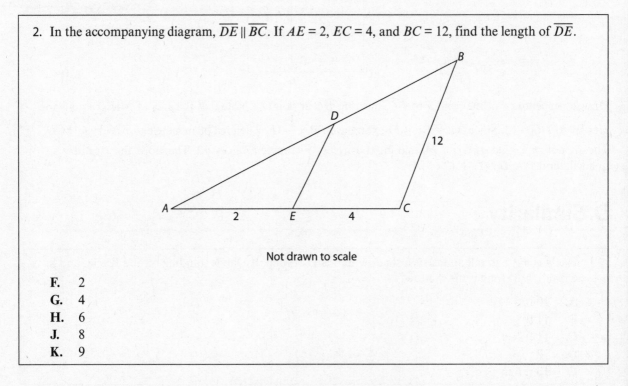

Not drawn to scale

    F.   2
    G. 4
    H. 6
    J.   8
    K. 9

G is correct. Because $\overline{DE} \parallel \overline{BC}$, congruent corresponding angles are formed with $\angle DEA \cong \angle BCA$ and $\angle ADE \cong \angle ABC$, and thus $\triangle ADE \sim \triangle ABC$. Since the triangles are similar, their corresponding sides are in proportion and $\dfrac{DE}{BC} = \dfrac{AE}{AC}$. Notice that $EC = 4$ may not be used in this proportion because $\overline{EC}$ is not a side of either triangle. To find DE, solve $\dfrac{DE}{BC} = \dfrac{AE}{AC}$ or $\dfrac{DE}{12} = \dfrac{2}{6}$ or $DE = 4$.

---

3. In the accompanying diagram, $\overline{AB} \parallel \overline{CD}$ and $\overline{AD}$ intersects $\overline{BC}$ at E. If $AB = 6$, $CD = 9$, and $BC = 30$, what is the length of $\overline{BE}$?

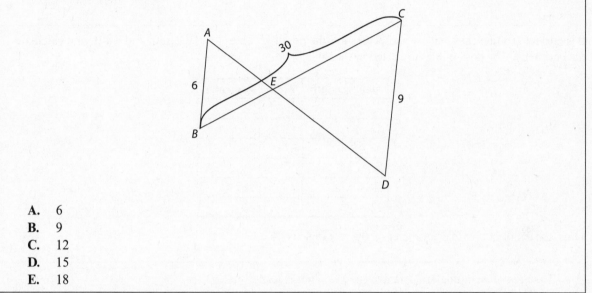

    A. 6
    B. 9
    C. 12
    D. 15
    E. 18

C is correct. Since $\overline{AB} \parallel \overline{CD}$, pairs of congruent alternate interior angles are formed, $\angle B \cong \angle C$ and $\angle A \cong \angle D$, and so $\triangle ABE \sim \triangle DCE$. Since the triangles are similar, corresponding sides are in proportion and $\dfrac{BE}{AB} = \dfrac{EC}{DC}$. To find BE, use x as the length of $\overline{BE}$ and $(30 - x)$ as the length of $\overline{EC}$: $\dfrac{x}{6} = \dfrac{30 - x}{9}$ or $9x = 6(30 - x)$ or $9x = 180 - 6x$ or $15x = 180$ or $x = 12$.

---

4. $\triangle LMN$ is similar to $\triangle PQT$. The area of $\triangle LMN$ is 16, and the length of its shortest side is 2. If the area of $\triangle PQT$ is 36, what is the length of its shortest side?

    F. 3
    G. 4.5
    H. 6
    J. 9
    K. 22

F is correct. Since $\triangle LMN \sim \triangle PQT$, the ratio of the areas is equal to the square of the ratio of any corresponding sides. Since the two shortest sides are a pair of corresponding sides, $\dfrac{16}{36} = \left(\dfrac{2}{x}\right)^2$ or $\dfrac{4}{9} = \dfrac{4}{x^2}$ or $4x^2 = 36$ or $x^2 = 9$ or $x = \pm 3$. Since x must be positive, $x = 3$. The length of the shortest side of $\triangle PQT$ is 3.

E. Areas and Perimeters

1. If the area of a rectangle is 32 and the measures of the length and width of the rectangle are integers, what is the smallest possible perimeter of the rectangle?

    A. 12
    B. 24
    C. 36
    D. 64
    E. 66

B is correct. To find the smallest perimeter, find the possible values for the length and width and calculate the perimeter. The possibilities are listed in the table:

Area	Length	Width	Perimeter
32	1	32	66
32	2	16	36
32	4	8	24
32	8	4	24
32	16	2	36
32	32	1	66

Thus, the smallest possible perimeter of the rectangle is 24.

2. The area of an equilateral triangle is $9\sqrt{3}$. What is its perimeter?

    F. 6
    G. 12
    H. 18
    J. 24
    K. 36

H is correct. Since the area of the equilateral triangle is $9\sqrt{3}$ and $A = \dfrac{s^2\sqrt{3}}{4}$, then $\dfrac{s^2\sqrt{3}}{4} = 9\sqrt{3}$ or $s^2 = 4(9)$ or $s = \pm 6$. Since s is the length of a side, $s = 6$, and the perimeter is 3(6) or 18.

3. If two sides of a triangle measure 6 and 8, what is the largest possible area for the triangle?

    A. 7
    B. 24
    C. 32
    D. 48
    E. 64

B is correct.

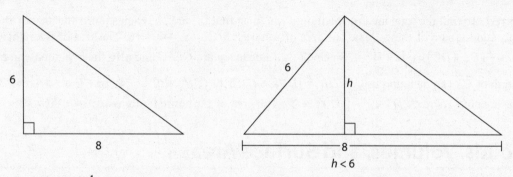

The area of a triangle is $\frac{1}{2}$(base)(height). The largest possible area for a triangle with two sides measuring 6 and 8 is the area of a right triangle with legs measuring 6 and 8. In this case, the area of the right triangle is $\frac{1}{2}$(6)(8) or 24. Notice that if the two sides 6 and 8 are not perpendicular, the altitude will be less than 6. Therefore, the area of the triangle would be less than 24.

4. In the accompanying diagram, *ABCD* and *CEFG* are squares. If *DE* = 2 and *DC* = 4, what is the area of the entire figure?

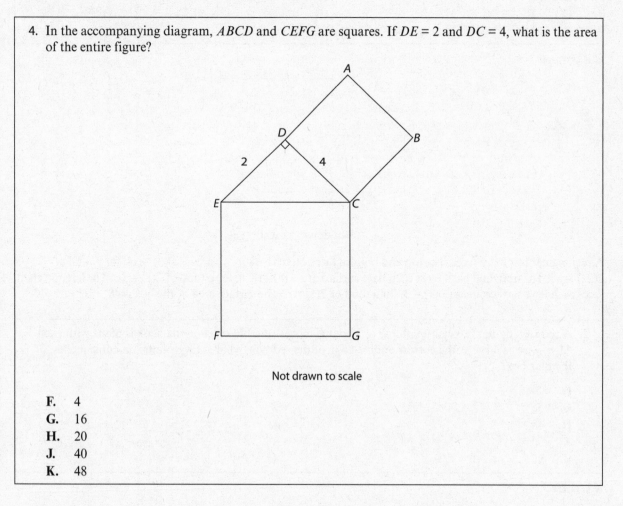

Not drawn to scale

F. 4
G. 16
H. 20
J. 40
K. 48

J is correct. To find the total area of the figure, you must find the area of each square, the area of the triangle, and the sum of these areas. The area of square $ABCD = s^2 = 4^2 = 16$. The area of the right $\triangle DEC = \frac{1}{2}(DE)(DC) = \frac{1}{2}(2)(4) = 4$. Since $\overline{CE}$ is a side in square $CEFG$ and also the hypotenuse in $\triangle DEC$, the length of $\overline{CE}$ can be found using $(CE)^2 = (DE)^2 + (DC)^2$ or $(CE)^2 = (2)^2 + (4)^2$ or $CE = \pm\sqrt{20}$ or $CE = \sqrt{20}$, and the area of square $CEFG = s^2 = \left(\sqrt{20}\right)^2 = 20$. The area of the entire figure is $16 + 4 + 20 = 40$.

F. Solids, Volumes, and Surface Areas

1. If the length, width, and height of a rectangular box measure 8, 3, and 1, respectively, what is the total surface area of the box?

   A.   24
   B.   35
   C.   70
   D.   72
   E.   144

C is correct.

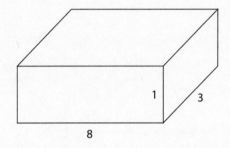

Not drawn to scale

A rectangular box has 6 faces. The top and bottom faces each have surface areas $(8)(3) = 24$, for a total of $2(24) = 48$. The front and back faces each have surface areas $(8)(1) = 8$, for a total of $2(8) = 16$. The left and right faces each have surface areas $(3)(1) = 3$, for a total of $2(3) = 6$. The surface area of the box is $48 + 16 + 6 = 70$.

2. A red rectangular box has a volume of 12 cubic inches. If a blue rectangular box is made with each edge twice as large as the corresponding edge of the red box, what is the volume, in cubic inches, of the blue box?

   F.   24
   G.   36
   H.   48
   J.   72
   K.   96

K is correct.

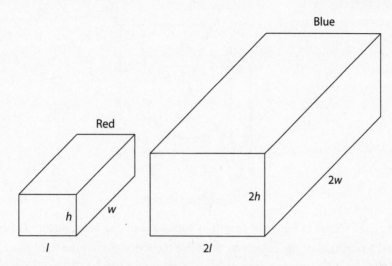

Since the volume of the red box is $(l)(w)(h)$ and the edges of the blue box are twice as large, the volume of the blue box is $(2l)(2w)(2h)$ or $8(lwh)$. The volume of the blue box is 8 times the volume of the red box, $8(12) = 96$.

---

3. If all faces of a pyramid (including the base) are equilateral triangles, and an edge of the pyramid measures 2 cm, what is the total surface area, in cm², of the pyramid?

   A. 4

   B. $3\sqrt{3}$

   C. $4\sqrt{3}$

   D. 8

   E. 16

C is correct. Since **all** faces of the pyramid are congruent equilateral triangles, the total surface area of the pyramid is 4 times the area of one of the triangles. Each edge of the pyramid is also a side of a triangle, and so the triangles are equilateral triangles with sides of length 2 cm, and the area of each triangle is

$A = \dfrac{s^2\sqrt{3}}{4} = \dfrac{(2)^2\sqrt{3}}{4} = \sqrt{3}$. The total surface area of the pyramid is therefore $4\sqrt{3}$ cm².

---

4. A sphere with a diameter measuring 3 cm is inscribed in a cube. What is the length of a diagonal, in centimeters, of the cube?

   F. 3

   G. $3\sqrt{2}$

   H. $3\sqrt{3}$

   J. 6

   K. 27

H is correct.

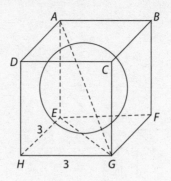

Not drawn to scale

Since the diameter of the sphere is 3 cm, the length of each edge of the cube, including edges $\overline{AE}$, $\overline{EH}$, and $\overline{HG}$, is 3 cm. To find a diagonal of the cube, you must use the Pythagorean theorem twice, first to find EG and then to find AG. Since $\overline{EG}$ is the hypotenuse in right triangle ΔEHG, $(EG)^2 = 3^2 + 3^2 = \sqrt{18}$. Since $\overline{AG}$ is the hypotenuse in right triangle ΔAEG, $(AG)^2 = 3^2 + (\sqrt{18})^2 = 9 + 18 = 27$ and $AG = \pm\sqrt{27} = \pm3\sqrt{3}$. The length of a diagonal is $3\sqrt{3}$ cm.

G. Properties of Circles

1. In the accompanying diagram, O is the center of the circle. If the area of sector AOB is 25π, what is the length of $\overarc{AB}$?

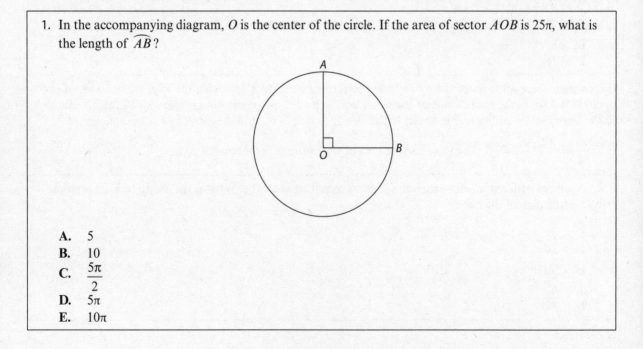

   A.   5
   B.   10
   C. $\dfrac{5\pi}{2}$
   D. 5π
   E. 10π

D is correct. First, find the radius of the circle. Use the proportion $\dfrac{\text{area of sector } AOB}{\text{area of a circle}} = \dfrac{90}{360}$, which is equivalent to $\dfrac{25\pi}{\pi r^2} = \dfrac{1}{4}$ or $r^2 = 4(25)$. Thus, $r = 10$. Now use another proportion to find the length of $\overset{\frown}{AB}$, $\dfrac{\text{length of } \overset{\frown}{AB}}{\text{circumference of a circle}} = \dfrac{90}{360}$ or $\dfrac{\text{length of } \overset{\frown}{AB}}{2\pi(10)} = \dfrac{1}{4}$. Thus, the length of $\overset{\frown}{AB} = 5\pi$.

---

2. In the accompanying diagram, $\overline{AB}$ and $\overline{CD}$ are diameters of the circle. If length of $\overset{\frown}{AD}$ is 4π, what is the total area of the shaded regions?

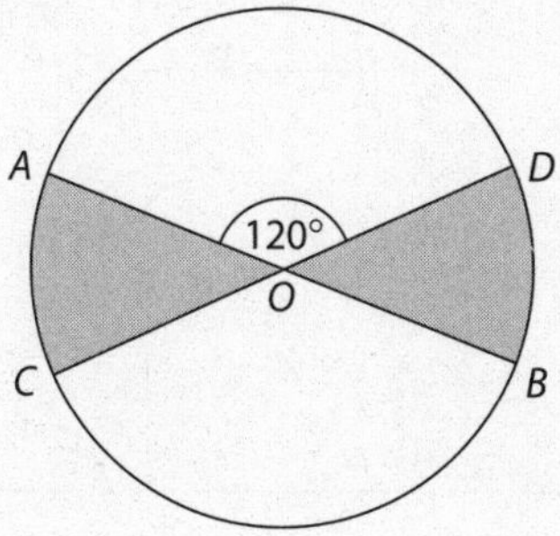

   F. 3π
   G. 6π
   H. 12π
   J. 24π
   K. 48π

H is correct. Begin by finding the area of the circle. To do that, you need to find the radius. Using the proportion $\dfrac{\text{length of } \overset{\frown}{AD}}{2\pi r} = \dfrac{120}{360}$, you have $\dfrac{4\pi}{2\pi r} = \dfrac{1}{3}$ or $r = 6$. The area of the circle is πr^2 or 36π. Since $\overline{AB}$ is a diameter, $m\angle DOB + 120 = 180$, and thus, $m\angle DOB = 60$. Also, $\angle AOC$ and $\angle DOB$ are vertical angles, and thus $m\angle AOC = 60$. Now use a proportion to find the area of sector DOB: $\dfrac{\text{area of sector } DOB}{\text{area of a circle}} = \dfrac{60}{360}$. The proportion is equivalent to $\dfrac{\text{area of sector } DOB}{36\pi} = \dfrac{1}{6}$ or area of sector $DOB = 6\pi$, and the total area of the shaded regions is $2(6\pi)$ or 12π.

3. In the accompanying diagram, a regular hexagon is inscribed in a circle. If $AB = 6$, what is the length of $\overset{\frown}{AB}$?

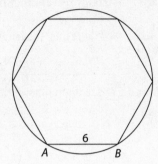

A. 2
B. π
C. 2π
D. 4π
E. 6π

C is correct.

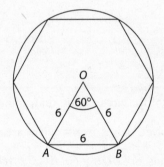

Draw radii $\overline{OA}$ and $\overline{OB}$. A regular hexagon is both equilateral and equiangular. Therefore, $m\angle AOB = \left(\dfrac{1}{6}\right)(360) = 60$. Also, $\overline{OA}$ and $\overline{OB}$ are radii and thus, $m\angle OAB = m\angle OBA = 60$, and $\triangle AOB$ is an equilateral triangle. To find the length of $\overset{\frown}{AB}$, use the proportion $\dfrac{\text{length of } \overset{\frown}{AB}}{\text{circumference of a circle}} = \dfrac{60}{360}$, which is equivalent to $\dfrac{\text{length of } \overset{\frown}{AB}}{2\pi(6)} = \dfrac{1}{6}$ or length of $\overset{\frown}{AB} = 2\pi$.

4. In the accompanying diagram, O is the center of the larger circle, and $\overline{OA}$ and $\overline{OB}$ are diameters of the smaller circles. If the length of $\overline{AB}$ is 12, what is the total area of the shaded regions?

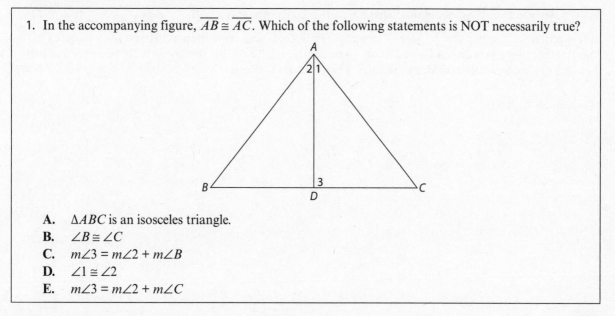

   F. 9π

   G. 18π

   H. 24π

   J. 27π

   K. 36π

G is correct. Since $\overline{OA}$ and $\overline{OB}$ are radii of the larger circle and $\overline{AB}$ is 12, you have $OA = OB = 6$. The area of the larger circle is $\pi(6)^2$ or 36π. The two smaller circles are congruent, and the length of the radius for each of the small circles is 3. The area of each small circle is $\pi(3)^2$ or 9π, and the total area of both small circles is 18π. Therefore, the area of the shaded regions is $36\pi - 18\pi$ or 18π.

H. Concept of Proof

1. In the accompanying figure, $\overline{AB} \cong \overline{AC}$. Which of the following statements is NOT necessarily true?

   A. $\triangle ABC$ is an isosceles triangle.

   B. $\angle B \cong \angle C$

   C. $m\angle 3 = m\angle 2 + m\angle B$

   D. $\angle 1 \cong \angle 2$

   E. $m\angle 3 = m\angle 2 + m\angle C$

D is correct. Examine the statement in each of the five choices. Choice A, $\triangle ABC$ is an isosceles triangle since $\overline{AB} \cong \overline{AC}$. Choice B, $\angle B \cong \angle C$ because the base angles of an isosceles triangle are congruent. Choice C, $m\angle 3 = m\angle 2 + m\angle B$ because the measure of an exterior angle of a triangle is equal to the sum of the measures of the two nonadjacent interior angles. Choice E, since $m\angle 3 \cong m\angle 2 + m\angle B$ and $\angle B \cong \angle C$, substituting $m\angle B$ with $m\angle C$ you have $m\angle 3 \cong m\angle 2 + m\angle C$. Regarding Choice D, in order to have $\angle 1 \cong \angle 2$, you must have sufficient information to show that $\triangle ABD \cong \triangle ACD$. Reviewing all the congruent parts of the two triangles, you have $\angle B \cong \angle C$, $\overline{AB} \cong \overline{AC}$, and $\overline{AD} \cong \overline{AD}$, which is equivalent to having a pair of congruent angles and two pairs of congruent sides. However, $\angle B$ and $\angle C$ are not the included angles, which means you could not use the theorem *s.a.s.* $\cong$ *s.a.s.* (side-angle-side) to prove the triangles congruent. Note that *a.s.s.* (angle-side-side) is not an acceptable method for proving triangles congruent. Thus, in this case, it is not necessarily true that $\angle 1 \cong \angle 2$.

---

2. If no member of Mary's family plays football, which of the following statements MUST be true?

    F. If Phillip does not play football, then Phillip is a member of Mary's family.
    G. If Jonathan is not a member of Mary's family, then he plays football.
    H. If Richard is not a member of Mary's family, then he does not play football.
    J. If Bill plays table tennis, then he is a member of Mary's family.
    K. If David plays football, then he is not a member of Mary's family.

K is correct. Use reasoning skills. Since no one in Mary's family plays football, if you play football you are not in Mary's family. Another approach is to use formal logic. Here are some of the rules of logic:

- Statement: If A, then B.
- Converse: If B, then A.
- Inverse: If not A, then not B.
- Contrapositive: If not B, then not A.

> **Note:** A statement and the contrapositive always have the same truth value.

In this problem, "No member of Mary's family plays football" can be written as "If you are a member of Mary's family, then you do not play football." The contrapositive of this statement is "If you play football, then you are not a member of Mary's family." Thus, Choice K is true.

I. Transformations

1. In the accompanying diagram, the graph of $y = f(x)$ is shown. Which of the following could be the graph of $f(x + 2)$?

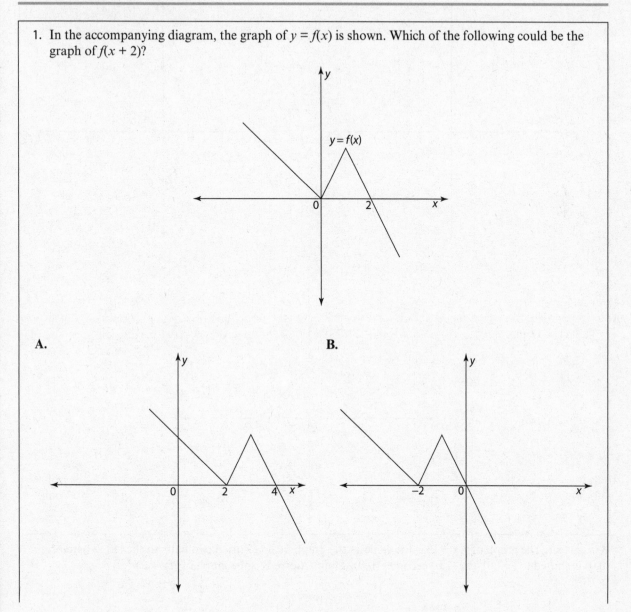

A.

B.

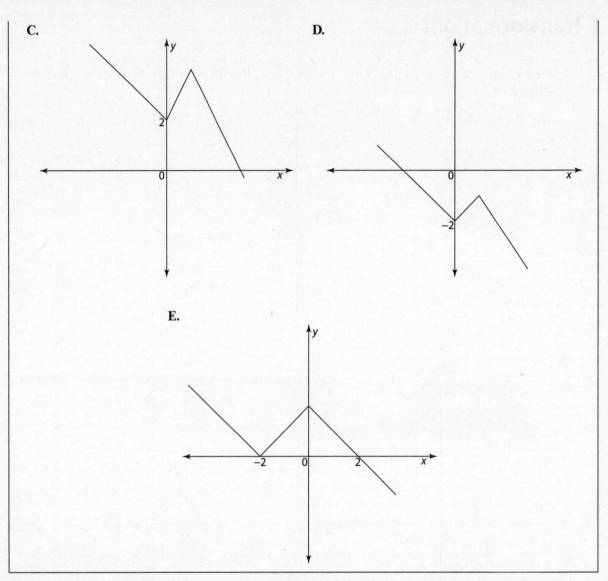

B is correct. The graph of $f(x + 2)$ is the same as the graph of $f(x)$ shifted two units to the left. Therefore, $(0,0)$ is shifted to $(-2,0)$ and $(2,0)$ becomes $(0,0)$. Thus, Choice B is the graph of $f(x + 2)$.

2. In the accompanying diagram, a triangle and the line $y = x$ are shown. Which of the following would be the image of the triangle reflected in the line $y = x$?

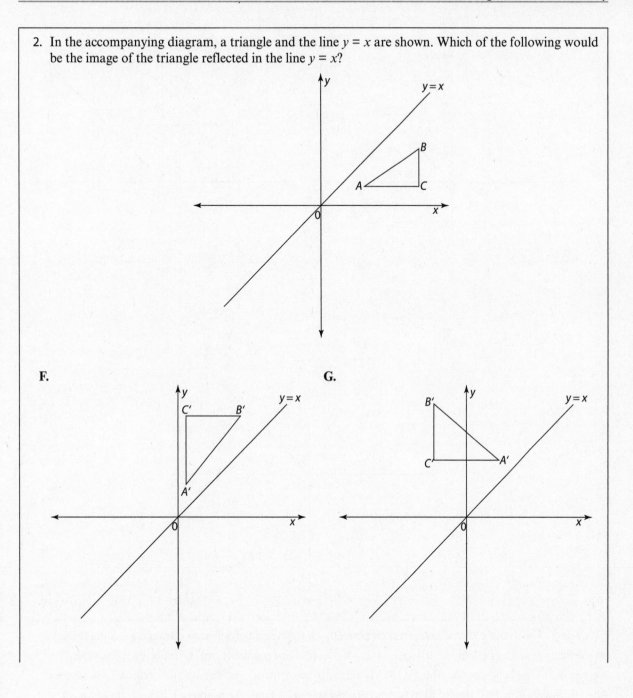

F.

G.

H.

J.

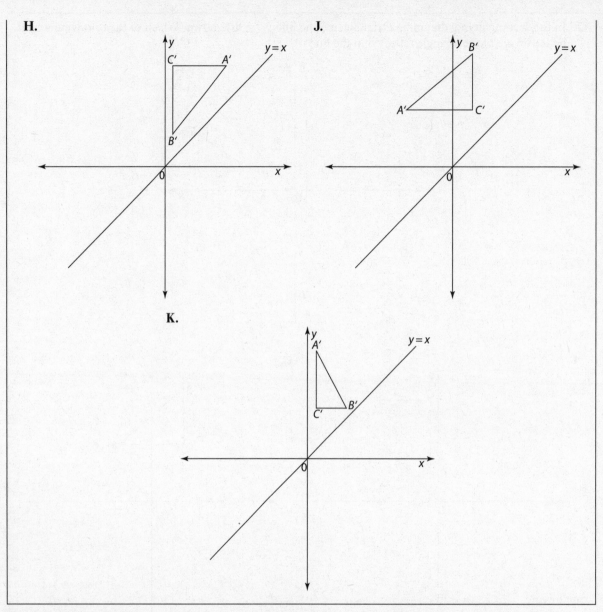

K.

F is correct. The triangle and its image match perfectly along the line of reflection. Imagine folding the graph on the line $y = x$. The base of the triangle, $\overline{AC}$ (a horizontal line segment), will be reflected to become a vertical line segment. The height of the triangle, $\overline{BC}$ (a vertical line segment), will become a horizontal line segment. Also, the image of $\triangle ABC$ should have vertex A below side $\overline{BC}$. Thus, the graph in Choice F is the image.

3. In the accompanying diagram, the figure is a regular hexagon. How many lines of symmetry does the hexagon have?

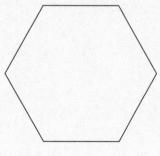

A. 1
B. 2
C. 3
D. 4
E. 6

E is correct.

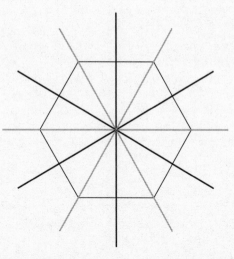

A line of symmetry divides a figure into two parts, each the mirror image of the other. As illustrated in the accompanying diagram, 6 such lines are possible.

XIII. Tackling Trigonometry

On the ACT Mathematics Test, there are fewer problems on trigonometry than on other topics. You'll be tested on many concepts of trigonometry, including trigonometry of the right triangle, properties of trigonometric functions of non-acute angles, laws of sine and cosine, and graphs of trigonometric functions. You are also expected to know how to work with trigonometric identities and solve trigonometric equations. The practice problems in this chapter are designed to help you review many of the trigonometry concepts. Work the problems, and check your answers with the given explanations.

A. Trigonometry of the Right Triangle

1. In the accompanying figure, $\triangle DEF$ is a right triangle with $m\angle F = 90$, $DF = 5$, and $EF = \sqrt{11}$. What is $\cos D$?

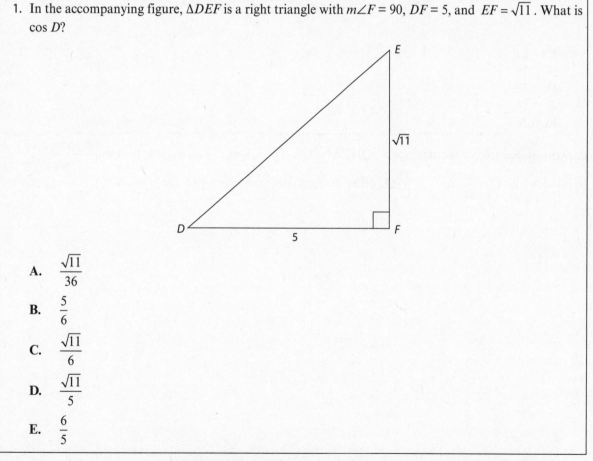

A. $\dfrac{\sqrt{11}}{36}$

B. $\dfrac{5}{6}$

C. $\dfrac{\sqrt{11}}{6}$

D. $\dfrac{\sqrt{11}}{5}$

E. $\dfrac{6}{5}$

B is correct. Remember the mnemonic SOHCAHTOA (see page 387). The cosine of an angle is the ratio $\dfrac{\text{adjacent leg}}{\text{hypotenuse}}$. In this case, $\cos D = \dfrac{DF}{DE}$. Using the Pythagorean theorem, you have $(DE)^2 = \left(\sqrt{11}\right)^2 + (5)^2$, which is equivalent to $(DE)^2 = 11 + 25$ or $(DE)^2 = 36$ or $DE = \pm 6$. Since $DE > 0$, you have $DE = 6$. Thus, $\cos D = \dfrac{5}{6}$.

2. In the accompanying figure, ΔABC is a right triangle with $m\angle B = 90$ and $BC = 12$. If $\tan C = \dfrac{2}{3}$, what is the length of $\overline{AB}$?

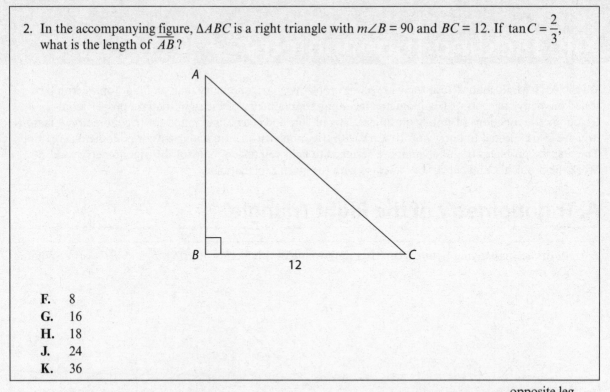

F. 8
G. 16
H. 18
J. 24
K. 36

F is correct. Remember the mnemonic SOHCAHTOA. The tangent of an angle is the ratio $\dfrac{\text{opposite leg}}{\text{adjacent leg}}$. In this case, $\tan C = \dfrac{AB}{BC}$ or $\dfrac{2}{3} = \dfrac{AB}{12}$. Solving the equation, you have $3AB = 2(12)$ or $AB = 8$.

3. A 20-ft ladder is leaning against a wall of a building. The wall is perpendicular to the ground. If the ladder makes an angle of 52° with the ground, what is the distance, to the nearest tenth of a foot, from the foot of the ladder to the bottom of the wall?

   A.   12.3
   B.   12.4
   C.   15.7
   D.   15.8
   E.   25.6

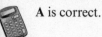

A is correct.

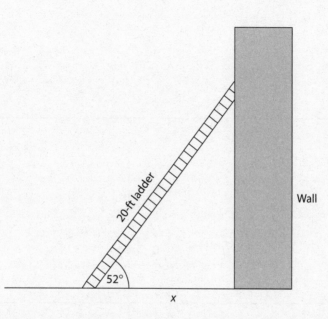

Let x be the distance from the foot of the ladder to the bottom of the wall. Applying the cosine ratio, you have $\cos 52° = \dfrac{x}{20}$. Using a calculator, you have $\cos 52° = 0.6157$, and therefore, $0.6157 = \dfrac{x}{20}$ or $x = 12.314$ ft. Thus, the distance is 12.3 ft.

B. Trigonometric Functions of Non-Acute Angles

1. If $\cos\theta = \dfrac{-5}{13}$ and $\pi < \theta < \dfrac{3\pi}{2}$, what is the value of $\sin\theta$?

   A. $\dfrac{-12}{13}$

   B. $\dfrac{-5}{13}$

   C. $\dfrac{5}{13}$

   D. $\dfrac{5}{12}$

   E. $\dfrac{12}{13}$

A is correct.

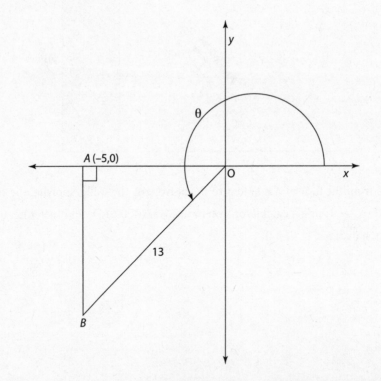

One approach is to draw θ as illustrated in the accompanying figure. Using the Pythagorean theorem, you have $5^2 + (AB)^2 = 13^2$, which is equivalent to $25 + (AB)^2 = 169$ or $(AB)^2 = 144$ or $AB = \pm12$. Since AB is the length of a side of right $\triangle AOB$, $AB = 12$; however, note that the coordinates of point B are $(-5,-12)$. Remember the mnemonic CAST for determining the sign of a trigonometric function in each of the four quadrants.

The letter A in the first quadrant indicates that all functions are positive in that quadrant. The letter S in the second quadrant indicates that only sine and cosecant are positive in that quadrant. The letter T in the third quadrant indicates that only tangent and cotangent are positive in that quadrant. And lastly, the letter C in the fourth quadrant indicates that only cosine and secant are positive in that quadrant.

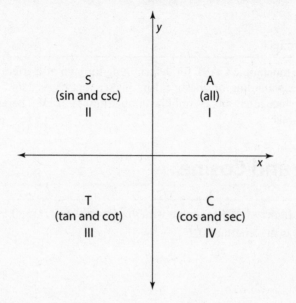

The sine ratio is negative in the third quadrant. Thus, $\sin\theta = \dfrac{-12}{13}$.

---

2. If $\sin\theta = -0.5$, which of the following could be true?

F. $\theta = \dfrac{\pi}{6}$

G. $\theta = \dfrac{\pi}{3}$

H. $\theta = \dfrac{5\pi}{6}$

J. $\theta = \dfrac{7\pi}{6}$

K. $\theta = \dfrac{5\pi}{3}$

J is correct. One approach is to substitute the value of θ in each of the five choices in the equation $\sin\theta = -0.5$ and see which is true. In Choice F, $\sin\left(\dfrac{\pi}{6}\right) = \dfrac{1}{2} \neq -0.5$; in Choice G, $\sin\left(\dfrac{\pi}{3}\right) = \dfrac{\sqrt{3}}{2} \neq -0.5$; in Choice H, $\sin\left(\dfrac{5\pi}{6}\right) = \dfrac{1}{2} \neq -0.5$; in Choice J, $\sin\left(\dfrac{7\pi}{6}\right) = -0.5$; and in Choice K, $\sin\left(\dfrac{5\pi}{3}\right) = \dfrac{-\sqrt{3}}{2} \neq -0.5$.

3. If $\sin \theta > 0$ and $\tan \theta < 0$, in which quadrant does θ lie?

   A. Quadrant I
   B. Quadrant II
   C. Quadrant III
   D. Quadrant IV
   E. Cannot be determined

B is correct. Remember the mnemonic CAST for determining the sign of a trigonometric function in each of the four quadrants (see explanation for question 1 in this section, pages 216–217). Since $\sin \theta > 0$, θ could lie in quadrant I or II, and since $\tan \theta < 0$, θ could lie in quadrant II or IV. Therefore, θ lies in quadrant II, thus satisfying both conditions.

C. Laws of Sine and Cosine

1. In the accompanying figure, $\triangle DEF$ is shown with $m\angle F = 100$, $m\angle D = 30$, and $EF = 12$. Which of the following expressions is the length of $\overline{DF}$?

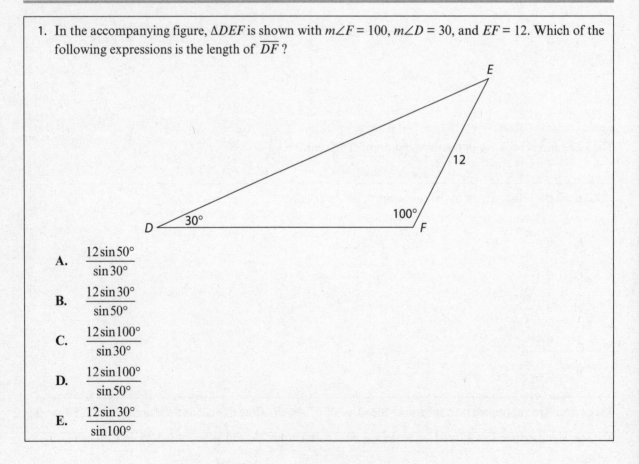

   A. $\dfrac{12 \sin 50°}{\sin 30°}$

   B. $\dfrac{12 \sin 30°}{\sin 50°}$

   C. $\dfrac{12 \sin 100°}{\sin 30°}$

   D. $\dfrac{12 \sin 100°}{\sin 50°}$

   E. $\dfrac{12 \sin 30°}{\sin 100°}$

A is correct. The Law of Sines states that the ratios of the sines of the angles of a triangle to the lengths of the sides opposite those angles are equal. Applying the Law of Sines, you have $\dfrac{\sin 30°}{12} = \dfrac{\sin E}{DF}$. Since $m\angle F = 100$ and $m\angle D = 30$, $m\angle E = 180 - 100 - 30 = 50$. Therefore, $\dfrac{\sin 30°}{12} = \dfrac{\sin 50°}{DF}$, which is equivalent to $(DF)\sin 30° = 12\sin 50°$ or $DF = \dfrac{12\sin 50°}{\sin 30°}$.

2. In the accompanying figure, $\triangle ABC$ is shown with $AB = 8$, $AC = 5$, and $BC = 10$. Which of the following expressions is the measure of $\angle B$?

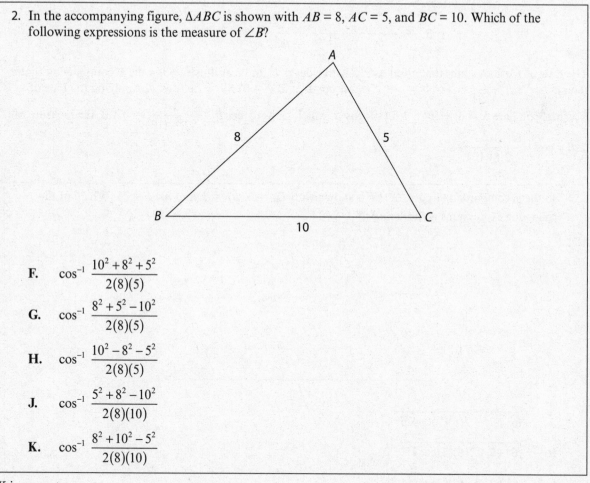

   F. $\cos^{-1}\dfrac{10^2 + 8^2 + 5^2}{2(8)(5)}$

   G. $\cos^{-1}\dfrac{8^2 + 5^2 - 10^2}{2(8)(5)}$

   H. $\cos^{-1}\dfrac{10^2 - 8^2 - 5^2}{2(8)(5)}$

   J. $\cos^{-1}\dfrac{5^2 + 8^2 - 10^2}{2(8)(10)}$

   K. $\cos^{-1}\dfrac{8^2 + 10^2 - 5^2}{2(8)(10)}$

K is correct.

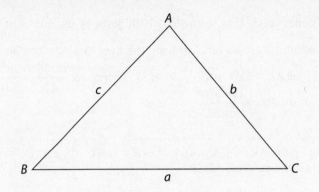

The Law of Cosines states that given $\triangle ABC$ with sides a, b, and c as illustrated in the accompanying figure, then $c^2 = a^2 + b^2 - 2ab \cos C$, $b^2 = a^2 + c^2 - 2ac \cos B$, and $a^2 = b^2 + c^2 - 2bc \cos A$. Applying the Law of Cosines, you have $5^2 = 8^2 + 10^2 - 2(8)(10) \cos B$, which leads to $\cos B = \dfrac{8^2 + 10^2 - 5^2}{2(8)(10)}$. Thus, the measure of $\angle B = \cos^{-1} \dfrac{8^2 + 10^2 - 5^2}{2(8)(10)}$.

3. In the accompanying figure, $\triangle DEF$ is shown with $DF = 6$, $EF = 7$, and $m\angle F = 25$. Which of the following expressions is the length of $\overline{DE}$?

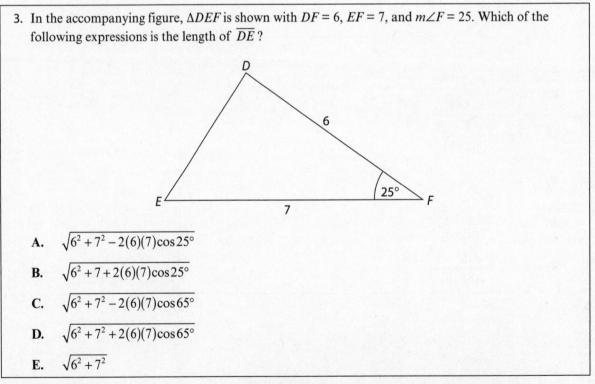

A. $\sqrt{6^2 + 7^2 - 2(6)(7)\cos 25°}$

B. $\sqrt{6^2 + 7 + 2(6)(7)\cos 25°}$

C. $\sqrt{6^2 + 7^2 - 2(6)(7)\cos 65°}$

D. $\sqrt{6^2 + 7^2 + 2(6)(7)\cos 65°}$

E. $\sqrt{6^2 + 7^2}$

A is correct. The Law of Cosines states that given $\triangle ABC$ with sides a, b, and c as illustrated in the accompanying figure, then $c^2 = a^2 + b^2 - 2ab \cos C$, $b^2 = a^2 + c^2 - 2ac \cos B$, and $a^2 = b^2 + c^2 - 2bc \cos A$. Applying the Law of Cosines, you have $(DE)^2 = 6^2 + 7^2 - 2(6)(7) \cos 25°$ or $DE = \pm\sqrt{6^2 + 7^2 - 2(6)(7)\cos 25°}$. Since $DE > 0$, you have $DE = \sqrt{6^2 + 7^2 - 2(6)(7)\cos 25°}$.

D. Graphs of Trigonometric Functions

1. The graph of a function $y = f(x)$ is shown in the accompanying figure. Which of the following could be the function f?

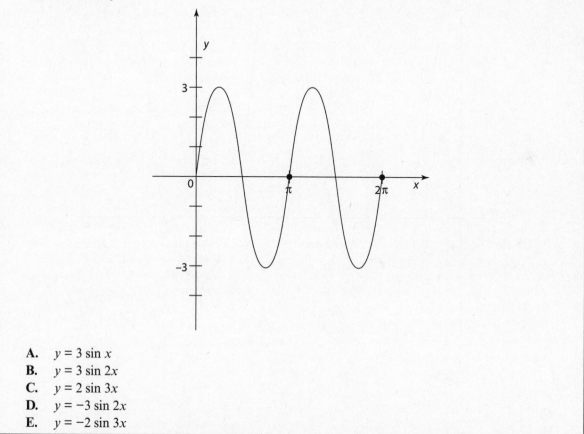

   A. $y = 3 \sin x$
   B. $y = 3 \sin 2x$
   C. $y = 2 \sin 3x$
   D. $y = -3 \sin 2x$
   E. $y = -2 \sin 3x$

B is correct. Since all five choices involve the sine function, you can assume that the given graph is that of a sine function. The given graph completes one cycle of the sine curve from $x = 0$ to $x = \pi$, which implies that the period of the function is π. Using the formula, $\text{period} = \dfrac{2\pi}{\text{frequency}}$, you have $\pi = \dfrac{2\pi}{\text{frequency}}$ or the frequency is 2. The graph also indicates that the range of f is $-3 \le y \le 3$, which means the amplitude of f is 3. Thus, the sine function is $y = 3 \sin 2x$, where the amplitude is 3 and the frequency is 2.

2. In the accompanying figure, the graph of a function $y = a \cos x + d$ is shown. What is the value of a?

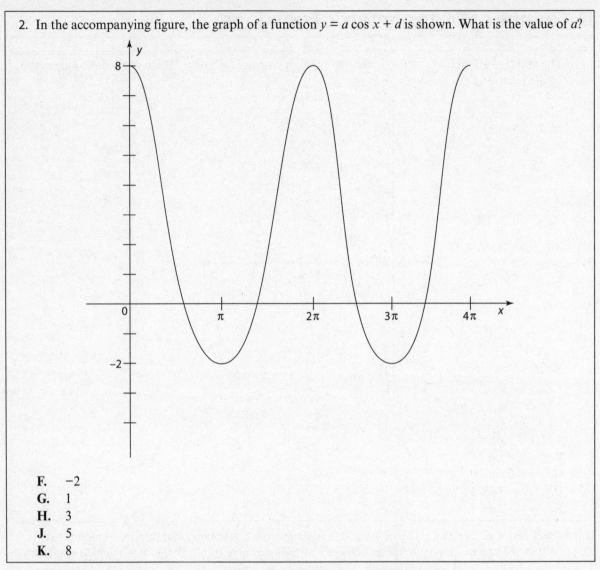

   F. -2
   G. 1
   H. 3
   J. 5
   K. 8

J is correct. The graph shows that the range of f is $-2 \le y \le 8$. The midline of the graph can be found using the formula $y = \left(\dfrac{1}{2}\right)$(maximum value of y + minimum value of y). Thus, you have $y = \dfrac{8+(-2)}{2} = 3$. Thus, $y = 3$ is the midline, and the amplitude of the function is $8 - 3$ or 5. Therefore, the equation of the function is $y = 5\cos x + 3$, which means $a = 5$.

E. Trigonometric Identities

1. For all values of θ such that $0 < \theta < \dfrac{\pi}{2}$, which of the following is equivalent to $\csc\theta(1 - \cos^2\theta)$?

   A. $\sin\theta$
   B. $\cos\theta$
   C. $\csc\theta$
   D. $\sec\theta$
   E. $\sin^2\theta$

A is correct. Beginning with the Pythagorean identity $\sin^2\theta + \cos^2\theta = 1$, you can derive $\sin^2\theta = 1 - \cos^2\theta$.

Also using the reciprocal identity $\csc\theta = \dfrac{1}{\sin\theta}$, you can rewrite $\csc\theta(1 - \cos^2\theta)$ as $\dfrac{1}{\sin\theta}(\sin^2\theta)$, which is equivalent to $\sin\theta$.

2.

θ	sin θ	cos θ
30°	$\dfrac{1}{2}$	$\dfrac{\sqrt{3}}{2}$
45°	$\dfrac{\sqrt{2}}{2}$	$\dfrac{\sqrt{2}}{2}$
60°	$\dfrac{\sqrt{3}}{2}$	$\dfrac{1}{2}$

Given the accompanying table of values and that $\sin(A + B) = \sin A \cos B + \cos A \sin B$, which of the following is the value of $\sin 75°$?

   F. $\sqrt{3}$

   G. 3

   H. $1 + \sqrt{6}$

   J. $\dfrac{1 + \sqrt{3}}{2}$

   K. $\dfrac{\sqrt{2} + \sqrt{6}}{4}$

K is correct. Applying the formula $\sin(A + B) = \sin A \cos B + \cos A \sin B$, you have $\sin 75° = \sin(30° + 45°) = \sin 30° \cos 45° + \cos 30° \sin 45°$. Using the given table of values,

$$\sin 75° = \left(\frac{1}{2}\right)\left(\frac{\sqrt{2}}{2}\right) + \left(\frac{\sqrt{3}}{2}\right)\left(\frac{\sqrt{2}}{2}\right) = \frac{\sqrt{2}}{4} + \frac{\sqrt{6}}{4} = \frac{\sqrt{2} + \sqrt{6}}{4}.$$

F. Solving Trigonometric Equations

1. If $2 \cos \theta - 1 = 0$ and $0° < \theta < 90°$, what is the value of θ in degrees?

   A. $\dfrac{1}{2}$

   B. 30

   C. 45

   D. 60

   E. 120

D is correct. Adding 1 to both sides of the equation, $2 \cos \theta - 1 = 0$, you have $2 \cos \theta = 1$, which is equivalent to $\cos\theta = \dfrac{1}{2}$. Therefore, $\cos^{-1}(\cos\theta) = \cos^{-1}\left(\dfrac{1}{2}\right)$ or $\theta = \cos^{-1}\left(\dfrac{1}{2}\right)$. Using a calculator, you will find $\cos^{-1}\left(\dfrac{1}{2}\right) = 60°$ and thus, $\theta = 60°$.

2. If $2 \sin^2 x = \sin x$ and $0 < x < \dfrac{\pi}{2}$, what is the value of x?

   F. 0

   G. $\dfrac{\pi}{6}$

   H. $\dfrac{\pi}{4}$

   J. $\dfrac{\pi}{3}$

   K. $\dfrac{\pi}{2}$

G is correct. Begin by solving for $\sin x$. Rewrite $2 \sin^2 x = \sin x$ as $2 \sin^2 x - \sin x = 0$. Factoring out $\sin x$, you have $\sin x(2 \sin x - 1) = 0$, which implies $\sin x = 0$ or $2 \sin x - 1 = 0$. If $\sin x = 0$, then $x = 0$, π, or 2π. If $2 \sin x - 1 = 0$, then $\sin x = \dfrac{1}{2}$, and $x = \dfrac{\pi}{6}$ or $\dfrac{5\pi}{6}$. Since $0 < x < \dfrac{\pi}{2}$, the only solution is $x = \dfrac{\pi}{6}$.

XIV. Understanding Probability and Statistics

On the ACT Mathematics Test, you'll be tested on your understanding of probability and statistics concepts, which include the following:

- Counting principles and simple probability
- One-way and two-way tables
- Mean, median, and mode
- Bar graphs and line graphs
- Box-and-whisker plots and stem-and-leaf plots
- Scatterplots and a line or curve of best fit
- Normal distribution and standard deviation

The practice problems in this chapter are designed to help your review of many of these concepts. Work the problems, and check your answers with the given explanations.

A. Counting Problems

1. At a restaurant, the menu consists of 2 varieties of salad, 5 different entrées, and 3 desserts, of which one is apple pie. If the Tuesday night dinner special consists of 1 salad, 1 entrée, and apple pie for dessert, how many different Tuesday night dinner specials are there?

   A. 5
   B. 7
   C. 10
   D. 15
   E. 30

C is correct. Use the Fundamental Counting Principle to determine the number of different dinner specials. Since there are 2 choices for salad, 5 choices for the entrée, and 1 choice for dessert because dessert must be apple pie, there are (5)(2)(1), or 10 different dinner specials.

2. The junior class is holding an election for president, vice president, and secretary, and 6 students are candidates. If any of the candidates could be elected president, vice president, or secretary, but no one can hold more than one position, how many different outcomes are possible?

   F. 6
   G. 20
   H. 36
   J. 72
   K. 120

K is correct. This is a permutation problem because order matters (you could have the same three students elected to different positions). For example, Mary could be elected president, Bill vice president, and Janet secretary; or Bill could be elected president, Janet vice president, and Mary secretary. Thus, the number of different outcomes is $_6P_3$, which is 6(5)(4) or 120.

---

3. What is the total number of distinct diagonals that can be drawn in an octagon? (An octagon has 8 sides.)

   A. 7
   B. 20
   C. 28
   D. 40
   E. 56

B is correct.

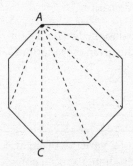

There are 8 vertices in an octagon. From each vertex, 5 diagonals can be drawn. You have (8)(5) or 40 diagonals. However, each diagonal was counted twice. For example, a diagonal drawn from vertex A to C is the same as the diagonal drawn from vertex C to A. Therefore, the total number of distinct diagonals in an octagon is $\dfrac{40}{2}$ or 20.

---

4. If the local post office has only three denominations of stamps available—$0.01 stamps, $0.10 stamps, and $0.20 stamps—how many different sets of the three kinds of stamps can be used to make $0.41?

   F. 4
   G. 5
   H. 8
   J. 9
   K. 10

J is correct. This problem involves not only selecting from three subgroups of stamps, but also factoring in the values of these stamps. This is not a permutation or combination problem. To solve this problem, list all the possible outcomes. Summarizing the outcomes, you have the following table:

$0.01	$0.10	$0.20
1	0	2
1	2	1
11	1	1
21	0	1
1	4	0
11	3	0
21	2	0
31	1	0
41	0	0

There are 9 possible combinations of stamps to make $0.41.

B. Probability

1. If a number is randomly selected from the set {1, 2, 3, 4, 5, 6, 7, 8, 9}, what is the probability that it will be a prime number?

   A. $\dfrac{2}{9}$

   B. $\dfrac{3}{9}$

   C. $\dfrac{4}{9}$

   D. $\dfrac{5}{9}$

   E. 3

C is correct. $P(\text{a prime number}) = \dfrac{\text{number of prime numbers in the set}}{\text{total number of elements in the set}}$.

There are 4 prime numbers in the set: 2, 3, 5, 7. There are 9 numbers in total. Therefore, the probability of getting a prime number is $\dfrac{4}{9}$.

2. Janet labeled all her books in her classroom as either fiction or nonfiction. She has 30 nonfiction books. If a book is picked at random, the probability that it is fiction is $\dfrac{3}{5}$. What is the total number of books in her classroom?

   F. 50
   G. 60
   H. 75
   J. 90
   K. 150

H is correct. Since $P(\text{fiction}) = \dfrac{3}{5}$, $P(\text{nonfiction}) = 1 - \dfrac{3}{5} = \dfrac{2}{5}$. Use x to represent the total number of books. There are 30 nonfiction books. Therefore, $\dfrac{\text{the number of nonfiction books}}{\text{total number of books}} = \dfrac{2}{5}$ or $\dfrac{30}{x} = \dfrac{2}{5}$, which is equivalent to $2x = 30(5)$ or $x = 75$. There are 75 books in total in Janet's classroom.

---

3. Victoria has 3 quarters and 2 dimes in her piggybank. If 2 coins are taken out of the piggybank at random, what is the probability that both coins are dimes?

    A. $\dfrac{1}{20}$

    B. $\dfrac{1}{10}$

    C. $\dfrac{2}{5}$

    D. $\dfrac{2}{3}$

    E. $\dfrac{4}{5}$

B is correct. $P(2 \text{ dimes}) = \dfrac{\text{number of ways of picking 2 dimes}}{\text{total number of ways of picking 2 coins from 5 coins}}$. The number of ways of picking 2 dimes is $_2C_2$ or 1. The number of ways of picking 2 coins from 5 coins is $_5C_2$ or 10. Therefore, $P(2 \text{ dimes}) = \dfrac{1}{10}$. Another approach is as follows:

$$P(2 \text{ dimes}) = P(\text{first coin is a dime}) \times P(\text{second coin is a dime}) = \dfrac{2}{5}\left(\dfrac{1}{4}\right) = \dfrac{1}{10}$$

---

4. In a box, there are 10 red balls and 8 blue balls. What is the minimum number of balls that have to be removed in order for the probability of picking 1 red ball at random from the box to be $\dfrac{2}{3}$?

    F. 0
    G. 2
    H. 3
    J. 4
    K. 6

H is correct. The probability of picking 1 red ball equaling $\dfrac{2}{3}$ implies that the total number of balls in the box has to be divisible by 3. Initially, there are 10 red and 8 blue balls in the box totaling 18, which is divisible by 3. However, the probability of picking 1 red ball is $\frac{10}{18}$, which is $\frac{5}{9}$, not $\frac{2}{3}$. The next number divisible by 3 is 15. If there are 15 balls in the box and the probability of picking a red ball is $\frac{2}{3}$, then you have $\frac{x}{15} = \frac{2}{3}$, x being the number of red balls. Solve the proportion and note that $x = 10$. So you need 10 red balls and 5 blue balls. Since there are 10 red and 8 blue balls initially, you must remove 3 blue balls from the box.

---

5. What is the expected value of a discrete random variable x whose probability distribution is shown below?

x_i	$p(x_i)$
5	$\frac{1}{5}$
10	$\frac{1}{10}$
15	$\frac{1}{5}$
20	$\frac{3}{10}$
30	$\frac{1}{5}$

A. 5
B. 10
C. 15
D. 17
E. 25

D is correct. The expected value of a probability distribution is given as $\sum_{i=1}^{n} x_i \cdot p(x_i)$. In this case, the expected value is $5\left(\frac{1}{5}\right) + 10\left(\frac{1}{10}\right) + 15\left(\frac{1}{5}\right) + 20\left(\frac{3}{10}\right) + 30\left(\frac{1}{5}\right) = 17$.

C. One-Way Tables and Two-Way Tables

Tables and bar graphs are used to show the relationship between two categorical variables. Data can be shown as frequency counts or as relative frequencies. Relative frequencies for two-way tables can also be displayed as relative frequencies for the entire table, for rows, or for columns. Try the following practice problems.

1. Two hundred and forty students signed up for an after-school sports program. Each student selected one and only one of four sports available: basketball, football, soccer, and tennis. Their selections are summarized in a relative frequency table below.

Relative Frequency Table				
Sports	Basketball	Football	Soccer	Tennis
Percent	45	12.5	35	7.5

How many students signed up for tennis?

   A.   8
   B.   15
   C.   18
   D.   32
   E.   33

C is correct. The table shows that 7.5% of students signed up for tennis. Convert 7.5% to either a decimal, .075, or a fraction, $\dfrac{7.5}{100}$. Thus, the number of students who signed up for tennis is $(240)\dfrac{7.5}{100}$ or 18, Choice C. Note that you could also have used a proportion to solve the problem: $\dfrac{7.5\%}{100\%} = \dfrac{x}{240}$ or $x = 18$.

Use the following information to answer questions 2–4.

Fifty third graders were asked which subject they like more: math or science. Their responses are summarized in a two-way frequency table below.

Frequency Table			
	Math	Science	Total
Boys	13	10	23
Girls	9	18	27
Total	22	28	50

2. To the nearest tenth, what percent of the third graders who like science more than math are girls?

   F.   27.0
   G.   36.0
   H.   54.0
   J.   64.3
   K.   66.7

J is correct. The science column shows that there are 28 students who prefer science, and of the 28 students, 18 are girls. Thus, the percent of the 28 students who are girls is $\left(\dfrac{18}{28}\right)(100\%) \approx 64.286\% \approx 64.3\%$, Choice J.

3. Below is a partially constructed relative frequency table based on the information provided earlier on the 50 third graders.

Relative Frequency Table

	Math	Science	Total
Boys	0.26	0.20	0.46
Girls	x		
Total		y	1.00

What is the value of $x + y$?

A. 0.18
B. 0.56
C. 0.74
D. 37
E. 74

C is correct. Remember that this is a relative frequency table. Based on the frequency table provided earlier, there are 9 girls who prefer math and there are 50 students total. Thus, $x = \dfrac{9}{50} = 0.18$. Similarly, there are 28 students who chose science out of 50; therefore, $y = \dfrac{28}{50} = 0.56$. The value of $(x + y)$ is = 0.18 + 0.56 = 0.74, Choice C. A completely constructed relative frequency table is shown below.

Relative Frequency Table

	Math	Science	Total
Boys	0.26	0.20	0.46
Girls	0.18	0.36	0.54
Total	0.44	0.56	1.00

4. Below is a partially constructed relative frequency of row table based on the information provided earlier on the 50 third graders.

Relative Frequency of Row Table

	Math	Science	Total
Boys	56.5%	43.5%	100%
Girls		x	100%
Total			100%

What is the value of x in percent?

F. 33.3
G. 36
H. 44
J. 56
K. 66.7

K is correct. Remember that this is a relative frequency of row table. Based on the frequency table provided earlier, there are 18 girls who prefer science out of a total of 27 girls. Thus, $x = \dfrac{18}{27}(100\%) \approx 66.7\%$, Choice K. A complete relative frequency of row table is shown below.

Relative Frequency of Row Table

	Math	Science	Total
Boys	56.5%	43.5%	100%
Girls	33.3%	66.7%	100%
Total	44%	56%	100%

5. A furniture manufacturer has three factories that make tables and chairs. In the month of January, the three factories together produced 200 tables and 600 chairs. The production levels of the three factories are shown below in a relative frequency of column table.

Relative Frequency of Column Table

	Tables	Chairs	Total
Factory A	0.20	0.33	0.3
Factory B	0.50	0.40	0.425
Factory C	0.30	0.27	0.275
Total	1.00	1.00	1.00

How many chairs did Factory B produce in the month of January?

- **A.** 100
- **B.** 160
- **C.** 200
- **D.** 240
- **E.** 340

D is correct. The conditional frequency for Factory B under the Chairs column is 0.40, which means Factory B produced 40 percent of the total number of chairs made by the three factories. Since the three factories together produced 600 chairs, Factory B made (600)(0.40) or 240 chairs, Choice D. (It might be helpful to see the complete relative frequency of column table as shown below. Please note that you do not need to construct a complete frequency table to answer the question.)

Relative Frequency of Column Table

	Tables	Chairs	Total
Factory A	40	200	240
Factory B	100	240	340
Factory C	60	160	220
Total	200	600	800

6. A baker asked 40 of her customers which pie they like more: apple or pumpkin. Their responses are summarized in a stacked bar graph below.

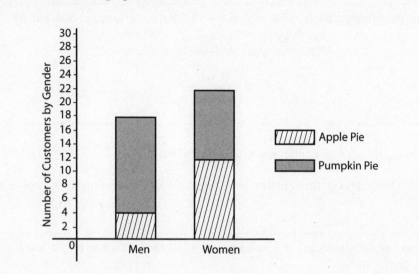

If one person is randomly selected from all the customers who prefer apple pie, what is the probability that the person selected is a woman?

F. $\dfrac{1}{4}$

G. $\dfrac{5}{11}$

H. $\dfrac{11}{20}$

J. $\dfrac{6}{11}$

K. $\dfrac{3}{4}$

K is correct. The stacked bar graph shows that of the customers who prefer apple pie, 4 are men and 12 are women. The total number of customers who prefer apple pie is 16. Thus, the probability of a woman being picked from all the customers who prefer apple pie is $\dfrac{12}{16}$ or $\dfrac{3}{4}$. (It might be helpful to see a frequency table for the stacked bar graph. Please note that you do not need to construct a frequency table for the stacked bar graph to answer the question.)

Frequency Table			
	Apple Pie	Pumpkin Pie	Total
Men	4	14	18
Women	12	10	22
Total	16	24	40

D. Mean, Median, and Mode

---

1. If the average (arithmetic mean) of 6, m, and n is 10, what is the average of m and n?

    A. 4
    B. 12
    C. 18
    D. 24
    E. 36

B is correct. Knowing the average implies knowing the sum. Since $\dfrac{6+m+n}{3}=10$, you know that $6 + m + n$ = 30 by multiplying both sides of the equation by 3. Then $m + n = 24$, and the average of m and n is $\dfrac{m+n}{2}$, which is $\dfrac{24}{2}$ or 12.

---

2. If the average (arithmetic mean) of x and $3x - 4$ is p and the average of $6 - 2x$ and $14 - 2x$ is q, what is the average of p and q?

    F. 4
    G. 16
    H. $4 - 2x$
    J. $2x + 4$
    K. $8x + 16$

F is correct. Since the average of x and $3x - 4$ is p, you have $p = \dfrac{(x)+(3x-4)}{2} = \dfrac{4x-4}{2} = 2x-2$. Similarly, $q = \dfrac{(6-2x)+(14-2x)}{2} = \dfrac{20-4x}{2} = 10-2x$. The average of p and q can be obtained by $\dfrac{(2x-2)+(10-2x)}{2} = \dfrac{8}{2} = 4$.

---

3. Rebecca's test grades in her math class for the first quarter are 90, 84, 80, 92, 84, and 98. Of the 6 grades in the first quarter, if p is the mean, q is the median, and r is the mode, which of the following inequalities is true?

    A. $r < q < p$
    B. $r < p < q$
    C. $p < r < q$
    D. $q < p < r$
    E. $p < q < r$

A is correct. The mean is the average: $p = \dfrac{90 + 84 + 80 + 92 + 84 + 98}{6} = 88$. The median is q, which is the middle value of 80, 84, 84, 90, 92, 98 or $\dfrac{84 + 90}{2} = 87$. The mode is r, which is the value that appears the most often: 84. Thus, $r < q < p$.

---

4. Given $3x - 2$, $-\dfrac{1}{x}$, and x^2, if x^2 is the median, which of the following could be the value of x?

   F. -3

   G. -2

   H. $-\dfrac{1}{2}$

   J. $\dfrac{1}{2}$

   K. 3

H is correct. Substitute the given numbers into the three expressions:

x	$3x - 2$	x^2	$-\dfrac{1}{x}$
-3	-11	9	$\dfrac{1}{3}$
-2	-8	4	$\dfrac{1}{2}$
$-\dfrac{1}{2}$	$-3\dfrac{1}{2}$	$\dfrac{1}{4}$	2
$\dfrac{1}{2}$	$-\dfrac{1}{2}$	$\dfrac{1}{4}$	-2
3	7	9	$-\dfrac{1}{3}$

Notice that when $x = -\dfrac{1}{2}$, you have $-3\dfrac{1}{2}$, $\dfrac{1}{4}$, and 2, making x^2 the median.

E. Bar Graphs and Line Graphs

1. In the accompanying diagram, the line graph shows the number of books sold by Whitman Bookstore in each month from January to May. What percent of the number of books sold in February is equal to the number of books sold in May?

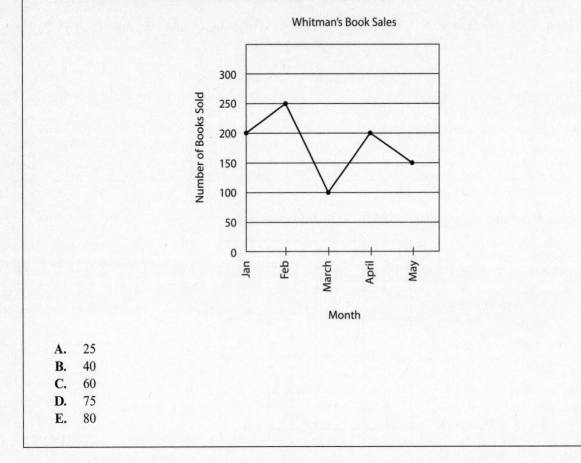

Whitman's Book Sales

A. 25
B. 40
C. 60
D. 75
E. 80

C is correct. According to the graph, you know that the number of books sold in February is 250 and the number of books sold in May is 150. Use the proportion $\dfrac{150}{250} = \dfrac{x}{100\%}$, which is equivalent to $x = \dfrac{100(150)}{250}\%$ or 60%.

2. In 2016, students who attended Washington High School or Adams High School were allowed to participate in only one sport for the year: tennis, soccer, swimming, or basketball. Based on the information provided in the accompanying bar graph, how many more students at Washington High School than at Adams High School participated in a sport in 2016?

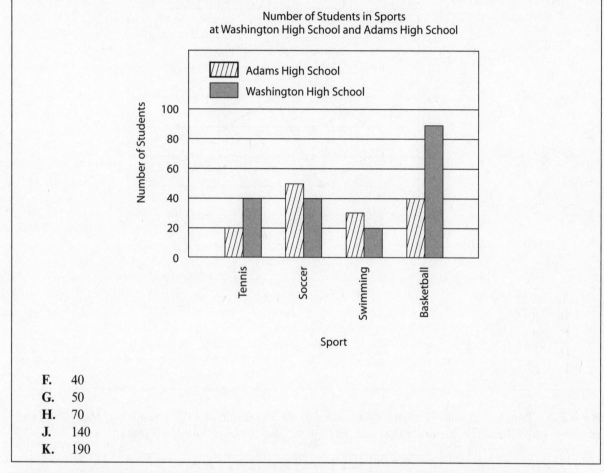

Number of Students in Sports
at Washington High School and Adams High School

F.　40
G.　50
H.　70
J.　140
K.　190

G is correct. At Washington High School, 40 students played tennis, 40 played soccer, 20 swam, and 90 played basketball, totaling 40 + 40 + 20 + 90 = 190 students who participated in a sport. At Adams High School, 20 students played tennis, 50 played soccer, 30 swam, and 40 played basketball, totaling 20 + 50 + 30 + 40 = 140 students who participated in a sport. The difference between the number of students who participated in a sport at Washington High School and at Adams High School is 190 – 140 = 50.

3. In the accompanying diagram, the double line graph shows the revenues and expenses of Concord Electronics for the past 5 years. Which year had the greatest profit?

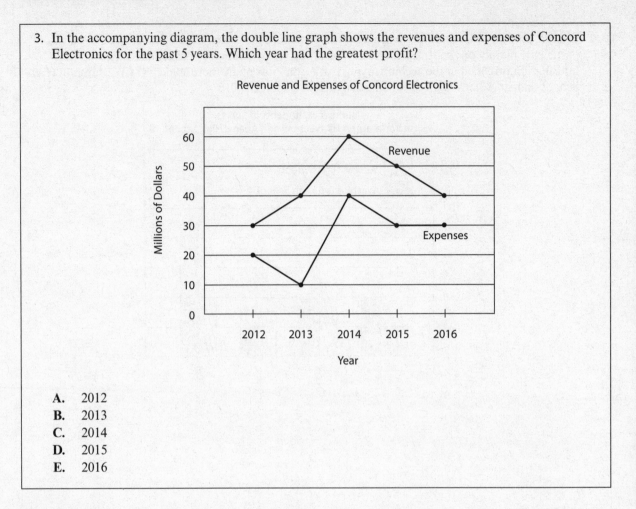

Revenue and Expenses of Concord Electronics

A. 2012
B. 2013
C. 2014
D. 2015
E. 2016

B is correct. Profit = Revenue – Expenses. According to the line graph, in 2013, revenue was $40 million and expenses were $10 million. Profit for that year was $30 million, the largest for the 5 years.

	2012	2013	2014	2015	2016
Revenue	30	40	60	50	40
Expenses	20	10	40	30	30
Profit	10	30	20	20	10

F. Box-and-Whisker Plots and Stem-and-Leaf Plots

1. The box-and-whisker plot below represents the midterm grades of students in a geometry class.

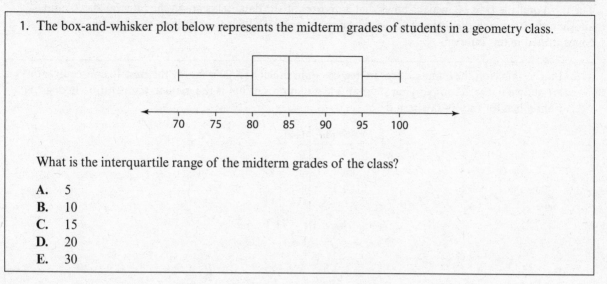

What is the interquartile range of the midterm grades of the class?

A. 5
B. 10
C. 15
D. 20
E. 30

C is correct. The given box-and-whisker plot shows that the lowest midterm grade is 70, highest is 100, first quartile Q_1 is 80, second quartile Q_2 (or median) is 85, and the third quartile Q_3 is 95.

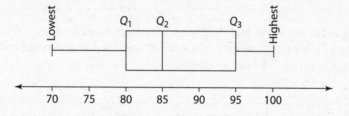

The interquartile range is the difference between the third quartile and the first quartile ($Q_3 - Q_1$). Thus, the interquartile range is $95 - 80 = 15$.

2. Given a box-and-whisker plot as shown below, which of the following intervals contains the quarter of data in which the data items are most concentrated?

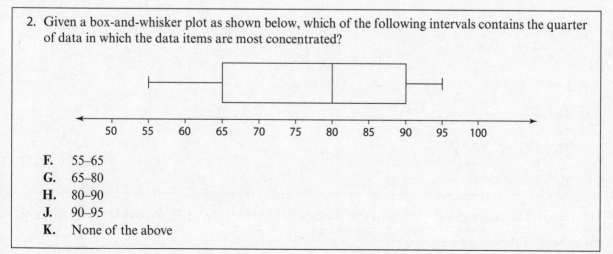

F. 55–65
G. 65–80
H. 80–90
J. 90–95
K. None of the above

J is correct. The first quartile Q_1 is 65, which shows that a quarter of the data items are in the interval 55–65. The second quartile or median Q_2 is 80, indicating that a quarter of the data items are in the interval 65–80. The third quartile Q_3 is 90, which shows that a quarter of the data items are in the interval 80–90, and another quarter are in the interval 90–95. Since the interval 90–95 is the smallest, the data items are most concentrated in this interval.

3. In a certain city, the temperatures in degrees Fahrenheit at 8:00 a.m. for the past 10 consecutive days are shown in the accompanying stem-and-leaf diagram. What is the median temperature in degrees Fahrenheit for the 10-day period?

Stem	Leaf
4	9
5	2, 4, 4, 6
6	2, 2, 5
7	0, 1

Key: 7|1 = 71°F

    A.   54
    B.   55
    C.   56
    D.   59
    E.   62

D is correct. According to the stem-and-leaf diagram, the temperatures for the past 10 days are 49, 52, 54, 54, 56, 62, 62, 65, 70, and 71. Since the median of a data set arranged in numerical order is the middle number, the median temperature is $\frac{56+62}{2}$ or 59°F.

4. What is the mean of the set of data represented by the stem-and-leaf plot shown below?

Stem	Leaf
1	5
2	
3	7, 8, 8
4	0, 2

Key: 4|2 = 42

    F.   2.3
    G.   28
    H.   35
    J.   38
    K.   42

H is correct. The stem-and-leaf plot shows that the data items are 15, 37, 38, 38, 40, and 42. Thus, the mean (or average) of these numbers is $\frac{15+37+38+38+40+42}{6} = 35$.

G. Scatterplots and a Line or Curve of Best Fit

When solving problems involving scatterplots or a line of best fit, it is helpful to remember the following:

- A **line or curve of best fit** is a line or curve that best describes a set of data points. Some of the common curves are those of quadratic, cubic, polynomial, logarithmic, and exponential functions.
- A **correlation coefficient, r,** indicates how strong the correlation is between two variables. The closer $|r|$ is to 1, the stronger the correlation. For example, $r = -0.9$ indicates a stronger correlation than $r = 0.8$.
- If $r > 0$, the slope of the regression line is positive, and if $r < 0$, the slope is negative.

---

1. Which of the following values of a correlation coefficient represents data with the strongest linear correlation between two variables?

   A.   −0.92
   B.   0
   C.   0.85
   D.   1.2
   E.   2.1

A is correct. The correlation coefficient, r, is always $-1 \leq r \leq 1$. If $r > 0$, the slope of the regression line is positive, and if $r < 0$, the slope of the regression line is negative. To determine the strength of a linear relationship between the two variables, you look at $|r|$. The closer the $|r|$ is to 1, the stronger the linear relationship between the two variables. Among the choices given, $|-0.92| = 0.92$, Choice A, is the closest to 1.

Use the following information to answer questions 2–4.

Twenty students took a math test. The scatterplot in the accompanying figure shows, for ten students, the relationship between the number of hours a student studied for the test and the student's grade for the test. The figure also shows the line of best fit for all twenty students.

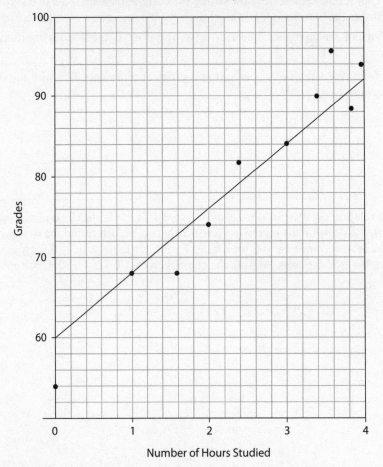

Grades of 10 Students for a Math Test and the Number of Hours They Studied for the Test

2. According to the line of best fit, which of the following is the predicted grade for a student who studied 2 hours for the test?

   F.   74
   G.   76
   H.   78
   J.   82
   K.   84

G is correct. Since the student studied 2 hours for the test, go to 2 on the *x*-axis and then go up to the point on the line of best fit. Notice that the corresponding *y*-value for *x* = 2 is 76, Choice G.

3. Based on the line of best fit, what was the minimum number of hours a student had to study in order to earn a grade of 96 or higher?

   A. 3.6
   B. 4.5
   C. 5
   D. 5.5
   E. 6

B is correct. Begin by finding the slope of the line of best fit. Pick any two points on the line with integer coordinates; for example, (4, 92) and (3, 84). The slope is $\dfrac{92-84}{4-3} = 8$, which means that for every additional hour of study, a student's grade goes up 8 points. Remember, you already have the point (4, 92), which means that a student studying 4 hours would receive a grade of 92. A grade of 96 is 4 more points than 92. Thus, a student needs to study an additional half-hour; that is, a student has to study a total of 4.5 hours in order to receive a grade of 96 or higher, Choice B.

4. Of the ten students whose grades are on the scatterplot, how many have an actual grade within 4 points of the predicted grade by the line of best fit?

   F. 3
   G. 5
   H. 6
   J. 7
   K. 9

J is correct. Students who studied 0, 1.6, and 3.6 hours received grades of 54, 68, and 96, respectively. Their grades were more than 4 points from the predicted grades by the line of best fit. The other seven students had grades all within 4 points of their predicted grades, Choice J.

5. The scatterplot of a set of data points is shown in the accompanying diagram. Which of the following equations could best model the data?

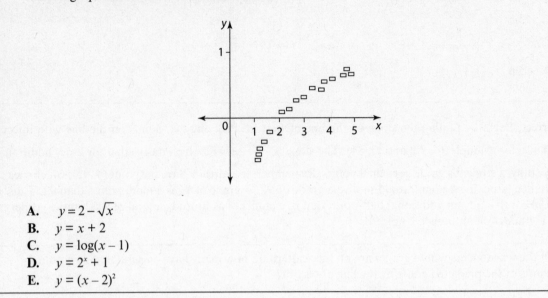

A. $y = 2 - \sqrt{x}$
B. $y = x + 2$
C. $y = \log(x - 1)$
D. $y = 2^x + 1$
E. $y = (x - 2)^2$

C is correct. Enter the equation of each choice into the calculator and examine its graph. The graph of $y = \log(x - 1)$ best models the data, Choice C.

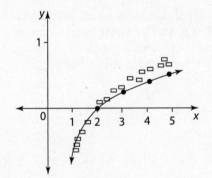

6. The number of elephants in a region in Asia from 2010 to 2015 is shown in the scatterplot below. The line of best fit is also shown.

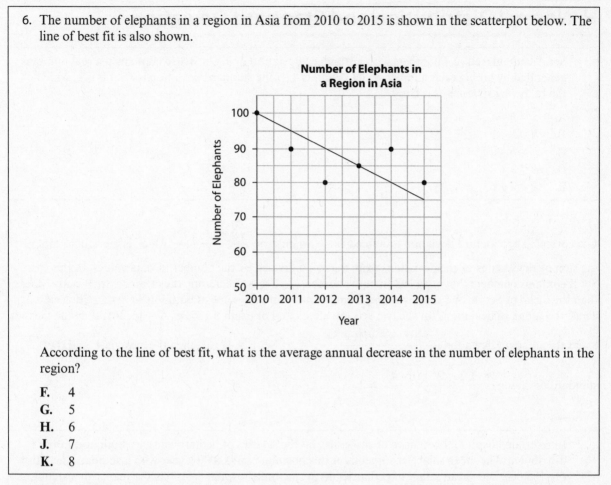

Number of Elephants in a Region in Asia

According to the line of best fit, what is the average annual decrease in the number of elephants in the region?

F.   4
G.   5
H.   6
J.   7
K.   8

G is correct. From the line of best fit, select two points with integer coefficients; for example, (2010, 100) and (2013, 85).The slope of the line is $m = \dfrac{y_2 - y_1}{x_2 - x_1}$, and in this case, $m = \dfrac{100 - 85}{2010 - 2013} = -5$. Thus, the yearly decrease in the number of elephants in the region is 5, Choice G.

H. Normal Distribution and Standard Deviation

---

1. Set A contains ten real numbers with a standard deviation of h. Set B also contains ten real numbers generated by taking each number in Set A minus 4. If the standard deviation for Set B is k, which of the following statements is true?

   A. $k = h - 4$
   B. $k = h - 2$
   C. $k = h$
   D. $k = h + 4$
   E. $k = h + 6$

C is correct. The standard deviation is defined as $\sqrt{\text{variance}}$ or $\sqrt{\dfrac{\sum(x_i - \bar{x})^2}{n}}$, which is the square root of the sum of the squares of the deviations from the mean divided by the number of data values. In this case, Set B contains numbers that are 4 less than the numbers in Set A. Therefore, the mean of Set B is also 4 less than the mean of Set A, and the deviations from the mean are the same in both sets or $k = h$, Choice C. Thus, the standard deviations for the two sets are identical. For example, if Set A = {6, 10}, then the mean is 8 and the standard deviation is $\sqrt{\dfrac{(6-8)^2 + (10-8)^2}{2}} = 2$. If Set B = {2, 6}, then the mean is 4, and the standard deviation is $\sqrt{\dfrac{(2-4)^2 + (6-4)^2}{2}} = 2$.

---

2. In a certain hospital, the salaries of surgeons and the salaries of pediatricians are both normally distributed. The mean salary of surgeons at this hospital is $400,000 a year with a standard deviation of $100,000. The mean salary of pediatricians at the same hospital is $250,000 a year with a standard deviation of $50,000. Dr. Smith, a surgeon, has an annual salary of $450,000, and Dr. Lee, a pediatrician, has an annual salary of $300,000. Which of the following statements is true?

   F. In the hospital, Dr. Smith's salary is in a higher percentile among all the surgeons than Dr. Lee's salary percentile among all the pediatricians.
   G. In the hospital, Dr. Lee's salary is in a higher percentile among all the pediatricians than Dr. Smith's salary percentile among all the surgeons.
   H. The salaries of both doctors are in the same percentile in their respective groups.
   J. Dr. Lee's salary is greater than the salary of more than half of the surgeons at the hospital.
   K. There is insufficient information to determine which doctor's salary is in a higher percentile in their respective groups.

G is correct.

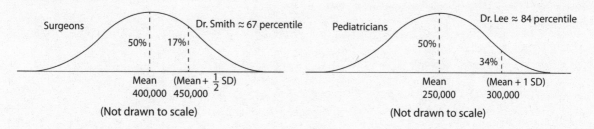

Dr. Smith's salary is a half standard deviation above the mean, while Dr. Lee's salary is 1 standard deviation above the mean. Thus, Dr. Lee's salary is relatively higher among all the pediatricians in the hospital than Dr. Smith's salary among all the surgeons, Choice G.

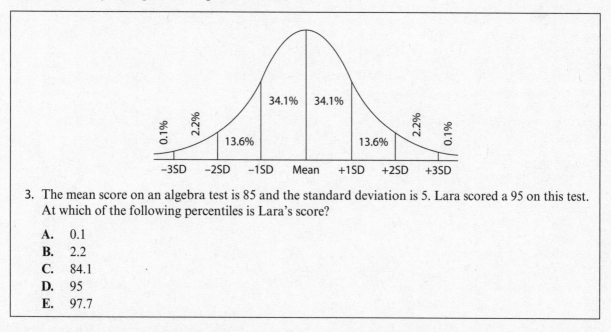

3. The mean score on an algebra test is 85 and the standard deviation is 5. Lara scored a 95 on this test. At which of the following percentiles is Lara's score?

   A. 0.1
   B. 2.2
   C. 84.1
   D. 95
   E. 97.7

E is correct. The mean score is 85 and the standard deviation is 5. Therefore, Lara's score of 95 is 2 standard deviations above the mean. The normal distribution curve shows that only 2.3% (2.2% + 0.1%) of the test scores are at the 97.7th (100 − 2.3) percentile.

XV. Science Test

A. Overview

The ACT Science Test includes 40 multiple-choice questions, which, historically, are distributed over 7 different passages. You will find between 5 and 7 questions that follow the text and data presented in any passage; the exact number of questions depends on the passage type under consideration.

No calculator is allowed, but it is completely unnecessary anyway. Any math calculations you will be asked to do involve simple arithmetic, and often it is not a specific calculation that matters as much as understanding the pattern or trend in the data displayed. In some instances, interpolation or extrapolation of graphs or data tables will be required.

The content of the ACT Science Test mirrors subject matter from the curricula typically found in the core science courses completed between grades 9 and 12 in American secondary schools. These include content from the following disciplines (examples of topics shown in parentheses):

- *Earth/Space Sciences* (geology, astronomy, meteorology, oceanography, and environmental sciences)
- *Biology* (biochemistry, cell biology, genetics, evolution, microbiology, botany, zoology, and ecology)
- *Chemistry* (properties and states of matter, chemical bonding, chemical reactions, solutions, acids and bases, kinetics and equilibria, gas laws, and organic chemistry)
- *Physics* (mechanics, energy, thermodynamics, electromagnetism, fluids, solids, and optics)

You should be prepared to take this test if you are in the process of completing a college-preparatory science course of study in secondary school (three years or more of science) and you have already completed two such courses. To ensure that you have a solid foundation in both the physical and life sciences and have been exposed to a wide range of topics within each discipline, it is helpful (but not required or necessary) to have completed a course in biology and a course in the physical sciences (or equivalents).

An important fact to remember is that this test is primarily concerned with your ability to think scientifically, not with your ability to recall specific information from any one discipline or course. Students taking this test are at different points in their science program, and the sequence of courses within the course of study can also vary greatly from school to school. This test must accommodate a diverse student pool with a wide range of specific scientific knowledge; most of the information necessary to understand a passage is presented either directly or implicitly within the passage itself. You may find it helpful, however, to include in your ACT science preparation some review of fundamental/core concepts from the science courses you have already completed. Doing so may help you proceed through the passages and complete analyses more efficiently.

B. General Strategies

Remember that pacing yourself throughout the test is essential for maximizing your success. Managing 40 questions distributed over 7 different passages in a 35-minute period can be stressful and doesn't allow much time for review of passages. (This amounts to an average of 5 minutes per section, but recall that sections will vary in the number of questions asked depending on the passage type.) It is highly recommended that you practice sample science questions in an authentic, test-like environment as much as possible, as you are more likely to be relaxed and confident on the actual test day. In other words, practice, practice, practice! The Cram Plans presented in this book will help you organize your practice schedule given your specific time frame for review.

To think like a scientist, you should base your conclusions on a logical analysis of facts and objective observations. The **scientific method** is the organized approach to solving a problem and/or answering a question using logic and reasoning and integrating past scientific knowledge. It generally follows the sequence of steps below:

1. **Observation** involves using one or more of the five senses to perceive the world. Observations can be qualitative in nature (that is, involve the use of descriptive words) or quantitative in nature (that is, involve the use of descriptive numbers). An example of qualitative data is color (for example, blue or yellow); an example of quantitative data is length in meters (for example, 0.025 m or 1.37×10^{-6} cm).

2. **Forming a hypothesis** involves creating a statement that uses the independent and dependent variables present in an experimental design (see step 3) to predict the outcome of an experiment. A hypothesis is something of an "educated guess" based on direct observation and past scientific knowledge. A hypothesis should be testable and the tests replicable in order to be scientifically valid.

3. **Experimentation** varies widely, depending upon the scientific discipline involved, the specific subject matter under investigation, and the exact question posed, but it is preferred to involve some form of controlled laboratory design. This includes a means of manipulating the independent variable and recording data describing the effect in the dependent variable. The independent variable is the factor that is selected by the experimenter to be altered during the course of the experiment and is the lone difference between the control group and the experimental group (assuming a simple, two-group design). The dependent variable is the observed result or outcome of the alteration of the independent variable. Data involving the independent and dependent variables are recorded throughout the experiment and organized into tables, as are any qualitative data that may be significant.

4. **Data analysis** involves using the data collected during experimentation to create graphs, charts, and other visual representations that help clarify patterns in the data and determine the relationship between the independent and dependent variables tested in the experiment. Calculations are often performed to manipulate the data and to understand relationships between data values. Mathematical models or other models may be generated to demonstrate a principle revealed by the data.

5. **Forming a conclusion** includes a summary of the findings of the experiment and a statement of support or rejection of the hypothesis. Assuming the experimental controls are in place, any difference in the dependent variable between the control and experimental groups can be attributed to the independent variable, and the hypothesis is supported. If no difference between the control and experimental groups is observed, the hypothesis is rejected and a new hypothesis might be proposed, including observations made and conclusions drawn during the current experiment. Only when a concept has stood the test of countless scientific experimentation over time (that is, is supported by overwhelming evidence) and helps establish an overarching idea or guiding principles to explain a natural phenomenon, might it be considered a theory (for example, the theory of relativity and the theory of evolution by natural selection).

Remember that scientific reasoning skills are emphasized over recall of any specific scientific content on the ACT Science Test. Do not use precious time memorizing such specific content before the ACT; your time is better spent practicing a variety of sample problems and exposing yourself to a variety of data presentation formats. The more exposure you have to concepts and experimental scenarios from a variety of scientific disciplines, and the more you practice reading and interpreting data presented in a variety of chart, table, and graphic forms, the more comfortable you will be addressing the passages and questions on the actual test. In addition to the sample problems and visual examples in this book, you can find countless other graphic and visual presentations of data in science textbooks and in (print or digital) journals and news articles. For more specific information, review the next section, "Visual Representations of Data."

C. Visual Representations of Data

The likelihood of formulating the correct answer for most of the questions in the ACT Science Test is directly related to your ability to read and interpret visual data. Understanding the way that data tables are organized and the way that graphs are structured will make it easier to understand the different displays of data that you are likely to encounter on the ACT Science Test, and will thus help to maximize your score. Descriptions of data tables and graphs are provided below along with examples from various science contexts. After reviewing those, it will be helpful to regularly review tables and graphs that you encounter in science and math textbooks, newspaper articles, and other sources of visual data displays. Limitless examples are available online.

1. Understanding Data Tables

A data table is a set of related data values organized into a series of vertical columns and horizontal rows creating a grid (or matrix). Data tables are useful in organizing, managing, and understanding large volumes of data and for discerning patterns and relationships between variables. There are often descriptive titles that summarize the nature of the data presented using the independent and dependent variables. The far left column generally contains data representing the independent variable; other columns usually contain information pertaining to the dependent variable.

An example of the range of recorded wavelengths and frequencies of light is shown in the following table:

Color of Light	Wavelength (nm)	Frequency (THz)
Red	780–622	384–482
Orange	622–597	482–503
Yellow	597–577	503–520
Green	577–492	520–610
Blue	492–455	610–659
Violet	455–390	659–769

Here, the color of observed light is the independent variable, and the wavelength of observed light (measured in nanometers) and the frequency of observed light (measured in terahertz) are the dependent variables. Note that the units used are given in parentheses in the heading of each column after the column title.

2. Understanding Graphs

Line graphs can show more detail than other types of graphs and are used when the independent variable (*x*-axis) represents a continuous quantity (for example, temperature in degrees Celsius). When the independent variable is instead a qualitative factor (e.g., whether the test subject received a pharmaceutical drug or a placebo), a bar graph is more appropriately used.

An example of a bar graph is shown here to represent the frequency that an interviewer received an affirmative response to a survey question:

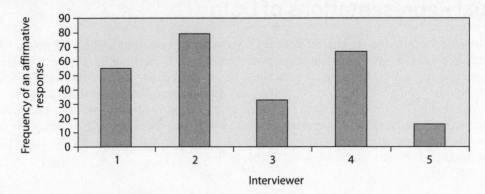

An example of a line graph is shown here to demonstrate the relationship between time (independent variable) and the growth of a plant seedling (dependent variable):

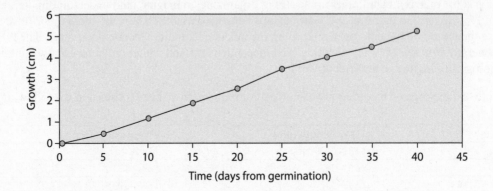

Line graphs you will encounter are likely to demonstrate data with one or more of the following trends:

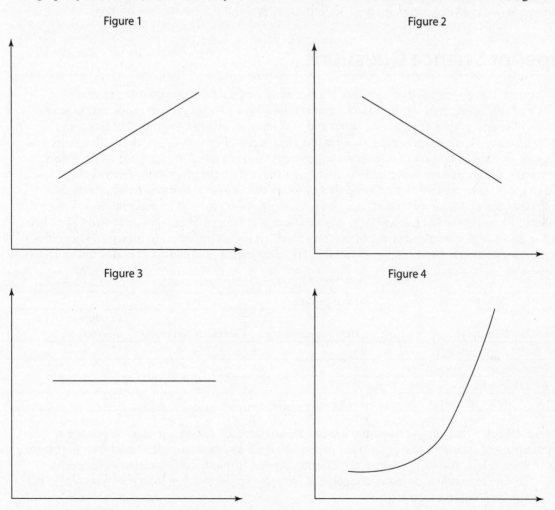

In Figure 1, the relationship between variables is direct and positive; as the value of x increases, so does the value of y. In Figure 2, the relationship between variables can be described as inverse and negative; as the value of x increases, the value of y decreases. In Figure 3, there is likely no meaningful relationship between variables; as x increases, y remains constant. Finally, in Figure 4, the relationship demonstrated is exponential; as x increases, y increases exponentially.

To summarize the approach to interpreting any visual representation of data, consider the following:

1. Read the labels and units carefully. Understand the type of measurement presented.
2. Consider the trend of data presented. Describe a relationship between the independent and dependent variables.
3. Extrapolate (extend the given data points in a logical predictive manner beyond what is directly presented) when appropriate to predict results. A line of best fit is typical for linear graphs.
4. Interpolate between points on a graph or in a data table to predict values to be expected at that point.

Don't forget to review figures in science and math textbooks and in newspaper, magazine, and journal articles to expose yourself to a wide variety of scientific contexts and representations of data.

D. Types of Science Questions

The ACT Science Test is composed of passages of three main types: data representation, research summaries, and conflicting viewpoints. A data representation–type passage presents information in any combination of charts, graphs, figures, and tables and asks that you analyze and interpret this data. A research summary–type passage presents information in a series of related tables, charts, diagrams, and graphs that all represent a portion of a scientific experiment. You are asked to analyze the data, assess the experimental design, and make predictions about results based on the given data. A conflicting viewpoints–type passage presents two or more alternate hypotheses or explanations for an observable natural phenomenon and asks you to compare and contrast the positions and to make inferences using the data provided. Regardless of the passage type, you should expect to see information presented to you in a combination of descriptive text and visual forms. Be aware that not all information presented is significant to the particular question at hand (i.e., don't feel that you must use all information provided if it is irrelevant to your analysis).

ACT Science Test Summary	Passage Type		
	Data Representation	Research Summaries	Conflicting Viewpoints
Number of questions per passage	5	6	7
Number of passages on ACT Science Test	3	3	1
Total number of questions on ACT Science Test	15	18	7
Percent of ACT Science Test	37.5%	45%	17.5%

In Passages I–III below, five sample questions are presented after each passage in order to provide a sufficient sampling of questions that you should expect to see for any passage type. Remember that on the actual ACT Science Test, you will be asked to primarily respond to questions associated with research summaries and data representation passage types, and only to respond to seven total questions within the one conflicting viewpoints passage.

Passage I: Data Representation Example (Biology Context)

Transpiration is a process that occurs in plants as they lose water from tiny pores called stomata on the underside of their leaves. Plants must open their stomata to allow the diffusion of CO_2 into the leaf for photosynthesis, but they must balance this with the rate of water loss through transpiration. Transpiration is significant to a plant's physiology in that it drives the movement of water from the surrounding soil into plant roots via osmosis, the passive transport of water across a cell membrane. The quantity of transpirational water loss in leaves with the same surface areas but experiencing four environmental conditions (normal, windy, hot, and humid) was recorded in a botany laboratory. The recorded data are shown in Table 1.

Time (min.)	Total Transpirational Water Loss (mL)			
	Normal	+ Wind	+ Heat	+ Humidity
5	0.2	0.3	0.2	0.05
10	0.5	0.6	0.4	0.15
15	0.7	1.1	0.7	0.35
20	1.0	1.5	1.1	0.45
25	1.2	1.8	1.5	0.5

Table 1

1. According to Table 1, which type of condition is likely to encourage the least amount of transpiration from a plant leaf?

   A. normal
   B. windy
   C. hot
   D. humid

D is correct. High humidity (simulated in the lab through heavy misting of the plant leaf) was associated with only 0.5 mL of transpirational water loss, the lowest value of any of the four environmental conditions, including the normal control group. More water was present in the air and thus a smaller gradient was present to affect the movement of water from the leaf into the atmosphere.

2. Imagine the researcher ran out of time to complete the experiment and was only able to collect data to the 23-minute interval. The total transpirational water loss (in mL) expected for the plant in the hot environment is:

   F. 1.7
   G. 1.3
   H. 0.9
   J. 0.6

G is correct. Interpolation occurs between the provided data of 1.1 mL and 1.5 mL for minutes 20 and 25, respectively. The only logical value that lies between these two values is 1.3 mL.

3. Which of the following graphs is consistent with the data presented in Table 1?

A.

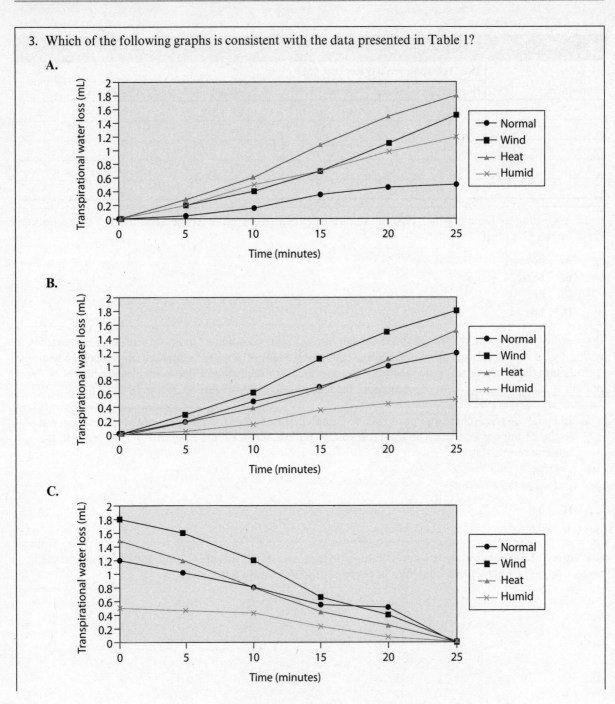

D.

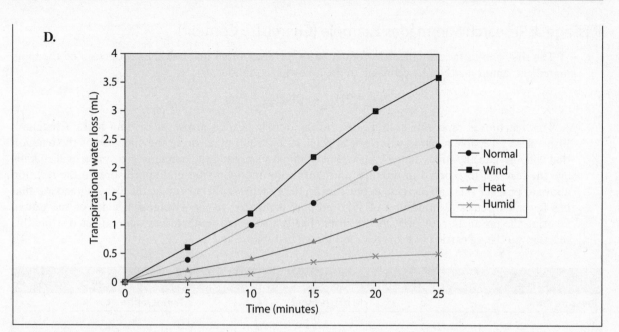

B is correct. According to the data, the humid environment lost the least amount of water over time and the windy environment lost the most (for the reasons outlined earlier). Only the Choice B graph correctly displays all four lines.

4. What type of specific indoor environment could be inferred to necessitate the most frequent watering schedule for a common houseplant?

    F. A dark hallway

    G. Near an air conditioner

    H. Under a table lamp

    J. In a bathroom with a shower

G is correct. The fan involved in the operation of the air conditioner would simulate the windy environment in the experiment. A plant directly in the airflow would likely require a more frequent watering schedule due to increased transpiration.

5. Which of the following inferences is consistent with the data presented in this passage?

    A. A plant in a hot, windy environment will transpire more than a plant in either a hot environment or a windy environment.

    B. A plant in a very humid environment will transpire more than a plant in a moderately humid environment.

    C. A plant in a very hot, sunny desert will transpire more in the winter than in the summer.

    D. A plant in the dark will transpire equally if the environment is humid or dry.

A is correct. Since increased heat was associated with increased transpiration, and increased wind was also associated with increased transpiration, it is logical to infer that an environment that included both increased heat and wind would result in more transpiration than was recorded in either of the individual situations.

Passage II: Research Summaries Example (Chemistry Context)

The first step in the commercial production of fertilizer often involves the production of the main ingredient, ammonia (NH_3), according to the following equation:

$$N_{2(g)} + 3H_{2(g)} \leftrightarrow 2NH_{3(g)} + \text{heat}$$

This reaction is reversible as indicated by the double-headed arrow. According to Le Chatelier's Principle, a reversible reaction will work to reach equilibrium by favoring the direction of the reaction that will alleviate any stress on the system. For example, increasing the pressure on a system will encourage the reaction to proceed in the direction that favors the reduction of the pressure. In the reaction above to produce NH_3, an increase in pressure on the system would encourage the forward reaction that has fewer molecules (2 molecules of NH_3 product compared to the 4 total molecules of reactants), favoring the production of NH_3 for fertilizer. The pressure and temperature were adjusted while this reaction was being carried out; the data are shown in Tables 1 and 2.

Table 1		
Pressure (atm)	% NH_3 present	Temperature (°C)
50	40	200
100	70	200
200	80	200
300	90	200

Table 2		
Temperature (°C)	% NH_3 present	Pressure (atm)
200	90	400
300	80	400
400	50	400
500	30	400

Although applying Le Chatelier's Principle helps to understand the conditions under which the maximum amount of NH_3 can be generated, these conditions are not always practical in a real-world industrial setting. The same reaction was tested under a wider range of pressures and more detailed temperature data were recorded. The data were used to generate Figure 1. The pressure and temperature conditions that were determined to be economically and otherwise practically feasible are shaded in the figure.

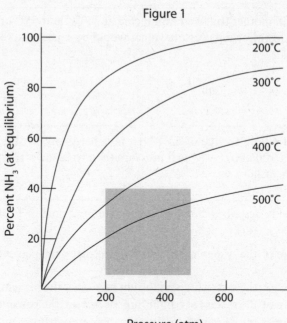

Figure 1

Once ammonia is produced, it often is converted into other products for easier storage and handling. For instance, ammonia can first be converted into nitric acid (HNO_3) through oxidation, and that HNO_3 product can be combined with NH_3 to produce the final ammonium nitrate (NH_4NO_3) fertilizer product according to the following reactions:

$$NH_3 + 2O_2 \rightarrow HNO_3 + H_2O$$
$$NH_3 + HNO_3 \rightarrow NH_4NO_3$$

Although it is a desirable fertilizer because of its high nitrogen content, NH_4NO_3 must be stored and handled appropriately due to certain physical and chemical characteristics of the compound. Although stable at temperatures below 210°C, it will spontaneously decompose at or above that temperature and can become part of an explosive, self-sustaining reaction if certain catalysts are present. The solubility of NH_4NO_3 in water at various temperatures is shown in Table 3.

Table 3	
Temperature (°C)	Solubility of NH_4NO_3 (g/100 mL H_2O)
0	119
20	190
40	286
60	421
80	630
100	1,024

6. According to Table 1, if another trial were conducted at 200°C and 55% of NH_3 were present at equilibrium, which of the following pressure values would be expected to be present?

    F.   40 atm

    G.   70 atm

    H.   250 atm

    J.   340 atm

G is correct. According to Table 1, a value of 55% NH_3 falls between the observed values of 40% NH_3 (at 50 atm) and 70% NH_3 (at 100 atm). A logical pressure then to associate with 55% NH_3 is 70 atm, a value that falls between the other two.

7. Which statement correctly describes the trend in the data presented in Table 2 when pressure is held constant?

    A.   As the temperature of the system at equilibrium decreases, the percent of NH_3 present remains constant.

    B.   As the temperature of the system at equilibrium increases, the percent of NH_3 present increases.

    C.   As the temperature of the system at equilibrium decreases, the percent of NH_3 present decreases.

    D.   As the temperature of the system at equilibrium increases, the percent of NH_3 present decreases.

D is correct. As the temperature values increase in the first column of Table 2, the corresponding percentages of NH_3 present at equilibrium decrease. For example, 200°C is associated with 90% NH_3, while 400°C is associated with 50% NH_3.

8. Using the data presented in Figure 1, which scenario for the production of NH_3 is both economically feasible and allows for a minimum of 30% NH_3 present at equilibrium?

    F.   150 atm; 300°C

    G.   250 atm; 400°C

    H.   300 atm; 300°C

    J.   550 atm; 200°C

G is correct. To be economically feasible, the point representing the set of conditions described must lie within the shaded area and at a point that is above 30% on the y-axis. The only option provided that meets the criteria is at 250 atm and 400°C. Any pressure value below 200 atm or above 500 atm would not qualify, nor would any temperature below 300°C.

9. If one industrial chemist wants to store the NH_4NO_3 by dissolving it in water at 50°C, what is a possible quantity of compound that could be dissolved in 100 mL of water according to the information presented in Table 3?

   A. 179 g
   B. 260 g
   C. 408 g
   D. 512 g

C is correct. Using the information in Table 3, the maximum quantity of NH_4NO_3 that can be completely dissolved in 100 mL of water at 40°C is 286 grams and at 60°C is 421 grams. The mass then that can be dissolved at 50°C must be between 286 and 421 grams; 408 grams meets this criterion.

10. The equilibrium constant (K_{eq}) is an important part of the proportion that predicts the concentrations of reactants and products present in a system at equilibrium such that for the generic reaction

$$aA + bB \rightarrow cC + dD, \; K_{eq} = \frac{[C]^c [D]^d}{[A]^a [B]^b}.$$

   For the initial ammonia synthesis reaction $N_{2\,(g)} + 3H_{2\,(g)} \leftrightarrow 2NH_{3\,(g)}$ + heat, the $K_{eq} = 4.50 \times 10^{-5}$ at 450°C. When the synthesis is repeated but the temperature is raised to 500°C, the $K_{eq} = 1.50 \times 10^{-5}$. Which statement best explains the significance of these results?

   F. As the temperature increases, the reverse reaction is favored to relieve the system of the added temperature stress; relatively less NH_3 will be present.
   G. As the temperature increases, the pressure also increases; this favors the reverse reaction and relatively more NH_3 will be present.
   H. As the temperature increases, the forward reaction is favored to relieve the system of the added temperature stress; relatively less NH_3 will be present.
   J. As the temperature increases, the pressure decreases; this favors the forward reaction and relatively less NH_3 will be present.

F is correct. According to Le Chatelier's Principle, a reversible reaction at equilibrium will favor the direction of the reaction that acts to relieve any stress placed on the system. If the temperature increases, then the reverse reaction will be favored to use heat energy; relatively less NH_3 will then be present.

Passage III: Conflicting Viewpoints Example (Earth/Space Sciences Context)

Much debate currently rages regarding the appropriate reaction to the global warming crisis. The world emissions of CO_2, a critical greenhouse gas that directly contributes to global warming, has increased dramatically the past 50 years. This increase can be directly attributed in part to the burning of fossil fuels (like oil, natural gas, and coal) for energy. Data regarding global CO_2 emissions from 1970 to 2015 and global use of fossil fuels throughout the 1970s are presented in Figures 1 and 2, respectively.

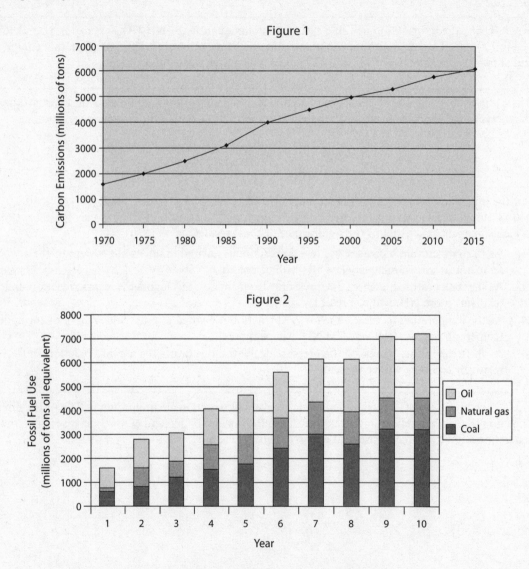

Figure 1

Figure 2

As efforts are made to convert U.S. energy sources to renewable, more environmentally friendly options, different opinions arise regarding the type of renewable energy source that should be invested in to replace the current need for energy being met chiefly by the burning of fossil fuels. Relative global use of different conventional and renewable energy sources spanning more than two decades is shown in Figure 3.

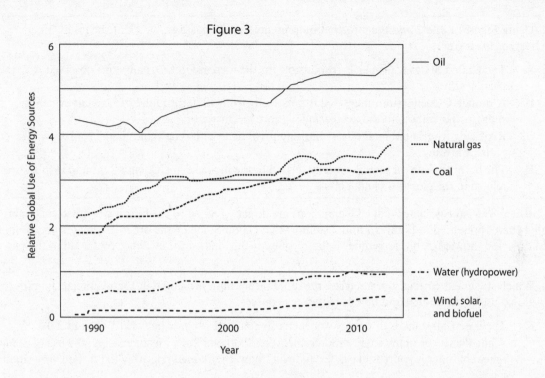

Figure 3

Viewpoint 1

Although much recent discussion of global warming and alternative energy sources has included the concepts of wind, solar, and water power, these energy sources are unreliable (e.g., cloudy days can interfere with solar power) and are not equally distributed across the country (e.g., low solar intensity in northern regions).

In order to encourage the United States to burn less fossil fuels for energy and thus to emit less of the greenhouse gas CO_2, the infrastructure must be converted to support the burning of biofuels like ethanol instead. When the corn or soybean is being grown, the plant is absorbing significant quantities of CO_2 from the atmosphere to use for photosynthesis. It thus naturally acts to detoxify the air of a greenhouse gas. When the ethanol is later burned for fuel, the CO_2 produced from the combustion is negated by the earlier absorption. Ethanol thus has a carbon-neutral footprint.

Viewpoint 2

While some biofuels might be useful and responsible renewable energy sources, soybean- and corn-based ethanol is actually contributing to global warming. The benefit gained from the absorption of CO_2 during the natural plant growth process is canceled out from the CO_2 released during the combustion process that allows the ethanol to be used as a fuel. Additionally, natural forests are being cleared and fields that are currently being used as farmlands are being converted to biofuel fields. This makes ethanol a producer of CO_2 when the global effect is considered.

A better alternative is utilizing a combination of renewable energy sources, like wind and solar. While it is true that not all countries and local regions have equal access to all forms of energy, if efforts are combined at all levels of government within the United States, and if those efforts are then coordinated between the United States and neighboring countries, and if multiple energy sources are utilized, the United States and its neighbors can free themselves of their dependence on burning fossil fuels, producing fewer CO_2 emissions and contributing less to global warming in the future.

11. Using Figures 1 and 2 and the information presented in the passage, which of the following statements is true?

    A. The United States is primarily responsible for the increase in CO_2 emissions observed over the past 50 years.

    B. Although CO_2 emissions increased dramatically from 1970 through 2015, recent evidence suggests that emissions are decreasing in more recent years.

    C. Replacing traditional methods of burning fossil fuels with renewable energy sources will reverse global warming.

    D. The burning of fossil fuels is directly related to the increase in CO_2 emissions and is thus directly related to the global warming crisis.

D is correct. The passage states that CO_2 emissions are directly related to the burning of fossil fuels, and the parallel curves presented in Figures 1 and 2 support that claim. Some of the other statements may seem true based on prior knowledge, but remember to base your conclusions on the evidence presented in the passage.

12. Which statement correctly summarizes the more recent data presented in Figure 3 regarding the global use of traditional and renewable energy sources?

    F. The use of all sources of energy was increasing at a steady rate between 1990 and 2010.

    G. While the use of many energy sources between 1990 and 2010 was increasing, the use of some renewable energy sources like solar and wind power remained relatively flat or had very slight increases.

    H. The use of hydropower and coal increased at the same rate from 1990 to 2010.

    J. While the use of all fossil fuels has continued to increase, the use of renewable energy like solar, wind, and biofuels actually decreased between 1990 and 2010.

G is correct. Figure 3 shows that the curves for all forms of energy except wind, solar, and biofuels are sloping upward over time and thus are increasing in usage. The curve for wind, solar, and biofuels is basically flat throughout the time period, a sharp contrast from the other curves.

13. According to Viewpoint 1, which statement is supported regarding ethanol?

    A. Burning ethanol is better than burning traditional oil because burning ethanol is not associated with releasing CO_2.

    B. Ethanol produces as much CO_2 as it absorbs, thus it is a carbon-neutral fuel.

    C. Ethanol is better for the environment because it is extracted from plants and is thus a natural alternative.

    D. Ethanol is not a suitable replacement for oil even though it is considered renewable.

B is correct. The main argument presented in Viewpoint 1 supports the use of ethanol as a biofuel and states that such biofuels are desirable because the plants grown for the process absorb as much CO_2 as they release when burned for energy.

14. Which of the following statements is consistent with Viewpoint 2 and presents a point of conflict with Viewpoint 1?

    F. Ethanol from soybeans is associated with less CO_2 than ethanol from corn and is thus preferable as a biofuel.

    G. Plants need CO_2 for photosynthesis and are therefore consumers of CO_2.

    H. If CO_2 emission data associated with using ethanol for fuel include the amount of land cleared for new biofuel fields, ethanol is a net producer of CO_2.

    J. Alternative energy like wind, water, and solar power is associated with fewer CO_2 emissions than the combustion of any fuel, traditional or renewable.

H is correct. The main argument presented in Viewpoint 2 contradicts that which is presented in Viewpoint 1. It claims that the biofuel fields are replacing farmlands and natural forests and thus are actually contributing to the global CO_2 emissions.

15. Which of the following statements might logically be made as a rebuttal from Viewpoint 1 to the perspective presented in Viewpoint 2?

    A. The efforts required to coordinate efforts at local and state levels within the United States and then between the United States and its neighbors are too complicated and expensive to be dependable or practical.

    B. Very few successful attempts have been made in recent years to increase the use of solar and wind power, so future attempts are also likely to be ineffective.

    C. Ethanol and other biofuels should be part of the combination of renewable energy sources to replace fossil fuels even though they are a net producer of CO_2.

    D. Nuclear energy should be utilized as much as possible because it is not associated with the same limitations as is ethanol.

A is correct. The only rebuttals that can be made logically with the evidence provided in the passage are that the solution presented in Viewpoint 2 would be ineffective for some reason or that the data can be challenged or contradicted by other data. The notion of coordinating efforts among different governments, countries, and energy sources speaks to the potential ineffectiveness of this solution.

XVI. Writing Test

The ACT Writing Test is an essay in which you demonstrate your writing and thinking skills. This section of the ACT is optional and is administered after the four sections of the ACT are completed. If you choose to take the Writing Test, you will receive a separate Writing Test subscore that does not affect any of the other scores as well as a combined English/Writing score. The essay score is not calculated into the composite score.

You will be required to write a 40-minute essay response to a prompt. The prompt will present three perspectives on a debatable issue that is familiar to high school students. You are asked to consider the strengths and weaknesses of the three perspectives on the issue, state and support your own position, and explain how your position relates to the three given perspectives. In your analysis of the issue and explanation of your position, you should refer to all three perspectives. Your position may be similar to one or more of the three perspectives, a qualification of one or more of the perspectives, or an original perspective. Past questions have concerned high school dress codes, mandated community service, and the role of social media in society.

The scorers will evaluate your essay on your ability to:

- weigh and understand three perspectives on a complex issue.
- explicate and support your own perspective on the issue with reasons and examples.
- organize your ideas in a logical manner.
- demonstrate your knowledge of the conventions of standard written English.

Two trained scorers will evaluate your essay on a 6-point scale in four domains:

- **Ideas and analysis:** Your understanding of the complexities of the issue, ability to generate reasonable supporting evidence, logical evaluation of the three given perspectives, and appropriate and effective use of rhetorical strategies.
- **Development and support:** Your ability to support your claims with relevant reasons, appropriate examples, and effective references to the three given perspectives.
- **Organization:** Your ability to implement an effective and logical organization plan with appropriate use of transitional words and phrases within and between paragraphs.
- **Language use:** Your knowledge of the conventions of standard written English and your ability to use diction, voice, and style to accomplish your persuasive purpose.

The score in each domain is the sum of the two scorers' grades, so you will receive a score ranging from 2 to 12 in each domain. The domain scores are then converted to a scaled score from 1 to 36 (which is not necessarily the sum of the scores of the two scorers).

The graders know you are writing this essay under pressure in 40 minutes so they are not looking for a highly polished piece of writing. Rather, they hope to see a thoughtful (and legible) first draft.

The rubric is included after the diagnostic test in Chapter IV (see pages 70–72).

A. Approach to the Essay: Reading Critically and Annotating (4–6 minutes)

Reading critically is the first (and often most important) step. As you read the prompt and the three perspectives, think about the points of view on the issue. Write notes in the margins as you read. Note the strengths and weaknesses of each perspective. How are they different? What is your own position on the issue? What are the reasons you feel this way? What examples could you use to support your position? How are these examples present in or missing from the given perspectives? Your answers to these questions will help you formulate your response.

Note: To support your position, do not ignore the counterargument (the other side of an issue). Most likely, the perspectives will include antithetical viewpoints. You strengthen your argument by defining the counterargument and then explaining why your position is stronger. Also, you don't have to completely agree or disagree with a perspective; you can qualify an issue (limit or restrict the argument). The issues presented are complex; under some conditions, you might support one side, while under other conditions, you might support the other. In this case, your thesis would clearly state the conditions affecting your position. Refer to the three perspectives as you sharpen your focus and develop support for your position.

B. Approach to the Essay: Planning (3–5 minutes)

It is helpful to begin your planning by considering the prewriting questions in the "Planning Your Essay" section of the prompt. The questions will guide you to evaluate the strengths and weaknesses of the three perspectives. Then, review your notes and write a thesis sentence, a one-sentence assertion that presents the position that your examples will prove. If you are still not sure exactly where you stand on the issue, do some brainstorming first: Think of all the examples, reasons, and ideas in the three perspectives and consider the evidence given to support each position; then, determine on which side your argument will be stronger.

After you know your position, plan your essay. List your main points in the prewriting space provided in your test booklet. These notes can be very brief: your position and a brief evaluation of the three given perspectives.

Always write from strength: It is important to choose logical, appropriate examples and specific references to support your thesis. You should avoid hypothetical examples or very broad generalizations; the strength of your essay is in the specific details. In addition, to ensure that you have something to write about, it is helpful to be aware of current debates in education and other fields. Read the newspapers and pay particular attention to issues that concern schools and high school students.

C. Approach to the Essay: Writing (24–26 minutes)

1. State Thesis Clearly in Introductory Paragraph

It is always to your advantage to pique your reader's interest in the opening paragraph. However, in a timed writing, you don't need a long introductory paragraph. Get to the point quickly so you have time to develop your argument. Make sure you establish your position and set up the development of your analysis of the three perspectives and your supporting examples. Explaining the context of the issue is a good beginning point; in other words, set the scene. Clarify why this issue is a topic of debate. For example, if you are responding to a prompt asking you to consider three perspectives for or against mandatory dress codes in schools, you might begin by discussing a situation in which some students arrive at school dressed inappropriately. You might give some specific examples of this ill-chosen attire. You would then state your position on the issue: Does the inappropriate dress warrant a change in a school's dress code? Should the school consider requiring school uniforms? Or, is clothing just an expression of individual creativity that should be appreciated? Is there a middle ground? What insights do the three perspectives offer on the issue? Your answers to these questions form the basis of your thesis statement.

2. Develop Your Examples

In the topic sentence of each body paragraph, state the example or the reason that you will develop. As you present your argument, refer to the given perspectives and focus your comments on the evidence that supports or refutes each. Then explain the reason/example so the reader understands why it supports your thesis. Try to give specific details. If you are writing about articles of clothing, describe them; about social media, give the websites and apps; about magazines, name them; about extracurricular activities, list the clubs.

3. Organize Coherently

Many students ask about a "formula" for the essay or about the required numbers of paragraphs. There is no specific plan or correct number of paragraphs to guarantee success on the Writing Test. The number of paragraphs will depend on the number of examples you choose to support your argument. Paragraphing should be logical: Each time you begin a new point, begin a new paragraph. As you develop your examples, be sure to use transitional phrases. These words and phrases are the key to coherence, and graders are trained to spot them. When you begin a new paragraph, use a phrase like "*Another* advantage to school uniforms . . ." or "Uniformity in dress *also* fosters school unity."

Use transitional phrases within the paragraph as well to help your ideas flow logically. Transitional words and phrases link ideas and indicate the relationship of ideas within a sentence, a paragraph, or a passage. They are essential tools for a writer who wants to achieve a clear and logical flow of ideas.

Important Transitional Words and Phrases	
Words used to indicate an example	**Words used to show a result**
for example for instance specifically	consequently hence accordingly therefore
Words used to indicate a reason	**Words used to indicate more information**
as because since due to	besides in addition moreover furthermore
Words used to contrast	**Words used to show similarity**
although but however in contrast nevertheless whereas while yet on the other hand still despite	another similarly likewise also again in the same way too equally
Words used to establish time relationships	**Words used for emphasis**
before during after at last at this point later soon next until recently then then again once at the same time	indeed clearly to be sure without doubt assuredly

4. Analyze the Perspectives

The perspectives will state three points of view. You may choose to agree with one (or more) or you may present an original point of view. Whatever you choose, be sure to state the opposing position (the counterargument) and explain your reasons for rejecting this perspective. This technique indicates your awareness of the complexity of the issue. Too often students make the mistake of reducing a complex issue to simple black-and-white terms and supporting one of the given perspectives while ignoring the others. Introduce the opposing positions with transitional words or phrases: "Granted, according to Perspective Three . . ." or "As Perspective One states, it may be true that . . ." or "Supporters of Perspective Two argue that . . ." and then respond to the position with your argument. For example:

> Perspective Two argues that teenagers use their clothing to express their artistic individuality, but painted and ripped jeans that reveal an inordinate amount of skin are a distraction in the classroom.

5. Use Active Verbs

To make your writing lively rather than flat, avoid state-of-being verbs (forms of the verb *to be*) and weak passive sentences. Also, avoid phrases like "I believe" and "I think" and clichés.

> *Weak:* I think people who dress to impress are silly.
>
> *Strong:* Clothing expresses both individuality and creativity.

6. Vary Sentence Structure

Most students have a tendency to write simple and compound sentences that follow the subject-verb pattern. Since you will have very little time to revise your essay, be aware of sentence structure as you write.

Start a sentence with a participial phrase:

> *Instead of:* I find it difficult to decide what to wear to school.
>
> *Write:* Standing in front of my closet, I search in vain for something comfortable to wear to school.

Start with a subordinate clause:

> When I get ready for school, I waste precious minutes deciding what to wear.

Start with an adverb:

> Frequently, students use their attire to express their individuality and creativity.

D. Proofread (2–3 minutes)

Try to allow time to read over your essay. Be sure your writing is legible. If you see a mistake, change it by crossing out neatly or erasing carefully. You may insert a word or phrase above the line with a caret (^).
Do not write in the margins outside the black lines in your test booklet. *Note:* Do not plan to write a rough draft, revise, and then copy it over into the test booklet. You will most likely not have enough time to recopy the essay.

E. Sample Essay Questions

1. Sample A

Video Games and Violence

A large number (according to some sources, 97%) of children and teenagers spend hours of every day playing video games. These games provide stress relief, excitement, and instant gratification in the form of rewards and opportunity for more play. However, many worry that video-game playing is addictive and that the violent nature of many of the games may result in aggressive behavior. They advocate limitations on the availability of games, expressing fear that constant exposure to violent acts may cause young people to become less sensitive to the pain and suffering of others. Others contend that game players are very aware of the difference between the fantasy world of the game and the real world.

Read the three perspectives below and consider the conflicting positions on the link between playing video games and violence

Perspective 1	Perspective 2	Perspective 3
A majority of the research on the dangers of video games is deeply flawed and no causal link has been established between video-game playing and acts of violence. In fact, violent video games may provide a safe outlet for aggressive and angry feelings and may actually have the effect of reducing criminal behavior.	In the media, violent video games have been blamed for school shootings, increases in bullying, and violence toward women. Access to games should be restricted because many of the games desensitize players to violence, reward players for imitating violent acts, and teach children that violence is an appropriate way to settle disputes.	In *Brown v. Entertainment Merchants Association*, the Supreme Court ruled "Like the protected books, plays, and movies that preceded them, video games communicate ideas—and even social messages—through many familiar literary devices (such as characters, dialogue, plot, and music) and through features distinctive to the medium (such as the player's interaction with the virtual world)."

Essay Task

Your task is to construct a well-written, well-organized essay in which you consider the issue of restrictions on access to video games. As you plan and write your essay, be sure to

- consider the effectiveness of the three perspective given above
- develop your own perspective on the issue
- clarify ways in which your perspective is similar to or different from the three perspectives given above

You may choose to defend, challenge, or qualify any part of the three given perspectives. Whatever your position, be sure to back up your assertions with reason and detailed examples.

Planning Your Essay

The space below is for you to plan your essay. As you plan, think about the following ideas:

Strengths and weaknesses of each of the three given perspectives:

- What aspects do they address and what aspects do they disregard?
- Is the perspective persuasive? Why or why not? To whom might each appeal?

Experience or knowledge that will help you evaluate the issue:

- How strong is your position?
- What evidence (reasons, facts, examples) will you offer to support your position?

2. Sample B

Using Technology in Classrooms

More and more schools are using technology to support teaching and learning in the classroom. Advocates say technology has the power to transform teaching by ushering in a new model of connected teaching: computers and hand-held devices increase student engagement, accelerate learning, provide links to resources, and personalize learning. Some educators, however, are concerned about over-reliance on electronics, fearing the computer will replace human-to-human interaction in the classroom.

Read the three perspectives below and consider the conflicting positions on the issue of the use of technology in classrooms.

Perspective 1	Perspective 2	Perspective 3
Computer-based technologies support the thinking process, motivate students' interest in diverse topics, and help teachers prepare students for the future.	Technology may not translate into more effective teaching. In fact, it may promote passive learning. Because no evidence exists to prove a causal link between information technology and increased learning, more money should be spent on hiring better teachers than on buying the latest electronic gadgets.	Technology is a great leveler of opportunities. In low socioeconomic areas where home computers are unaffordable, school-based technology promotes equity by reducing the disparity in resources available to students.

Essay Task

Your task is to construct a well-written, well-organized essay in which you consider the issue of the use of technology in classrooms. As you plan and write your essay, be sure to

- consider the effectiveness of the three perspective given above
- develop your own perspective on the issue
- clarify ways in which your perspective is similar to or different from the three perspectives given above

You may choose to defend, challenge, or qualify any part of the three given perspectives. Whatever your position, be sure to back up your assertions with reason and detailed examples.

Planning Your Essay

The space below is for you to plan your essay. As you plan, think about the following ideas:

Strengths and weaknesses of each of the three given perspectives:

- What aspects do they address and what aspects do they disregard?
- Is the perspective persuasive? Why or why not? To whom might each appeal?

Experience or knowledge that will help you evaluate the issue:

- How strong is your position?
- What evidence (reasons, facts, examples) will you offer to support your position?

XVII. Full-Length Practice Test with Answer Explanations

Format of the ACT Practice Test

The Practice Test will cover four content areas: English, Mathematics, Reading, and Science. These tests are designed to measure your ability in these four areas and to predict your success in college. Each question on the test is numbered. Choose the best answer for each question and fill in the corresponding circle on the answer sheet provided.

For each question, be sure to fill in only one circle on your answer sheet. If you erase, do so completely, as the scoring device will pick up any stray marks. (Although this is a practice test and is not being mechanically scored, you should practice the way you would like to perform on the actual test.)

Your score will be based on the number of questions you have answered correctly during the time allowed for each section. No points will be deducted for incorrect answers. You should answer all questions, even if you are unsure and have to guess. It is advantageous to you to answer every question on the test.

If you finish a section before the allotted time runs out, you may not work on any other section. You may not go back to a previous section or move ahead to work on the next section.

You may use any open spaces on your test booklet for scrap.

The Practice Test also includes the optional Writing Test. The Writing Test is an essay in which you demonstrate your writing and thinking skills. It is administered after the four sections of the ACT are completed. For more on the Writing Test, see Chapter XVI.

Timing: You will need 3 hours and 35 minutes to complete the Practice Test.

Test	# of Questions	# of Minutes
English	75	45
Mathematics	60	60
Reading	40	35
Science	40	35
Writing	1	40

After you complete the test, use the Answer Key (pages 346–347), the Scoring Worksheets (page 369), and the Raw Score Conversions chart (page 371) to obtain your scaled scores.

To score the Writing Test (Essay), refer to the rubric on pages 70-72 and to the sample essays and their evaluations starting on page 365.

Answer Sheet

Section 1: English Test

1 Ⓐ Ⓑ Ⓒ Ⓓ	26 Ⓕ Ⓖ Ⓗ Ⓙ	51 Ⓐ Ⓑ Ⓒ Ⓓ
2 Ⓕ Ⓖ Ⓗ Ⓙ	27 Ⓐ Ⓑ Ⓒ Ⓓ	52 Ⓕ Ⓖ Ⓗ Ⓙ
3 Ⓐ Ⓑ Ⓒ Ⓓ	28 Ⓕ Ⓖ Ⓗ Ⓙ	53 Ⓐ Ⓑ Ⓒ Ⓓ
4 Ⓕ Ⓖ Ⓗ Ⓙ	29 Ⓐ Ⓑ Ⓒ Ⓓ	54 Ⓕ Ⓖ Ⓗ Ⓙ
5 Ⓐ Ⓑ Ⓒ Ⓓ	30 Ⓕ Ⓖ Ⓗ Ⓙ	55 Ⓐ Ⓑ Ⓒ Ⓓ
6 Ⓕ Ⓖ Ⓗ Ⓙ	31 Ⓐ Ⓑ Ⓒ Ⓓ	56 Ⓕ Ⓖ Ⓗ Ⓙ
7 Ⓐ Ⓑ Ⓒ Ⓓ	32 Ⓕ Ⓖ Ⓗ Ⓙ	57 Ⓐ Ⓑ Ⓒ Ⓓ
8 Ⓕ Ⓖ Ⓗ Ⓙ	33 Ⓐ Ⓑ Ⓒ Ⓓ	58 Ⓕ Ⓖ Ⓗ Ⓙ
9 Ⓐ Ⓑ Ⓒ Ⓓ	34 Ⓕ Ⓖ Ⓗ Ⓙ	59 Ⓐ Ⓑ Ⓒ Ⓓ
10 Ⓕ Ⓖ Ⓗ Ⓙ	35 Ⓐ Ⓑ Ⓒ Ⓓ	60 Ⓕ Ⓖ Ⓗ Ⓙ
11 Ⓐ Ⓑ Ⓒ Ⓓ	36 Ⓕ Ⓖ Ⓗ Ⓙ	61 Ⓐ Ⓑ Ⓒ Ⓓ
12 Ⓕ Ⓖ Ⓗ Ⓙ	37 Ⓐ Ⓑ Ⓒ Ⓓ	62 Ⓕ Ⓖ Ⓗ Ⓙ
13 Ⓐ Ⓑ Ⓒ Ⓓ	38 Ⓕ Ⓖ Ⓗ Ⓙ	63 Ⓐ Ⓑ Ⓒ Ⓓ
14 Ⓕ Ⓖ Ⓗ Ⓙ	39 Ⓐ Ⓑ Ⓒ Ⓓ	64 Ⓕ Ⓖ Ⓗ Ⓙ
15 Ⓐ Ⓑ Ⓒ Ⓓ	40 Ⓕ Ⓖ Ⓗ Ⓙ	65 Ⓐ Ⓑ Ⓒ Ⓓ
16 Ⓕ Ⓖ Ⓗ Ⓙ	41 Ⓐ Ⓑ Ⓒ Ⓓ	66 Ⓕ Ⓖ Ⓗ Ⓙ
17 Ⓐ Ⓑ Ⓒ Ⓓ	42 Ⓕ Ⓖ Ⓗ Ⓙ	67 Ⓐ Ⓑ Ⓒ Ⓓ
18 Ⓕ Ⓖ Ⓗ Ⓙ	43 Ⓐ Ⓑ Ⓒ Ⓓ	68 Ⓕ Ⓖ Ⓗ Ⓙ
19 Ⓐ Ⓑ Ⓒ Ⓓ	44 Ⓕ Ⓖ Ⓗ Ⓙ	69 Ⓐ Ⓑ Ⓒ Ⓓ
20 Ⓕ Ⓖ Ⓗ Ⓙ	45 Ⓐ Ⓑ Ⓒ Ⓓ	70 Ⓕ Ⓖ Ⓗ Ⓙ
21 Ⓐ Ⓑ Ⓒ Ⓓ	46 Ⓕ Ⓖ Ⓗ Ⓙ	71 Ⓐ Ⓑ Ⓒ Ⓓ
22 Ⓕ Ⓖ Ⓗ Ⓙ	47 Ⓐ Ⓑ Ⓒ Ⓓ	72 Ⓕ Ⓖ Ⓗ Ⓙ
23 Ⓐ Ⓑ Ⓒ Ⓓ	48 Ⓕ Ⓖ Ⓗ Ⓙ	73 Ⓐ Ⓑ Ⓒ Ⓓ
24 Ⓕ Ⓖ Ⓗ Ⓙ	49 Ⓐ Ⓑ Ⓒ Ⓓ	74 Ⓕ Ⓖ Ⓗ Ⓙ
25 Ⓐ Ⓑ Ⓒ Ⓓ	50 Ⓕ Ⓖ Ⓗ Ⓙ	75 Ⓐ Ⓑ Ⓒ Ⓓ

Section 2: Mathematics Test

1 Ⓐ Ⓑ Ⓒ Ⓓ Ⓔ	31 Ⓐ Ⓑ Ⓒ Ⓓ Ⓔ
2 Ⓕ Ⓖ Ⓗ Ⓙ Ⓚ	32 Ⓕ Ⓖ Ⓗ Ⓙ Ⓚ
3 Ⓐ Ⓑ Ⓒ Ⓓ Ⓔ	33 Ⓐ Ⓑ Ⓒ Ⓓ Ⓔ
4 Ⓕ Ⓖ Ⓗ Ⓙ Ⓚ	34 Ⓕ Ⓖ Ⓗ Ⓙ Ⓚ
5 Ⓐ Ⓑ Ⓒ Ⓓ Ⓔ	35 Ⓐ Ⓑ Ⓒ Ⓓ Ⓔ
6 Ⓕ Ⓖ Ⓗ Ⓙ Ⓚ	36 Ⓕ Ⓖ Ⓗ Ⓙ Ⓚ
7 Ⓐ Ⓑ Ⓒ Ⓓ Ⓔ	37 Ⓐ Ⓑ Ⓒ Ⓓ Ⓔ
8 Ⓕ Ⓖ Ⓗ Ⓙ Ⓚ	38 Ⓕ Ⓖ Ⓗ Ⓙ Ⓚ
9 Ⓐ Ⓑ Ⓒ Ⓓ Ⓔ	39 Ⓐ Ⓑ Ⓒ Ⓓ Ⓔ
10 Ⓕ Ⓖ Ⓗ Ⓙ Ⓚ	40 Ⓕ Ⓖ Ⓗ Ⓙ Ⓚ
11 Ⓐ Ⓑ Ⓒ Ⓓ Ⓔ	41 Ⓐ Ⓑ Ⓒ Ⓓ Ⓔ
12 Ⓕ Ⓖ Ⓗ Ⓙ Ⓚ	42 Ⓕ Ⓖ Ⓗ Ⓙ Ⓚ
13 Ⓐ Ⓑ Ⓒ Ⓓ Ⓔ	43 Ⓐ Ⓑ Ⓒ Ⓓ Ⓔ
14 Ⓕ Ⓖ Ⓗ Ⓙ Ⓚ	44 Ⓕ Ⓖ Ⓗ Ⓙ Ⓚ
15 Ⓐ Ⓑ Ⓒ Ⓓ Ⓔ	45 Ⓐ Ⓑ Ⓒ Ⓓ Ⓔ
16 Ⓕ Ⓖ Ⓗ Ⓙ Ⓚ	46 Ⓕ Ⓖ Ⓗ Ⓙ Ⓚ
17 Ⓐ Ⓑ Ⓒ Ⓓ Ⓔ	47 Ⓐ Ⓑ Ⓒ Ⓓ Ⓔ
18 Ⓕ Ⓖ Ⓗ Ⓙ Ⓚ	48 Ⓕ Ⓖ Ⓗ Ⓙ Ⓚ
19 Ⓐ Ⓑ Ⓒ Ⓓ Ⓔ	49 Ⓐ Ⓑ Ⓒ Ⓓ Ⓔ
20 Ⓕ Ⓖ Ⓗ Ⓙ Ⓚ	50 Ⓕ Ⓖ Ⓗ Ⓙ Ⓚ
21 Ⓐ Ⓑ Ⓒ Ⓓ Ⓔ	51 Ⓐ Ⓑ Ⓒ Ⓓ Ⓔ
22 Ⓕ Ⓖ Ⓗ Ⓙ Ⓚ	52 Ⓕ Ⓖ Ⓗ Ⓙ Ⓚ
23 Ⓐ Ⓑ Ⓒ Ⓓ Ⓔ	53 Ⓐ Ⓑ Ⓒ Ⓓ Ⓔ
24 Ⓕ Ⓖ Ⓗ Ⓙ Ⓚ	54 Ⓕ Ⓖ Ⓗ Ⓙ Ⓚ
25 Ⓐ Ⓑ Ⓒ Ⓓ Ⓔ	55 Ⓐ Ⓑ Ⓒ Ⓓ Ⓔ
26 Ⓕ Ⓖ Ⓗ Ⓙ Ⓚ	56 Ⓕ Ⓖ Ⓗ Ⓙ Ⓚ
27 Ⓐ Ⓑ Ⓒ Ⓓ Ⓔ	57 Ⓐ Ⓑ Ⓒ Ⓓ Ⓔ
28 Ⓕ Ⓖ Ⓗ Ⓙ Ⓚ	58 Ⓕ Ⓖ Ⓗ Ⓙ Ⓚ
29 Ⓐ Ⓑ Ⓒ Ⓓ Ⓔ	59 Ⓐ Ⓑ Ⓒ Ⓓ Ⓔ
30 Ⓕ Ⓖ Ⓗ Ⓙ Ⓚ	60 Ⓕ Ⓖ Ⓗ Ⓙ Ⓚ

CUT HERE

Section 3: Reading Test

1 Ⓐ Ⓑ Ⓒ Ⓓ		26 Ⓕ Ⓖ Ⓗ Ⓙ	
2 Ⓕ Ⓖ Ⓗ Ⓙ		27 Ⓐ Ⓑ Ⓒ Ⓓ	
3 Ⓐ Ⓑ Ⓒ Ⓓ		28 Ⓕ Ⓖ Ⓗ Ⓙ	
4 Ⓕ Ⓖ Ⓗ Ⓙ		29 Ⓐ Ⓑ Ⓒ Ⓓ	
5 Ⓐ Ⓑ Ⓒ Ⓓ		30 Ⓕ Ⓖ Ⓗ Ⓙ	
6 Ⓕ Ⓖ Ⓗ Ⓙ		31 Ⓐ Ⓑ Ⓒ Ⓓ	
7 Ⓐ Ⓑ Ⓒ Ⓓ		32 Ⓕ Ⓖ Ⓗ Ⓙ	
8 Ⓕ Ⓖ Ⓗ Ⓙ		33 Ⓐ Ⓑ Ⓒ Ⓓ	
9 Ⓐ Ⓑ Ⓒ Ⓓ		34 Ⓕ Ⓖ Ⓗ Ⓙ	
10 Ⓕ Ⓖ Ⓗ Ⓙ		35 Ⓐ Ⓑ Ⓒ Ⓓ	
11 Ⓐ Ⓑ Ⓒ Ⓓ		36 Ⓕ Ⓖ Ⓗ Ⓙ	
12 Ⓕ Ⓖ Ⓗ Ⓙ		37 Ⓐ Ⓑ Ⓒ Ⓓ	
13 Ⓐ Ⓑ Ⓒ Ⓓ		38 Ⓕ Ⓖ Ⓗ Ⓙ	
14 Ⓕ Ⓖ Ⓗ Ⓙ		39 Ⓐ Ⓑ Ⓒ Ⓓ	
15 Ⓐ Ⓑ Ⓒ Ⓓ		40 Ⓕ Ⓖ Ⓗ Ⓙ	
16 Ⓕ Ⓖ Ⓗ Ⓙ			
17 Ⓐ Ⓑ Ⓒ Ⓓ			
18 Ⓕ Ⓖ Ⓗ Ⓙ			
19 Ⓐ Ⓑ Ⓒ Ⓓ			
20 Ⓕ Ⓖ Ⓗ Ⓙ			
21 Ⓐ Ⓑ Ⓒ Ⓓ			
22 Ⓕ Ⓖ Ⓗ Ⓙ			
23 Ⓐ Ⓑ Ⓒ Ⓓ			
24 Ⓕ Ⓖ Ⓗ Ⓙ			
25 Ⓐ Ⓑ Ⓒ Ⓓ			

Section 4: Science Test

1 Ⓐ Ⓑ Ⓒ Ⓓ		26 Ⓕ Ⓖ Ⓗ Ⓙ	
2 Ⓕ Ⓖ Ⓗ Ⓙ		27 Ⓐ Ⓑ Ⓒ Ⓓ	
3 Ⓐ Ⓑ Ⓒ Ⓓ		28 Ⓕ Ⓖ Ⓗ Ⓙ	
4 Ⓕ Ⓖ Ⓗ Ⓙ		29 Ⓐ Ⓑ Ⓒ Ⓓ	
5 Ⓐ Ⓑ Ⓒ Ⓓ		30 Ⓕ Ⓖ Ⓗ Ⓙ	
6 Ⓕ Ⓖ Ⓗ Ⓙ		31 Ⓐ Ⓑ Ⓒ Ⓓ	
7 Ⓐ Ⓑ Ⓒ Ⓓ		32 Ⓕ Ⓖ Ⓗ Ⓙ	
8 Ⓕ Ⓖ Ⓗ Ⓙ		33 Ⓐ Ⓑ Ⓒ Ⓓ	
9 Ⓐ Ⓑ Ⓒ Ⓓ		34 Ⓕ Ⓖ Ⓗ Ⓙ	
10 Ⓕ Ⓖ Ⓗ Ⓙ		35 Ⓐ Ⓑ Ⓒ Ⓓ	
11 Ⓐ Ⓑ Ⓒ Ⓓ		36 Ⓕ Ⓖ Ⓗ Ⓙ	
12 Ⓕ Ⓖ Ⓗ Ⓙ		37 Ⓐ Ⓑ Ⓒ Ⓓ	
13 Ⓐ Ⓑ Ⓒ Ⓓ		38 Ⓕ Ⓖ Ⓗ Ⓙ	
14 Ⓕ Ⓖ Ⓗ Ⓙ		39 Ⓐ Ⓑ Ⓒ Ⓓ	
15 Ⓐ Ⓑ Ⓒ Ⓓ		40 Ⓕ Ⓖ Ⓗ Ⓙ	
16 Ⓕ Ⓖ Ⓗ Ⓙ			
17 Ⓐ Ⓑ Ⓒ Ⓓ			
18 Ⓕ Ⓖ Ⓗ Ⓙ			
19 Ⓐ Ⓑ Ⓒ Ⓓ			
20 Ⓕ Ⓖ Ⓗ Ⓙ			
21 Ⓐ Ⓑ Ⓒ Ⓓ			
22 Ⓕ Ⓖ Ⓗ Ⓙ			
23 Ⓐ Ⓑ Ⓒ Ⓓ			
24 Ⓕ Ⓖ Ⓗ Ⓙ			
25 Ⓐ Ⓑ Ⓒ Ⓓ			

CUT HERE

Section 5: Writing Test

CUT HERE

Section 1: English Test

45 Minutes—75 Questions

Directions: The English Test consists of five passages. In each passage, words and phrases are underlined and numbered. Following each passage are corresponding questions (on the actual exam, passages appear in the left-hand column, with corresponding questions in the right-hand column). Each question offers four alternatives for the underlined part. Consider the choices and then select the one that best fits the requirements of standard written English. Be sure to take into account the style and tone of the whole passage. If you think the word or phrase is correct as written, choose "NO CHANGE." For some of the questions, you will see a number in a box, which corresponds to a similar number within the passage. These questions ask about a section of the passage or about the passage as a whole. It is a good idea to read through the entire passage before you begin to answer the questions.

Passage I

The Fiddling Emperor

History is filled with stories of dubious origin. One of the <u>most notable stories are</u> the tale of
¹
Nero, Emperor of Rome in the first century A.D., <u>who ostensibly</u> "fiddled while Rome burned."
²
According to rumor, Nero stood on a hillside overlooking the city of Rome and "fiddled" while the city was destroyed by flames. In fact, some <u>sources crediting</u> Nero with setting the fire so that
³
<u>they</u> could have a free hand in rebuilding the city to
⁴
his liking. While this may be true, historians wonder

1.
   A. NO CHANGE
   B. most notable are
   C. most notable stories is
   D. most is

2. Which of the following alternatives would NOT be acceptable?

   F. who supposedly
   G. who some say
   H. who purportedly
   J. whom they say

3.
   A. NO CHANGE
   B. sources credits
   C. sources credit
   D. would have credited

4.
   F. NO CHANGE
   G. he
   H. them
   J. it

about the "fiddling" image, for violins (or fiddles) <u>were not invented</u> until the eleventh century.
5

The writings of the ancient Romans yield some clues to the mystery. Nero was born into a family of Roman nobility. <u>When his father died and his mother</u>
6
Agrippa married Claudius, the emperor of Rome. When his stepfather <u>adopted him; Nero</u> became the
7
official heir to the empire. Upon the death of Claudius, probably by poison administered by Agrippa, Nero, then sixteen years old, became emperor. 8

5.
A. NO CHANGE
B. have not been invented
C. were not being invented
D. were not inventing

6.
F. NO CHANGE
G. Since his father died, and his mother
H. His father dying, his mother
J. His father died and his mother

7.
A. NO CHANGE
B. adopted him Nero
C. adopted him: Nero
D. adopted him, Nero

8. The writer is considering adding the following sentence at this point in the paragraph:

The first emperor of Rome was Augustus.

Would this addition be appropriate here?

F. Yes, because it clarifies Nero's role in the dynasty begun by Augustus.
G. Yes, because it is a detail that provides information important to the topic.
H. No, because it is not a relevant detail.
J. No, because this sentence contradicts a point made earlier in the paragraph.

At first, under the tutelage of his mother and Seneca, Nero <u>originally appeared</u> to be a benign ruler, involved in fostering interest in theater, music, and the arts. He increased <u>trade, supported</u> athletic competitions. As his power and confidence increased, Nero disassociated himself from his mother and engaged in wilder pursuits. <u>Indeed</u>, his behavior became so erratic and characterized by excess indulgences in wicked activities that some thought him mad. He dismissed former advisors, <u>having his mother murdered and becoming</u> a cruel and ruthless dictator. Eventually, he even had his wife assassinated to make way for a new woman with whom he <u>had fallen</u> in love.

9.
  A. NO CHANGE
  B. appeared from the start
  C. appeared
  D. in the beginning appeared

10.
  F. NO CHANGE
  G. trade and supported
  H. trade and he supports
  J. trade, but he supported

11. For the sake of logic and coherence, which would be the best transitional phrase to use?
  A. NO CHANGE
  B. Nevertheless
  C. In contrast
  D. However

12.
  F. NO CHANGE
  G. have his mother murdered and become
  H. to have his mother murdered and to become
  J. had his mother murdered, and became

13.
  A. NO CHANGE
  B. has fell
  C. has fallen
  D. had fell

By 64 A.D., Nero's behavior had become totally outrageous. Then came the great fire in Rome. ☐14 A rumor started that while the fire burned and the citizens ran for their lives, the emperor climbed up on a distant rooftop and sang. From this apparent disregard for the lives of his people arose the tale that Nero fiddled while Rome burned. We may never know the truth, but we do know that he didn't actually fiddle. ☐15

14. Suppose the writer wants to add the following detail at this point in the essay:

> According to the historian Tacitus, it was " . . . the most terrible and destructive fire which Rome had ever experienced."

Would this addition be appropriate here?

F. Yes, because the severity of the fire dramatizes the story of Nero's callousness.
G. Yes, because if it had not been a huge fire, the story of Nero would never have been known.
H. No, because the reader does not know if Tacitus is a reliable witness.
J. No, because Nero was not really playing the fiddle anyway.

Question 15 asks about the essay as a whole.

15. Suppose the writer had decided to write a scholarly essay delineating Nero's role in the history of the Roman Empire. Would this essay fulfill the writer's goal?

A. Yes, because the essay is scholarly in tone and provides accurate historical details.
B. Yes, because the essay fully explicates Nero's role in the history of the Roman Empire.
C. No, because so much of the essay is fictional and the tone is sarcastic rather than serious.
D. No, because the essay presents both historical and questionable information with a focus on Nero's reputation.

Passage II

Memories

Memories of my grandparents unravel like a reel of old 8-millimeter film. Some parts <u>are clear, the images intact</u> and decipherable. Others are fuzzy,
    16
transparent, and vague. They look like charcoal <u>drawings' that</u> have become smudged and faded
            17
with time. Whole sections are <u>missing: gaps appear</u>
                                        18
that account for the years when no memories exist.

The movie begins with impressions <u>due to the</u>
                                            19
<u>fact of a large</u> room with a wildly patterned carpet.
    19
My dad tells me <u>they were</u> the apartment my grand-
                    20
parents lived in when I was a young child.

16. All of the following would be acceptable here EXCEPT:
    F. are clear: the images are intact
    G. being clear with images that are intact
    H. are clear, and the images are intact
    J. are clear; the images are intact

17.
    A. NO CHANGE
    B. drawing's which
    C. drawings, who
    D. drawings that

18.
    F. NO CHANGE
    G. missing and gaps appear
    H. missing with gaps that appear
    J. missing gaps

19.
    A. NO CHANGE
    B. coming from a large
    C. of a large
    D. largely coming out of a

20.
    F. NO CHANGE
    G. they're
    H. it's
    J. this was

I have impressions of noise and laughter, food and music. Then I hear a crackling sound as the film breaks, and there is nothing on the screen but white light. 21

I was only four years old when my grandparents retired and moved to Hibiscus Island, Florida, a mystical place of warmth and palm trees that existed in my imagination as a fantasy world of exotic plants and mysterious creatures. It was too costly and expensive to travel to visit them, and they
22
rarely ventured up north. I grew up without knowing that special bond between grandparents and the offspring of their offspring. 23

21. If the writer were to delete the preceding sentence, the essay would primarily lose:

   A. a thematic reference that provides a transition from this paragraph to the next one.

   B. a detail that explains why the grandparents moved to the south.

   C. a description of the movie that summarizes the points made previously.

   D. nothing at all since this sentence is not relevant to the rest of the paragraph.

22.

   F. NO CHANGE

   G. extravagant and costly

   H. expensive

   J. costly, so

23. The writer is considering replacing the period at the end of this sentence with a comma and adding the following information to the sentence.

   that unconditional love that never scolded or reprimanded.

If the writer made this addition, the sentence would:

   A. gain an interesting point that clarifies and explains.

   B. lose a critical transition.

   C. distract the reader with contradictory information.

   D. present an inappropriate opinion.

The images emerge again with a hazy glow of color and sunlight as somehow my parents arranged a trip to Florida. The airplane ride unfolds as a series of crystal clear episodes as <u>my brothers and I</u>
₂₄
board the plane. I can recall the rumbling of the propellers, the sticky feel of the vinyl seats beneath my legs, the faint feeling of nausea as the plane <u>lands, and my</u> unbridled excitement as we walk
₂₅
down the steps off the plane, and I see my first palm tree. The house my grandparents lived in was just as magical as it had been in my mind. <u>Hibiscus flowers</u>
₂₆
<u>are in full bloom, and lemon trees and banana trees</u>
₂₆
<u>grow in the backyard; in a moment of sense mem-</u>
₂₆
<u>ory, I can smell the tang of lemons in the air.</u> The
₂₆
movie speeds up as kaleidoscopic impressions crowd together. My grandparents welcome us, <u>but being</u>
₂₇
<u>that they</u> are just two old people who are strangers
₂₇
to me. I feel that I should know them, but there have been no shared experiences to create a bond. <u>Nevertheless,</u> we have fun as together we stroll on
₂₈
beaches that are white and soft and gather seashells to take home.

24.
 F. NO CHANGE
 G. my brothers and me
 H. myself and my brothers
 J. my brothers with myself

25.
 A. NO CHANGE
 B. lands; my
 C. landing and my
 D. lands with my

26. Given that all of the choices are true, which BEST conveys the sense of "magical"?

 F. NO CHANGE
 G. The hibiscus flowers that grow all over the island have given it the name Hibiscus Island.
 H. My grandfather was an avid gardener who liked to cultivate fruit trees in his yard.
 J. I never knew that bananas grow upside down on a plant and that lemons aren't always yellow.

27.
 A. NO CHANGE
 B. but they
 C. however, they
 D. they

28.
 F. NO CHANGE
 G. Thus
 H. Consequently
 J. Moreover

From the <u>street vendors stands</u>, we buy strange
29
foods, briny clams, and creamy frozen custard. And

then it is over. The film snaps and the movie ends. 30

Passage III

A Russian Jewel

Tourists preparing for their first trip to Russia

may imagine dreary, gray cinder-block buildings

<u>with poorly, and badly paved</u> ice-covered streets.
31
They may envision a land populated by men wear-

ing fur hats and women with babushkas

<u>(brightly printed head scarves)</u> and peasant dress.
32
True, parts of Russia do resemble this portrait, but

certainly not the city of St. Petersburg, formerly

named Leningrad. Founded by Tsar Peter I, and the

capital of Russia until 1918, <u>tourists will discover</u>
33
<u>that St. Petersburg</u> is located on Neva Bay in the
33

29.

    A. NO CHANGE

    B. street's vendor's stands

    C. street vendors stand's

    D. street vendors' stands

30. Which of the following sentences, if included here, would best conclude the essay?

    F. It wasn't a real movie, but just a dream that I had.

    G. It is so important for a child to have grandparents in his or her life.

    H. My brothers have completely different memories of the role my grandparents played in our lives.

    J. I don't get the satisfaction of a happy ending, or any ending, for we never get the chance to meet again.

31.

    A. NO CHANGE

    B. with poorly paved

    C. both poorly and badly paved

    D. surrounded with poorly, paved

32. The writer is considering deleting the parenthetical information. If this change was made, the paragraph would primarily lose

    F. a personal comment.

    G. an explanatory detail.

    H. a historical footnote.

    J. a colorful metaphor.

33.

    A. NO CHANGE

    B. tourists, visiting St. Petersburg, which

    C. it is St. Petersburg that

    D. St. Petersburg

Gulf of <u>Finland, this</u> historically and architec-
₃₄
turally rich city is reminiscent of a colder, more

northern Venice.

First, one is struck by the beauty of the waterways,

the Neva River and its tributaries that crisscross the

city. <u>Bridges that traverse</u> the small rivers and canals
₃₅
and connect the islands that house some of the oldest

buildings in the city. On warm summer weekends,

residents <u>who</u> gather on the shores of some of the
₃₆
nearly one hundred islands to sunbathe and swim.

<u>Because of the city's northern latitude,</u> summer twi-
₃₇
light can last until midnight.

The beauty of the physical setting is matched by

the magnificence of the baroque and neoclassical

architecture. Perhaps the <u>best known and most</u>
₃₈
<u>famous</u> museum in the world and one of the <u>largest:</u>
₃₈   ₃₉
<u>the</u> Hermitage is the official state museum of
₃₉

34.
   F. NO CHANGE
   G. Finland; this
   H. Finland. For example,
   J. Finland, however,

35.
   A. NO CHANGE
   B. Bridges traverse
   C. Bridges, traverse the
   D. Bridges that are traversing

36.
   F. NO CHANGE
   G. Omit the underlined portion.
   H. which
   J. that

37. Which of the following would NOT be an
acceptable replacement for the underlined
part?
   A. As the city is located in a northern
latitude
   B. Being that the city is very far north
   C. Since the city is far north
   D. Just as in other cities in northern
latitudes

38.
   F. NO CHANGE
   G. most famously known
   H. best known
   J. most known and famous

39.
   A. NO CHANGE
   B. largest; the
   C. largest. The
   D. largest, the

St. Petersburg, its collection, housed in several
40

buildings, numbers over three million masterpieces

including works by Leonardo da Vinci,

Michelangelo, Rembrandt, Renoir, Cezanne,

Manet, and Monet. 41 The most spectacular

museum building and one of the biggest tourist

attractions are the Winter Palace, founded by
42

Catherine the Great, an avid collector of art. The
43

museum's coffers were enriched by wartime acquisi-

tions as the Red Army marched through Germany

and appropriated assets as they passed. In addition

to the Hermitage, the Stock Exchange, the Summer

Garden and Summer Palace of Peter the Great, and

Palace Square are breathtaking examples of opu-

lent edifices.

40.
- **F.** NO CHANGE
- **G.** St. Petersburg; whose
- **H.** St. Petersburg's collection
- **J.** St. Petersburg. Its

41. At this point, the writer wants to add a sentence that indicates the extraordinary nature of the museum's collection. Which alternative would best fulfill the writer's goal?

- **A.** Claude Monet was the founder of the French Impressionist movement.
- **B.** The collection contains exquisite examples of art that encompass the entire history of mankind, from ancient treasures to contemporary works.
- **C.** Located on the banks of the River Neva, the museum fills ten buildings with works of art.
- **D.** Tourists wait in line, sometimes for hours, to visit the museum's collections of fine artwork.

42.
- **F.** NO CHANGE
- **G.** attractions is
- **H.** attractions were
- **J.** attractions being

43. Which choice best shows that Catherine the Great was passionate about collecting art?

- **A.** NO CHANGE
- **B.** a collector of art
- **C.** a strong and materialistic queen
- **D.** who loved to decorate her palaces

The center of St. Petersburg also holds attractions for tourists. Visitors and natives alike love to shop on the most famous street in the city, Nevsky Prospekt. 44

This truly magnificent Russian city, with exquisite churches, impressive monuments, and breathtaking physical beauty, will remain an indelible memory to all who visit this vibrant metropolis. 45

44. Given that all of the following are true, which would be the most appropriate to add on to the preceding sentence to fulfill the writer's goal of highlighting the importance of this street? (Change the period to a comma first.)

   F. St. Petersburg's main avenue and one of the best-known streets in Russia.

   G. known at the beginning of the twentieth century as Avenue of the 25th of October.

   H. prospekt being the Russian equivalent of avenue.

   J. extending from the Admiralty to the railway station.

Question 45 asks about the essay as a whole.

45. Suppose the writer's goal had been to write an essay about those cities in Russia that exemplify baroque architecture. Does this essay fulfill that goal?

   A. Yes, because the writer discusses the specific characteristics of the baroque style.

   B. Yes, because the writer describes St. Petersburg as a uniquely baroque city.

   C. No, because the essay is an overview of the attractions of a single city.

   D. No, because the writer never fully discusses the architecture of this particular city.

Passage IV

The Artist

Rosa Bonheur was the best pupil of her father, Raymond B. Bonheur. In Bordeaux, France, they lived together the peaceful life of artists. <u>Her father being already</u> a well-known painter when his daugh-
46
ter was born. After a time, the Bonheurs moved to Paris where young Rosa could have better <u>opportu-</u>
47
<u>nities; it was there</u> that she put on men's clothing,
47
which she wore for the rest of her life. She wore a workingman's blouse and trousers and tramped about looking more like a man than a woman with her short hair. This made everybody stare at her <u>and think her very odd</u>. It was then that her enemies,
48
<u>mostly those who were both jealous or envious</u> of
49
her work, said that she dressed in this manner in order to attract attention. Today, most people <u>now believe</u> she dressed so because it was the most
50
comfortable and convenient costume for her.

46.
F. NO CHANGE
G. Her father was
H. Her father was being
J. Her father, being

47.
A. NO CHANGE
B. opportunities, it was there
C. opportunities which she had; it was there
D. opportunities; there

48.
F. NO CHANGE
G. and they had thought she was odd
H. to think her very odd
J. which made them think she was very odd

49.
A. NO CHANGE
B. most of them who were jealous
C. those whom were jealous and envious
D. mostly those who were jealous

50.
F. NO CHANGE
G. believe now
H. believe
J. have believed

She went to all sorts of <u>places; the stockyards,</u> [51] slaughter houses, and all around the streets of Paris—to learn of things and people, especially of animals, which she wished most to paint. She could hardly have <u>traveled so free</u> [52] had she worn women's clothing.

Rosa Bonheur exhibited her first painting in 1841, twelve years before her beloved father died; thus, he <u>would have had</u> [53] the happiness of knowing that the daughter whom he had taught so lovingly was on the road to success and fortune. That year she painted only two little <u>pictures—one of rabbits, the other of sheep and goats—but</u> [54] they were so splendidly done that all the critics knew a great female artist had arrived.

Soon her work began to be bought by the French Government, which was a sure sign of her power. She was already much beloved by the people. In the meantime, art lovers in America and others in England had heard of Mademoiselle Bonheur, but heard far less about her painting <u>as</u> [55] about her mas-

51.
   A. NO CHANGE
   B. places—the stockyards,
   C. places; the stockyards;
   D. places, she went to the stockyards,

52.
   F. NO CHANGE
   G. traveled with the freedom
   H. traveled so freely
   J. been traveling so free

53.
   A. NO CHANGE
   B. had
   C. would of had
   D. had to have

54. Which of the following alternatives to the underlined portion would NOT be acceptable?
   F. pictures (one of rabbits, the other of sheep and goats), but
   G. pictures, one of rabbits and the other of sheep and goats, but
   H. pictures one of rabbits and the other of sheep and goats but
   J. pictures: one of rabbits and one of sheep and goats. However,

55.
   A. NO CHANGE
   B. rather than
   C. as than
   D. than

culine garb. She was considered mostly an eccentric

woman, however once the art world saw her great
       _____
          56

painting, "The Horse Fair," the artist was no longer

judged by the clothes she wore but by her art. [57]

Finally, she received the cross of the Legion of

Honour and was made a member of the Institute of

Antwerp.

Rosa Bonheur lived near Fontainebleau until the

Franco-Prussian War broke out. Then she and oth-

ers began to fear that her studio and pictures would
    _____
       58

be destroyed, and the artist stopped her work and
              ___
              59

prepared to go elsewhere. But the Crown Prince of

Prussia himself ordered that Mademoiselle Bonheur

should not even be disturbed. Her work had made

her belong to all the world, and all the world would
                                 _____
                                        60

protect her if need be.
_____
    60

56.
  F. NO CHANGE
  G. woman: however
  H. woman however,
  J. woman; however,

57. In the preceding sentence, the writer would
    like to underscore the change in the public's
    attitude toward Rosa Bonheur. Which of the
    following choices would best accomplish that
    goal?

  A. Leave the sentence as it is now.
      OR Replace the sentence with one of the
      choices below:
  B. When the people saw "The Horse Fair,"
      they knew Rosa Bonheur was a great
      painter of animals.
  C. Rosa Bonheur did not enjoy a good
      reputation as an artist because many
      people thought her weird.
  D. In public, Rosa Bonheur's behavior
      caused a scandal, but in private, she was
      a serious artist.

58.
  F. NO CHANGE
  G. have begun to fear
  H. begin fearing
  J. are beginning to fear

59.
  A. NO CHANGE
  B. omit this word
  C. because
  D. so

60.
  F. NO CHANGE
  G. the entire population of the people of
      the world were willing to protect her
  H. all the other people would protect her
  J. protecting her would be done by all the
      world

Passage V

A Divine Dessert

[1]

Chocolate—just the word ignites cravings that cannot be satisfied until one consumes a piece of the smooth, silky confection. What is it about chocolate that ignites such passion in the hearts of self-confessed "chocoholics"? Some researchers say the response is purely physical: It is the caffeine that is present in chocolate that <u>provide</u> the feeling of plea-
61
sure that is <u>associated to</u> indulging in a rich piece of
62
chocolate. Others attribute the sense of well-being to the presence of chemicals like theobromine, a mild stimulant. Whatever it is, for many, chocolate is undeniably addicting.

[2]

Chocolate has a fascinating history. It begins with the Maya <u>who are people who live</u> in the rain-
63
forests of South America. <u>No one know</u> exactly
64
when, but about 2,000 years ago, these ancient people discovered that when they harvested the fruit of

61.
A. NO CHANGE
B. providing
C. provides
D. provided

62.
F. NO CHANGE
G. associated for
H. associated in
J. associated with

63.
A. NO CHANGE
B. Omit the underlined portion.
C. whom lived
D. the name of the people who lived

64.
F. NO CHANGE
G. No one knows
H. No one who knows
J. Not knowing

the cacao tree, roasted the seeds, <u>and they ground</u>₆₅ the seeds to a paste, and mixed this paste with water and spices, they would have a frothy and spicy beverage. This drink played an important role in their social activities and in <u>the religious rituals performed by them</u>₆₆.

[3]

Like any other novelty, chocolate inspired invention and creativity. Using their culinary skills, <u>chocolate began to be used by chefs</u>₆₇ to flavor pastries and desserts. A dramatic change came about <u>in 1828</u>₆₈ when the Dutch chocolate maker van Houten developed a machine that reduced the cocoa butter in the cacao bean and pressed it into a disc shape. This led to the evolution of the chocolate <u>bar, and, as they say,</u>₆₉ "the rest is history."

65.
A. NO CHANGE
B. and grinding
C. they ground
D. ground

66.
F. NO CHANGE
G. their religious rituals
H. those religious rituals that were performed by them
J. performing religious rituals

67.
A. NO CHANGE
B. chocolate was used by chefs
C. chefs began the use of chocolate
D. chefs began to use chocolate

68. Which of the following would NOT be an acceptable placement for the underlined phrase?
F. where it is now
G. at the beginning of the sentence (before *A dramatic change*).
H. after *van Houten*
J. after *butter*

69.
A. NO CHANGE
B. bar; and as they say;
C. bar and, as, they say,
D. bar, and as they say

[4]

Credit for bringing chocolate to Europe is usually given to Christopher Columbus. <u>Moreover</u>, choco-
[70]
late did not become an overnight sensation. It was not until Spanish chefs replaced the chili pepper used by the Maya with sugar that chocolate bever-ages became popular. At first, this <u>drink was a luxury</u>,
[71]
for only the wealthy elite could afford to purchase it from Spanish merchants. Spain's exclusive hold on chocolate, however, did not last. Other European countries <u>began cultivating</u> the cacao tree in their
[72]
colonies, and soon the common people were able to enjoy the taste of chocolate.

[5]

Although chocolate has been accused of every "health crime" under the sun including causing acne, tooth decay, and obesity, recent studies have <u>touted the benefits</u> of consuming chocolate.
[73]
Scientists have discovered that chocolate can reduce

70.
    F. NO CHANGE
    G. However
    H. Clearly
    J. Despite this

71.
    A. NO CHANGE
    B. drink was a high-priced item
    C. drink was luxurious
    D. drink was over the top

72.
    F. NO CHANGE
    G. began to cultivate
    H. began the cultivation for
    J. began in the cultivation of

73. Which of the following would NOT be an acceptable replacement for the underlined portion?
    A. publicized the positive qualities
    B. laid on thick the good points
    C. promoted the advantages
    D. announced the healthful nature

high blood pressure and <u>is contributing</u> to overall
74
heart health. For true chocolate-lovers, however, the most important benefit is how chocolate makes them feel when they indulge. A piece of good dark chocolate or rich milk chocolate melting on the tongue is one of life's simple pleasures. ☐75☐

74.
  F. NO CHANGE
  G. contribute
  H. be a contributor
  J. make a contribution

Question 75 asks about the essay as a whole.

75. For the sake of the logic and coherence of this essay, paragraph 4 would be best placed:

  A. where it is now.
  B. after paragraph 5.
  C. before paragraph 2.
  D. before paragraph 3.

IF YOU FINISH BEFORE TIME IS CALLED, CHECK YOUR WORK ON THIS
SECTION ONLY. DO NOT WORK ON ANY OTHER SECTION IN THE TEST.

Section 2: Mathematics Test

60 Minutes—60 Questions

Directions: Solve each problem and fill in the corresponding circle on the answer sheet. Figures are not necessarily drawn to scale. You may use a permitted graphing calculator.

1. For all values of x, which of the following is equivalent to $(x^2 - 3) - (4x^2 - 5x + 1)$?

   A. $-3x^2 - 5x - 2$
   B. $-3x^2 - 5x + 4$
   C. $-3x^2 + 5x - 4$
   D. $3x^2 - 5x - 2$
   E. $3x^2 - 5x + 4$

2. In the accompanying diagram, what is the value of x?

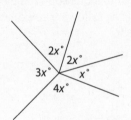

   F. 15
   G. 30
   H. 45
   J. 60
   K. 90

3. If $\dfrac{3}{ab} = 6$, then $ab =$

   A. $\dfrac{1}{18}$

   B. $\dfrac{1}{6}$

   C. $\dfrac{1}{2}$

   D. 2

   E. 18

4. In the accompanying figure, $\overline{BD}$ and $\overline{AE}$ intersect at point C, and $AB = AC$. If $m\angle DCE = 40$, what is the measure of $\angle A$?

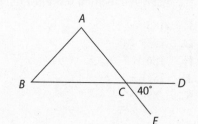

   F. 40
   G. 60
   H. 80
   J. 100
   K. 120

5. If $2(4^k) = 2^5$, what is the value of k?

   A. 0
   B. 1
   C. 2
   D. 3
   E. 4

6. Two similar triangles have perimeters 16 and 36, respectively. If the shortest side of the smaller triangle is 4, what is the length of the shortest side of the larger triangle?

   F. 3
   G. 6
   H. 9
   J. 12
   K. 18

7. Given the sequence 7, 11, 15, 19, . . . , what is the 8th term of the sequence?

    A.   31
    B.   35
    C.   39
    D.   56
    E.   60

8. Karen took four math tests and her scores were 96, 85, 92, and 99. What is the sum of the mean and median scores of the four tests?

    F.   183
    G.   185
    H.   186
    J.   187
    K.   189

9. For all values of $x \neq 0$, which of the following is equivalent to $\dfrac{2x^4 + 6x^2 - 4x}{2x}$?

    A. $x^3 + 6x^2 - 4x$
    B. $x^3 + 6x - 4$
    C. $x^3 - 3x + 2$
    D. $x^3 + 3x - 2$
    E.   48

10. What is the largest 3-digit integer that is divisible by 11?

    F.   911
    G.   979
    H.   990
    J.   993
    K.   999

11. If a square and an equilateral triangle have the same perimeter, and the area of the square is 36, what is the length of a side of the triangle?

    A.   4
    B.   6
    C.   8
    D.   10
    E.   12

12. In the xy-plane, the point $(-12, k)$ lies on the line $2x - 3y = 6$. What is the value of k?

    F. -10
    G. -6
    H.   6
    J.   10
    K.   15

13. If 50% of k is 20, what is $\dfrac{1}{4}$ of k?

    A. $\dfrac{5}{2}$
    B.   5
    C.   10
    D.   40
    E.   160

14. On a coordinate plane, two lines l and m are parallel. If an equation of line l is $y = 2x - 4$, which of the following could be an equation of line m?

    F. $y + 2x = 4$
    G. $y + 2x = -4$
    H. $y - 2x = 0$
    J. $y = \dfrac{1}{2}x - 4$
    K. $y = -\dfrac{1}{2}x - 4$

15. For all real values of x, which of the following is equivalent to $(2x - 3)(x + 1)$?

    A. $2x^2 - 3$
    B. $2x^2 - 5x - 3$
    C. $2x^2 - x + 3$
    D. $2x^2 - x - 3$
    E. $2x^2 + x - 3$

16. On a coordinate plane diagram, the vertices of $\triangle ABC$ are $A(-1, -1)$, $B(3, -1)$, and $C(3, 3)$. What is the degree measure of $\angle ACB$?

    F. 15
    G. 30
    H. 45
    J. 60
    K. 75

17. If $abc = 0$ and $bcd = 1$, which of the following must be true?

    I. $a = 0$
    II. $bc > 0$
    III. $d = 1$

    A. I only
    B. II only
    C. III only
    D. I and II only
    E. I, II, and III

18. The function $p(x)$ is defined as $p(x) = \sqrt{x}$. If $p(4k) = 8$, what is the value of k?

    F. 2
    G. 4
    H. 8
    J. 16
    K. 32

19. If the sum of three consecutive even integers is 138, what is the numerical value of the middle integer?

    A. 40
    B. 42
    C. 44
    D. 46
    E. 48

20. What is the slope of the line whose x-intercept is -3 and whose y-intercept is 4?

    F. $\dfrac{-4}{3}$

    G. $\dfrac{-3}{4}$

    H. $\dfrac{3}{4}$

    J. $\dfrac{4}{3}$

    K. Cannot be determined

21. What is the mean of the set of data represented by the stem-and-leaf plot shown below?

Stem	Leaf
2	0, 1, 1
4	3
6	
8	0, 5
Key: 5|1 = 51	

    A. 21
    B. $28.\overline{3}$
    C. 32
    D. 42.5
    E. 45

22. What positive integer has the property such that six more than twice the number is the same as four times the number?

    F. -3
    G. -1
    H. 1
    J. 3
    K. 6

23. Given the scatterplot in the accompanying figure, which of the following could be the approximate value of its correlation coefficient?

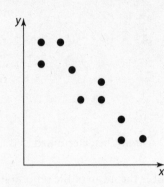

    A.   −0.91
    B.   −0.15
    C.   0.25
    D.   0.87
    E.   0.95

24. Mary bought two kinds of pens. One kind cost $2 each, and the other cost $3 each. If Mary spent a total of $48 on the pens, and she bought twice as many of the more expensive pens than of the cheaper pens, how many of the $2 pens did Mary buy?

    F.   2
    G.   4
    H.   5
    J.   6
    K.   8

25. Which of the following is a solution to the equation $x^2 + 9 = 6x$?

    A.   −6
    B.   −3
    C.   0
    D.   3
    E.   9

26. In the accompanying diagram, $y = g(x)$. How many values of x is $g(x) = 3$?

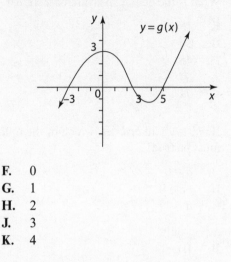

    F.   0
    G.   1
    H.   2
    J.   3
    K.   4

27. Karen has 3 quarters, 4 dimes, 6 nickels, and 2 pennies in her bag. If she takes a coin at random from her bag, what is the probability that the coin is NOT a quarter?

    A. $\dfrac{1}{15}$

    B. $\dfrac{1}{5}$

    C. $\dfrac{3}{5}$

    D. $\dfrac{11}{15}$

    E. $\dfrac{4}{5}$

Use the following information to answer questions 28 and 29.

The scatterplot in the accompanying figure shows the number of minutes a student studied for a math quiz and the grade the student received on the quiz. The line of best fit is also shown.

Quiz Grades vs. Study Time

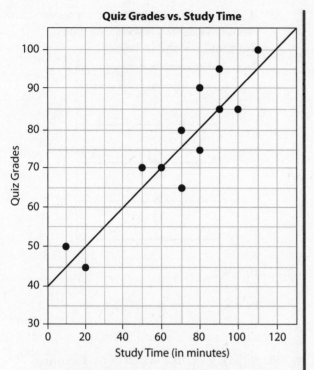

28. If $g = ht + k$ is the equation of the line of best fit, where g represents a student's grade on the quiz and t represents the number of minutes the student studied for the quiz, what is the value of h?

    F. -2

    G. $-\dfrac{1}{2}$

    H. $\dfrac{1}{2}$

    J. 1

    K. 2

29. If a student wished to receive a grade of no lower than 80 on the quiz, what is the minimum number of minutes he must study according to the line of best fit?

    A.   60

    B.   70

    C.   80

    D.   90

    E.   100

30. Which of the following is an even function?

    F. $y = 2x - 1$

    G. $y = 4x + 2$

    H. $y = (x - 2)^4$

    J. $y = x^2 - 3$

    K. $y = x^2 - 4x - 12$

31. In the accompanying diagram, the figure is a rectangular prism. If $HG = 8$, $FG = 4$, $CG = 2$, and n is the midpoint of HG, what is the length of $\overline{AN}$?

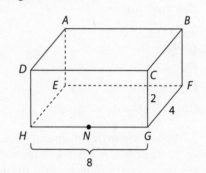

    A.   4

    B.   6

    C.   12

    D.   18

    E.   36

32. If the distance between $A(-2, 5)$ and $B(6, k)$ is 8, what is the value of k?

    F. -5

    G.   2

    H.   5

    J.   10

    K.   25

33. If $\dfrac{m}{n} = -2$, what is the value of $2\left(\dfrac{m}{n}\right)^2$?

    A. -16

    B. -8

    C.   6

    D.   8

    E.   16

305

34. If $3k - 2$ is divided by 4, the remainder is 2. Which of the following could be the value of k?

    F.   1
    G.   2
    H.   3
    J.   4
    K.   5

35. In the complex numbers, where $i = \sqrt{-1}$, which of the following is equivalent to $(1 + 3i)(1 - i)$?

    A. -3
    B.   5
    C. $-2 + 4i$
    D. $4 + 2i$
    E. $-4 + 2i$

36. In the accompanying diagram, the equation of the circle is $x^2 + y^2 = 9$ and the equation of the line is $y = 2x$. Which of the following sets of inequalities define the shaded region?

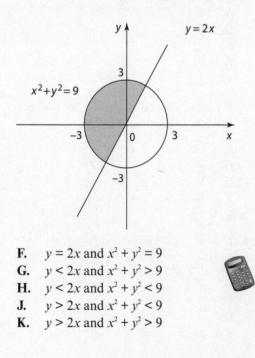

    F. $y = 2x$ and $x^2 + y^2 = 9$
    G. $y < 2x$ and $x^2 + y^2 > 9$
    H. $y < 2x$ and $x^2 + y^2 < 9$
    J. $y > 2x$ and $x^2 + y^2 < 9$
    K. $y > 2x$ and $x^2 + y^2 > 9$

37. What is the expected value of a discrete random variable x whose probability distribution is shown below?

x_i	$p(x_i)$
2	$\dfrac{1}{2}$
4	$\dfrac{1}{6}$
6	$\dfrac{1}{6}$
8	$\dfrac{1}{6}$

    A.   4
    B.   4.5
    C.   5
    D.   6
    E.   8

38. If $(2x)^2 < 2x$, then which of the following could be a value of x?

    F. $\dfrac{1}{4}$
    G. $\dfrac{1}{2}$
    H. $\dfrac{3}{4}$
    J.   1
    K.   2

39. The average height of Janet, Karen, and Mary is 5 ft 4 in. Karen is 5 ft 6 in tall, and she is the tallest of the three. Janet is the shortest. If no two girls have the same height and all heights are integral inches, what is the least possible height for Janet?

    A.   5 ft
    B.   5 ft 1 in
    C.   5 ft 2 in
    D.   5 ft 3 in
    E.   5 ft 6 in

40. If y is a positive integer, $y = x^2$ and $x = -y^2$, what is the value of y?

   F. −2
   G. −1
   H. 0
   J. 1
   K. 2

Use the following information to answer questions 41–43.

In the accompanying figure, $\triangle ABC$ is shown with vertices $A(3, 4)$, $B(1, 1)$, and $C(7, 1)$.

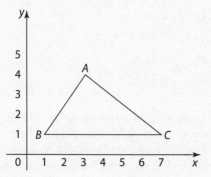

41. If line l (not shown) is perpendicular to $\overrightarrow{AB}$, what is the slope of line l?

   A. $\dfrac{-3}{2}$

   B. $\dfrac{-2}{3}$

   C. $\dfrac{-1}{5}$

   D. $\dfrac{2}{3}$

   E. $\dfrac{3}{2}$

42. If $\triangle A'B'C'$ is the image of $\triangle ABC$ reflected in the x-axis, which of the following are the coordinates of A'?

   F. (−3, −4)
   G. (−3, 4)
   H. (−4, 3)
   J. (3, −4)
   K. (4, −3)

43. If $\triangle A''B''C''$ is the image of $\triangle ABC$ under a dilation of 2 about the origin, what is the area of $\triangle A''B''C''$ in square units?

   A. $4\dfrac{1}{2}$

   B. 9
   C. 18
   D. 36
   E. 72

44. The accompanying graph summarizes the sales of a company over 6 years. Between which 2 years is the increase in sales the greatest?

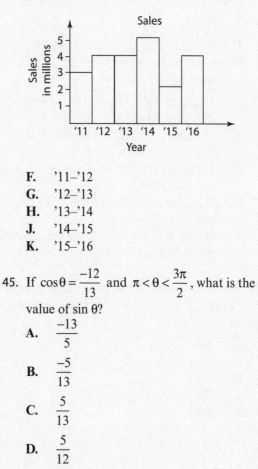

   F. '11–'12
   G. '12–'13
   H. '13–'14
   J. '14–'15
   K. '15–'16

45. If $\cos\theta = \dfrac{-12}{13}$ and $\pi < \theta < \dfrac{3\pi}{2}$, what is the value of $\sin\theta$?

   A. $\dfrac{-13}{5}$

   B. $\dfrac{-5}{13}$

   C. $\dfrac{5}{13}$

   D. $\dfrac{5}{12}$

   E. $\dfrac{12}{13}$

46. In the accompanying diagram, $AB = 14$, $m\angle ABC = 30°$, and $m\angle C = 90°$. What is the length of $\overline{AC}$?

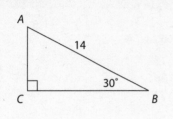

F. 7
G. $7\sqrt{2}$
H. $7\sqrt{3}$
J. $14\sqrt{2}$
K. $14\sqrt{3}$

47. If every student in Mrs. Smith's class is on the honor roll, which of the following statements must be true?

A. If John is on the honor roll, he is in Mrs. Smith's class.
B. If Mary is not on the honor roll, she is not in Mrs. Smith's class.
C. If George is not in Mrs. Smith's class, he is not on the honor roll.
D. If Nancy is in Mrs. Smith's class, she is not on the honor roll.
E. If Jean is not in Mrs. Smith's class, she is on the honor roll.

48. What is the surface area of a sphere, in square inches, if the volume of the sphere is 288π cubic inches?

F. 36π
G. 144π
H. 288π
J. 384π
K. 845π

49. The graph of a function $y = f(x)$ is shown in the accompanying figure. Which of the following could be the function f?

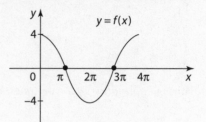

A. $y = \cos 4x$
B. $y = -4 \cos x$
C. $y = 2 \cos 4x$
D. $y = 4\cos\dfrac{x}{2}$
E. $y = 4 \cos 2x$

50. In an xy-coordinate plane, point C with coordinates $(4, 0)$ is the center of a circle and point A with coordinates $(4, 5)$ is on the circle. Which of the following could be the coordinates of point B, if B is also a point on the circle?

F. $(-3, 4)$
G. $(0, 0)$
H. $(1, 4)$
J. $(4, 3)$
K. $(4, 10)$

51. If $-3 \le p \le -1$ and $-2 \le q \le 2$, which of the following represents all possible values of pq?

A. $-6 \le pq \le -2$
B. $-5 \le pq \le 1$
C. $-2 \le pq \le 6$
D. $-2 \le pq \le 2$
E. $-6 \le pq \le 6$

52. In the accompanying diagram, $DE = 6$, $EF = 10$, and $m\angle E = 40$. The length of $\overline{DF}$ is given by which of the following expressions?

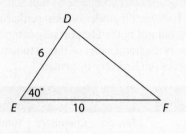

   F.   8
   G. $6 \sin 40°$
   H. $10 \tan 40°$
   J. $6^2 + 10^2 - 2(6)(10) \cos 40°$
   K. $\sqrt{36 + 100 - 120 \cos 40°}$

53. In the accompanying diagram, two concentric circles have O as their centers, $\overline{OA}$ is a radius of the larger circle, and $AB = 2$. If the circumference of the larger circle is 16π, what is the circumference of the smaller circle?

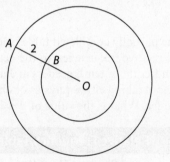

Not drawn to scale

   A. 4π
   B. 8π
   C. 10π
   D. 12π
   E. 14π

54. A recreational fishing boat charges $20 per adult and $10 per child for a 4-hour fishing trip, plus $2 per fish caught during the trip. If a family of two adults and three children went fishing on the boat, and at the end of the trip paid a total charge of $82, how many fish did the family catch?

   F.   1
   G.   4
   H.   6
   J.   8
   K.   21

55. If $\log A = h$ and $\log B = k$, what is the value of $\log\left(\dfrac{A^2}{B}\right)$ in terms of h and k?

   A. $h^2 - k$
   B. $2h - k$
   C. $2h + k$
   D. $\dfrac{h^2}{k}$
   E. $h^2 + k$

56. What is the matrix product $\begin{bmatrix} -2 & 1 \end{bmatrix}\begin{bmatrix} 3 \\ -4 \end{bmatrix}$?

   F. $\begin{bmatrix} -6 & -4 \end{bmatrix}$
   G. $[-2]$
   H. $[-10]$
   J. $[2]$
   K. $\begin{bmatrix} -6 \\ -4 \end{bmatrix}$

57. In the accompanying diagram, *ACDE* is a rectangle and the region above the rectangle is a semicircle. If the area of the rectangle is 32 and the length of $\overline{CD}$ is twice the length of $\overline{ED}$, what is the perimeter of the figure *ABCDE*?

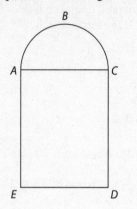

A. 20
B. 24
C. $20 + 2\pi$
D. $20 + 4\pi$
E. $24 + 4\pi$

58. In the accompanying figure, *ABCD* is a rhombus with diagonals $\overline{BD}$ and $\overline{AC}$ intersecting at *E*. If *BC* = 8 and *AC* = 8, what is the $m\angle ADE$?

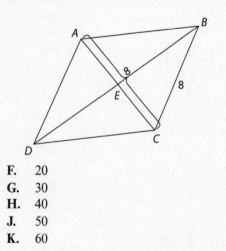

F. 20
G. 30
H. 40
J. 50
K. 60

Use the following information to answer questions 59 and 60.

The tenth-grade class at Jefferson High School has 124 students. Every tenth grader is taking either physics or chemistry, but not both. The partially completed table below shows the frequencies of these students taking either physics or chemistry by gender.

Frequency Table			
	Physics	Chemistry	Total
Male	28		68
Female		25	
Total			124

59. What is the total number of tenth graders at Jefferson High School taking physics?

A. 28
B. 31
C. 40
D. 59
E. 68

60. The partially completed table below shows the relative frequencies, to the nearest hundredth, of tenth graders at Jefferson High School taking either physics or chemistry by gender. What is the value of *x* + *y*?

Relative Frequency Table			
	Physics	Chemistry	Total
Male	*x*	0.32	
Female		*y*	0.45
Total	0.48		1

F. 0.03
G. 0.20
H. 0.23
J. 0.43
K. 0.55

IF YOU FINISH BEFORE TIME IS CALLED, CHECK YOUR WORK ON THIS SECTION ONLY. DO NOT WORK ON ANY OTHER SECTION IN THE TEST.

Section 3: Reading Test

35 Minutes—40 Questions

Directions: The Reading Test consists of four passages, each followed by 10 questions. After reading a passage, select the best answer and fill in the corresponding circle on the answer sheet. You may look back in the passages as you answer the questions.

Passage I

PROSE FICTION: The following is an excerpt from the novel *A Room with a View* written by E. M. Forster in 1908. Lucy Honeychurch and Miss Bartlett are traveling through Italy together.

"The Signora had no business to do it," said Miss Bartlett, "no business at all. She promised us south rooms with a view close together, instead of which here are north
(5) rooms, looking into a courtyard, and a long way apart. Oh, Lucy!"

"And a Cockney, besides!" said Lucy, who had been further saddened by the Signora's unexpected accent. "It might be London." She
(10) looked at the two rows of English people who were sitting at the table; at the row of white bottles of water and red bottles of wine that ran between the English people; at the portraits of the late Queen and the late Poet
(15) Laureate that hung behind the English people, heavily framed; at the notice of the English church (Rev. Cuthbert Eager, M. A. Oxon.), that was the only other decoration of the wall. "Charlotte, don't you feel, too, that we might
(20) be in London? I can hardly believe that all kinds of other things are just outside. I suppose it is one's being so tired."

"This meat has surely been used for soup," said Miss Bartlett, laying down her fork.
(25) "I want so to see the Arno. The rooms the Signora promised us in her letter would have looked over the Arno. The Signora had no business to do it at all. Oh, it is a shame!"

"Any nook does for me," Miss Bartlett con-
(30) tinued; "but it does seem hard that you shouldn't have a view."

Lucy felt that she had been selfish. "Charlotte, you mustn't spoil me: of course, you must look over the Arno, too. I meant
(35) that. The first vacant room in the front—"

"You must have it," said Miss Bartlett, part of whose travelling expenses were paid by Lucy's mother—a piece of generosity to which she made many a tactful allusion.

(40) "No, no. You must have it."

"I insist on it. Your mother would never forgive me, Lucy."

"She would never forgive me."

The ladies' voices grew animated, and—if
(45) the sad truth be owned—a little peevish. They were tired, and under the guise of unselfishness they wrangled. Some of their neighbours interchanged glances, and one of them—one of the ill-bred people whom one does meet
(50) abroad—leant forward over the table and actually intruded into their argument. He said:

"I have a view, I have a view."

Miss Bartlett was startled. Generally at a pension people looked them over for a day or
(55) two before speaking, and often did not find out that they would "do" till they had gone. She knew that the intruder was ill-bred, even before she glanced at him. He was an old man, of heavy build, with a fair, shaven face and
(60) large eyes. There was something childish in those eyes, though it was not the childishness of senility. What exactly it was Miss Bartlett did not stop to consider, for her glance passed on to his clothes. These did not attract her. He

(65) was probably trying to become acquainted with them before they got into the swim. So she assumed a dazed expression when he spoke to her, and then said: "A view? Oh, a view! How delightful a view is!"

(70) "This is my son," said the old man; "his name's George. He has a view too."

"Ah," said Miss Bartlett, repressing Lucy, who was about to speak.

"What I mean," he continued, "is that you (75) can have our rooms, and we'll have yours. We'll change."

The better class of tourist was shocked at this, and sympathized with the new-comers. Miss Bartlett, in reply, opened her mouth as (80) little as possible, and said "Thank you very much indeed; that is out of the question."

"Why?" said the old man, with both fists on the table.

"Because it is quite out of the question, (85) thank you."

"You see, we don't like to take—" began Lucy. Her cousin again repressed her.

"But why?" he persisted. "Women like looking at a view; men don't." And he (90) thumped with his fists like a naughty child, and turned to his son, saying, "George, persuade them!"

"It's so obvious they should have the rooms," said the son. "There's nothing else to (95) say."

He did not look at the ladies as he spoke, but his voice was perplexed and sorrowful. Lucy, too, was perplexed; but she saw that they were in for what is known as "quite a (100) scene," and she had an odd feeling that whenever these ill-bred tourists spoke the contest widened and deepened till it dealt, not with rooms and views, but with—well, with something quite different, whose existence she had (105) not realized before. Now the old man attacked Miss Bartlett almost violently: Why should she not change? What possible objection had she? They would clear out in half an hour.

Miss Bartlett, though skilled in the delica-(110) cies of conversation, was powerless in the presence of brutality. It was impossible to snub any one so gross. Her face reddened with displeasure. She looked around as much as to say, "Are you all like this?" And two little old (115) ladies, who were sitting further up the table, with shawls hanging over the backs of the chairs, looked back, clearly indicating "We are not; we are genteel."

"Eat your dinner, dear," she said to Lucy, (120) and began to toy again with the meat that she had once censured.

Lucy mumbled that those seemed very odd people opposite.

"Eat your dinner, dear. This pension is a (125) failure. To-morrow we will make a change."

1. The main purpose of the passage is to:

   A. expose the hazards of traveling to foreign countries.
   B. defend the British subjects who transport their culture as they immigrate.
   C. reveal the class consciousness of two women.
   D. confirm the snobbish pre-conceptions of British travelers toward their Italian hosts.

2. The effect of the repetition of the phrase "English people" in the second paragraph (lines 7–22) is to:

   F. suggest the Signora's belief that most tourists prefer the similar to the exotic.
   G. underscore the pervasive imperialism of the British Empire.
   H. contrast with the authenticity of the Signora's Italian accent.
   J. allude to the close cultural ties between Britain and Italy.

3. The relationship between Miss Bartlett and Lucy Honeychurch suggests:

   A. they are social equals on an educational mission.

   B. Miss Bartlett is a wealthy woman who has employed Lucy Honeychurch as a companion.

   C. the two women share a mutual dislike but are forced together by circumstances.

   D. Miss Bartlett acts as a chaperone and companion to Lucy Honeychurch.

4. The description of the "two little old ladies" (lines 114–118) implies that they:

   F. try to ignore and remain aloof from the scene erupting around them.

   G. sympathize with Lucy Honeychurch and Miss Bartlett as they cope with the embarrassment of ill-mannered companions.

   H. believe the kindness of George and his father should be rewarded.

   J. are perplexed by the many-layered social dimensions of the drama unfolding before them.

5. The attitudes of Lucy Honeychurch and Miss Bartlett toward the offer of a room exchange is best described as:

   A. suspicion toward the surprisingly forward outburst of the old man.

   B. warm appreciation of a generous suggestion.

   C. amusement at the chivalrous and gentlemanly offer.

   D. admiration for the courage of the old man to assert himself in such lofty company.

6. The author's use of the words "attacked" (line 105), "violently" (line 106), and "brutality" (line 111) suggests:

   F. the encounter in the pension epitomizes a clash of social values.

   G. the arrival of the new-comers is marred by a physical assault.

   H. the old man, a former soldier, is unable to cast off his propensity for violence.

   J. a foreshadowing of the impending hostility between those who have just arrived and those who have been in residence for some time.

7. Which of the following best describes Lucy Honeychurch's response to the old man as opposed to Miss Bartlett's?

   A. Lucy is confused, while Miss Bartlett is affronted.

   B. Lucy is angry, while Miss Bartlett is conciliatory.

   C. Lucy is amenable, while Miss Bartlett is confused.

   D. Lucy is exhilarated, while Miss Bartlett is indifferent.

8. All of the following contrasts are present in the passage EXCEPT:

   F. subtlety versus brutality

   G. politeness versus impropriety

   H. senility versus mental sharpness

   J. peevishness versus decorum

9. The author implies the "something quite different" (lines 103–104) refers to:

   A. social strata.

   B. nationalistic feeling.

   C. gender distinctions.

   D. imperialism.

10. The tone of the phrase "a piece of generosity to which she made many a tactful allusion" (lines 38–39) is best described as:

   F. didactic.
   G. sorrowful.
   H. strident.
   J. ironic.

Passage II

SOCIAL SCIENCE: The following passage is an excerpt from *Politics,* an essay written by Ralph Waldo Emerson in 1844.

The theory of politics which has possessed the mind of men, and which they have expressed the best they could in their laws and in their revolutions, considers persons and
(5) property as the two objects for whose protection government exists. Of persons, all have equal rights, in virtue of being identical in nature. This interest of course with its whole power demands a democracy. Whilst the rights
(10) of all as persons are equal, in virtue of their access to reason, their rights in property are very unequal. One man owns his clothes, and another owns a county. This accident, depending primarily on the skill and virtue of the
(15) parties, of which there is every degree, and secondarily on patrimony, falls unequally, and its rights of course are unequal. Personal rights, universally the same, demand a government framed on the ratio of the census; property
(20) demands a government framed on the ratio of owners and of owning. Laban,* who has flocks and herds, wishes them looked after by an officer on the frontiers . . . and pays a tax to that end. Jacob has no flocks or herds . . . and
(25) pays no tax to the officer. It seemed fit that

Laban: a biblical figure, brother-in-law to Isaac. Laban owns many sheep which are tended by his son-in-law, Jacob.

Laban and Jacob should have equal rights to elect the officer who is to defend their persons, but that Laban and not Jacob should elect the officer who is to guard the sheep and cattle.
(30) And if questions arise whether additional officers or watch-towers should be provided, must not Laban and Isaac, and those who must sell part of their herds to buy protection for the rest, judge better of this, and with more right,
(35) than Jacob, who, because he is a youth and a traveller, eats their bread and not his own?

In the earliest society the proprietors made their own wealth, and so long as it comes to the owners in the direct way, no other opinion
(40) would arise in any equitable community than that property should make the law for property, and persons the law for persons.

But property passes through donation or inheritance to those who do not create it. Gift,
(45) in one case, makes it as really the new owner's, as labor made it the first owner's: in the other case, of patrimony, the law makes an ownership which will be valid in each man's view according to the estimate which he sets on the
(50) public tranquillity.

It was not however found easy to embody the readily admitted principle that property should make law for property, and persons for persons; since persons and property mixed
(55) themselves in every transaction. At last it seemed settled that the rightful distinction was that the proprietors should have more elective franchise than non-proprietors, on the Spartan principle of "calling that which is just, equal;
(60) not that which is equal, just."

That principle no longer looks so self-evident as it appeared in former times, partly, because doubts have arisen whether too much weight had not been allowed in the laws to
(65) property, and such a structure given to our usages as allowed the rich to encroach on the poor, and to keep them poor; but mainly

(70) because there is an instinctive sense, however obscure and yet inarticulate, that the whole constitution of property, on its present tenures, is injurious, and its influence on persons deteriorating and degrading; that truly the only interest for the consideration of the State is persons; that property will always follow

(75) persons; that the highest end of government is the culture of men; and if men can be educated, the institutions will share their improvement and the moral sentiment will write the law of the land.

(80) If it be not easy to settle the equity of this question, the peril is less when we take note of our natural defences. We are kept by better guards than the vigilance of such magistrates as we commonly elect. Society always consists

(85) in greatest part of young and foolish persons. The old, who have seen through the hypocrisy of courts and statesmen, die and leave no wisdom to their sons. They believe their own newspaper, as their fathers did at their age.

(90) With such an ignorant and deceivable majority, States would soon run to ruin, but that there are limitations beyond which the folly and ambition of governors cannot go. Things have their laws, as well as men; and things

(95) refuse to be trifled with. Property will be protected. Corn will not grow unless it is planted and manured; but the farmer will not plant or hoe it unless the chances are a hundred to one that he will cut and harvest it. Under any

(100) forms, persons and property must and will have their just sway. They exert their power, as steadily as matter its attraction. Cover up a pound of earth never so cunningly, divide and subdivide it; melt it to liquid, convert it to gas;

(105) it will always weigh a pound; it will always attract and resist other matter by the full virtue of one pound weight:—and the attributes of a person, his wit and his moral energy, will exercise, under any law or extinguishing tyr-

(110) anny, their proper force,—if not overtly, then covertly; if not for the law, then against it; if not wholesomely, then poisonously; with right, or by might.

11. According to the author, what is "the Spartan principle" (lines 58–60)?

   A. A decision becomes just by being unequal.

   B. A decision that is just is automatically equal.

   C. Any decision that accepts the superiority of wealth is just.

   D. An elected person is automatically a just person.

12. According to the passage, what should be the primary interest of the state?

   F. guarding the borders of a nation

   G. defending property ownership

   H. protecting the rights of its citizens

   J. securing political power based on ownership of land

13. The word "sway" (line 101) most nearly means:

   A. move from side to side.

   B. indecisiveness.

   C. wavering.

   D. influence.

14. The author believes that the "deceivable majority" (lines 90–91) is:

   F. those who are young and naïve.

   G. the old and foolish people.

   H. those who believe that democracy is inevitable.

   J. the hypocritical politicians.

15. The passage contains all of the following EXCEPT:

   A. a biblical allusion.

   B. a farming analogy.

   C. a rhetorical question.

   D. a startling statistic.

16. The main argument of the passage is that:

   F.   a truly democratic government is impossible because of the acquisitive nature of human beings.

   G.   for the good of the economic health of the nation, property must receive primary consideration from a responsible government.

   H.   if a democratic government fulfills its responsibility to protect and educate its citizens, economic prosperity will naturally follow.

   J.   those who gain wealth by acquiring property are morally indebted to those who have less.

17. The "accident" (line 13) to which the author refers is the:

   A.   naturally occurring inequality in wealth.
   B.   protection of the government.
   C.   clash between the interests of the state and the rights of individuals.
   D.   failure of a system of government to provide protections to its citizens.

18. According to the passage, one may gain wealth through all of the following EXCEPT:

   F.   a gift.
   G.   an inheritance.
   H.   skill.
   J.   vigilance.

19. The purpose of the example of the corn (lines 96–99) is to:

   A.   elucidate an economic principle.
   B.   clarify an agricultural disagreement.
   C.   present a humorous example.
   D.   compare inherited wealth to acquired wealth.

20. It can be inferred from the example of Laban and Jacob (lines 21–29) that the author believes:

   F.   workers are entitled to share in the profits of a business enterprise.

   G.   the owners of a business must incur the expense of protecting it.

   H.   employees must expect their employer to charge them for the costs of their food and safety.

   J.   a worker has the right to bear arms to defend the products of his labor.

Passage III

HUMANITIES: The following is the Preface to *The House of the Seven Gables* written by Nathaniel Hawthorne in 1851.

When a writer calls his work a Romance, it need hardly be observed that he wishes to claim a certain latitude, both as to its fashion and material, which he would not have felt
(5) himself entitled to assume had he professed to be writing a Novel. The latter form of composition is presumed to aim at a very minute fidelity, not merely to the possible, but to the probable and ordinary course of man's experi-
(10) ence. The former—while, as a work of art, it must rigidly subject itself to laws, and while it sins unpardonably so far as it may swerve aside from the truth of the human heart—has fairly a right to present that truth under cir-
(15) cumstances, to a great extent, of the writer's own choosing or creation. If he think fit, also, he may so manage his atmospherical medium as to bring out or mellow the lights and deepen and enrich the shadows of the picture. He will
(20) be wise, no doubt, to make a very moderate use of the privileges here stated, and, especially, to mingle the Marvelous rather as a slight, delicate, and evanescent flavor, than as any portion of the actual substance of the dish
(25) offered to the public. He can hardly be said, however, to commit a literary crime even if he disregard this caution.

In the present work, the author has proposed to himself—but with what success, fortunately, it is not for him to judge—to keep undeviatingly within his immunities. The point of view in which this tale comes under the Romantic definition lies in the attempt to connect a bygone time with the very present that is flitting away from us. It is a legend prolonging itself, from an epoch now gray in the distance, down into our own broad daylight, and bringing along with it some of its legendary mist, which the reader, according to his pleasure, may either disregard, or allow it to float almost imperceptibly about the characters and events for the sake of a picturesque effect. The narrative, it may be, is woven of so humble a texture as to require this advantage, and, at the same time, to render it the more difficult of attainment.

Many writers lay very great stress upon some definite moral purpose, at which they profess to aim their works. Not to be deficient in this particular, the author has provided himself with a moral,—the truth, namely, that the wrong-doing of one generation lives into the successive ones, and, divesting itself of every temporary advantage, becomes a pure and uncontrollable mischief; and he would feel it a singular gratification if this romance might effectually convince mankind—or, indeed, any one man—of the folly of tumbling down an avalanche of ill-gotten gold, or real estate, on the heads of an unfortunate posterity, thereby to maim and crush them, until the accumulated mass shall be scattered abroad in its original atoms. In good faith, however, he is not sufficiently imaginative to flatter himself with the slightest hope of this kind. When romances do really teach anything, or produce any effective operation, it is usually through a far more subtle process than the ostensible one. The author has considered it hardly worth his while, therefore, relentlessly to impale the story with its moral as with an iron rod,—or,

rather, as by sticking a pin through a butterfly,—thus at once depriving it of life, and causing it to stiffen in an ungainly and unnatural attitude. A high truth, indeed, fairly, finely, and skillfully wrought out, brightening at every step, and crowning the final development of a work of fiction, may add an artistic glory, but is never any truer, and seldom any more evident, at the last page than at the first.

The reader may perhaps choose to assign an actual locality to the imaginary events of this narrative. If permitted by the historical connection,—which, though slight, was essential to his plan,—the author would very willingly have avoided anything of this nature. Not to speak of other objections, it exposes the romance to an inflexible and exceedingly dangerous species of criticism, by bringing his fancy-pictures almost into positive contact with the realities of the moment. It has been no part of his object, however, to describe local manners, nor in any way to meddle with the characteristics of a community for whom he cherishes a proper respect and a natural regard. He trusts not to be considered as unpardonably offending by laying out a street that infringes upon nobody's private rights, and appropriating a lot of land which had no visible owner, and building a house of materials long in use for constructing castles in the air. The personages of the tale—though they give themselves out to be of ancient stability and considerable prominence—are really of the author's own making, or at all events, of his own mixing; their virtues can shed no luster, nor their defects redound, in the remotest degree, to the discredit of the venerable town of which they profess to be inhabitants. He would be glad, therefore, if—especially in the quarter to which he alludes—the book may be read strictly as a Romance, having a great deal more to do with the clouds overhead than with any portion of the actual soil of the County of Essex.

21. The purpose of the first paragraph of the passage is to:

    A. distinguish between two literary genres.
    B. contrast the purpose of Romantic literature with that of nonfiction.
    C. explain why the author has chosen a particular setting for his work.
    D. argue that an author should not commit the literary sin of embellishment.

22. It may be inferred that the author believes that:

    F. non-fiction is the genre best suited to teaching morals.
    G. romantic literature should tell a love story with a happy ending.
    H. an author has an obligation to be as realistic as possible, even in a work of fiction.
    J. a work of fiction should have a moral purpose.

23. The author uses the contrast between "gray in the distance" (line 36) and "our own broad daylight" (line 37) to:

    A. suggest that it is far better to place characters in recognizable times and places than to build imaginary kingdoms.
    B. connect bygone times with contemporary settings.
    C. stress the importance of color and clarity in storytelling.
    D. contrast the romantic nature of historical fiction with fanciful descriptions of New England towns.

24. The author would most likely define a Romance as:

    F. a relationship in which the most tender affections are engaged.
    G. a tale of legendary heroes who have powers beyond those of mortal men and women.
    H. a literary form in which a writer may take liberties with style and content.
    J. a historical chronology with accurate details.

25. The phrase "minute fidelity" (lines 7–8) most likely means:

    A. minor particulars.
    B. close faithfulness.
    C. trivial occurrences.
    D. ordinary events.

26. In lines 63–65 ("In good faith . . . of this kind") the author reveals himself to be:

    F. boastful.
    G. secure.
    H. imaginative.
    J. modest.

27. It can be inferred that the author feels that a reader who wishes "to assign an actual locality to the imaginary events" (lines 81–82) is:

    A. making a regrettable mistake.
    B. coming to a wise decision.
    C. committing an unpardonable sin.
    D. doing a favor to the author.

28. According to the author, "to impale the story with its moral" (lines 70–71) is similar to "sticking a pin through a butterfly" (lines 72–73) in that both:

F. are acts of cruelty and violence.

G. create a disharmony between the perpetrator and the witness.

H. cause an unnatural stiffness and awkwardness.

J. add artistic glory to a literary work.

29. It can be inferred that the moral of *The House of the Seven Gables* concerns:

A. the error of thinking one is above moral laws.

B. the inflexibility of those who judge others by harsh standards.

C. the passing of wrong-doing from one generation to those that follow.

D. the nature of good versus evil.

30. The author uses all of the following as contrasts in the passage EXCEPT:

F. clouds overhead versus actual soil.

G. evanescent flavor versus actual substance.

H. a subtle process versus an ostensible one.

J. mellow lights versus enriched shadows.

Passage IV

NATURAL SCIENCE: Passage A, an article written by a space enthusiast in 2013, is a discussion of the ongoing investigation into the presence of water on the planet Mars. Passage B is adapted from "NASA's Curiosity Rover Team Confirms Ancient Lakes on Mars," an article posted on the NASA website on October 8, 2015.

Passage A

The mystery of how Mars changed from a warm, wet world to a cold, dry, rocky, bleak planet has intrigued scientists for decades. The apparent lack of water on Mars poses a per-
(5) plexing dilemma—how to explain all the geological features that seem to indicate flowing water. While most scientists embrace the idea that water once flowed across the Martian surface, how long it flowed, the amounts that
(10) flowed, and the climatic conditions under which it flowed are still debated. For now, images of channels, meanders, and eroded landforms on Mars strongly tantalize as ghosts of flowing water.

(15) With information retrieved from the Mars rover Opportunity—still going strong after almost a decade of cruising the Martian landscape—researchers hope to add to their growing store of evidence. With the additional
(20) inflow of information from the newest Mars rover, Curiosity, which landed in August 2012, researchers have accumulated support for the theory that water, essential for the formation of life as we know it, once streamed on the red
(25) planet.

To try to account for this water, the scientific community is debating theories of climate change on Mars that present two very different views of the planet and of life and water
(30) on Mars: If Mars has always had the climate we find today, huge quantities of water must have been released over a short period of time to create the water-related landforms found on the surface, many of which require significant
(35) amounts of water to form. These great quantities of water would have to have shaped the surface quickly, before evaporating or boiling away. Also, life would not have had a chance to evolve in such short-lived bodies of water.
(40) Alternately, if Mars once had a warmer, wetter climate, water could have existed over a long period of time, altered the surface gradually, and allowed for the possible formation of life. These different water scenarios give rise to
(45) different views of the planet's evolution. Regardless of whether water existed for long or short periods of time, it probably escaped into space and/or sank into the ground to become permafrost.

(50) The necessity of water to the evolution of life-forms is the trigger that keeps researchers seeking confirmation of its presence on Mars.

319

The first clues that water once flowed on Mars appeared in the photographs sent back to (55) Earth in 1971 by the orbiting Mariner 9 spacecraft. Images of riverbeds and canyons led scientists to the tentative hypothesis that running water had formed these topographical features. What appeared to be ice caps on the (60) north and south poles of the planet also pointed to the presence of water. It is also possible that the red dust that covers the surface of the planet may conceal a layer of ice.

Studying water on Mars gives scientists (65) insight into how planets evolve, how water accumulates, how climates develop, and, possibly, how life begins. For these reasons, understanding the story of water is central to most of NASA's planetary missions.

Passage B

(70) A new study from the team behind NASA's Mars Science Laboratory/Curiosity has confirmed that Mars was once, billions of years ago, capable of storing water in lakes over an extended period of time.

(75) Using data from the Curiosity rover, the team has determined that, long ago, water helped deposit sediment into Gale Crater, where the rover landed more than three years ago. "Observations from the rover suggest that (80) a series of long-lived streams and lakes existed at some point between about 3.8 to 3.3 billion years ago, delivering sediment that slowly built up the lower layers of Mount Sharp," said Ashwin Vasavada, Mars Science Laboratory (85) project scientist at NASA's Jet Propulsion Laboratory in Pasadena, California, and co-author of the new Science article to be published Friday, Oct. 9, 2015. The findings build upon previous work that suggested there were (90) ancient lakes on Mars, and add to the unfolding story of a wet Mars, both past and present. Last month, NASA scientists confirmed current water flows on Mars.

"What we thought we knew about water on (95) Mars is constantly being put to the test," said Michael Meyer, lead scientist for NASA's Mars Exploration Program at NASA Headquarters in Washington. "It's clear that the Mars of billions of years ago more closely (100) resembled Earth than it does today. Our challenge is to figure out how this more clement Mars was even possible, and what happened to that wetter Mars."

"During the traverse of Gale, we have (105) noticed patterns in the geology where we saw evidence of ancient fast-moving streams with coarser gravel, as well as places where streams appear to have emptied out into bodies of standing water," Vasavada said. "The prediction (110) was that we should start seeing water-deposited, fine-grained rocks closer to Mount Sharp. Now that we've arrived, we're seeing finely laminated mudstones in abundance that look like lake deposits."

(115) The mudstone indicates the presence of bodies of standing water in the form of lakes that remained for long periods of time, possibly repeatedly expanding and contracting during hundreds to millions of years. These lakes (120) deposited the sediment that eventually formed the lower portion of the mountain. "Paradoxically, where there is a mountain today there was once a basin, and it was sometimes filled with water," said John Grotzinger, (125) the former project scientist for Mars Science Laboratory at the California Institute of Technology in Pasadena, and lead author of the new report. "We see evidence of about 250 feet (75 meters) of sedimentary fill, and based (130) on mapping data from NASA's Mars Reconnaissance Orbiter and images from Curiosity's camera, it appears that the water-transported sedimentary deposition could have extended at least 500 to 650 feet (150 to (135) 200 meters) above the crater floor."

Questions 31–34 ask about Passage A.

31. Which of the following statements best represents the findings about the presence of water on Mars at the time Passage A was written?

   A. Scientists have found irrefutable evidence that water is currently present on Mars.

   B. Scientists doubt they will ever find evidence that water flowed on Mars.

   C. The ice caps indicate that any water found on Mars today is frozen.

   D. Geologic evidence indicates that some form of water was once present on Mars.

32. The first clues that Mars had water resources came from:

   F. the chemistry lab aboard the Mars rover Opportunity.

   G. images taken by video cameras aboard Curiosity.

   H. photographs sent by Mariner 9 spacecraft.

   J. astronauts who landed on the surface of Mars.

33. The primary purpose of the second paragraph (lines 15–25) is to:

   A. present the most current information on the search for water on Mars.

   B. challenge the original hypothesis about the waterless surface of Mars.

   C. provide historical context to the NASA rover program.

   D. specify the source of the debate over the presence of water on Mars.

34. According to the passage, investigations into the possibility of the presence of water on Mars will yield insight into all of the following EXCEPT:

   F. how climates develop.

   G. how life begins.

   H. how planets evolve.

   J. how volcanoes are formed.

Questions 35–37 ask about Passage B.

35. Which of the following statements can be inferred from the remarks of Michael Meyer?

   A. The climate on Mars was once harsher and drier than it is now.

   B. The climate on Mars was once less harsh and less dry than it is now.

   C. The climate on Mars was once harsher and damper than it is now.

   D. The climate on Mars was once milder and drier than it is now.

36. Which of the following best describes the organizational pattern of the fourth paragraph (lines 104–114)?

   F. Observation, prediction, confirmation

   G. Prediction, observation, hypothesis

   H. Hypothesis, confirmation, observation

   J. Observation, experiment, confirmation

37. The "findings" referred to in the second paragraph, line 88, refer to:

   A. the sediment that drifted down from the top of Mount Sharp 2 billion years ago.

   B. the data sent to Earth by the Curiosity rover that prove there is presently water in the Gale Crater.

   C. the absence of mudstone on the lower layers of Mount Sharp.

   D. evidence that 3.3 to 3.8 billion years ago the surface of Mars was marked by lakes and streams.

Questions 38–40 ask about both passages.

38. Both Passage A and Passage B explicitly underscore which of the following ideas?

    F. The possibility that life once existed and may still exist in some form on Mars is real.

    G. The data received from the Curiosity rover far exceeded the NASA scientists' expectations.

    H. The key to unlocking the mystery of water on Mars lies in the topography of the landforms on the planet.

    J. Through an ever-widening range of exploration, the rover Curiosity will eventually discover bodies of water on Mars.

39. The author of Passage A chooses such words and phrases as "apparent" (line 4), "seem" (line 6), "For now" (line 11), and "probably" (line 47). The author of Passage B uses such words and phrases as "confirmed" (lines 71–72 and 92) and "It's clear" (line 98). Which of the following is the most likely explanation for this difference in word choice?

    A. The author of Passage A has more credible scientific qualifications than the author of Passage B.

    B. The number of photographs sent by the rover Curiosity has declined in the past 3 years.

    C. Data accumulated in the 2 years that elapsed between the publications of the articles yielded important confirmatory evidence.

    D. The author of Passage A relies on data from Mariner 9 while the author of Passage B relies on data from Curiosity.

40. Unlike the author of Passage A, the author of Passage B supports his assertions with which of the following?

    F. Geological evidence

    G. Photographs from Curiosity and Mariner 9

    H. References to Martian climate change

    J. Quotes from experts

IF YOU FINISH BEFORE TIME IS CALLED, CHECK YOUR WORK ON THIS SECTION ONLY. DO NOT WORK ON ANY OTHER SECTION IN THE TEST.

Section 4: Science Test

35 Minutes—40 Questions

Directions: The Science Test consists of seven passages; each passage is followed by several questions. After reading each passage, select the best answer to each question and fill in the corresponding circle on the answer sheet. Refer to the information in the passages as often as necessary to respond to the questions. Use of a calculator is NOT permitted on this test.

Passage I

The most common type of light bulb still employed worldwide today is the incandescent bulb popularized by Thomas Edison in the late 1800s. In recent years, new types of light bulbs have been introduced to consumers, including the halogen and compact fluorescent light (CFL). Although each type of bulb employs electricity as the initial energy source, each bulb utilizes a different mechanism of energy transfer to emit light. Incandescent bulbs use heat to produce light from a filament; halogen bulbs improve on this mechanism by sealing the filament in an envelope filled with inert gas. CFLs involve the emission of UV light from a gas contained within a tube; this UV light in turn excites a phosphor coating such that it emits visible light.

Various light bulb types were tested for the character and quality of light produced. The data are shown in Table 1. (*Note:* W = watts, a unit of power; lm = lumens, a measure of output from a light source.)

Table 1				
Bulb type	**Power (W)**	**Light output (lm)**	**Light efficiency (lm/W)**	**Operating temperature (°K)**
Incandescent	40	500	12.5	2800
	60	850	14.2	3100
	100	1700	17.0	3300
Halogen	60	1150	19.2	3200
	100	2400	24.0	3500
CFL	20	1200	60.0	2700

The industry-standard equivalencies between the color temperature of the bulb (used to indicate light quality to the consumer) and the actual maximum operating temperature of the bulb are shown in Table 2.

Table 2	
Color temperature	**Maximum temperature (°K)**
Soft white	3000
Bright white	3500
Cool white	4000
Daylight	5000

Many consumers are concerned not only with the quality of the light their bulbs can provide, but also with the electricity used to power such bulbs and any pollution associated with the production of the bulbs. Relevant information regarding the energy use and costs for various bulb types is summarized in Table 3. (*Note:* kWh = kilowatt hour, the typical unit of measurement used by electric companies.) The levels of mercury, a known environmental toxin and health hazard, associated with incandescent and CFL bulbs are shown in Figure 1. No mercury is associated with halogen bulbs.

Table 3	
Consumer concern	**Formula**
Electricity used (kWh)	$\dfrac{\text{Power (W)} \times \text{time used (hours)}}{1000 \text{ (W/kW)}}$
Greenhouse gas emissions (pounds of pollution)	Electricity used (kWh) × (1.58 pounds/kWh)

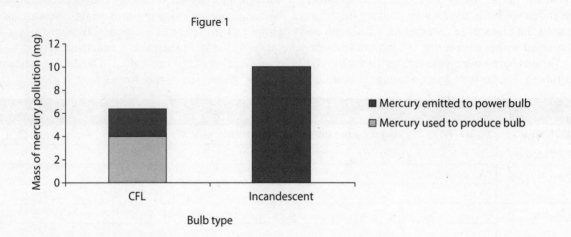

Figure 1

1. If an incandescent bulb with a power of 80 W were tested, which of the following is a likely value for its light efficiency?

    A.   10.5 lm/W

    B.   15.8 lm/W

    C.   18.2 lm/W

    D.   22.1 lm/W

2. Which of the following graphs correctly summarizes the relationship between power of bulb and light output for all light bulb types according to the data in Table 1?

F.

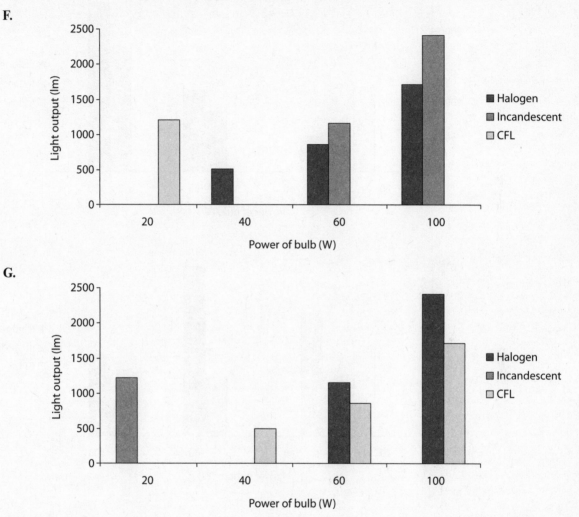

G.

H.

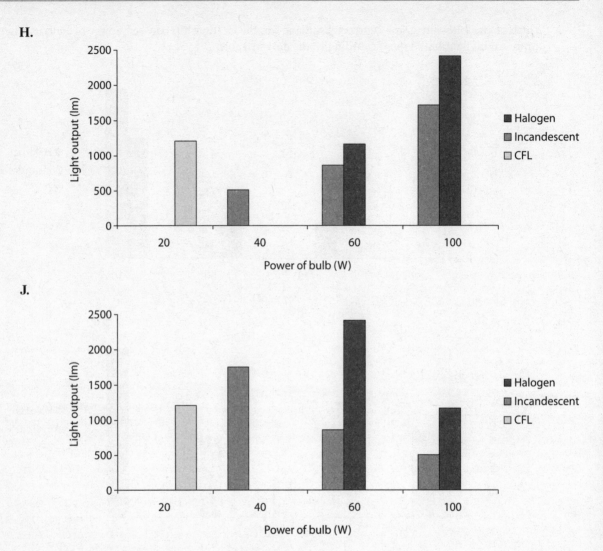

J.

3. If a 100 W halogen bulb were being marketed to consumers, what color temperature is likely to be claimed on the packaging?

    A.   soft white

    B.   bright white

    C.   cool white

    D.   daylight

4. Which of the following statements is supported by the data in Table 1 regarding bulb type, power, and light efficiency?

    F.   A higher-powered bulb is always more efficient in producing light, regardless of bulb type.

    G.   Within incandescent bulbs, the lower the power, the higher the efficiency.

    H.   Bulb type is more significant than power in predicting light efficiency.

    J.   High-powered halogen bulbs have the best efficiency overall.

5. In order to estimate the electricity used to power a CFL bulb for 24 hours, which mathematical model should be used?

A. $\dfrac{60 \text{ W} \times 24 \text{ h}}{1000 \text{ W/kW}}$

B. $\dfrac{20 \text{ W} \times 24 \text{ h}}{100 \text{ W/kW}}$

C. $\dfrac{60 \text{ W} \times 12 \text{ h}}{1000 \text{ W/kW}}$

D. $\dfrac{20 \text{ W} \times 24 \text{ h}}{1000 \text{ W/kW}}$

6. If consumers are interested in reducing the amount of greenhouse gases and potential mercury contamination, which of the following bulbs is most appropriate?

F. 40 W incandescent
G. 60 W incandescent
H. 100 W incandescent
J. 20 W CFL

Passage II

Bacteria represent most of the organisms on Earth that are limited to asexual modes of reproduction. Since they are unable to introduce genetic diversity into their offspring during reproduction as do sexually reproducing organisms, and since genetic diversity enhances not only offspring but also species survival, bacteria have evolved different, non-reproductive mechanisms for achieving the same goals. One of these is called transformation and involves a bacterium picking up and expressing short segments of DNA from its surroundings.

Bacteria can be encouraged to transform in a laboratory setting for biotechnological research purposes. For example, the *E. coli* bacterium can transform such that it takes up and expresses the human insulin gene for diabetic therapy. Before bacteria can be called successful transformants in the lab, they are encouraged to take up foreign DNA through one of two means: electroporation or chemical transformation.

Experiment 1

During electroporation, short bursts of a high-voltage current are passed through a solution containing bacteria. The bacterial cell membranes become leaky in response, and the cells become more likely to pick up free DNA molecules present in the solution and become transformants.

A research group uses the electroporation method to transform *E. coli* bacteria in different environments (Petri dishes, or *plates*). The gene they insert provides the trait of ampicillin-resistance; transformed bacteria will not be affected by the presence of the ampicillin antibiotic. The presence of ampicillin (or other antibiotics, like penicillin) is fatal in bacteria that lack the specific antibiotic-resistance gene. The total numbers of bacterial colonies present in each Petri dish after a 24-hour incubation period are displayed in Table 1. (*Note:* NM = the standard nutrient medium required for growing bacteria; lawn = many indistinguishable colonies; amp = ampicillin; pen = penicillin.)

Table 1		
	Untreated *E. coli*	Transformed *E. coli*
NM	Lawn	Lawn
NM/amp	0	13
NM/pen	0	0

Experiment 2

During chemical transformation, bacteria are exposed to solutions that chemically and/or thermally alter their cell membranes enough to make the DNA molecules pass through the membrane and into the cell. The research group follows the same procedure as described in Experiment 1 except that chemical transformation by means of heat-shock at 42 °C is employed instead to encourage the uptake of the ampicillin-resistance gene. The data are shown in Table 2.

Table 2		
	Untreated *E. coli*	Transformed *E. coli*
NM	Lawn	Lawn
NM/amp	0	18
NM/pen	1	0

To compare the results from Experiments 1 and 2, the research group calculates the transformation efficiency. Transformation efficiency is a measure of the number of cells within the colonies of a bacterial culture that take up the DNA of interest; it is described by the number of transformants per given mass of plated DNA and is calculated according to the following formula:

$$\text{Transformation efficiency} = \frac{\text{Number of transformed cells}}{\text{Quantity of DNA plated (μg)}}$$

7. From the data presented in Table 1, *E. coli* colonies grew in what type of environments?

   A. NM only
   B. NM/amp only
   C. NM/pen only
   D. NM/amp or NM

8. Which of the statements below is supported by the data in Tables 1 and 2?

   F. There is clear evidence that the bacteria in the plates containing penicillin were transformed, while those in the ampicillin-containing plates were not.
   G. The untreated *E. coli* produced more colonies in both experiments than did the transformed *E. coli*.
   H. Both mechanisms of transformation were effective in growing colonies, but chemical transformation produced more total colonies than electroporation.
   J. The presence of a bacterial lawn in the NM plates indicates inefficient transformation.

9. What is the purpose of the NM plate in Experiments 1 and 2?

    A. It shows the set of conditions that prevent bacterial growth.
    B. It acts as a control group to demonstrate the plate conditions in which both untreated and transformed bacteria will grow.
    C. It demonstrates the conditions necessary for growing the antibiotics used in the experiments.
    D. It acts as an experimental group and can be used to calculate the transformation efficiency of the experiment.

10. Which of the following statements might provide an explanation for the one colony observed in the NM/pen plate in Table 2?

    F. A researcher must have transformed a bacterium with the ampicillin-resistance gene by mistake.
    G. A bacterium must have had a natural resistance to the penicillin antibiotic, so that bacterium was unaffected by penicillin and produced a visible colony.
    H. A researcher must have transformed a bacterium with the penicillin-resistance gene by mistake.
    J. The penicillin used in the experiments must have been ineffective.

11. In Experiment 1, 0.01 µg of DNA was plated. What is the corresponding transformation efficiency?

    A. 1300 transformants/µg DNA
    B. 2600 transformants/µg DNA
    C. 13,000 transformants/µg DNA
    D. 15,000 transformants/µg DNA

12. If twice as much DNA were plated in the transformation conducted in Experiment 2 than in Experiment 1, which of the following statements would be supported?

    F. The chemical method of transformation demonstrated higher transformation efficiency than that using electroporation.
    G. The transformation efficiency is not dependent upon the quantity of DNA plated, so there would be no difference in transformation efficiency between the two methods.
    H. The chemical method of transformation is concluded to be the most effective method under any conditions.
    J. The electroporation method of transformation demonstrated higher transformation efficiency than that using chemical transformation.

Passage III

Burning of hydrocarbon fuels occurs in the typical internal combustion engine according to the following generalized, unbalanced reaction:

$$C_xH_y + O_2 \rightarrow CO_2 + H_2O + heat$$

Complete combustion data (including the relative number of CO_2 molecules produced per fuel molecule and the heat of combustion of the fuel in kJ/mol) for specific hydrocarbon fuels were collected using a bomb calorimeter and are shown in Table 1.

Table 1			
Hydrocarbon fuel	Chemical formula	CO_2 molecules produced	Heat (kJ/mol)
Methane	CH_4	1	890
Ethane	C_2H_6	2	1555
Propane	C_3H_8	3	2208
Butane	C_4H_{10}	4	2861
Octane	C_8H_{18}	8	5472

More recently, alternative fuel sources have become more readily available and are often considered to be more environmentally friendly and/or easier to transport and store than some of the more traditional hydrocarbon fuels. Some data on the combustion of two alternative fuels are shown in Table 2.

Table 2			
Alternative fuel	Chemical formula	CO_2 molecules produced	Heat (kJ/mol)
Methanol	CH_3OH	1	726
Ethanol	CH_3CH_2OH	2	1300

13. According to the data presented in Table 1:

   A. propane produces more heat per molecule than does butane.
   B. methane produces more heat per molecule than does ethane.
   C. butane produces more heat per molecule than does octane.
   D. butane produces more heat per molecule than does propane.

14. If hexane, C_6H_{14}, were analyzed and the data placed in Table 1, which of the following heat values is a logical measurement?

   F. 1580 kJ/mol
   G. 2600 kJ/mol
   H. 4160 kJ/mol
   J. 5750 kJ/mol

15. A hydrocarbon can be converted into an alcohol by replacing a hydrogen atom with an alcohol (–OH) functional group. Which of the following statements is then consistent with the information presented in Tables 1 and 2?

   A. A hydrocarbon fuel has a higher heat of combustion than an alcohol molecule with the same number of carbon atoms.
   B. An alcohol molecule releases relatively more CO_2 molecules than a hydrocarbon fuel with the same number of carbon atoms.
   C. A hydrocarbon fuel has a lower heat of combustion than an alcohol molecule with the same number of carbons.
   D. An alcohol molecule releases relatively fewer CO_2 molecules than a hydrocarbon fuel with the same number of carbon atoms.

16. The production of CO_2 has been linked to global warming because CO_2 acts as a greenhouse gas, trapping radiation in Earth's atmosphere. If a goal then is to limit CO_2 production while reaching a minimum heat of combustion of 3000 kJ/mol, which of the following is the worst option for a fuel choice according to the data in Tables 1 and 2?

F. using 3 molecules of ethanol
G. using 4 molecules of methane
H. using 2 molecules of ethane
J. using 1 molecule of octane

17. Instead of pure oxygen, engines are primarily supplied air, a mixture of approximately 78% nitrogen gas (N_2), 21% oxygen gas (O_2), and 1% other trace gases. The air-fuel ratio (AFR) describes the proportion of air to fuel that is necessary for the complete combustion of the fuel with no production of excess exhaust gases. Calculating the AFR is important when analyzing engine efficiency and performance. If an AFR is too low, then complete combustion of the gas cannot occur and undesirable CO (carbon monoxide) will be present after combustion. Alternatively, an AFR that is too high results in a lower heat transfer from the combustion products than desired. A graph demonstrating the relationship between the AFR and CO production is shown in the following figure:

Which of the following options is the optimal AFR for a gasoline fuel?

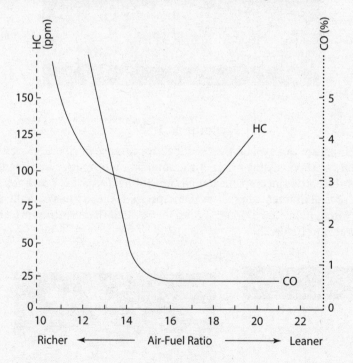

A. 14
B. 16
C. 19
D. 20

Passage IV

The theory of evolution is central to understanding the history of life on Earth and the planet's current levels of biodiversity. Still being debated, however, is the rate at which evolution occurs. Researchers and professors of evolutionary biology regularly examine the fossil record, which provides strong structural evidence for evolution. This evidence is contained in the remains of organisms that had been preserved over geologic time in layers of sedimentary rock called strata. The distribution of fossils within the strata provides a relative date for the fossils, while radioactive dating can provide an absolute date of the fossils' age.

Several students of evolutionary biology were presented with the scenario illustrated in Figure 1 and asked to explain how Species 2 and 3 present in stratum 2 evolved given the ancestral species present in stratum 1. Everyone agreed that stratum 1, the lowest layer containing any fossils, provides evidence that Species 1 was in abundance in that time period and showed diversity in size. The students were divided into two groups and asked to use the data in Figure 1 to defend one of two hypotheses regarding the rate at which evolution occurs.

Figure 1

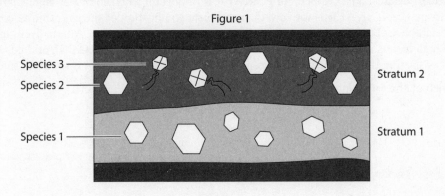

Hypothesis 1

The concept of phyletic gradualism can explain the "sudden" appearance of Species 3 in stratum 2. Most large-scale evolutionary changes are actually the result of the summation of many small changes over geologic time. Because the fossil record is incomplete, not all transitional forms are preserved in any stratum. Although Species 3 possesses several different characters than Species 1, those traits actually accumulated slowly over millions of years within many transitional species that existed that were not preserved in the fossil record. This is demonstrated in Figure 2:

Figure 2

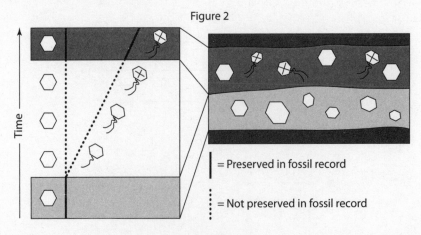

| = Preserved in fossil record

┊ = Not preserved in fossil record

Hypothesis 2

The concept of punctuated equilibrium can explain the sudden appearance of Species 3 in stratum 2. The most important factor affecting the rate of evolution is the rate of environmental change. Most of the time the environment is not changing, but periodically there are large-scale, drastic changes in the environment that influence evolution to act quickly. Adaptation by a population happens relatively quickly, and then the population reaches equilibrium and stasis resumes. This explains how Species 3 very quickly accumulated new traits from Species 1 while Species 2 continued to exist in much the same form as did Species 1. This is demonstrated in Figure 3:

Figure 3

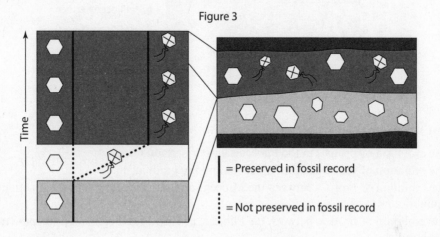

= Preserved in fossil record

= Not preserved in fossil record

18. According to Hypothesis 1:

    F.   the gradual change in form that occurs is not always well-preserved in the fossil record.
    G.   the gradual change in form is not influenced by environmental change.
    H.   there is no evidence to support punctuated equilibrium.
    J.   the fossil record shows that the rate of evolution never changes.

19. The major difference between Hypotheses 1 and 2 concerns:

    A.   whether evolution occurs.
    B.   the rate at which evolution occurs.
    C.   if mutation contributes to evolution.
    D.   if natural selection leads to evolution.

20. The following figure demonstrates the evolution of foraminiferans (forams), a type of protist, as preserved in the fossil record over three epochs:

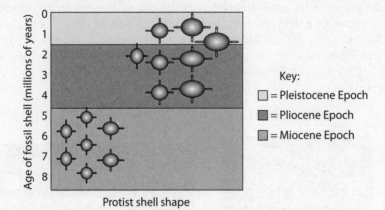

Which of the following conclusions is illogical?

F. The evolution of protists in the Pliocene supports gradualism.
G. The evolution of protists in the Miocene supports gradualism.
H. The evolution of protists between the Miocene and the Pliocene supports punctuated equilibrium.
J. The evolution of protists between the Pliocene and the Pleistocene supports punctuated equilibrium.

21. Which of the following is true regarding the two hypotheses presented?

A. Hypothesis 1 involves a short generation time between strata; Hypothesis 2 involves a longer time.
B. The entire fossil record provides more support for Hypothesis 1 than Hypothesis 2.
C. Both hypotheses involve the notion of transitional forms, although they differ in number of transitional forms that occur.
D. Both hypotheses attempt to explain gaps in the fossil record as periods of very little environmental change.

22. Data were collected regarding the evolution of trilobites, an early arthropod present in the Cambrian Period. An evolutionary lineage was established based on the number of "ribs" possessed by a trilobite species. The results are shown in the following figure:

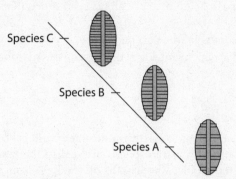

Which of the following is a logical conclusion?

F. Trilobite evolution provides strong evidence for the support of punctuated equilibrium because rapid change happened quickly.

G. Trilobite evolution provides strong evidence for the support of phyletic gradualism because the gaps in the fossil record of trilobites can be explained by missing transitional forms.

H. Trilobite evolution provides strong evidence for the support of phyetic equilibrium because change accumulated relatively slowly over time.

J. Trilobite evolution provides inconclusive evidence; neither hypothesis is strongly supported.

23. A third idea regarding evolutionary rates, called punctuated gradualism, has also been proposed. Punctuated gradualism suggests that a species remains in stasis (a period of virtually no change) until it experiences short bursts of change that may or may not result in speciation (the production of a new species from its ancestor). This third hypothesis is:

A. in conflict with both Hypotheses 1 and 2.

B. more closely aligned with Hypothesis 2 because of the inclusion of rapid change in a short amount of time.

C. in conflict with Hypothesis 2 because of the lack of an intermediate form.

D. more closely aligned with Hypothesis 1 because of the inclusion of rapid change that does not necessarily result in speciation.

24. Which of the following conclusions is most consistent with the entirety of the data presented in Passage IV?

    F. Evolution most typically occurs at a very slow and steady pace.

    G. The rate of evolution can be gradual or can occur in short, quick bursts depending on the specific situation present.

    H. Evolution is most predictable when examined over a very short time frame.

    J. The rate of evolution is dependent solely on the rate of environmental change experienced by the population over time.

Passage V

Ozone (O_3) is an important component of Earth's atmosphere with both positive and negative associations. Ozone is found at its highest levels in the stratosphere, also called the ozone layer. Here, the ozone serves a helpful function in filtering out the smaller wavelengths of UV light from the sun that would otherwise pose serious health threats to all forms of life on Earth. Ozone is typically generated in the stratosphere according to the following sequential reactions:

$$(1)\ O_2 \xrightarrow{\ \text{UV light}\ } 2O_2$$

$$(2)\ O + O_2 \longrightarrow O_3$$

Ozone found in the lower troposphere, also called low-level ozone, is considered a major pollutant by environmental advocates and is recognized as such by governmental agencies. Although not directly produced from automobiles, fossil fuel power plants, or oil refineries, ozone is produced when UV light acts on their nitrous oxide emissions. At this level of the atmosphere, different wavelengths of UV light are present that can break N_2O molecules down into NO (nitric oxide) and O (free oxygen). Once the O atoms are formed, reaction number 2 (above) proceeds to form ozone.

Typical ozone concentrations at increasing altitudes in Earth's atmosphere are shown in Figure 1.

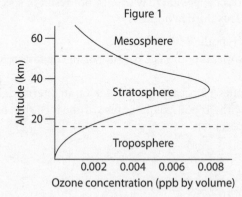

Figure 1

The low-level ozone levels in a major metropolitan city were collected over a decade. Average daily levels of ozone for each month in year 6 of the study are presented in Figure 2 (where month 1 = January, etc.), while a summary of the average daily levels of ozone (in parts per billion, or ppb) for each year in the study are listed in Table 1.

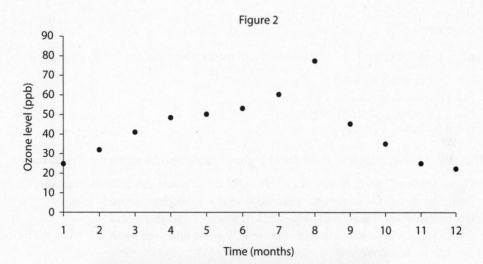

Figure 2

Table 1	
Year	Average ozone level (ppb)
1	34
2	35
3	38
4	39
5	33
6	43
7	39
8	39
9	41
10	42

25. Using the data presented in Figure 1, which statement correctly represents the relationship between altitude and ozone concentrations?

    A. As altitude increases, ozone concentration increases, peaks, then decreases.
    B. As altitude decreases, ozone concentration increases, peaks, then decreases.
    C. As altitude increases, ozone concentration decreases then increases.
    D. As altitude decreases, ozone concentration decreases then increases.

26. According to the data in Figure 2, a month in which this city experienced low-level ozone levels averaging approximately 50 ppb is:

    F. January
    G. May
    H. July
    J. November

27. According to the passage, both stratospheric and tropospheric ozones are directly produced from:

    A. UV light reacting with N_2O.
    B. free O atoms reacting with O_2 in the air.
    C. O_2 atoms combining with each other.
    D. UV light reacting with O_2.

28. Considering the information in Table 1 and Figure 2, which of the following conclusions is logical?

    F. Ozone levels will reach hazardous levels in the next decade unless drastic measures are taken.
    G. Ozone levels will fall in the next year; beyond that it becomes unpredictable.
    H. Ozone levels will remain relatively stable throughout the next decade.
    J. Ozone levels will continue to rise in the next 5 years, although levels will continue to fluctuate throughout any given year.

29. Guidelines for issuing smog alerts are summarized in the following table.

Category	Air quality index	Low-level ozone (ppb)
Green/safe	0–50	0–59
Yellow/moderate	51–100	60–75
Orange/potentially unhealthy	101–150	76–95
Red/unhealthy	151–200	96–115
Purple/very unhealthy	201–300	116–374
Maroon/hazardous	301–500	375 and above

Using this and the data in Figure 2, the corresponding air quality index for the city in August would be:

    A. green.
    B. yellow.
    C. orange.
    D. red.

Passage VI

Hooke's Law describes the behavior of springs when a force is applied that results in an extension, the difference between the initial length (X_0) and the stretched length (X) of the spring (see Figure 1). Hooke's Law states that the extension of the spring is directly proportional to the magnitude of the force applied. It also states that, due to the elastic nature of the spring, the spring will return to its original length once the force is removed.

Figure 1

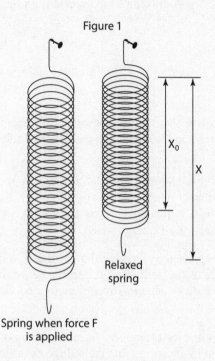

X_0

X

Relaxed
spring

Spring when force F
is applied

Both aspects of Hooke's Law apply up until the spring is stretched to its elastic limit; beyond this position the spring will have a permanent extension and will behave differently when new forces are applied. Students in a physics class measure the extension of three different springs as increasing force is applied. Their data are shown in Table 1. (*Note:* N = Newtons, a unit of force.)

Table 1			
	Extension (mm)		
Force applied (N)	Spring A	Spring B	Spring C
1	0.5	2.2	1.4
2	1	4.4	2.8
5	2.5	11	7
10	5	22	14
12	6	26.4	16.8

30. If Spring C is retested using a force of 8 N, what approximate extension is likely to be measured?

    F.   7 mm
    G.   11 mm
    H.   15 mm
    J.   18 mm

31. An unknown force is applied to Spring A and results in an extension of 0.25 mm. What magnitude of force was applied?

    A.   0.5 N
    B.   0.75 N
    C.   1.5 N
    D.   2.0 N

32. The spring constant (k) is a measure of the rigidity or strength of a spring. The higher the k value, the more resistant a spring is to an extension. According to the data in Table 1, which is true regarding the tested springs?

    F.   The spring constant for Spring B is greater than that for Spring A.
    G.   Spring A has the highest k value of all springs tested.
    H.   The spring constant for Spring C is greater than that for Spring A.
    J.   Spring B has the highest k value of all springs tested.

33. The restoring force (F_r) is the force exerted by a spring that returns it to its original conformation after a stretch. It is equal to the opposite of the product of the spring constant (k in Newtons per meter) and the resultant extension of the spring (x in mm) according to the following formula:

$$F_r = -kx$$

The negative product indicates that the restoring force from the spring is applied in the opposite direction as the initial force applied to the spring that caused the extension.

If a student is told that the spring constant of an unknown spring is 2.2 N/mm and that a force had been applied to the spring such that it was extended by 11 mm, then the restoring force exerted by the spring is:

    A.   −24.2 N
    B.   −1.1 N
    C.   −0.2 N
    D.   24.2 N

34. A curious student disassembles his retractable pen. He compresses the small spring against his desk a few times and reassembles the pen; the pen remains functional. He takes it apart again, but this time pulls on each end of the spring simultaneously before reinserting it. This time, the pen does not work properly. Which statement correctly explains what has happened?

F. The summation of the forces exerted by the student during the compression and the stretch is greater than the potential energy of the spring.

G. The spring exerted a force on the student that was stronger than the force exerted by the student on the spring.

H. The force exerted by the student when he stretched the spring extended it beyond its elastic limit, so it remains permanently extended.

J. The elastic limit of the spring exceeded the maximum force applied by the student, so the spring bent.

Passage VII

Environmental engineers worked with public health researchers to compare methods of freshwater filtration. Primary concerns were the removal of both *Cryptosporidium* and *Giardia*, two water-borne protozoans that can cause mild to severe gastrointestinal disease in humans.

Information about four municipal water treatment plants was gathered by the engineers. Main features of the treatment plants and the effectiveness of the removal of *Cryptosporidium* oocysts and *Giardia* cysts are reported in Table 1.

Table 1					
Plant	Primary treatment	Secondary treatment	Disinfection	% removal of *Cryptosporidium* oocysts	% removal of *Giardia* cysts
1	Screening, grit separation	Oxidation, sedimentation	None	92.7	93.5
2	Screening, grit separation, sedimentation	Activated sludge	Chlorination	87.0	85.1
3	Screening, grit separation, sedimentation	Activated sludge	Chlorination	96.6	97.0
4	Screening, grit separation, sedimentation	Activated sludge	Filtration	97.9	98.6

A variety of water purification means were then tested in the lab. The removal efficiency was calculated and the data recorded in Table 2. (*Note:* The units for removal efficiency are in $\log_{10}$ form; an efficiency of 1-log translates to 90%, 2-log to 99%, log-3 to 99.9%, etc.)

Table 2		
Purification process	*Cryptosporidium*	*Giardia*
Chlorine	0	0–2
Chlorine dioxide	0	0–2
UV light	0–4	0–4
Slow sand filtration	1.2–3.7	1.2–3.5
Membrane filtration	2–3	2–2.7

One final concern to be addressed by the research team was the relationship between the removal of turbidity (cloudiness) of the water and the removal of protozoans. Specifically, it was hypothesized that the clarity of the water is an indicator of the successful removal of protozoans. The removal efficiencies for turbidity and for *Cryptosporidium* are related in Figure 1.

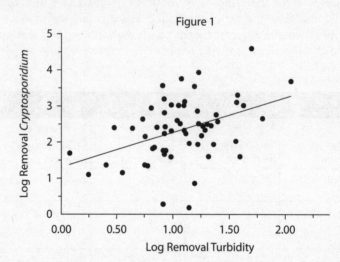

Figure 1

35. According to the data in Table 1, which treatment plant was most successful at removing *Giardia* cysts?

    A. Plant 1

    B. Plant 2

    C. Plant 3

    D. Plant 4

36. Which of the following statements regarding the type of treatment methods employed is supported by the data presented in Table 1?

   F. Plant 1 was more successful removing *Cryptosporidium* than *Giardia*.
   G. Plants 2, 3, and 4 all employed the same primary and secondary treatment methods yet varied in the ability to remove protozoan cysts and oocysts.
   H. Plants that did not use a disinfectant method were the least successful with removing *Giardia* cysts.
   J. Plants that used chlorination experienced the most success with removing protozoan cysts and oocysts.

37. According to the data in Table 2, the maximum removal efficiency of *Giardia* by UV light is:

   A. 90%
   B. 99%
   C. 99.9%
   D. 99.99%

38. The most reliable and effective purification method for both protozoan types according to the laboratory data is:

   F. UV light.
   G. chlorination.
   H. membrane filtration.
   J. slow sand filtration.

39. According to the data in Figure 1, which of the following is true?

   A. As the efficiency of the turbidity removal increases, the efficiency of the *Cryptosporidium* removal also increases.
   B. As the efficiency of the turbidity removal increases, the efficiency of the *Cryptosporidium* removal decreases.
   C. When low levels of turbidity are removed, high levels of *Cryptosporidium* are removed.
   D. When high levels of turbidity are removed, low levels of *Cryptosporidium* are removed.

40. According to the data in Tables 1 and 2, which of the following methods is LEAST effective overall in removing protozoans like *Cryptosporidium* and *Giardia* from water?

   F. Filtration
   G. Oxidation
   H. Chlorination
   J. UV light

IF YOU FINISH BEFORE TIME IS CALLED, CHECK YOUR WORK ON THIS SECTION ONLY. DO NOT WORK ON ANY OTHER SECTION IN THE TEST.

Section 5: Writing Test

40 Minutes

Social Media

Almost 75% of all American adults use some form of social media, whether it be just checking in on their Facebook page once a week or tweeting minute-by-minute updates on Twitter. Many of these sites post extensive biographical material, allow other users to access this information, and connect users with friends, acquaintances, and virtual strangers. Some say social media has brought people closer together, afforded access to intellectual and emotional support, and established a forum for circulating information (both factual and fictional). Others fear the sites are wasting time that could be far more productive, depersonalizing human interaction, putting young people in danger of predators, and propagating misleading and fabricated data.

Read the three perspectives below and consider the conflicting positions on the role of social media in today's society.

Perspective 1	Perspective 2	Perspective 3
Social media provides a pathway to increased social interaction. Families, friends, and business associates all point out that they have established stronger relationships by connecting on social media. Students, also, connect with their teachers regularly and use the sites to work cooperatively with their peers.	Social media is often the source of misinformation, rumors that range from merely silly (President Obama gave part of Arizona to Mexico) to downright dangerous (a prominent community member was spotted performing in a strip club). In addition, some young people are so distracted by social media that their grades suffer, and they are unable to interact with others face-to-face.	Social media both helps and hinders law enforcement. By posting the activities of accused criminals on social media, law enforcement officers have been able to track down offenders who (foolishly) post their misdeeds on social media. Conversely, information posted on social media can give predators access to private information and allow gangs and terrorist groups to recruit members.

Essay Task

Your task is to construct a well-written, well-organized essay in which you discuss the impact of social media on the American public. As you plan and write your essay, be sure to

- consider the effectiveness of the three perspectives given above
- develop your own perspective on the issue
- clarify ways in which your perspective is similar to or different from the three perspectives given above

You may choose to defend, challenge, or qualify any part of the three given perspectives. Whatever your position, be sure to back up your assertions with reason and detailed examples.

Planning Your Essay

The space below is for you to plan your essay. As you plan, think about the following ideas:

Strengths and weaknesses of each of the three given perspectives:

- What aspects do they address and what aspects do they disregard?
- Is the perspective persuasive? Why or why not? To whom might each appeal?

Experience or knowledge that will help you evaluate the issue:

- How strong is your position?
- What evidence (reasons, facts, examples) will you offer to support your position?

IF YOU FINISH BEFORE TIME IS CALLED, CHECK YOUR WORK ON THIS SECTION ONLY. DO NOT WORK ON ANY OTHER SECTION IN THE TEST.

Scoring the Practice Test

Answer Key

Section 1: English Test

1. C (UM)	17. D (UM)	33. D (UM)	49. D (RH)	65. D (UM)
2. J (UM)	18. F (UM)	34. G (UM)	50. H (RH)	66. G (UM)
3. C (UM)	19. C (RH)	35. B (UM)	51. B (UM)	67. D (RH)
4. G (UM)	20. J (UM)	36. G (UM)	52. H (UM)	68. J (RH)
5. A (UM)	21. A (RH)	37. B (RH)	53. B (UM)	69. A (UM)
6. J (UM)	22. H (RH)	38. H (RH)	54. H (RH)	70. G (RH)
7. D (UM)	23. A (RH)	39. D (UM)	55. D (RH)	71. A (RH)
8. H (RH)	24. F (UM)	40. J (UM)	56. J (UM)	72. G (UM)
9. C (RH)	25. A (UM)	41. B (RH)	57. A (RH)	73. B (RH)
10. G (UM)	26. F (RH)	42. G (UM)	58. F (UM)	74. G (UM)
11. A (RH)	27. B (UM)	43. A (RH)	59. D (RH)	75. D (RH)
12. J (UM)	28. F (RH)	44. F (RH)	60. F (RH)	UM = Usage/ Mechanics
13. A (UM)	29. D (UM)	45. C (RH)	61. C (UM)	
14. F (RH)	30. J (RH)	46. G (UM)	62. J (UM)	RH = Rhetorical Skills
15. D (RH)	31. B (RH)	47. A (UM)	63. B (RH)	
16. G (UM)	32. G (RH)	48. F (RH)	64. G (UM)	

Section 2: Mathematics Test

1. C (EA)	11. C (GT)	21. E (PS)	31. B (GT)	41. B (AG)
2. G (GT)	12. F (AG)	22. J (EA)	32. H (AG)	42. J (GT)
3. C (EA)	13. C (EA)	23. A (PS)	33. D (EA)	43. D (GT)
4. J (GT)	14. H (AG)	24. J (AG)	34. J (EA)	44. K (PS)
5. C (EA)	15. D (EA)	25. D (EA)	35. D (AG)	45. B (GT)
6. H (GT)	16. H (GT)	26. H (AG)	36. J (GT)	46. F (GT)
7. B (AG)	17. A (EA)	27. E (PS)	37. A (PS)	47. B (GT)
8. J (PS)	18. J (AG)	28. H (PS)	38. F (EA)	48. G (GT)
9. D (EA)	19. D (EA)	29. C (PS)	39. B (EA)	49. D (GT)
10. H (EA)	20. J (AG)	30. J (AG)	40. J (AG)	50. H (AG)

51. E (AG)	55. B (AG)	59. D (PS)	GT = Plane Geometry/ Trigonometry	PS = Probability/ Statistics
52. K (GT)	56. H (AG)	60. J (PS)		
53. D (GT)	57. C (GT)	EA = Pre-Algebra/ Elementary Algebra	AG = Intermediate Algebra/Coordinate Geometry	
54. H (EA)	58. G (GT)			

Section 3: Reading Test

1. C (AL)	10. J (AL)	19. A (SS)	28. H (AL)	37. D (SS)
2. G (AL)	11. B (SS)	20. G (SS)	29. C (AL)	38. H (SS)
3. D (AL)	12. H (SS)	21. A (AL)	30. J (AL)	39. C (SS)
4. G (AL)	13. D (SS)	22. J (AL)	31. D (SS)	40. J (SS)
5. A (AL)	14. F (SS)	23. B (AL)	32. H (SS)	AL = Arts/ Literature
6. F (AL)	15. D (SS)	24. H (AL)	33. C (SS)	
7. A (AL)	16. H (SS)	25. B (AL)	34. J (SS)	SS = Social Studies/Sciences
8. H (AL)	17. A (SS)	26. J (AL)	35. B (SS)	
9. A (AL)	18. J (SS)	27. A (AL)	36. F (SS)	

Section 4: Science Test

1. B (RS)	10. G (RS)	19. B (CV)	28. J (DR)	37. D (RS)
2. H (RS)	11. A (RS)	20. J (CV)	29. C (DR)	38. H (RS)
3. B (RS)	12. J (RS)	21. C (CV)	30. G (DR)	39. A (RS)
4. H (RS)	13. D (DR)	22. G (CV)	31. A (DR)	40. H (RS)
5. D (RS)	14. H (DR)	23. B (CV)	32. G (DR)	DR = Data Representation
6. J (RS)	15. A (DR)	24. G (CV)	33. A (DR)	
7. D (RS)	16. J (DR)	25. A (DR)	34. H (DR)	RS = Research Summaries
8. H (RS)	17. B (DR)	26. G (DR)	35. D (RS)	
9. B (RS)	18. F (CV)	27. B (DR)	36. G (RS)	CV = Conflicting Viewpoints

Answer Explanations

Section 1: English Test

Passage I

1. **C.** Subject/verb agreement: The singular subject **one** needs the singular form of the verb **is.**

2. **J.** Pronoun case: The objective pronoun **whom** is incorrect because **who** is the subject of the verb **fiddled.** All other answer choices create a grammatically correct sentence.

3. **C.** Verb formation: The plural subject **sources** needs the present tense (plural) of the verb **credit.**

4. **G.** Pronoun/antecedent agreement: The singular (masculine) pronoun **he** is needed to refer to the singular antecedent **Nero.**

5. **A.** Verb tense: The verb phrase is correct because the past tense is needed.

6. **J.** Sentence structure: The sentence is not complete; it is a fragment and requires a main clause.

7. **D.** Punctuation: An introductory adverb clause must be followed by a comma.

8. **H.** Rhetorical strategy: The suggested sentence is not relevant to the paragraph and should be omitted.

9. **C.** Redundancy: The sentence begins with **At first**, so **originally** is redundant.

10. **G.** Punctuation: The sentence needs the conjunction **and** instead of a comma between the verbs.

11. **A.** Logic and Coherence: **Indeed** is the correct transitional word to use for emphasis.

12. **J.** Parallelism: The verbs **had** and **became** are needed to be parallel with the verb **dismissed.**

13. **A.** Verb tense: The past perfect tense is correct in this sentence.

14. **F.** Rhetorical strategy: The additional sentence adds specific details that heighten the effect of the description.

15. **D.** Purpose: This essay would not qualify as a scholarly essay. It is an informal investigation of the history behind a common saying.

Passage II

16. **G.** Verb tense/Punctuation: The -ing form of a verb cannot be used without a helping verb. All the other choices are punctuated correctly.

17. **D.** Punctuation: No apostrophe is needed because there is no possession in this sentence.

18. **F.** Punctuation: The sentence correctly uses the colon before an explanation.

19. **C.** Wordiness: The phrase **due to the fact** is a wordy expression.

20. **J.** Pronoun/antecedent agreement: The singular antecedent **room** needs the singular pronoun reference **this.**

21. **A.** Organization: The sentence provides a transition into the next paragraph.

22. **H.** Redundancy: The words **costly, extravagant,** and **expensive** mean the same thing; only one is necessary.

23. **A.** Rhetorical strategy: The phrase clarifies **that special bond.**

24. **F.** Pronoun case: **I** is the correct nominative pronoun because it is the subject of the verb **board.**

25. **A.** Punctuation: The comma is used correctly before a conjunction that connects items in a series.

26. **F.** Style: The sentence as it is written best conveys the **magical** quality of the garden.

27. **B.** Verb formation: The -ing form of the verb cannot be used without a helping verb.

28. **F.** Coherence: The sentence contrasts with the preceding sentence, so **nevertheless** is the correct transitional word to use here.

29. **D.** Punctuation: The apostrophe is needed to indicate the plural possessive **vendors'.**

30. **J.** Organization: This choice is the most effective and relevant conclusion to the essay.

Passage III

31. **B.** Redundancy: **poorly** and **badly** denote the same condition, so it is redundant to use both words.

32. **G.** Rhetorical strategy: The parenthetical information provides an explanatory detail.

33. **D.** Modification: The introductory participial phrase **Founded by Tsar Peter I, and the capital of Russia until 1918,** modifies **St. Petersburg,** which must follow the comma.

34. **G.** Sentence structure: This sentence has a comma splice error. The semicolon is needed to join two main clauses.

35. **B.** Sentence structure: The word **that** must be omitted so **Bridges** can be the subject of the verb **traverse.**

36. **G.** Sentence structure: The word **who** must be omitted so **residents** can be the subject of the verb **gather.**

37. **B.** Style: **Being that** is considered a stylistically inappropriate expression when used to mean **because.**

38. **H.** Redundancy: **best known** and **famous** denote the same thing; only one is needed.

39. **D.** Punctuation: The comma rather than the colon is used after an introductory participial phrase.

40. **J.** Sentence structure: This is a run-on sentence that needs to be separated into two sentences.

41. **B.** Rhetorical strategy: The details in Choice B best reflect the extraordinary quality of the collection.

42. **G.** Subject/verb agreement: The **Winter Palace** is the singular subject of the verb **is.**

43. **A.** Style: The phrase **an avid collector of art** best conveys Catherine's passion.

44. **F.** Rhetorical strategy: Choice F is the most relevant to the importance of the street.

45. **C.** Rhetorical strategy: The essay does not focus on baroque architecture; it is an overview of the highlights of a city.

Passage IV

46. **G.** Verb formation: The -ing form of the verb cannot be used without a helping verb.

47. **A.** Punctuation: The semicolon is appropriately used to join two main clauses.

48. **F.** Rhetorical strategy: The sentence is correct; all the other choices are wordy or use awkward phrasing.

49. **D.** Redundancy/awkwardness: **Jealous** and **envious** have essentially the same meaning and **both** needs **and** rather than **or. Whom** cannot be used as a subject.

50. **H.** Redundancy: The sentence begins with the word **Today,** so **now** is redundant.

51. **B.** Punctuation: The dash is used to set off a list that functions as an appositive for **all sorts of places.** Notice that a dash is used later in the sentence at the end of the list (a clue because the list is set off by dashes).

52. **H.** Adjective/adverb confusion: The adverb **freely** (not the adjective **free**) is needed to modify the verb **traveled.**

53. **B.** Verb tense: The past tense **had** is needed rather than the present perfect conditional.

54. **H.** Rhetorical strategy/punctuation: All of the constructions are acceptable except Choice H, which has no appropriate punctuation.

55. **D.** Diction: The appropriate word to use in comparisons using **less** is **than.**

56. **J.** Punctuation: When **however** is used to join two main clauses, it must be preceded by a semicolon and followed by a comma.

57. **A.** Rhetorical strategy: The original sentence best accomplishes the goal of emphasizing the change in attitude toward Rosa Bonheur.

58. **F.** Verb tense: The past tense is correct in this sentence.

59. **D.** Style: The word **so** best conveys the logical relationship of the ideas in the sentence.

60. **F.** Style: The sentence is stylistically effective as it is.

Passage V

61. **C.** Subject/verb agreement: The singular form of the verb **provides** is needed because the subject, **that,** refers to a singular antecedent, **caffeine.**

62. **J.** Idiom: The correct idiom is **associated with.**

63. **B.** Wordiness: The underlined portion is wordy and unnecessary to the meaning of the sentence.

64. **G.** Verb tense: The correct verb form is **No one knows.**

65. **D.** Parallelism: The verb **ground** is needed to be parallel with the verbs **harvested** and **roasted.**

66. **G.** Parallelism: The phrase **their religious rituals** parallels the phrase **their social activities.**

67. **D.** Misplaced modification and Style: Whenever possible, avoid the use of the passive voice (**chocolate began to be used by chefs**). In this sentence, the use of the passive voice creates a modification error: The phrase **Using their culinary skills** modifies **chocolate** rather than **chefs.**

68. **J.** Logic and coherence: Putting the phrase **in 1828** after **butter** is not a logical placement.

69. **A.** Punctuation: The sentence is correctly punctuated.

70. **G.** Logic and coherence: **However** is needed to convey the contrasting ideas between this sentence and the preceding sentence.

71. **A.** Style: The sentence contains the most appropriate wording for the style of the passage.

72. **G.** Idiom: The correct idiom is **began to cultivate.**

73. **B.** Style: Choice B uses an inappropriately slangy tone.

74. **G.** Parallelism: The verb **contribute** parallels the verb **reduce.**

75. **D.** Logic and coherence: To follow the chronological order of the essay, the most logical placement for paragraph 4 is before paragraph 3.

Section 2: Mathematics Test

1. **C.** Applying the distributive property, you have $x^2 - 3 - 4x^2 + 5x - 1$, which is equivalent to $-3x^2 + 5x - 4$.

2. **G.** The sum of the measures of all the angles is 360. Thus, $2x + 2x + 4x + x + 3x = 360$ or $12x = 360$ or $x = 30$.

3. **C.** Since $\dfrac{3}{ab} = 6$, you have $3 = 6ab$. Thus, $ab = \dfrac{3}{6}$ or $\dfrac{1}{2}$.

4. **J.** Since $m\angle DCE = 40$, $m\angle ACB = 40$ because $\angle ACB$ and $\angle DCE$ are vertical angles. Since $AB = AC$, $m\angle B = m\angle ACB = 40$. In $\triangle ABC$, $m\angle A + \angle B + m\angle ACB = 180$. Thus, $m\angle A + 40 + 40 = 180$ or $m\angle A = 100$.

5. **C.** Rewrite $2(4^k) = 2^5$ as $2(2^2)^k = 2^5$, then as $2(2^{2k}) = 2^5$, and then as $(2^1)(2^{2k}) = 2^5$, and finally as $2^{(1 + 2k)} = 2^5$. Set $1 + 2k = 5$, and you have $k = 2$.

6. **H.** Set up a proportion, $\dfrac{4}{16} = \dfrac{x}{36}$, with x being the shortest side of the larger triangle. Cross-multiply and you have $16x = 4(36)$ or $x = 9$.

7. **B.** This is an arithmetic sequence with a common difference of 4. The nth term of an arithmetic sequence is $a_0 + (n - 1)d$, where a_0 is the first term. In this case, the 8th term is $7 + (8 - 1)(4)$ or 35.

8. **J.** The mean of the four tests is $\dfrac{96 + 85 + 92 + 99}{4}$ or 93. The median is $\dfrac{96 + 92}{2}$ or 94. Thus, the sum of the mean and median is $93 + 94$ or 187.

9. **D.** The expression is equivalent to dividing each term in the numerator by the denominator $2x$. Therefore, $\dfrac{2x^4}{2x} + \dfrac{6x^2}{2x} - \dfrac{4x}{2x} = x^3 + 3x - 2$. Remember, when dividing monomials with the same base, you subtract the exponents.

10. **H.** Only two of the numbers, 979 and 990, among the five choices are divisible by 11. But 990 is the larger number.

11. **C.** Since the area of the square is 36, a side of the square is 6. The perimeter of the square is 4(6) or 24, which is the same as the perimeter of the equilateral triangle. Thus, a side of the triangle is $\frac{24}{3}$ or 8.

12. **F.** Since $(-12,k)$ lies on the line $2x - 3y = 6$, the coordinates of $(-12,k)$ satisfy the equation of the line. Therefore, $2(-12) - 3k = 6$ or $-24 - 3k = 6$, which is equivalent to $-3k = 30$ or $k = -10$.

13. **C.** Since 50% is equivalent to $\frac{1}{2}$, you have $\left(\frac{1}{2}\right)k = 20$. Multiply both sides by $\frac{1}{2}$ and you have $\frac{1}{4}k = 10$.

14. **H.** If two lines are parallel, then their slopes are equal. The slope-intercept form of a line is $y = mx + b$. The slope of the line $y = 2x - 4$ is 2. The equation $y - 2x = 0$ is equivalent to $y = 2x$, and thus its slope is 2.

15. **D.** Applying the distributive property, you have $(2x - 3)(x + 1) = 2x^2 + 2x - 3x - 3$, which is equivalent to $2x^2 - x - 3$.

16. **H.** Note that $AB = 4$, $BC = 4$, and $\triangle ABC$ is a right triangle. Since $AB = BC$, $\triangle ABC$ is an isosceles right triangle. Thus, $m\angle ACB = 45°$.

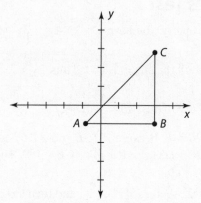

17. **A.** Since $bcd = 1$, you know that all three variables, b, c, and d, cannot be 0. Since $abc = 0$ and $b \neq 0$ and $c \neq 0$, you have $a = 0$. The product bc could be either positive or negative. And $bcd = 1$ does not require $d = 1$.

18. **J.** If $p(4k) = 8$, then $\sqrt{4k} = 8$. Squaring both sides, you have $4k = 64$, or $k = 16$.

19. **D.** Begin with $x + (x + 2) + (x + 4) = 138$. You have $3x + 6 = 138$ or $3x = 132$ or $x = 44$. Thus, the middle integer $x + 2$ is 46.

20. **J.** Since the x-intercept is -3 and the y-intercept is 4, the line passes through the points $(-3, 0)$ and $(0, 4)$. The slope of the line is $m = \dfrac{4 - 0}{0 - (-3)} = \dfrac{4}{3}$.

21. **E.** The stem-and-leaf plot shows that the data items are 20, 21, 21, 43, 80, and 85. Thus, the mean (or average) of these numbers is $\dfrac{20 + 21 + 21 + 43 + 80 + 85}{6} = 45$.

22. **J.** Begin with $2x + 6 = 4x$. You have $6 = 2x$ or $x = 3$. Thus, the number is 3.

23. **A.** The points in the scatterplot approximate a straight line with a negative slope. The data has a strong negative linear correlation. Thus, the linear correlation coefficient for the line of best fit could be -0.91, Choice A.

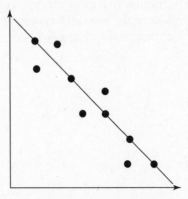

24. **J.** Let x represent the number of \$2 pens and $2x$ represent the number of \$3 pens. Then $2(x) + 3(2x) = 48$ or $8x = 48$ or $x = 6$. Mary bought 6 \$2 pens.

25. **D.** Rewrite $x^2 + 9 = 6x$ in standard form and obtain $x^2 - 6x + 9 = 0$. Factor $x^2 - 6x + 9 = 0$, and you have $(x - 3)(x - 3) = 0$. Set $x - 3 = 0$ and $x = 3$.

26. **H.** Draw the line $y = 3$, which is horizontal and parallel to the x-axis, crossing the y-axis at $y = 3$. This line intersects $g(x)$ at 2 points. Thus, there are 2 x-values.

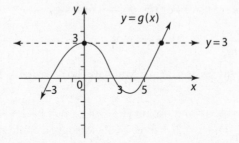

27. **E.** There are a total of 15 coins and 12 of the 15 are not quarters. Thus, the probability of getting a coin that is not a quarter is $\dfrac{12}{15}$ or $\dfrac{4}{5}$.

28. **H.** Inspecting the line of best fit in the given figure, note that the points $(0, 40)$, $(60, 70)$, and $(90, 85)$ are all on the line. Use two of the points, say $(0, 40)$ and $(60, 70)$, and obtain the slope; slope $= \dfrac{70 - 40}{60 - 0} = \dfrac{30}{60} = \dfrac{1}{2}$. Since at $t = 0$, $g = 40$, the equation of the line of best fit is $g = \dfrac{1}{2}t + 40$, and $h = \dfrac{1}{2}$.

29. **C.** The equation of the line of best fit is $g = \dfrac{1}{2}t + 40$. Since the student wanted a grade of 80 or higher, you have $\dfrac{1}{2}t + 40 \geq 80$ or $t \geq 80$. Thus, the minimum number of minutes the student must study for the

quiz is 80. Alternatively, you could arrive at the same conclusion by inspecting the graph. Note that the intersection of the lines $g = 80$ and $t = 80$ is on the line of best fit.

30. **J.** If a function, f, is an even function, then $f(x) = f(-x)$. In Choice J, let $y = f(x)$ and compare $f(x)$ and $f(-x)$. Since $f(x) = x^2 - 3$ and $f(-x) = (-x)^2 - 3 = x^2 - 3$, they are equal. Thus, $y = x^2 - 3$ is an even function. Another approach to the problem is to look at the graph of the function. The graph of an even function is symmetrical with respect to the y-axis. The graph of $y = x^2 - 3$ is symmetrical with respect to the y-axis as shown in the accompanying diagram.

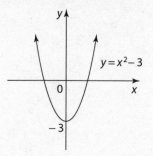

31. **B.** Note that $\triangle HEN$ is a right triangle with $EH = 4$ and $HN = 4$. Using the Pythagorean theorem or 45°-45° right-triangle relationship, $EN = 4\sqrt{2}$. Now, look at the right triangle AEN. Note that $AE = 2$ and $EN = 4\sqrt{2}$. Using the Pythagorean theorem, you have $(AN)^2 = (2)^2 + (4\sqrt{2})^2$ or $(AN)^2 = 4 + 32 = 36$ or $AN = 6$.

32. **H.** Using the distance formula, you have $\sqrt{(6-(-2))^2 + (k-5)^2} = 8$ or $\sqrt{8^2 + (k-5)^2} = 8$. Squaring both sides, you have $64 + (k-5)^2 = 64$ or $(k-5)^2 = 0$ or $k = 5$.

33. **D.** Since $\dfrac{m}{n} = -2$, then $2\left(\dfrac{m}{n}\right)^2 = 2(-2)^2 = 2(4) = 8$.

34. **J.** Substituting $k = 4$ in the expression $3k - 2$, you have $3(4) - 2$ or 10. Then divide 10 by 4, and you have a remainder of 2.

35. **D.** Apply the distributive property and obtain $(1 + 3i)(1 - i) = 1 - i + 3i - 3i^2 = 1 + 2i - 3i^2$. Since $i^2 = -1$, $1 + 2i - 3i^2 = 1 + 2i - 3(-1) = 1 + 2i + 3$ or $4 + 2i$. Also, you could have entered $(1 + 3i)(1 - i)$ into your calculator and obtained the same answer.

36. **J.** Since the shaded region is inside the circle, the inequality is $x^2 + y^2 < 9$. The region is also above the line $y = 2x$. Therefore, the inequality is $y > 2x$. The points in the shaded region must satisfy both inequalities. Thus, the points in the shaded region are points satisfying both $y > 2x$ and $x^2 + y^2 < 9$.

37. **A.** The expected value of a probability distribution is given as $\sum\limits_{i=1}^{n} x_i \cdot p(x_i)$. In this case, the expected value is $2\left(\dfrac{1}{2}\right) + 4\left(\dfrac{1}{6}\right) + 6\left(\dfrac{1}{6}\right) + 8\left(\dfrac{1}{6}\right) = 4$.

38. **F.** Substituting $x = \dfrac{1}{4}$ into the inequality, you have $\left(2\left(\dfrac{1}{4}\right)\right)^2 < 2\left(\dfrac{1}{4}\right)$ or $\left(\dfrac{1}{2}\right)^2 < \dfrac{1}{2}$ or $\dfrac{1}{4} < \dfrac{1}{2}$. The inequality holds.

39. **B.** Since the average height is 5 ft 4 in, the sum of their heights is 3 times 5 ft 4 in or 16 ft. Since Karen is the tallest and Karen is 5 ft 6 in tall, the maximum possible height for Mary is 5 ft 5 in. Thus, the least possible height for Janet is as follows: 16 ft – (5 ft 6 in + 5 ft 5 in) = 5 ft 1 in.

40. **J.** If $y = x^2$ and $x = -y^2$, then $y = (-y^2)^2$ or $y = y^4$. Rewriting the equation, you get $y^4 - y = 0$ or $y(y^3 - 1) = 0$. So $y = 0$ or $y^3 = 1$ or $y = 1$. Since y is a positive integer, $y = 1$.

41. **B.** Since line l is perpendicular to $\overrightarrow{AB}$, the slopes of line l and $\overrightarrow{AB}$ are negative reciprocals. The slope of $\overrightarrow{AB}$ is $\dfrac{4-1}{3-1} = \dfrac{3}{2}$. Thus, the slope of line l is $\dfrac{-2}{3}$.

42. **J.** The image of a point (x, y) reflected in the x-axis is $(x, -y)$. Therefore, the image of $A(3, 4)$ reflected in the x-axis is $A'(3, -4)$.

43. **D.** The area of a triangle is $\dfrac{1}{2}(\text{base})(\text{height})$. For $\triangle ABC$, note that $BC = 6$ and let $\overline{BC}$ be the base.

    The height is the altitude from point A to $\overline{BC}$, and the altitude is 3. Therefore, the area of $\triangle ABC$ is

    $\dfrac{1}{2}(6)(3) = 9$. Since $\triangle A''B''C''$ is the image of $\triangle ABC$ under a dilation of 2, $\triangle ABC$ is similar to $\triangle A''B''C''$. Thus, $\left(\dfrac{1}{2}\right)^2 = \dfrac{\text{area } \triangle ABC}{\text{area } \triangle A''B''C''}$, or $\dfrac{1}{4} = \dfrac{9}{\text{area } \triangle A''B''C''}$, and the area of $\triangle A''B''C''$ is $(4)(9)$ or 36.

44. **K.** Between '15 and '16, the increase is 2 million, the greatest increase.

45. **B.**

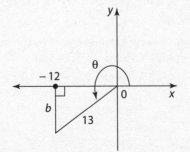

    Using the Pythagorean theorem, you have $b^2 + 12^2 = 13^2$, which is equivalent to $b^2 + 144 = 169$ or $b = \pm 5$. Since θ is in the third quadrant and the sine function is negative in the third quadrant, you have $\sin\theta = \dfrac{-5}{13}$.

46. **F.** Since $\sin B = \dfrac{AC}{AB}$, you have $\sin 30° = \dfrac{AC}{14}$ or $AC = 14 \sin 30°$. Since $\sin 30° = \dfrac{1}{2}$, $AC = 14\left(\dfrac{1}{2}\right) = 7$.

    Another approach to the problem is to note that $\triangle ABC$ is a 30°–60° right triangle. Thus, the length of the side opposite the 30° angle is equal to $\dfrac{1}{2}$ the length of the hypotenuse.

47. **B.** The statement "Every student in Mrs. Smith's class is on the honor roll" is equivalent to "If a student is in Mrs. Smith's class, the student is on the honor roll." A statement and its contrapositive

always have the same truth value. The contrapositive in this case is "If a student is not on the honor roll, the student is not in Mrs. Smith's class." Thus, the statement in Choice B is true.

48. **G.** Since the volume of a sphere is $\frac{4}{3}\pi r^3$, set $288\pi = \frac{4}{3}\pi r^3$ and obtain $r = 6$. Thus, the surface area of $4\pi r^2$ is $4\pi(6)^2$ or 144π.

49. **D.** Since all five choices involve the cosine function, you can assume that the given graph is that of a cosine function. The given graph completes one cycle of the cosine curve from $x = 0$ to $x = 4\pi$, which implies that the period of the function is 4π. Using the formula $\text{period} = \dfrac{2\pi}{\text{frequency}}$, you have

$4\pi = \dfrac{2\pi}{\text{frequency}}$ or the frequency is $\frac{1}{2}$. The graph also indicates that the range of the f is $-4 \le y \le 4$, which means the amplitude of f is 4. Thus, the cosine function is $y = 4\cos\dfrac{x}{2}$, where the amplitude is 4 and the frequency is $\frac{1}{2}$.

50. **H.** Since $\overline{CA}$ is a radius of the circle, the length of the radius of the circle is $\sqrt{(4-4)^2 + (5-0)^2} = 5$. Because B is a point on the circle, $\overline{CB}$ must also be a radius with length 5. Using the distance formula with each choice, only when the coordinates of B are $(1, 4)$ does the length equal $\sqrt{(4-1)^2 + (0-4)^2} = \sqrt{3^2 + 4^2} = 5$.

51. **E.** The smallest possible value for pq is -6. We get $pq = -6$ when $p = -3$ and $q = 2$. The largest possible value for pq is 6 when $p = -3$ and $q = -2$. Thus, $-6 \le pq \le 6$.

52. **K.** The law of cosine states that in a triangle, $\triangle ABC$, $c^2 = a^2 + b^2 - 2ab\cos C$, where a, b, and c are lengths of the sides opposite angles A, B, and C, respectively. In this case, $(DF)^2 = 6^2 + 10^2 - 2(6)(10)\cos 40°$ or $DF = \sqrt{36 + 100 - 120\cos 40°}$.

53. **D.** Since the circumference of the larger circle is 16π and $C = 2\pi r$, the radius $OA = 8$. Thus, $OB = 8 - (2) = 6$, and the circumference of the smaller circle is $2\pi(6)$ or 12π.

54. **H.** Two adults and three children cost $2(\$20) + 3(\$10) = \$70$. So $\$82 - \$70 = \$12$ for the fish caught. Thus, $\dfrac{\$12}{\$2} = 6$ fish.

55. **B.** Applying the properties of the logarithmic functions, you have $\log\dfrac{A^2}{B} = \log A^2 - \log B = 2\log A - \log B$. Since $\log A = h$ and $\log = k$, the expression $2\log A - \log B$ is equivalent to $2h - k$.

56. **H.** Since $\begin{bmatrix} -2 & 1 \end{bmatrix}$ is a 1×2 matrix and $\begin{bmatrix} 3 \\ -4 \end{bmatrix}$ is a 2×1 matrix, the product $\begin{bmatrix} -2 & 1 \end{bmatrix}\begin{bmatrix} 3 \\ -4 \end{bmatrix}$ is a 1×1 matrix. Carrying out the matrix multiplication, you have $[(-2)(3) + (1)(-4)]$ or $[-10]$.

57. **C.** Let $x = ED$ and $2x = CD$. Then $x(2x) = 32$ or $2x^2 = 32$ or $x^2 = 16$ or $x = 4$. Thus, $ED = 4$, $CD = 8$, $AE = 8$, and the diameter $AC = 4$. The circumference of the semicircle is $\frac{1}{2}(2\pi r) = \frac{1}{2}(2\pi(2)) = 2\pi$. Therefore, the perimeter of $ABCDE$ is $8 + 8 + 4 + 2\pi$ or $20 + 2\pi$.

58. **G.** A rhombus has four congruent sides, diagonals bisecting each other, and diagonals perpendicular to each other. In this case, $BC = AD = 8$, $AE = 4$, and $\triangle AED$ is a right triangle. Note that $\overline{AD}$ is the hypotenuse and that AD is twice AE. Thus, $\triangle AED$ is a 30°-60° right triangle and $m\angle ADE$ is 30.

59. **D.** Inspecting the Total column on the right side of the table, you see that the total number of female students is equal to $124 - 68$ or 56. Looking at the row labeled "Female," note that the number of female students taking physics is $56 - 25$ or 31. Also note the column labeled "Physics" shows that the total number of tenth graders taking physics is $28 + 31$ or 59. Please note that there are other approaches to solving the problem. A completed frequency table is shown below.

Frequency Table			
	Physics	**Chemistry**	**Total**
Male	28	40	68
Female	31	25	56
Total	59	65	124

60. **J.** Inspecting the Total column on the right, the relative frequency of male students is $1 - 0.45$ or 0.55. Looking at the row labeled "Male," the relative frequency of male students taking physics, x, is $0.55 - 0.32$ or 0.23. Looking at the row labeled "Total," the relative frequency of the total number of students taking chemistry is 0.52; therefore, the Chemistry column yields that $y = 0.52 - 0.32$ or $y = 0.20$. Thus, $x + y = 0.23 + 0.20 = 0.43$. Please note that there are other approaches to solving the problem.

A completed relative frequency table is shown below.

Relative Frequency Table			
	Physics	**Chemistry**	**Total**
Male	0.23	0.32	0.55
Female	0.25	0.20	0.45
Total	0.48	0.52	1

Section 3: Reading Test

Passage I

1. **C.** The main purpose of the passage is to introduce the characters and their positions in society. The interactions reveal how two upper-class women respond to an offer they consider as "vulgar" as the man making the offer. As the incident erupts into a "scene" (line 100), the awareness of class differences becomes paramount.

2. **G.** The passage is set in Italy, yet the English tourists are surrounded by portraits of English monarchs and served by an Italian host with a British accent. As Lucy says, "It might be London." The author establishes the pervasive influence of England.

3. **D.** The clues scattered throughout the passage reveal that Miss Bartlett is the companion to a younger woman, Lucy. Miss Bartlett says, "Eat your dinner, dear," and we know Lucy's mother is paying Miss Bartlett's expenses.

4. **G.** Miss Bartlett makes eye contact with the two women, and they exchange a look of understanding and shared experience.

5. **A.** The offer is clearly unexpected and obtrusive. Miss Bartlett is "startled" (line 53), and the others are shocked by the familiarity and forwardness of the old man.

6. **F.** The words connote violence, not physical but social. The women are shocked, and the aggressiveness of the old man is like a verbal assault.

7. **A.** Lucy is "perplexed" and has "an odd feeling" about the situation (lines 98–100). Miss Bartlett is obviously insulted by the offer of a room exchange.

8. **H.** There is no evidence of senility; in fact, according to the passage, "it was not the childishness of senility" (lines 61–62).

9. **A.** The passage implies that the "something" goes beyond the rooms and the views into larger realms. The emphasis on the men being "ill-bred" suggests class differences.

10. **J.** The irony arises from Miss Bartlett making **many** references to Lucy's mother paying Miss Bartlett's expenses, which is NOT a tactful thing to do.

Passage II

11. **B.** According to the passage, when something is just (fair) we automatically say it is equal.

12. **H.** The passage states (lines 72–79) the government should be most concerned with the welfare of its people.

13. **D.** In context, the word most nearly means *influence*.

14. **F.** The deceivable majority refers to "young and foolish persons" (line 85).

15. **D.** There are no startling statistics in the passage. The biblical allusion (Choice A) is the story of Laban. The farming analogy (Choice B) is the example of corn (lines 96–99), and the rhetorical question (Choice C) occurs on lines 30–36.

16. **H.** The author states the main idea clearly in lines 74–79: " . . . that property will always follow persons; that the highest end of government is the culture of men; and if men can be educated, the institutions will share their improvement and the moral sentiment will write the law of the land."

17. **A.** The "accident" to which the author refers is the "rights in property" (line 11) or the amount of wealth a person accumulates.

18. **J.** The author mentions all of the choices except "vigilance" as a way to accumulate wealth (skill: line 14; gift: line 44; inheritance or patrimony: lines 44 and 47).

19. **A.** The corn example (lines 96–99) elucidates the economic principle of profit. A farmer will not plant corn unless he expects to make money from this endeavor.

20. **G.** The author states that Laban, the employer, should select and pay those who guard his flock (lines 21–29).

Passage III

21. **A.** The author makes it clear at the beginning of the passage that he is writing a Romance, which he wants to distinguish from a Novel.

22. **J.** The only choice that can be supported by the passage is Choice J. The author states that he does not want to be "deficient" (line 49) in providing himself and the reader with a moral.

23. **B.** In the sentence before these phrases, the author states that he wants "to connect a bygone time with the very present" (lines 33–34).

24. **H.** In the first sentence, the author says that a Romance gives the writer "latitude" or leeway in presenting his tale. The rest of the paragraph explains his view that a writer of Romance may take liberties with reality, unlike the writer of a Novel.

25. **B.** The phrase "minute fidelity" refers to the close faithfulness to reality to which the writer of a Novel must adhere.

26. **J.** The author modestly states that he doesn't flatter himself by thinking his work will have a great impact on the reader.

27. **A.** When the author says, "The reader may perhaps choose to assign an actual locality to the imaginary events of this narrative . . . the author would very willingly have avoided anything of this nature" (lines 81–86), he suggests the reader would be making a regrettable mistake.

28. **H.** The author describes the effect of being heavy-handed with a moral as the same as that of sticking a pin in a butterfly: "at once depriving it of life, and causing it to stiffen in an ungainly and unnatural attitude" (lines 73–75).

29. **C.** The author states his moral on lines 52–53: "the wrong-doing of one generation lives into the successive ones."

30. **J.** The author uses all of the choices as contrasts except Choice J; he uses both phrases in Choice J to refer to the way he plans to "manage his atmospherical medium" (line 17).

Passage IV

31. **D.** The passage states that "most scientists embrace the idea that water once flowed across the Martian surface," (lines 7–9), but they haven't found irrefutable evidence (Choice A). They aren't doubtful, so Choice B is incorrect. No physical evidence of frozen water has been found on the ice caps (Choice C); its existence there is speculative.

32. **H.** While the passage refers to the chemistry lab on Opportunity (Choice F) and video cameras aboard Curiosity (Choice G), the photographs from Mariner 9 (1971) are credited with showing the first clues to the existence of water. Astronauts (Choice J) are not mentioned in the passage.

33. **C.** By referring to the Mars rover Opportunity (operating for the past ten years) and the latest rover, Curiosity, the paragraph provides a brief historical context. The second paragraph doesn't present the most current information (Choice A), or challenge a hypothesis (Choice B), or specify the source of a debate (Choice D).

34. **J.** The passage specifically states, "Studying water on Mars gives scientists insight into how planets evolve, how water accumulates, how climates develop, and, possibly, how life begins" (lines 64–67). The formation of volcanoes is not mentioned.

35. **B.** Michael Meyer states, "Our challenge is to figure out how this more clement Mars was even possible, and what happened to that wetter Mars." His remarks indicate that at some time in the past Mars' climate was more clement (less harsh) and wetter (less dry). Choice A is incorrect because it wasn't harsher and drier. Choice C is incorrect because it wasn't harsher. Choice D is incorrect because it wasn't milder and drier.

36. **F.** The fourth paragraph begins with an observation (". . . we have noticed . . ."), then makes a prediction ("The prediction was that we should start seeing water-deposited, fine-grained rocks . . ."), and concludes with a confirmation (" . . . we're seeing finely laminated mudstones . . ."). Choice F offers the only accurate organizational pattern of the paragraph. The paragraph doesn't begin with a prediction (Choice G) or a hypothesis (Choice H). Choice J is incorrect because there is no experiment in the paragraph.

37. **D.** According to the second paragraph, "The findings build upon previous work that suggested there were ancient lakes on Mars . . ." The findings being referred to are discussed earlier in the paragraph in a quote from Ashwin Vasavada: "Observations from the rover suggest that a series of long-lived streams and lakes existed at some point between about 3.8 to 3.3 billion years ago, delivering sediment that slowly built up the lower layers of Mount Sharp." Choice A is incorrect because the sediment built up Mount Sharp; it didn't drift down from the top. Choice B is incorrect because there is no evidence that the data sent to Earth by the Curiosity rover proves there is presently water in the Gale Crater. Choice C is incorrect because there is mudstone in the lower layers of Mount Sharp.

38. **H.** Both passages cite geologic findings ("rocky," "coarser gravel," "mudstones") and topographical features ("riverbeds and canyons," "Gale Crater," "Mount Sharp") that describe landforms on Mars. Only Passage A discusses the possibility of life on Mars (Choice F). There is no evidence in either passage for Choice G. Choice J is speculation that isn't explicitly supported by either passage.

39. **C.** The language in Passage A is more speculative and less definite than the language in Passage B because of the 2-year interval between them. In that interval, scientists found confirmatory data of the presence of water on Mars. There is no evidence to suggest that the author of Passage A has more credible scientific qualifications than the author of Passage B (Choice A) or that a decline in the number of photographs sent by the rover Curiosity would affect the language of the passages (Choice B). Choice D is inaccurate: Both authors include data from Curiosity.

40. **J.** Unlike the author of Passage A, the author of Passage B supports his assertions with quotes from experts (Ashwin Vasavada and Michael Meyer). Choice F is incorrect because both authors refer to geological evidence. Choice G is incorrect because Passage A refers to photographs from Curiosity and Mariner 9; Passage B doesn't refer to Mariner 9. Choice H is incorrect because both passages refer to Martian climate change.

Section 4: Science Test

Passage I

1. **B.** According to Table 1, an incandescent bulb with a power of 80 W should fall between the values shown for the 60 and 100 W values (14.2 and 17.0 lm/W, respectively). This is supported by a gradual increase in light efficiency values for incandescent bulbs over the range of 40–100 W. The only appropriate option is 15.8 lm/W.

2. **H.** This chart correctly shows the wattage of each bulb and its corresponding light output (e.g., the only 20 W bulb tested was a CFL that gave a light output of 1200 lm). Note that three incandescent bulbs were tested, two halogens, and only one CFL; there are different numbers of columns present for each wattage displayed.

3. **B.** The 100 W halogen bulb is associated with an operating temperature of 3500°K and a light output of 2400 lm according to Table 1. Using the index in Table 2, this corresponds most closely with a rating of bright white.

4. **H.** The CFL light output data are most convincing in the support of the notion that bulb type is a more significant predictor of light output than is power of the bulb. The CFL bulb demonstrated the lowest power rating of any bulb tested (20 W), yet produced more light than a 60 W halogen bulb that uses three times the power (1200 lm versus 1150 lm).

5. **D.** Substituting the values "20 W" for the power and "24 hours" for the time used into the equation $\dfrac{\text{Power (W)} \times \text{time used (hours)}}{1000 \text{ (W/kW)}}$ provides the correct model for determining the electricity used to power the CFL bulb.

6. **J.** The CFL bulb has a significantly lower power (20 W) than any of the incandescent bulbs (40, 60, and 100 W), so the greenhouse gas emissions for the CFL bulb will be a fraction (between 50% and 80% less) of the emissions associated with the incandescent bulbs. According to the information in Figure 1, more mercury is associated with the use of any incandescent bulb than with any CFL bulb; this is true even though no mercury is used to produce an incandescent bulb, while almost 4 mg are used to manufacture a CFL bulb.

Passage II

7. **D.** Both types of *E. coli* grew significantly in the NM plates (i.e., bacterial lawns were present), while 13 colonies were observed in the NM/amp plate. No colonies were observed in the NM/pen plate. Only the NM and NM/amp plates seemed to support the growth of *E. coli*.

8. **H.** Both methods of transformation were successful in producing colonies, but the chemical transformation associated with Experiment 2 produced more colonies (18) than did the electroporation used in Experiment 1 (13 colonies). The bacteria in the NM/pen plates generally did not survive because they had no antibiotic resistance to penicillin, which is unrelated to whether they were transformants. The presence of the bacterial lawn in the NM plates indicates that bacteria grew very easily under those conditions; this too is unrelated to whether they are transformants. The bacteria that did transform grew in the NM/amp plates, while the non-transformants did not.

9. **B.** The NM plate demonstrates the control conditions under which any type of *E. coli* can easily grow and reproduce. It represents a point of comparison for the experimental groups represented by the NM/amp and NM/pen plates.

10. **G.** The growth of one colony in the NM/pen plate in Experiment 2 is unexpected, as no bacteria used in the experiments were observed to tolerate the presence of the penicillin antibiotic in their environment. One original *E. coli* bacterium utilized must have possessed the penicillin-resistance trait and created a colony in the plate where no other bacteria could survive.

11. **A.** To calculate the transformation efficiency, substitute the quantity of DNA plated (0.01 µg) and the number of colonies observed (13) into the following equation:

$$\text{Transformation efficiency} = \frac{\text{Number of transformed cells}}{\text{Quantity of DNA plated (µg)}}$$

The resultant quotient is 1300 transformants/µg DNA.

12. **J.** If twice as much DNA were used in Experiment 2 than in Experiment 1, then the denominator in the equation above will change to 0.02 µg. Since the number of observed colonies in Experiment 2 was 18, the resultant quotient is 900 transformants per µg of DNA plated. Experiment 2 is then less efficient than Experiment 1 even though more total colonies were observed in Experiment 2 plates.

Passage III

13. **D.** According to the data presented in Table 1, butane produces 2861 kJ of heat per mole of fuel, while propane produces only 2208 kJ of heat. In fact, the more carbon atoms present in the hydrocarbon fuel, the more kJ of heat are associated.

14. **H.** A molecule of hexane has 6 carbon atoms present, so the quantity of heat produced through its combustion should fall somewhere between the values for the burning of butane with 4 carbon atoms and the burning of octane with 8 carbon atoms. Thus, it should fall between 2861 kJ/mol and 5472 kJ/mol, and the only appropriate value provided is 4160 kJ/mol.

15. **A.** When comparing three carbon-based fuels, methane (890 kJ/mol) has a higher heat of combustion than methanol (726 kJ/mol). Similarly, ethane (1555 kJ/mol) has a higher heat of combustion than ethanol (1300 kJ/mol). Thus, a hydrocarbon with a given number of carbon atoms is associated with a higher heat of combustion than an alcohol with the same number of carbon atoms.

16. **J.** According to the data, combusting 1 molecule of octane would produce enough heat (5472 kJ/mol) to satisfy the given set of conditions, and would also produce 8 molecules of CO_2. If one uses 4 molecules of methane or 2 molecules of ethane, sufficient heat would be generated, but only 4 CO_2 molecules would be produced. If 3 molecules of ethanol were combusted, 6 CO_2 molecules would be produced.

17. **B.** According to the graph, at an AFR of 16, the CO level is relatively low, as is the hydrocarbon level. At an AFR of 14, both levels are slightly higher than at an AFR of 16. Additionally, at AFRs of 19 and 20 the hydrocarbon levels increase significantly.

Passage IV

18. **F.** Hypothesis 1 clearly states that evolution happens gradually over time. It also argues that the fossil record is incomplete, and thus all change is not preserved. Although Choice H might also seem consistent with this hypothesis, there is no direct statement of this position, and change might happen gradually while not always at the same pace.

19. **B.** The main difference between the two hypotheses concerns the rate at which evolution occurs. Hypothesis 1 holds that evolution happens gradually over time, while Hypothesis 2 argues that evolution happens in short bursts of rapid change followed by long periods of relatively no change.

20. **J.** According to the figure, the time between the Pliocene and the Pleistocene demonstrates a period of relatively gradual change over time, similar to that observed within the Pliocene and within the Miocene. Between the Miocene and the Pliocene, forams demonstrated a period of very rapid change in shell shape, thus punctuated equilibrium is supported.

21. **C.** Hypothesis 1 argues that many transitional forms are often not well preserved in the fossil record; Figure 2 demonstrates these many forms as occurring gradually over time. Hypothesis 2 states that change happens very quickly; this is demonstrated in the single transitional form presented in Figure 3. Thus, the number of transitional forms is a point of conflict between the two hypotheses.

22. **G.** The figure demonstrates that trilobite evolution included the relatively slow accumulation of "ribs" (increased segmentation) over time. Thus, the concept of phyletic gradualism and Hypothesis 1 are supported by this example.

23. **B.** This third notion of punctuated gradualism includes the notion of quick bursts of change in a short period of time; it simply expands on the concept by including the idea that a new species may or may not be formed even when rapid change does occur.

24. **G.** When summarizing all of the data presented, it becomes clear that evolution happens very gradually in some instances (e.g., trilobites), and then in other cases happens very suddenly and then not at all again for a very long time (e.g., forams between the Miocene and the Pliocene).

Passage V

25. **A.** As the value for altitude increases from 20 km to 40 km, the corresponding ozone concentrations increase from 0.0025 ppb to over 0.006 ppb. The curve peaked just before this point (0.008 ppb, 35 km) and then, as altitude continued to increase to 60 km, the corresponding ozone concentration decreased to 0.002 ppb.

26. **G.** According to Figure 2, May (month 5) demonstrated an average ozone concentration of 50 ppb. April was slightly lower and June slightly higher.

27. **B.** The passage explains that an ozone molecule is created as a free oxygen atom collides with an oxygen gas molecule. This reaction produces O_3, ozone. UV light is involved in the production of free oxygen atoms through the splitting of oxygen gas molecules, and is thus indirectly involved.

28. **J.** Table 1 shows that, although there have been slight variations in this trend from one year to the next, overall the average annual ozone concentrations are gradually increasing. Figure 2 demonstrates that, within one year, average monthly ozone concentrations increased during the summer months, peaked in August, and then decreased to the initial values during the fall and winter months.

29. **C.** According to Figure 2, the average ozone concentration in August was 80 ppb. Since 80 ppb falls within the 76–95 ppb range, then August would require an orange alert to indicate that the air quality is potentially unhealthy.

Passage VI

30. **G.** Table 1 indicates that when Spring C was tested with a force of 5 N, the spring was extended by 7 mm. When tested with 10 N, it was extended by 14 mm. Thus, if an 8 N force were applied, Spring C would be extended by a distance between 7 mm and 14 mm. The 11 mm value meets this criterion.

31. **A.** When the unknown force was applied to Spring A, it was stretched by a distance of 0.25 mm, a shorter distance than observed in any of the initial trials. This indicates that the force is less than the 1 N force that resulted in a 0.5 mm extension. Additionally, the effect of the force on the spring is proportional to the force applied, so because the new stretch was half of the stretch at 1 N, then the force applied must be half of that value. The 0.5 N value meets these criteria.

32. **G.** The spring constant k is defined as a measure of a spring's rigidity: The higher the value of k, the more rigid the spring (i.e., the less it will extend). According to the data in Table 1, when the heaviest force was applied (12 N), Spring B extended the most (26.4 mm) and Spring A the least (6 mm). Thus, Spring A has the highest k value and Spring B the lowest.

33. **A.** Applying the values of $k = 2.2$ N/mm and $x = 11$ mm to the equation, $F_r = -kx$, the value of $F_r = -24.2$ N (the opposite product of 2.2 and 11).

34. **H.** The initial compression of the spring did not affect its functioning when replaced into the pen, but the extension that resulted from the stretching must have exceeded the elastic limit of the spring, the distance beyond which any extension will be permanent and will produce a different result when new forces are applied. That is why it no longer allowed the pen to function properly when the spring was reinserted into the pen the second time.

Passage VII

35. **D.** According to Table 1, Plant 4 recorded the highest efficiency of *Giardia* cyst removal at 98.6%. All other plants recorded values lower than 98.6%.

36. **G.** According to Table 1, Plants 2, 3, and 4 all employed the same primary and secondary methods of purification, yet the results ranged from 87% to 97.9% for *Cryptosporidium* and from 85.1% to 98.6% for *Giardia*. None of the other descriptions is consistent with the data provided.

37. **D.** According to Table 2, the maximum value for the removal of *Giardia* using UV light is 4-log. This is equivalent to a 99.99% removal.

38. **H.** According to the data in Table 2, chlorine, chlorine dioxide, and UV light have either no or unreliable effectiveness in removing *Cryptosporidium* and *Giardia* from water. Of the remaining methods, slow sand filtration and membrane filtration, the latter method demonstrated the highest and most reliable efficiency values for the removal of both types of protozoans (a minimum of 2-log for both *Cryptosporidium* and *Giardia*).

39. **A.** According to Figure 1, a clear and direct positive relationship is demonstrated between the efficiency of the turbidity removal and the efficiency of the *Cryptosporidium* oocyst (i.e., as the efficiency of the turbidity removal increases steadily, the efficiency of the removal of *Cryptosporidium* also increases steadily).

40. **H.** When summarizing the data presented in Tables 1 and 2, it becomes clear that the least effective method of purification of both types of protozoans is chlorination. The lab results in Table 2 indicate that chlorination was not at all effective in removing *Cryptosporidium* and was unreliably effective in removing *Giardia,* and the data in Table 1 demonstrate the lowest removal rates of both *Cryptosporidium* and *Giardia* in Plant 2, where chlorination was used.

Section 5: Writing Test

Sample Scored Essay A

Social media is everywhere—75% of American adults use it. In addition, as technology advances, social media is gaining an even larger place in individual's lives. Social media has a clear advantage: It connects individuals. However social media also has become an overpowering—even distracting—force in many individual's lives, sometimes even communicating incorrect information. Social media is a great asset for the community as long as its presence is limited, once its presence becomes overpowering, it becomes a detriment to society.

Social media within reason can connect individuals from across town or even across the country, creating closer knit communities. For example, in accordance with perspective one, social media allows students to connect with their teachers. At my school students rely on technology for not only incoming assignments but also extra help. It is 6 pm on a Tuesday night before an AP physics test and I can't solve a problem. What do I do? Do I scower the Internet for answers? No. I go onto an application, Edmodo, which connects students and teachers. I say thanks to this form of social media. Students can send messages, pictures, and videos to teachers, guaranteeing help with schoolwork, even after the bell has rung to end the day. Moreover, as perspective one states, social media connects both families and friends. One example of this is Skype, this application allows individuals to video chat from across the globe. While my cousins reside in Australia, thousands of miles away from me, I can chat and even "share" weekly dinners with them. If not for Skype, I would speak to my cousins on the phone and maybe see them once a year. Social media allows my family to stay connected wherever they are.

Furthermore, social media can help law enforcement. As stated in perspective three, criminal's will at times post activities on social media. For one, some criminals post evidence of their crimes, which is why law enforcement to convict those individuals. However, social media has other benefits. Every application includes tracking systems, and this can help police to locate possible criminals. For example, in 2006 an individual hacked onto Harvard's network. Through social media tracking, the school was able to track down this individual in under 24 hours. However, when social media takes over, that is when it becomes dangerous.

In order to keep social media as a benefit and safe, individuals have to recognize when they are becoming too relying. As perspective two stated, social media may sometimes provide incorrect information which is why individuals must be weary of all information. A prime example is the slenderman figure who created a social media page. Of course, this individual was not real—he was a make-believe character who created a website for children. However, many children believed his lies. They believed he lived in a castle in the woods and that he loved them. For this reason, when he asked two of those children to sacrafice their friend, they did—willingly. It was due to the ignorance of these children regarding information on the internet that they believed they would be "accepted" by the social media figure if they killed their friend. For slenderman, these girls attempted to murder their best friend—stabbing her 19 times. It is clear from this example that overpowering social media can be detrimental. Moreover, too much social media can control someone so much that they lose interest in other activities—school for example. For that reason perspective two is correct. As a result of this 24-hour distraction, some students are not paying much attention to school which results in lower grades. However, as stated earlier, if there is a limit on social media, the problem will not be so serious. Turning off smart phones, laptops, and tablets for a few hours every day will allow students to study more efficiently and effectively.

Overall, technology can be beneficial. However, when humans let it overpower them, it becomes a detriment.

Domain Scores

Ideas and Analysis: 4 (× 2 = 8)

The writer presents a reasonable analysis of the three perspectives. Although the thesis statement is a run-on sentence, it addresses the complexity of the argument (*Social media is a great asset for the community as long as its presence is limited, once its presence becomes overpowering, it becomes a detriment to society*). The writer's arguments show an understanding of the context; he clearly has thought about the benefits of social media as well as the damage it may do. The writer addresses the validity of the claims of the perspectives by giving personal and public examples (his family's experiences and the well-publicized Slenderman example).

Development and Support: 4 (× 2 = 8)

The evidence the writer uses to support this argument clarifies his understanding of the issue. His reasoning adequately illustrates his main points. For example, he uses the specific example of Skype to illustrate the power of social media to connect families and the Edmodo app to show the educational usefulness of online communication (although some may claim that Edmodo isn't social media). His understanding of the dangers of social media is clear in his explanations of the Slenderman narrative and of the distracting lure of the Internet for teenagers.

Organization: 4 (× 2 = 8)

The organizational pattern is clear and the ideas progress logically from the controlling idea that social media is a positive presence, as long as its influence is controlled. Transitional words and phrases (*furthermore, for example, a prime example, moreover*) highlight relationships between ideas and contribute to the coherence of this essay.

Language Use: 3 (× 2 = 6)

Language use is simplistic and sometimes unclear (*For one, some criminals post evidence of their crimes, which is why law enforcement to convict those individuals*). Word choice is sometimes awkward and inaccurate (*Do I scower the Internet for answers?* and *In order to keep social media as a benefit and safe, individuals have to recognize when they are becoming too relying*). Several sentences contain comma splice errors (*One example of this is Skype, this application allows individuals to video chat from across the globe*). While the frequent errors are distracting, they don't hinder understanding.

To calculate the Essay Score, add the Domain Scores: 8 + 8 + 8 + 6 = 30.

Using the conversion table on page 371, a Domain Score of **30** equals a scaled score of **23.**

Sample Scored Essay B

In today's society, social media surrounds us and connects us with other people. There are so many advantages for being able to communicate with others without being face-to-face. However, there are some disadvantages. By interacting via social media, misinformation can be spread. This is no way to use a key tool.

Different people have different perspectives on whether social media is helpful or harmful. The rumors that can spread through Facebook, Twitter, Instagram, etc. can clause a frenzy. Just recently a professional basketball player was found unconscious and word got around social media that he was dead. It is unbelievable how information can be tossed around and it ends with someone's life in hands. Its great that social media can be beneficial in interacting with people, but horrible for spreading rumors.

When the gossip goes viral, this also takes away from kids studying. When entertainment websites like E Online or Buzzfeed update their latest news, teenagers are the first ones to find out. With technology today, kids can easily spread the news by text messages or posting it on Facebook. Since it is so easy to get distracted by the latest gossip, some teenagers will spend more time on that rather than completing their work thoroughly. Just recently, a girl in my high school decided to drive while being drunk. She got into a horrible car crash. This news spread so quickly that everyone was worried for this girl, yet thinking how she could she do that to herself. No one did homework that night because everyone was on the phone or Twitter. Social media has such an impact on kids lives these days. It can possibly lead to dangers and can cause pain to a lot of people.

Some perspectives say social media provides a pathway to increased social interaction. Families, friends, and business associates all point out that they have established stronger relationships by connecting on social media. Students also connect with their teachers regularly and use the sites to work cooperatively with their peers. I agree with this perspective because I am on Facebook with a lot of my friends and my cousins.

The affects social media has can cause damage to anyone's reputation. As a community, not only teenagers, but everyone should be aware of the consequences of spreading false news. This can help or hinder the police when they are trying to catch a criminal. Some criminals even post about their crimes on Facebook! This can help the police catch them.

So is social media good or bad? Its both and its here to stay.

Domain Scores

Ideas and Analysis: 3 (× 2 = 6)

The writer responds vaguely to the three perspectives, although she merely copies part of Perspective 1 word-for-word from the prompt. She discusses (somewhat superficially) misinformation (and gives the example of the basketball player), social interaction (both positive and negative), and law enforcement (briefly). The thesis statement addresses some of the complexity of the issue by recognizing that there are both advantages and disadvantages to social media. The writer's ideas show an understanding of the context; she knows about the role of social media in disseminating information and misinformation, but she offers little analysis of the claims.

Development and Support: 3 (× 2 = 6)

The evidence the writer uses to support this argument is general, although she does cite the example of the basketball player and the girl from her school. Her reasoning, while not faulty, is vague (*Social media has such an impact on kids lives these days. It can possibly lead to dangers and can cause pain to a lot of people*). Other than referring to her Facebook friends, she offers little specific support for the positive role of social media.

Organization: 3 (× 2 = 6)

A rudimentary organizational pattern seems to be present, but it is not clear and purposeful. The writer attempts to develop one main idea in each paragraph but then drifts away from her point. The fifth paragraph, for example, begins with social media's role in damaging a reputation but shifts away from that topic to discuss its role in law enforcement.

Language Use: 3 (× 2 = 6)

Language use is simplistic and sometimes unclear (*This news spread so quickly that everyone was worried for this girl, yet thinking how she could she do that to herself*). Word choice and sentence structure are often awkward, simplistic, or inaccurate (*It is unbelievable how information can be tossed around and it ends with someone's life in hands*). While the frequent errors (*its* for *it's, affects* for *effects*) are distracting, they don't hinder understanding.

To calculate the Essay Score, add the Domain Scores: 6 + 6 + 6 + 6 = 24.

Using the conversion table on page 371, a Domain Score of **24** equals a scaled score of **19**.

Scoring Worksheets

Sections 1–4

English Test

Number Correct (Raw Score)

Usage/Mechanics (UM) Subscore Area   _____ (40)

Rhetorical Skills (RH) Subscore Area   _____ (35)

Total Number Correct for English Test (UM + RH)   _____ (75)

Mathematics Test

Number Correct (Raw Score)

Pre-Algebra/Elementary Algebra (EA) Subscore Area   _____ (16)

Intermediate Algebra/Coordinate Geometry (AG) Subscore Area   _____ (16)

Plane Geometry/Trigonometry (GT) Subscore Area   _____ (18)

Probability/Statistics   _____ (10)

Raw Score: Total Number Correct for Math Test (EA + AG + GT + PS)   _____ (60)

Reading Test

Number Correct (Raw Score)

Social Studies/Sciences (SS) Subscore Area   _____ (20)

Arts/Literature (AL) Subscore Area   _____ (20)

Total Number Correct for Reading Test (SS + AL)   _____ (40)

Science Test

Number Correct (Raw Score)

Data Representation (DR) Subscore Area   _____ (15)

Research Summaries (RS) Subscore Area   _____ (18)

Conflicting Viewpoints (CV) Subscore Area   _____ (7)

Total Number Correct for Science Test (DR + RS + CV)   _____ (40)

369

Test	Raw Score	Scale Score
English		
Mathematics		
Reading		
Science		
Sum of Scale Scores (English + Math + Reading + Science)		
Composite Score (sum ÷ 4)		

Scale Score	Section 1: English Test	Section 2: Mathematics Test	Section 3: Reading Test	Section 4: Science Test	Section 5: Writing Test	Scale Score
	Raw Score Conversions					
	Raw Scores					
36	75	60	40	40	47–48	36
35	74	59	38–39	—	45–46	35
34	73	58	37	39	44	34
33	70–72	55–57	36	—	43–42	33
32	69	54	35	38	41	32
31	68	53	34	—	40	31
30	67	50–52	33	37	39	30
29	66	49	32	36	37–38	29
28	64–65	48	31	35	35–36	28
27	63	44–47	29–30	33–34	34	27
26	62	41–43	28	32	33	26
25	57–61	39–40	27	31	32	25
24	55–56	37–38	26	29–30	31	24
23	53–54	35–36	25	28	29–30	23
22	50–52	34	24	25–27	28	22
21	49	33	23	23–24	26–27	21
20	47–48	30–32	22	21–22	25	20
19	43–46	27–29	21	18–20	23–24	19
18	39–42	25–26	20	17	22	18
17	37–38	22–24	19	16	21	17
16	34–36	19–21	18	14–15	20	16
15	30–33	15–18	16–17	12–13	19	15
14	29	12–14	14–15	10–11	18	14
13	26–28	09–11	12–13	09	17	13
12	24–25	08	10–11	08	16	12
11	22–23	06–07	09	07	15	11
10	20–21	05	07–08	06	14	10
9	19	04	06	05	13	9
8	15–18	—	05	04	12	8
7	13–14	03	—	03	11	7
6	10–12	02	04	—	10	6
5	09	—	03	02	9	5
4	06–08	—	02	—	—	4
3	04–05	01	—	01	—	3
2	02–03	—	01	—	—	2
1	00–01	00	00	00	8	1

Refer to the sample essays on pages 365–368 and to the rubric given at the end of the diagnostic test (pages 70–72) to calculate the raw score for your essay.

A. Using a Graphing Calculator

All the problems in the ACT Math Section can be done without a calculator. There are some problems, however, that can be solved easily by using a graphing calculator. Below are several illustrations of how to use a graphing calculator (TI-83 Plus) to solve some of the math questions on the Diagnostic Test.

Evaluating an Expression Involving the Imaginary Number *i* (From Diagnostic Test, Problem 30):

1. Given $i = \sqrt{-1}$, which of the following is equivalent to $2i(i^3 - 4i)$?

   A. -6
   B. $-6i^2$
   C. 6
   D. 7
   E. 10

TI-83 Plus Solution:

(Please note that the imaginary number *i* can be found as the second function of the decimal point key located at the bottom of the calculator.)

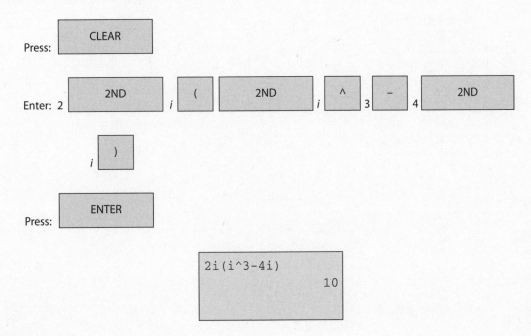

Correct Answer: **E**

Simplifying a Trigonometric Expression (From Diagnostic Test, Problem 29):

2. If $0 < \theta < \dfrac{\pi}{2}$, which of the following is equivalent to $\dfrac{\cos\theta}{\sqrt{1-\sin^2\theta}}$?

   F. -1

   G. $-2 - \cos 2x$

   H. $2 - \sin x$

   J. $1 + \cos\theta$

   K. 1

TI-83 Plus Solution:

Set the calculator in radian mode.

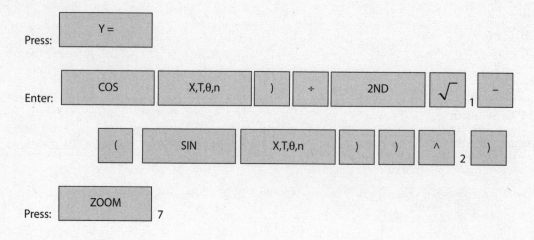

Press: Y =

Enter: COS   X,T,θ,n   )   ÷   2ND   √ 1   –

(SIN   X,T,θ,n   )   )   ^ 2   )

Press: ZOOM 7

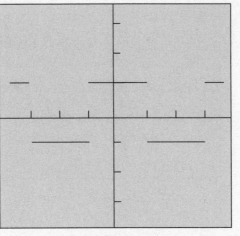

$[-2\pi, 2\pi]$ by $[-4, 4]$

Remember that $y = \dfrac{\cos\theta}{\sqrt{1 - \sin^2\theta}}$. Notice that $0 < \theta < \dfrac{\pi}{2}$, $y = 1$.

Correct Answer: **K**

Identifying an Odd or Even Function (From Diagnostic Test, Problem 22):

3. Which of the following is an odd function?

    A. $h(x) = 3x - 5$
    B. $k(x) = x^2 - 7x + 9$
    C. $p(x) = x^3 - 3$
    D. $q(x) = x^3 + 1$
    E. $f(x) = x^5 - 2x^3$

TI-83 Plus Solution:

Use the calculator to produce the graph of each equation in the five choices. The equation with a graph that has symmetry with respect to the *origin* is an odd function.

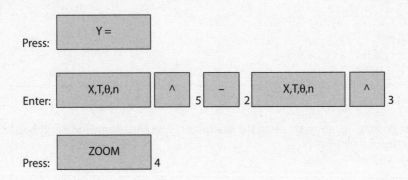

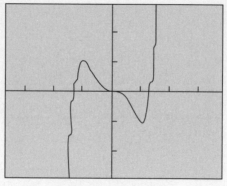

[–4.7, 4.7] by [–3.1, 3.1]

Correct Answer: **E**

Identifying an Equation of a Graph (From Diagnostic Test, Problem 10):

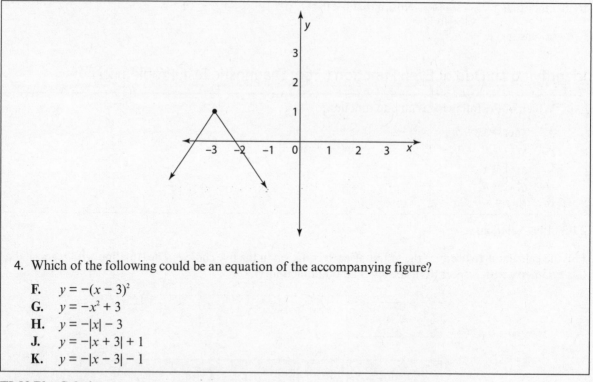

4. Which of the following could be an equation of the accompanying figure?

   F. $y = -(x - 3)^2$

   G. $y = -x^2 + 3$

   H. $y = -|x| - 3$

   J. $y = -|x + 3| + 1$

   K. $y = -|x - 3| - 1$

TI-83 Plus Solution:

Look at the graph of each equation by using the calculator. The equation whose graph matches the one in the given figure is the correct answer.

Press: Y =

Enter: (–) 2ND CATALOG

Select: ▷ abs (ENTER

Enter: X,T,θ,n + 3) + 1 ENTER

Press: ZOOM 6

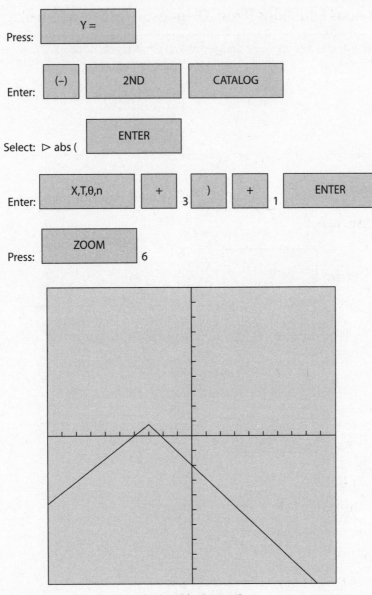

[–10, 10] by [–10, 10]

Correct Answer: **J**

Solving Simultaneous Equations (From Diagnostic Test, Problem 6):

5. If x is a negative integer, and $xy = -2$ and $y + x = 1$, what is the value of x?

    A. -2
    B. -1
    C. 0
    D. 1
    E. 2

TI-83 Plus Solution:

Write $xy = -2$ as $y = \dfrac{-2}{x}$ and $y + x = 1$ as $y = 1 - x$. Enter the two new equations into the calculator and look at the points of intersection.

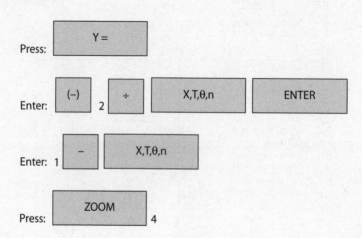

Press: Y =

Enter: (–) 2 ÷ X,T,θ,n ENTER

Enter: 1 – X,T,θ,n

Press: ZOOM 4

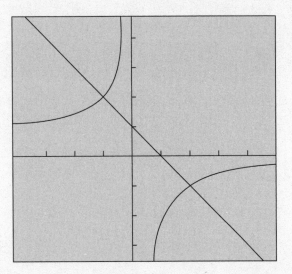

[–4.7, 4.7] by [–3.1, 3.1]

Notice that there are two intersection points $(-1,2)$ and $(2,-1)$. Since x is a negative integer, $x = -1$.

Correct Answer: **B**

B. Common Math Formulas and Theorems for the ACT

Real Numbers

- Primes
  - Prime numbers are 2, 3, 5, 7, 11, 13, . . .
  - 1 is not a prime number.
  - 2 is the only even prime number.
- Zero
  - 0 is the only number that is neither positive nor negative.
  - 0 is an even number.
  - If $ab = 0$, then either $a = 0$ or $b = 0$ or both equal 0.
- Even/Odd
  - even + even = even and (even)(even) = even
  - odd + odd = even and (odd)(odd) = odd
  - even + odd = odd and (even)(odd) = even

Use substitution to determine if an algebraic expression is even or odd.

Sequences

	*n*th term	Sum of the first *n* terms
Arithmetic sequences	$a_n = a_1 + (n-1)d$ a_1 = first term d = common difference	$s_n = (a_1 + a_n)\left(\dfrac{n}{2}\right)$ or $s_n = \left(\dfrac{n}{2}\right)\left[2a_1 + (n-1)d\right]$
Geometric sequences	$a_n = a_1 r^{n-1}$ a_1 = first term r = common ratio	$s_n = \dfrac{a_1 - a_1(r)^n}{1-r}$

Absolute Values

The absolute value of a number is never negative. It's either positive or zero.

For example: $|-3| = 3$, $|3| = 3$, and $|0| = 0$.

- The definition of the absolute value of a number is $|x| = \begin{cases} x, & \text{if } x \geq 0 \\ -x, & \text{if } x < 0 \end{cases}$.

- There are three common types of questions involving absolute value:
  - If $|x| = a$, $a > 0$, then solve the two equations $x = a$ or $x = -a$.
  - If $|x| > a$, $a > 0$, then solve the two inequalities $x < -a$ or $x > a$.
  - If $|x| < a$, $a > 0$, then either solve the two inequalities $x > -a$ and $x < a$ or solve $-a < x < a$.

Exponents

1. $(x^a)(x^b) = x^{a+b}$ e.g., $(x^3)(x^4) = x^7$

2. $\dfrac{x^a}{x^b} = x^{a-b}$, $x \neq 0$ e.g., $\dfrac{x^{10}}{x^4} = x^6$

3. $(ax^b)^c = (a^c)(x^{bc})$ e.g., $(2x^5)^3 = (2)^3(x^5)^3 = 8x^{15}$

4. $x^0 = 1$, $x \neq 0$ e.g., $(-4)^0 = 1$ but $-4^0 = -1$

5. $x^{-n} = \dfrac{1}{x^n}$, $x \neq 0$ e.g., $3^{-2} = \dfrac{1}{3^2}$

6. $x^{\frac{a}{b}} = \left(\sqrt[b]{x}\right)^a$ or $\sqrt[b]{x^a}$ e.g., $8^{\frac{2}{3}} = \left(\sqrt[3]{8}\right)^2$ or $\sqrt[3]{8^2}$ or $= 4$
   if $\sqrt[b]{x}$ exists

Direct and Inverse Variation

- When two non-zero quantities x and y are directly proportional, then:
  - $y = kx$ or $\dfrac{y}{x} = k$ for some constant k.
  - The graph is a line whose slope is k and the y-intercept is 0.
  - If (x_1, y_1) and (x_2, y_2) are points on the graph, then $\dfrac{x_1}{y_1} = \dfrac{x_2}{y_2}$.
- When two non-zero quantities x and y are inversely proportional, then:
  - $y = \dfrac{k}{x}$ or $xy = k$ for some constant k.
  - The graph is a hyperbola.
  - If (x_1, y_1) and (x_2, y_2) are points on the graph, then $(x_1)(y_1) = (x_2)(y_2)$.

Measurement of Angles

- The sum of the measures of the three angles of a triangle is $180°$.
- The measure of an exterior angle of a triangle is equal to the sum of the measures of the two nonadjacent interior angles.
- The measure of an exterior angle of a regular polygon with n sides is $\dfrac{360°}{n}$. The measure of an interior angle of a regular polygon with n sides is $\dfrac{(n-2)180°}{n}$.
- If two parallel lines are cut by a transversal, then the alternate interior angles are congruent.
- If two parallel lines are cut by a transversal, then the corresponding angles are congruent.
- If two lines intersect, then the vertical angles are congruent.

Properties of Triangles

- The Triangle Inequality: $c + d > e$

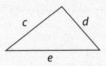

  The sum of the lengths of any two sides of a triangle is always greater than the length of the third side.

- If the lengths of two sides of a triangle are unequal, the measures of the angles opposite these sides are unequal and the greater angle lies opposite the greater side. Example: $BC > BA \Leftrightarrow m\angle A > m\angle C$.

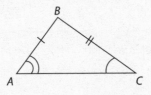

- The Pythagorean theorem: $a^2 + b^2 = c^2$

- Special Right Triangle: 30°-60° right triangle

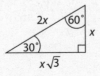

- Special Right Triangle: 45°-45° right triangle

Similarity

If two triangles are similar, then:

- The ratio of the *perimeters* is equal to the ratio of the lengths of any pair of corresponding line segments.
- The ratio of the *areas* is equal to the square of the ratio of the lengths of any pair of corresponding line segments.

Solids, Volumes, and Surface Areas

Shape	Volume	Surface Area
Cube	s^3	$6s^2$
Rectangular box	lwh	$2(lh + hw + lw)$
Right circular cylinder	$\pi r^2 h$	Total surface area: $2\pi r^2 + 2\pi rh$ Lateral surface area: $2\pi rh$
Sphere	$\dfrac{4}{3}\pi r^3$	$4\pi r^2$

Properties of Circles

Given a circle O with radius r and diameter d:

- Circumference: $C = 2\pi r$ or $C = \pi d$
- Area: $A = \pi r^2$

- The length of an arc: $\dfrac{\text{length } \overparen{AB}}{2\pi r} = \dfrac{m\angle AOB \text{ (in degrees)}}{360°}$

- The area of a sector: $\dfrac{\text{area of sector } AOB}{\pi r^2} = \dfrac{m\angle AOB \text{ (in degrees)}}{360°}$

Coordinate Geometry

Given $A(x_1, y_1)$ and $B(x_2, y_2)$:

- The midpoint of $\overline{AB}$: $\left(\dfrac{x_1 + x_2}{2}, \dfrac{y_1 + y_2}{2}\right)$. Think of a midpoint as the "average."
- The distance between A and B (the length of $\overline{AB}$): $d_{\overline{AB}} = \sqrt{(x_2 - x_1)^2 + (y_2 - y_1)^2}$.
- The slope of $\overline{AB}$: $m_{\overline{AB}} = \dfrac{y_2 - y_1}{x_2 - x_1}$.

Slopes and Lines

- The slope of the line through the points (x_1, y_1) and (x_2, y_2) is $\dfrac{y_2 - y_1}{x_2 - x_1}$. The slope of a line written in $y = mx + b$ form is m, e.g., the slope of the line $y = 3x - 2$ is 3.

- If two lines are parallel, their slopes are equal.
- If two lines are perpendicular, their slopes are negative reciprocals and the product of their slopes is -1.

Counting Principle

- If one activity can occur in m ways, and then following that a second activity can occur in n ways, then the number of ways both activities can occur in that order is mn.
- **Permutations**
  The number of permutations of n things taken r at a time is $_nP_r = \dfrac{n!}{(n-r!)}$. (Order matters.)
- **Combinations**
  The number of combinations of n things taken r at a time is $_nC_r = \dfrac{_nP_r}{r!}$. (Order *does not* matter.)

Probability

- Probability that an event A will occur is $P(A) = \dfrac{\text{number of ways event } A \text{ can occur}}{\text{total number of possible ways}}$.
- Probability that event A will occur is $0 \le P(A) \le 1$.
- Probability that event A will not occur is $P(\text{not } A) = 1 - P(A)$.
- Probability that event A or event B will occur is $P(A \cup B) = P(A) + P(B) - P(A \cap B)$.
- Expected Value (or mean) of a probability distribution $\{(x_1, p(x_1)), (x_2, p(x_2)), \dots (x_n, p(x_n))\}$ is
  $$\sum_{i=1}^{n}(x_i \cdot p(x_i)) = x_1 \cdot p(x_1) + x_2 \cdot p(x_2) + \dots + x_n \cdot p(x_n).$$

Mean, Median, and Mode

- The **mean** of a set of numbers or algebraic expressions is the average of the set. For example:
  - The average of 5, 6, and 10 is $\dfrac{5+6+10}{3}$ or 7.
  - The average of $x + 8$ and $5x - 4$ is $\dfrac{x+8+5x-4}{2}$ or $3x + 2$.
- The **median** of an ordered list of numbers is the middle value. For example:
  - The median of 2, 6, 10, 11, 14 is 10.
  - The median of 2, 6, 8, 20 is $\dfrac{6+8}{2}$ or 7.
- The **mode** of a list of numbers is the number that appears most often. For example:
  - The mode of 2, 3, 5, 5, 5, 6, 6, 8 is 5.
  - The mode of 2, 3, 6, 6, 8, 8, 12, 15 is 6 and 8.
- The range of a set of numbers is the difference between the maximum value and the minimum value. For example:
  - The range of 2, 6, 10, 11, 14 is 12.
  - The range of 2, 3, 5, 5, 5, 6, 6, 8 is 6.

Box-and-Whisker Plot

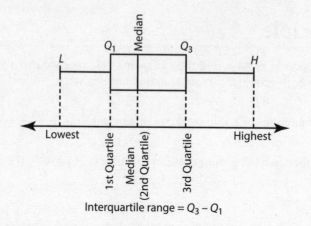

Interquartile range = $Q_3 - Q_1$

Normal Curve with Standard Deviation

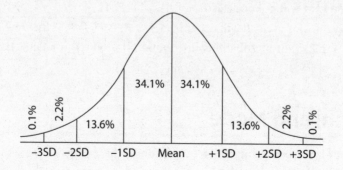

Quadratic Formula

- $ax^2 + bx + c = 0,\ a \neq 0$: $x = \dfrac{-b \pm \sqrt{b^2 - 4ac}}{2a}$

Equation of a Parabola

- $y = ax^2 + bx + c,\ a \neq 0$: axis of symmetry $x = \dfrac{-b}{2a}$

Equation of a Circle

- $(x - h)^2 + (y - k)^2 = r^2$ with center of circle (h, k), radius r

Trigonometric Functions

The mnemonic SOHCAHTOA, written as $S\frac{o}{h}C\frac{a}{h}T\frac{o}{a}$, may be helpful in remembering some of the trigonometric ratios.

$$\sin A = \frac{\text{opp}}{\text{hyp}} \qquad \cos A = \frac{\text{adj}}{\text{hyp}} \qquad \tan A = \frac{\text{opp}}{\text{adj}}$$

$$\csc A = \frac{\text{hyp}}{\text{opp}} \qquad \sec A = \frac{\text{hyp}}{\text{adj}} \qquad \cot A = \frac{\text{adj}}{\text{opp}}$$

Pythagorean Identities

- $\cos^2\theta + \sin^2\theta = 1$
- $1 + \tan^2\theta = \sec^2\theta$
- $\cot^2\theta + 1 = \csc^2\theta$

Quotient Identities

- $\tan\theta = \dfrac{\sin\theta}{\cos\theta}, \ \cot\theta = \dfrac{\cos\theta}{\sin\theta}$

Reciprocal Identities

- $\csc\theta = \dfrac{1}{\sin\theta}, \ \sec\theta = \dfrac{1}{\cos\theta}, \ \cot\theta = \dfrac{1}{\tan\theta}$

Functions of the Sum of Two Angles

- $\sin(A + B) = \sin A\cos B + \cos A\sin B$
- $\cos(A + B) = \cos A\cos B - \sin A\sin B$

Functions of the Double Angle

- $\sin 2A = 2\sin A\cos A$
- $\cos 2A = \cos^2 A - \sin^2 A$
- $\cos 2A = 2\cos^2 A - 1$
- $\cos 2A = 1 - 2\sin^2 A$

Law of Sines

- $\dfrac{a}{\sin A} = \dfrac{b}{\sin B} = \dfrac{c}{\sin C}$

Law of Cosines

- $c^2 = a^2 + b^2 - 2ab\cos C$
- $b^2 = a^2 + c^2 - 2ac\cos B$
- $a^2 = b^2 + c^2 - 2bc\cos A$

Properties of Logarithms

- $\log_a b = c \quad a^c = b$ with a and $b > 0$
- $\log_c(ab) = \log_c a + \log_c b$ with a, b, and $c > 0$
- $\log_c \dfrac{a}{b} = \log_c a - \log_c b$ with a, b, and $c > 0$
- $\log_c(a^b) = b\log_c a$ with a and $c > 0$
- $\log_c b = \dfrac{\log_a b}{\log_a c}$ Change of Base Formula with a, b, and $c > 0$

Graphs of Sine and Cosine

- $y = a\sin(bx - c) + d$ and $y = a\cos(bx - c) + d$
- Amplitude $= |a|$
- Frequency $= |b|$
- Period $= \dfrac{2\pi}{b}$
- Midline $y = d$
- Phase shift $= \dfrac{c}{b}$
- Left endpoint $x = \dfrac{c}{b}$
- Right endpoint $x = \dfrac{c}{b} + \dfrac{2\pi}{b}$